MW00534710

THE UNEXPECTED
ABIGAIL
ADAMS

ABIGAIL (SMITH) ADAMS
BENJAMIN BLYTH, 1766
Copy by JOHN ADAMS, 1795

THE UNEXPECTED
ABIGAIL
ADAMS

A Woman
"Not Apt to Be Intimidated"

JOHN L. SMITH, JR.

WESTHOLME
Yardley

Facing title page: Pastel portrait of Abigail Smith Adams by Benjamin Blyth, circa 1766, shortly after she married John Adams. (*Massachusetts Historical Society*)

© 2024 John L. Smith, Jr.

All rights reserved under International and Pan-American Copyright Conventions. No part of this book may be reproduced in any form or by any electronic or mechanical means, including information storage and retrieval systems, without permission in writing from the publisher, except by a reviewer who may quote brief passages in a review.

Westholme Publishing, LLC
904 Edgewood Road
Yardley, Pennsylvania 19067
Visit our Web site at www.westholmepublishing.com

ISBN: 978-1-59416-421-7
Also available as an eBook.

Printed in the United States of America.

For Nancy, Ami and Todd, Hunter and Alexis, Amber and Mario

Contents

Contents

Illustrations

(following page 124)

Prologue

The World of Abigail Adams

"If any young woman wants to have a nice, quiet life, I advise her not to marry an Adams."—Abigail Brown Brooks Adams, granddaughter-in-law to Abigail Adams

bigail Smith Adams—wife to President John Adams, family matriarch, selective feminist, second First Lady, and first presidential advisor in early America, certainly did not have "a nice, quiet life." Abigail Adams was not only an eyewitness to America's founding, but she helped to shape large portions of it working through her trusting husband, John Adams. Later in her life, Abigail looked back and firmly stated, "no man ever prospered in the world; without the consent and cooperation of his wife."[1] Abigail's unique contributions throughout her life led to the establishment and stability of the new form of democratic government in the world. It easily marked her as one of the Founders of the United States of America.

In total Abigail Adams famously wrote throughout her life approximately 2,300 letters. Culling through that sizable depository, this book shows a side of Abigail Adams through her own written words—light moments, incredibly sad or poignant moments, and historical moments—all told as they happened. Reading from her letters was like panning for gold, for they contain many nuggets of wisdom from Abigail. Many of them are included in a book for the first time.

The Importance of Letter Writing

The rich volume of letters left us by Abigail Adams—an undisciplined and natural writer—is the best collection that exists of first-person records in the entire pre- and post-Revolutionary War period and of the Founding Era. It spans a full fifty years, from 1765 to 1815.

Her eloquent letters were heavily edited and first published by her grandson Charles Francis Adams in 1840[2] and were the hit of the 1848 Woman's Rights Convention in Seneca Falls, New York. Since then, they have never been out of print. Despite her repeated calls to the letter recipients to "pray burn all my Letters,"[3] thankfully they did not. Writing by candlelight and quill pen throughout her life to John, friends, and family, Abigail proudly announced "My candle and my pen are all my companions."[4] Occasionally when writing in winter, Abigail found that the ink inside her reservoir had frozen solid.

In her book *Abigail Adams: A Writing Life*, Edith B. Gelles perfectly states that letter writing to Abigail was "therapeutic"[5]—freely expressing her thoughts and feelings late at night after the household and field management work was finished. Abigail had written to John, "my Pen is my only pleasure, and writing to you the composure of my mind."[6] These are the expressions which we find so captivating and so human, but they were meant to be read by the single individual to which they were addressed. Abigail was not writing her specific letter expecting that we in the twenty-first century would be reading it. She was often apologetic about her writing style to the recipient; if she could have imagined it, she would have been mortified at the thought of readers in a distant century. We are privileged to know her innermost feelings at critical times in history. She was an excellent, natural writer and we benefit from it.

Abigail lived in what was called the "golden age of letter writing." In the 1600s the notoriously unreliable English postal system had been reorganized and streamlined, which was reflected in the fledgling American colonies as well. But in the 1700s, the style of writing fundamentally changed as well. Previously words written in a letter reflected a stilted, formal, and unreadable style of prose. But it had all changed. The popular "self-help" books of the eighteenth century were style manuals on how to write various kinds of letters. The writing was formed in a new, revolutionary style as if the words were being simply spoken to the recipient. It was part of a young girl's education to practice writing letters for hours per day.

Abigail wrote in this new contemporary style. Many times, she would spell out phonetically a word of whose spelling she was unsure. Certain words were capitalized mid-sentence for emphasis, and the initial letter of a sentence was often not capitalized, as was practiced by many writers such as Thomas Jefferson. Abigail's and other letter-writers' own words are reproduced in their original form in this book. The primary language, spelling, punctuation, and capitalization, as foreign as it may seem to some readers today, has been retained. That's where the magic lives. Only rarely have brackets been used to add an explanation to help readers where the meaning may not be clear. To fully understand Abigail, we need to understand what and how she wrote. It's like listening to her speak to us.

She often freely quoted, as did John, phrases from favorite authors or biblical passages without the benefit of modern quotation marks. Most of her letters followed an outline style of (a) Acknowledging received letters from the recipient, (b) News of vital importance, (c) News of friends and family, including gossip, which was a key component of practical news. Another letter-writing practice of the day was to write a rough draft, then copy the letter over, correcting grammatical errors or the use of certain words, names, or phrases. Abigail's friend Mercy Otis Warren—a scholarly and disciplined poet and playwright—always copied a letter over. But Abigail, usually in a hurry, almost never copied over. She just issued in her letter a variation of "you may communicate this letter to her, if she can read it; but 'tis badly written, and I have not time to copy."[7]

Abigail gave passing fancy to spelling words correctly—or at least making the effort. In Abigail's time, dictionaries in America were rare.[8] Abigail sometimes experimented with spelling attempts on a separate piece of paper or in her letter as the following unedited sentence shows: "Nyork would be the balance in the scaile scale skaill, Scaill. (is it right now? it does not look so.)"[9] Spelling phonetically was still the style for nearly all colonials.

Often Abigail would start a letter to John with her now famous phrase, "My dearest friend." The meaning of the word "friend" used in that context was much different than what is implied today. John and Abigail, two married, loving people, often began their letters to the other with those words. Back then the word "friend" could imply a deep, loving relationship.

Reading the letters of Abigail Adams, allows the reader to understand her life and temporarily live in her extraordinary world. I have used full paragraph quotes by Abigail rather than short phrases as the next best thing to hearing Abigail herself speak to the reader.

Abigail's Support for Women's Rights

Abigail lived in an undisputed male-dominated world. White males held all the political and economic power in relationships in that patriarchal world. According to English law, which was the law in effect in colonial America,[10] every female of age was categorized as either a feme covert (married woman) or a feme sole (a widow or never-married woman). Under the doctrine of coverture, a married woman could not sign legal documents, enter contracts, own real property, keep any earned money, or get an education without her husband's approval. The law considered the wife and husband as one person—the husband. Legally the wife nearly ceased to exist. Along those same lines, if an unmarried woman had inherited a sizable amount of land or money, the very moment she said, "I do," she would be instantly penniless. The new husband now controlled all that she had and all that she would ever have.

Abigail Adams, as the self-assured woman she grew to become, was no fan of the common-law theory of coverture as she expressed to John in 1782, "Even in the freeest countrys our property is subject to the controul and disposal of our partners, to whom the Laws have given a soverign Authority."[11] This is why in those early colonial days it was so vitally important that the woman marry the right man from the start. With divorces rare or impossible, it was quite likely that the woman would be saddled with her choice of husband for life, for better or for worse. The worst would be bound to a brutal husband for life. It was fortunate that Abigail married John—a brilliant, supportive husband and father who was never threatened by Abigail's intelligence. In fact, he encouraged her intellectual growth throughout their entire lives.

It is often said that the marriage of John and Abigail Adams was a "marriage of equals." That may seem true in a simple sense and one that conveniently fits into a twenty-first-century model. Historically, however, the reality was different. Ultimately, John legally was always the lord and master of his domain, and that fact was absolutely accepted by both. But increasingly throughout their fifty-four-year-long marriage, John willingly and gratefully yielded husbandly power to Abigail because John could not be in two places doing two separate jobs at the same time: lawyer/congressman and farmer/father. Equally important, John had come to the realization that Abigail had the intelligence and good sense about events and people to trust her with anything. Abigail followed through with whatever task was asked of her and even gained superiority in challenges thrust upon her. But other than an earned sense of accomplishment, Abigail did not like her duties in the temporary male role such as running the farm. Many times, in her letters she likened her "deputy husband"[12] duties while being deprived of a supportive husband at home as her "sacrifices to my Country."[13]

Alternately, Abigail was pro-traditional female, as she was proud of her womanhood and the domestic home life that she and other women created. She did not consider domestic work as in any way inferior or less important than public life. She strongly felt that a woman's homemaking work led to a stable family, educated children, and a successful husband who built a career and supported local, state, and national politics—all of which led to the strength of a thriving new republic. She passionately believed and later vocalized that men were no smarter than women; she just felt that the naturally assigned gender roles were necessary for social stability. In some areas of women's rights today, Abigail is called a feminist. The Oxford English Dictionary supplies the definition of that word when used as a noun, "an advocate of women's rights on the basis of the equality of the sexes." In that sense then, Abigail could be called a feminist or more accurately, a "selective feminist" because of her seemingly contradictory non-feminist and feminist attitudes on various subjects in her life.

Educational Rights for Women
If Abigail had a vocal "Noble Cause" for her whole life, it was not "Remember the Ladies"; it was the lack of educational opportunities for girls and women. She recalled that in her younger years, "in this country you need not be told how much female Education is neglected, nor how fashonable it has been to ridicule Female learning."[14]

Despite Abigail's proud defense of female domesticity, she also felt very strongly that female intelligence did not cancel out being a good wife and mother. The two could and should coexist and she was living proof of it—reading and absorbing knowledge beginning from when she was a small child to later encouraging her nieces and granddaughters to do the same. She never quit reading and learning her entire life. She was finishing a biography of "Genll Jackson"[15] (Andrew Jackson) just two months before she died in 1818 at the age of seventy-three.

While once again reaffirming to Abigail that she had chosen well in her choice of a lifelong companion, John completely agreed with Abigail on the importance of educational opportunities for women. He wrote to Abigail one month following the vote for the Declaration of Independence, "Your Sentiments of the Importance of Education in Women, are exactly agreable to my own."[16] It was just one more thing that John and Abigail agreed upon in their long life together.

Political Rights for Women

Like marital and property rights, Abigail's world involved women having no political rights at all. Women were automatically banned from voting because at the time, only white men who owned property could vote. It was commonly felt that to cast an intelligent vote, one had to have "skin in the game"—a dependent reason to vote one way or the other. Besides, because women were entirely dependent upon the husband or father, the woman, if given the vote, would be heavily influenced to vote the way of their male dependent person, therefore casting an illegal two votes for every one person. It was also a common belief, then that women did not possess the critical analysis capabilities to understand the complexities of law and politics.

Alternately, more than simply a claim to marital and political rights, Abigail's well-known statement of "Remember the Ladies" was a sweeping claim for just status (not necessarily equal status) for women. She was not a fiery militant demanding the right to vote as she is sometimes portrayed. It is fair to say that the right to vote never realistically crossed her mind in her time; it would take the Nineteenth Amendment nearly 145 years later for that to happen. But history and progress often stumble forward in tiny steps. To address the wrongs of women's rights, "the American Revolution led to new laws. . . . One of its animating ideas. . . [was] that every person [woman] has the right to climb from degradation to dignity."[17]

Abigail as Witness to and Shaper of History

Abigail met in person or considered a friend nearly every important figure of the Revolutionary Era. Her list included George and particularly Martha Washington (whom she loved), Thomas Jefferson, Sally Hemings, Benjamin Franklin, Henry Knox, Paul Revere (he sometimes brought congressional correspondence to Abigail's house), Samuel and Elizabeth Adams, John and Dorothy Hancock, John and Sarah Jay, Marquis and Adrienne de Lafayette, John Paul Jones, Alexander Hamilton (whom Abigail hated), James and Elizabeth Monroe, and even King George III and Queen Charlotte of England, as well as King Louis XVI and Queen Marie Antoinette of France.

Abigail also functioned as John's trusted political advisor—and an early "chief of staff"—throughout their public time together, especially when John was president. She had a better sense of people and politics than John, even by his own admission. Although John was brilliant, when she was not with him, he often floundered or sank through his own paranoidal actions and words.

Abigail's Role as Family Physician

Medicine and medical knowledge in the late eighteenth century were still primitive. Abigail was born into and lived during that dangerous period of epidemics, diseases, and deaths.

As a young child, Abigail contracted rheumatic fever, an autoimmune disease that affects the heart and joints; a skin rash (probably impetigo) may have also accompanied the disease. Rheumatic fever was not contagious, and modern science has determined that it can result from not completely curing strep throat or scarlet fever in the person. Bouts of rheumatic fever kept young Abigail from being able to attend the local school. The disease also recurred many times throughout her adult life.

Abigail considered rheumatism as an inherited family malady, "that Hereditary Scourge the Rheumatism."[18] Other than rheumatism, ailments Abigail is known to have suffered from were arthritis, insomnia, headaches, smallpox, colds/allergies, eye inflammations, agues (aches), and fevers. It is possible that she had also contracted malaria in Philadelphia, judging from her successful use of quinine for her treatment. Some historians have speculated that Abigail also had diabetes but offer no evidence to support the claim. Because so many conditions went unidentified during this time, this list is incomplete.

Abigail very well might have developed other disorders and diseases that were common in Boston, New York City, Philadelphia, Amsterdam, London, and Paris. Diphtheria ("distemper"), pleurisy, influenza, whooping cough, dysentery, canker, scarlet fever, mumps, tuberculosis ("consumption"), yellow fever, "Cholera Morbis," typhoid fever, and various, vague "bilious intermittent" fevers, or "Hectics." Epidemics occurred in Boston and nearby areas nearly every year. The Boston dysentery epidemic in 1775 killed as many people as the Boston smallpox epidemic in 1776. Philadelphia was also well known as an epidemic hot spot every summer, necessitating the government to take a summer vacation.

Not only was an adult Abigail a skillful herbalist, but she also clearly understood the body-mind connection requiring the two to be in balance for good health. "I sensibly feel that the Health of the Body depends very Much upon the tranquility of the mind";[19] "the genial influence of the Sun is so necessary, both, to my health and Spirits; that I deplore his absence, if only hidden from me for a few days."[20]

When a person was diagnosed with a disease or disorder, Abigail's initial prescription was for a powerful laxative purgative to have the person pass any dangerous bodily waste. Calomel (mercury) was a widely used, if dangerous, product to empty the person's bowels.

Bleeding was a popular and widely used procedure to restore the natural balance of blood "humor" within a patient's circulatory system. It was felt that some illnesses were caused by a clogging of thick blood inside one's body. Throughout her life, Abigail was a firm believer in bleeding. Many of her discussions with an ill person ended with a form of this phrase "untill I was Bled which relieved me."[21] To her son, John Quincy, Abigail wrote, "I would advise you upon the approach of Spring to lose some Blood, the Headacks and flushing in your face with which you used to be troubled was occasiond by too great a Quantity of Blood in your Head."[22]

Sometimes the medicine of an era could kill you. Instead, some people used holistic folk remedies passed down in families for generations. As family pharmacist Abigail acknowledged the danger of lethal "phisick" medicines over holistic remedies, "the phisick part is bad enough I know."[23] Effective natural medicines Abigail recommended were nutmeg, rhubarb, cinnamon, chamomile flowers (in a poultice), "the Bark" (quinine), "Dropsies" (edema), laudanum (opium powder diluted in alcohol).

Abigail's Marketing and Investment Skills

During the Revolutionary War, colonial families struggled desperately to operate a business, run a farm, or just exist. State taxes still had to be paid and were sometimes higher than the amount residents used to pay to Great Britain. Inflation was rampant; money was scarce or counterfeited. Many families could not survive. Owing to Abigail's intelligence and willingness to take risks while John was constantly gone, she kept the family financially afloat. Her marketing skills to acquire in-demand goods that were scarce and resell them for profit saved the Adams family. Throughout the conflict, Abigail's shrewd investments in real estate, rare commodities, and government securities (loan office certificates) turned a handsome profit and made all the difference to the family's finances.

Simply expressed, Abigail "was an exemplary wife, mother, sister, daughter, friend, and patriot of early America."[24] Through her own words, this book attempts to capture the sometimes unexpected or surprising life of Abigail Adams, a remarkable woman for all times.

Part One

*A Young Woman of
Massachusetts*

Chapter One

"My Own Giddy Disposition"
1744–1762

In the sixtieth year of her life, Abigail Adams was in a reminiscing mood while writing to her eldest son, John Quincy Adams. She and her husband, John, had been retired for only four years from positions of international prominence that they had engaged in for nearly all their married lives. They were separated for much of that time.

She wistfully recalled to son John Quincy her earlier life experiences growing up in North Weymouth, Massachusetts, in the years from 1744 to 1764. She recollected that she had been a "giddy" girl but had always been comforted by her maternal Grandmother Quincy, who would quote to her "the old adage, wild colts make the best Horses."[1]

The essence of who Abigail Smith Adams became as an adult was formed in her early years growing up in Weymouth, the daughter of a liberal Congregationalist minister. Abigail was a member of an active and supportive family whose lineage stretched back to the very founding of the colony.[2] Abigail's first nineteen years molded her personality and her outlook on life. Her high intelligence, however, was inherent in her from the very beginning.

Abigail, who went by her childhood nickname of "Nabby," loved root-
ing through her father's large library in their parsonage home. She received no formal outside schooling because of her frequent illnesses. She
suffered from the effects of rheumatic fever, and consequentially was
fearful of the frequent epidemics that rolled through the area. Her
mother may have felt her own in-home education would be adequate
for a female of the day. But indeed, the education for Abigail and her
two sisters, Mary and Elizabeth, was apparently very adequate. It included reading, writing, religion, and arithmetic along with basic domestic skills to become competent homemakers and diligent wives
someday.

Abigail reportedly thrived in her own world of books, so additional
lessons in the French language were included in her curriculum.[3] As a
very young girl, she mastered the works of Alexander Pope, Jonathan
Swift, William Shakespeare, the now-forgotten poet James Thomson
(her favorite), and of course the Bible. She would quote relevant passages
from all those sources seemingly by heart in letters for the rest of her
life; some paraphrased, others right on the mark.

Many often-used passages in her future letters were from *The Seasons*,
a poem by Thomson. She would quote from it with amazing accuracy
in her writings, even if she was far from home. The premise of Thomson's poem was the comparison of the four seasons in nature to events
in a lifetime, and Abigail always saw parallels in her own life. With sim-
ilarities today to a young person quoting from a very meaningful song,
Abigail did the same from books and it seemed to give her a sense of
comfort.

Abigail's home education was conducted by her mother at first, and
then her father took over. This young, often shy, and stubborn girl of
her time was in good hands. Reverend William Smith, her enlightened
father, was a Harvard-educated ordained minister of the Weymouth
North Parish Church, having assumed that position in 1734. In 1738
the successful and established minister purchased a parsonage house
with acreage.[4]

Her father's brother, Isaac Smith, Sr., was one of the wealthiest mer-
chant-ship owners in Boston. Abigail would sometimes spend time visiting his luxurious Boston mansion on Queen Street not far from the
State House. Abigail recalled that she could get lost in the Smiths' luxurious library. Her cousin Isaac Smith, Jr., was a few years her junior.
By 1762 the two had even established a form of a juvenile pen pal club
where Abigail could try out her letter writing skills and French trans-

lation exercises. As they grew up and politics began to enter their lives, Abigail's cousin became a firm loyalist.

The Boston Smith family was part of a very prosperous merchant class clan. However, in 1740 when Reverend William Smith of Weymouth married, he married well. As soon as he took Elizabeth Quincy for his wife, he married into the notable Quincy clan of Braintree.

The Quincys were early founders of Massachusetts and even counted one of their English ancestors as a signer of the Magna Carta. Maternal grandmother Elizabeth Norton Quincy, a woman whom Abigail would always remember as kind and supportive, lived in a Braintree mansion called Mount Wollaston with her husband Colonel John Quincy. Colonel Quincy had also been Speaker in the Massachusetts House of Representatives and was still a powerful force in Braintree politics. On visits, John Adams was in awe of the Quincy's large home library, second only to Boston libraries. Young Abigail could always be found rummaging through her grandfather's books. One Christmas just after John and Abigail had married, they spent some of the day at the Quincy's house, where John, who didn't particularly like anybody, recorded in his diary that he seemed to like Elizabeth Quincy: "Went not to Christmas. Dined at Home. Drank Tea at Grandfather Quincys. . . . The old Lady as merry and chatty as ever."[5]

Reverend Smith and his family weren't overly rich, but then again Smith purposely gave the misleading impression that they were less affluent than they were. John Adams, when first meeting "Parson Smith," cynically wrote that he saw right through that little charade.

Abigail's mother, Elizabeth Quincy Smith, apparently was overprotective. And perhaps it was for a good reason that she seemed to keep Abigail close to her during her childhood: Nabby seemed to be one of those children who caught any illness going around. But even at age nineteen, Abigail complained to her "Unkle," Dr. Cotton Tufts: "My Mother makes bugbears sometimes, and then seems uneasy because I will not be scared by them."[6] Some of that animosity might have been simply adolescent chafing to establish one's own grown-up identity. Abigail and her two sisters sometimes wrote about that later in letters between themselves.

Other indications were that Elizabeth Smith, overall, was a loving and supportive parent. Many times, Abigail would accompany her mother on the social welfare rounds she would make caring for the sick and the poor of the parish. Stubborn though she was, Abigail was receiving lessons in life about charity and caring for those less fortunate that would form part of her personality for the rest of her life. And her youthful exposure to religious teachings all day, every day, and especially on the Sabbath would certainly be evident in all her letter writing for the next sixty years.

Elizabeth Smith would give birth to four children, three girls and a boy, during her marriage: Mary, December 9, 1741, the eldest sister and perhaps Abigail's closest friend in life, aside from John; Abigail herself, November 11, 1744; William Jr., unknown month, 1746; and Elizabeth, April or May 1750.[7]

Also living with the six members of the Smith family were four to five enslaved persons. Abigail Adams grew up in a Massachusetts household using the less harsh social euphemism: "servants." Perhaps this daily encounter with enslaved persons shaped Abigail's later strong vocal abolitionist viewpoints. History doesn't tell us how or why Reverend Smith came to own slaves. It is possible that he was given the slaves as a debt payment or maybe he purchased some or all of them.[8] At that time, slavery was legal and common in all thirteen colonies, although it was much more prevalent in the agrarian South. While a vocal northern minority of mostly Quakers maintained that slavery was a moral outrage, it was widely accepted nearly everywhere as a fact of life and was often an important marker of social position. Some religious tracts could even trace proslavery passages found in the Bible, thereby justifying it; it'll never be exactly known why a very devout religious man like Reverend Smith owned other human beings. However, we know the names of five of the Smith's slaves: Tom, who is mentioned in letters from Abigail to John just before they were married; Tom's wife Peg; Cato; Tower; and Phoebe.[9] Phoebe would go on to have quite a history as a freed person with an adult Abigail Adams.

Early visitors would have found Abigail's hometown of Weymouth, about ten miles south of Boston on Massachusetts Bay, to be a small farming and fishing village of about 1,200 people. "Weymouth you know, consists cheifly of Farmers, and has never been distinguished, unless for its Inactivity,"[10] Abigail's single sister Elizabeth Smith would later lament. It was surrounded by rolling hills and woods with the smell of salt water in the air, and six flat roads heading in and out of town in all directions, Weymouth offered some safety and security to all who lived there.

Even so, a long list of diseases and epidemics made up the everyday world of young Abigail and American colonists, regardless of social status: rheumatic fever, smallpox, mumps, measles, whooping cough, dysentery, typhus, malaria, yellow fever, scarlet fever, influenza, pneumonia, pleurisy, with various types of "ague," "flux," and "pox."[11] As previously mentioned, Abigail contracted rheumatic fever as a child. With one such bout, she was paralyzed for two weeks. She would suffer from repetitive episodes of rheumatic fever for her entire life. Some historical evidence also suggests she was diabetic (although it's unclear if that developed in her childhood), which could have aggravated her numerous other maladies.

The medical world that Abigail Smith Adams grew up in and indeed spent her entire life would seem very primitive to the twenty-first-century world of antibiotics, CAT scans, and robotic surgeries. Medical knowledge and medicine itself amounted to little more than primitive "quackery." In fact, Abigail mockingly used that term sometimes in letters to describe her own recommended home remedies: "You will find them an excellent Gaurd against the colds you are so subject to in winter. So much for Quackery."[12]

Abigail is mostly known for her prolific letter writing, many times undertaken late at night by flickering candlelight. In another reminiscent letter written when Abigail was sixty-seven years of age to her younger sister, Elizabeth ("Betsy"), she was remembering their childhood years and how their home education, while impressive for its subject variety, was lacking in grammar and handwriting. However, the following letter also introduces to us a new influential person in young Abigail's life, her future brother-in-law:

> you well know what our early Education was. neither Grammer or orthography [the spelling system of a language] were taught us— it was not then the fashion for females to know more than writing and a little arithmetic. no Books upon female Education were then in vogue no Accademies for Female instruction were then establishd. To our dear and venarable Brother Cranch do I attribute my early taste for Letters; and for the nurture & cultivation of those qualities which have Since afforded me much pleasure and Satisfaction. he it was who put proper Books into my hands—Who taught one to Love the Poets and to distinguish their Merrits—Milton Pope Tompson and Shakespear were amongst the first.[13]

The early male figure that Abigail wrote adoringly of was Richard Cranch, Mary Smith's eventual husband.

When discussing early male model figures in their lives, it's interesting that little if anything is ever mentioned in family records about their brother, William Smith, Jr. As the only son in the family, he was preordained by the longtime social custom of primogeniture to inherit the main estate of the parents. This chosen status of course included the early focus of attention and money to educate him instead of the three daughters, despite their having shown an independent passion for education. It's known that "Billy" was taught Latin and Greek by outside tutors and was privy to owning the best of English educational books sent from London. But it seemed for some unknown reason that the educational light never shone on Billy; he reportedly turned down a Harvard entrance invitation and went off to work. Billy would live a somewhat tragic life, accentuated by alcoholism, and which the adult sisters discussed in letters using veiled references to not advertise family shortcomings.

By summer 1759, Richard Cranch had zeroed in on one girl, Mary Smith, known as "Polly," the eldest of the daughters of Reverend William Smith. Sometimes John Adams would tag along with Cranch. On one of the visits to the Smith parsonage, John met fifteen-year-old Abigail Smith. He wasn't exactly impressed. Although in his diary he wrote, "Polly and Nabby are Wits," he also recognized in nearly the same paragraph that he was still smitten with Hannah Quincy—Abigail Smith's second cousin. In his diary entry,[14] John recalled the gentle qualities of Hannah (whom he called "H.Q."): "Tender and fond. Loving and compassionate." But the Smith sisters? John wrote, "P[arson] S[mith]s Girls have not this fondness, nor this Tenderness." He capped off his impression of the Smith sisters: "Are S Gils [Smith Girls] either Frank or fond, or even candid.—Not fond, not frank, not candid."[15]

To an even lesser extent, Adams did not have a nice initial impression of the girls' somewhat sneaky father, Reverend William Smith: "Parson Smith has no small share of Priest Craft.—He conceals his own Wealth, from his Parish, that they may not be hindered by knowing it from sending him Presents.—He talks very familiarly with the People, Men and Women of his Parish, to gain their affection.—He is [a] crafty designing Man.—He watches Peoples Looks and Behaviour.—I caught him, several times, looking earnestly at my face."[16]

In strangely prophetic words at year's end 1761, the two bachelor buddies—Cranch and Adams—co-wrote a short letter to Mary Smith, Richard's love interest and Abigail's sister. The second half of the letter, in Adams's handwriting, expresses a not-so-veiled interest by John in the now seventeen-year-old "Nabby." It had been two years since their first, lackluster meeting. John's words ironically feign jealousy about

Nabby's allegiance to the newly crowned King George III the year before: "to Mrs. Nabby. Tell her I hear she's about commencing a most loyal subject to young George—and altho my Allegiance has been hitherto inviolate I shall endeavour, all in my Power to foment Rebellion."[17]

On November 25, 1762, Mary Smith married Richard Cranch in the downstairs parlor room of Reverend Smith's parsonage, as Congregationalist Church regulations prohibited church weddings.[18]

Proper social and family etiquette dictated that daughters were betrothed and married in birth order, from oldest to youngest. This orderly transition provided time for families to adjust to the changes. It also would have given a spark of excitement to the daughter who was next in line for matrimony. In this case, it was Abigail.

Chapter Two

"As Speckled as You Desire to Be"

1762–1764

J ohn Adams and Abigail Smith began a formal courtship in 1762, since John felt he was in a suitable position to start seriously thinking about marriage. The year before, John's father had died from "throat distemper," leaving John the Braintree property and house.[1] This is the house that John and Abigail would live in throughout the Revolutionary War until they returned from Europe in 1788.[2] Property ownership made John a "freeholder" and gave him a voting seat in the Braintree town meetings.[3] Professionally, he was also admitted to practice in the highest appellate and trial court in the colony—the Superior Court of Judicature.

But it wasn't just a matter of money or position that sparked Adams's stronger interest in Abigail. It seemed she had also changed a lot emotionally in the two years since they had met. From that fizzled first encounter with the shy, awkward fifteen-year-old, Abigail had grown into a self-assured young woman whose "wit" that John initially noted had evolved into good-natured kidding. Now a more independent Abigail wrote that she would defend John from public charges of "Haughtiness," but confessed that he was certainly guilty of "Saucyness no Mortal can match."[4] Throughout their lives spent together, Abigail would continue to keep John's ego in check as no other person could.

Certainly, a now seventeen-year-old Abigail had also matured physically as well. She was at or near her adult height of five feet, one inch, with dark brown eyes and hair. She may have also had a naturally dark complexion, as was expressed years later. In July 1786 while serving as American ambassador to Great Britain, John and Abigail had been the guests of the British political radical Thomas Brand Hollis at his Essex country house. Four years later in a reply letter to Hollis, Abigail reminded Hollis of his words, "when you thought me an Egyptian."[5]

In 1762, when they first began their courtship, John's circuit-riding legal duties took him away from Abigail for extended lengths of time. When John was traveling, he would send Nabby short love notes.[6] One of the earliest and most famous of his early love letters from October 1762 was titled "Miss Adorable"[7] and reveals the type of close companionship they shared even during that early time. It was a whimsical letter disguised partly in lawyer humor as a third-person legal writ. The "court injunction" ordered Abigail to give John, "as many Kisses, and as many Hours of your Company after 9 O'Clock as he shall please to Demand and charge them to my Account." John kept up the lightheartedness by disguising his handwriting and using irregular spelling and grammar on the outside address cover to read: "to Mistris nabagil smith Of Waymoah this weth Ceare & Spead" ("To Mistress Abigail Smith of Weymouth this with care and speed").[8]

Judging from their letters to each other, most of the year 1763 appeared to have been a continuation of romantic fun, but with a deepening level of affection and commitment to each other. By spring of that year, they were using classic mythological pen names for each other which were very much in vogue with letter writers. He signed his letters as "Philander," which meant "lover of mankind"—kind of a stretch for John, or "Lysander," after a Spartan statesman. John would address his letters "To the great Goddess Diana,"[9] Abigail's pen name after the Roman goddess of the moon and the hunt.

They both realized that their strong, growing relationship was being built upon a foundation of something more than a fleeting desire. Their love, friendship, and trust in each other was developing as was described in a popular advice book of the period for young women: "True love is founded on esteem, in a correspondence of tastes and sentiments, and steals on the heart imperceptibly. . . . Genuine love is not founded in caprice; it is founded in nature, on honourable views, on virtue, on similarity of tastes."[10] Indeed, Abigail wrote to John late one night of their close connection, "there is a tye more binding than Humanity, and stronger than Friendship," while signing off with "Accept this hasty Scrawl warm from the Heart of Your Sincere, Diana."[11] As much as any virtuous eighteenth-century woman could say it: it was love.

Sometime in fall 1763, John must have asked Abigail to accompany him on a business trip, possibly to court in Worcester, because she wrote back to him, "The original design of this letter was to tell you, that I would next week be your fellow traveler provided I shall not be any encumberance to you, for I have too much pride to be a clog to any body. You are to determine that point."[12] It appears that they indeed traveled somewhere together in the third and fourth weeks in September 1763— as a presumably engaged, but still unmarried couple. However, by that time in Abigail's eyes, their two hearts "were both cast in the same mould."[13] Upon returning, Abigail wrote to her cousin Hannah Storer Green[14] a letter which Hannah acknowledged receiving, "wherein you give an account of your journey." But Abigail's letter to Hannah is missing, and we only have Hannah's reply letter[15] to tell us the details of the trip. It seems John and Abigail were very busy on the short trip and may have stayed with friends that John had in the Worcester[16] area. Hannah reacted to a joke that Abigail made in her letter that the journey had been anything but a "smooth road" and then she likened it to "Matrimony" and "Married Life."[17]

The rocky road toward matrimony, as Abigail expressed it, became rockier for her in the new year dawning of 1764. Just as she and John were agreeing on a date for their expected marriage, a smallpox epidemic hit Boston, some ten miles north of Weymouth. It started in December 1763 and raged on until July 1764. John's work frequently took him many, many miles from Weymouth and from Abigail. He knew that on his travels, he could certainly become infected with the virus and possibly die from it, or at the very least infect Abigail along with others in her family. John correctly felt that the responsible thing to do was for him to undergo smallpox inoculation.

Smallpox was the feared plague of its time. The outcome from naturally catching the infection, as opposed to inoculation, was death in as many as 30 percent of the cases. If they lived through it at all, a person could be disfigured; at the very least they carried the scars visibly for the rest of their life. Older colonists had almost all lived through a small-pox outbreak. Any living adults during that time usually had smallpox scars on their face or body. George Washington had contracted smallpox at the age of fifteen during a trip to Barbados with his half-brother. It was noted that he carried pockmarks on his nose for the rest of his life.

It was discovered that the best, but controversial, method for surviving smallpox was to be inoculated before catching it the "natural" way. That technique infected the patient with a usually milder case of the live virus and likely secured the patient lifelong immunity.

A drawback of inoculation was the weeks of quarantine demanded for the development of smallpox pustules. During this time John would be highly contagious to anyone on the outside that he encountered. Medical folklore of the time was unsure if anything John touched or even sent a letter to someone from his infected room would carry the smallpox "Distemper" with it. The commonly used fumigation treatment called for items such as letters, coming or going, to be "smoked." This involved holding letters with fire tongs for a long period of time in the smoke of a fire, the key obviously being not to singe the paper or let it catch on fire. John wrote these words of caution to Abigail: "I have one Request to make, which is that you would be very careful in making Tom, Smoke all the Letters from me, very faithfully, before you, or any of the Family reads them."[18]

Their system of safely sending and receiving letters during an epidemic worked well, neither Abigail nor any of her family became infected. By April 20, Abigail wrote, "I hope you smoke your Letters well, before you deliver them. Mamma is so fearful least I should catch the distemper, that she hardly ever thinks the Letters are sufficently purified. Did you never rob a Birds nest? Do you remember how the poor Bird would fly round and round, fearful to come nigh, yet not know how to leave the place—just so they say I hover round Tom whilst he is smoke-ing my Letters."[19] But in one particular letter, Abigail showed some immature and insensitive feelings toward Tom's work by telling John to "enclose the Letters in a cover, but seal only the out side, Tom makes bungling work opening them, and tares [tears] them sadly."[20]

By April 30, John was released from quarantine, having weathered "the distemper like an oak."[21] He had contracted only a mild form of smallpox of, by his own count, "about Eight or Ten, (for I have not yet counted them exactly) two of which only are in my Face, the rest scattered at Random over my Limbs and Body."[22] He was antsy and eager to get back to normal life.

In eighteenth-century nautical talk, ballast was heavy material like stones, lead, or iron that a ship's captain would place down in the hold along the keel line to lower the center of gravity. In rough seas and violent storms, ballast would keep the ship upright and prevent it from capsizing and sinking. To many historians, Abigail was John's ballast. Even at the young age of twenty-three, John had noted needing ballast in his life, "Ballast is what I want, I totter, with every Breeze."[23] Though brilliant, John knew that he could also be petty, jealous, at times paranoid, and prone to launching attacks upon people who he felt deserved it. He could verbally rip someone apart when he had finally taken all he could take which was usually at the end of a short fuse. Indeed, he would lash out many times in his life when Abigail wasn't nearby to reel him in and calm him down.

In the letter John coldly alerted Abigail to get her trousseau materials together and that "I shall leave orders for Brackett [a hired field hand], to go to Town, Wednesday or Thursday with an Horse Cart. You will get ready by that Time and ship aboard, as many Things as you think proper."[24]

But then John's words turned softer when he disclosed to Abigail that his separation from her and stress was noticeable even to himself. He needed her, "after so long a separation. My soul and Body have both been thrown into Disorder, by your Absence, and a Month or two more would make me the most insufferable Cynick, in the World. I see nothing but Faults, Follies, Frailties and Defects in any Body, lately. . . . But you who have always softened and warmed my Heart, shall restore my Benevolence as well as my Health and Tranquility of mind. You shall polish and refine my sentiments of Life and Manners."[25]

That wouldn't be the last time John asked for help from Abigail. Even as president of the United States, he was begging her to leave their farm and join him in the new federal capital of "City of Washington"[26] to keep him from capsizing and sinking from his own words.

However, Abigail also had encountered many problems and stress while collecting her trousseau in Boston. But she'd reminded herself not to complain or say hurtful things when, after all, they aren't "easily cured."

And there were problems with the cart that John had said he'd be sending to Boston to collect her wedding supplies. As part of the same letter and in a charming reply to John, Abigail wrote: "The cart you mentiond came yesterday, by which I sent as many things as the horse would draw the rest of my things will be ready the Monday after you return from Taunton. And—then Sir if you please you may take me."[27]

The October 25 wedding date was now quickly approaching. But sometime between October 4, the date of her last letter to John, and October 13, the date of her next letter and as Abigail was preparing to leave Boston, she became very sick and consequently down in the dumps: "I was in hopes that I should have been out the next day, but my disorder did not leave me as I expected and I am still confind extreemly weak, and I believe low spirited. The Doctor encourages me, tells me I shall be better in a few days. I hope to find his words true, but at present I feel, I dont know how, hardly myself."[28] Sure enough, Abigail recovered her health, and the wedding took place on schedule inside the parsonage house that she had grown up in. The small parlor just inside the front door served as its venue. The ceremony of course was performed by Reverend Smith, Abigail's father. Reportedly the Reverend gave a little, perhaps good-natured, dig at John by choosing this Bible passage from Matthew 11:18 folded into the wedding vows, "For John came neither eating nor drinking, and they say he hath a devil."[29] Misspelling Braintree as "Brantree," the town clerk recorded the marriage in the Weymouth Vital Records book: "ADAMS, John [of Brantree] and [Mrs.] Abigail Smith, Oct. 25, 1764."[30] John was twenty-nine years old and Abigail was twenty-eight days short of her twentieth birthday.

The new husband and wife immediately moved about four miles away from Weymouth into the saltbox house[31] that John had inherited from his father, along with its 166–188 acres.[32] Today it's called the John Quincy Adams birthplace. Their house was only a few hundred feet away from the proverbial mother-in-law house, living in what is now the John Adams birthplace.[33] Both houses sat on the "Old Coast Road," later renamed Franklin Street. The road ran from Plymouth to Boston, and road dust kicked up by frequent horses and carriages created a near-constant need for inside dusting, since window screening had not been invented yet. In the other direction behind the houses, the acres of pastureland, barns, and hills seemingly stretched out forever. A fine apple orchard would soon be added to the holdings. It was a leisurely walk up to the top of Penn's Hill, which amazingly still exists, as well as the two Adams households down below.

The newlyweds Mr. and Mrs. John Adams went about setting up a household with a long, bright lifetime together. Richard and Mary Cranch also moved about this time, but faced an uncertain future unlike John and Abigail. The Cranches were moving from Germantown to Salem, some twenty-five miles away. Mary told Abigail that Richard stood a better chance of a successful watch repair business in a more prosperous town like Salem. That may have been true, but either way, Abigail was sick about her older sister moving away and promised Mary that she and John would be visiting very soon.

Abigail's plan to visit her sister would have to wait, however. Abigail soon discovered that she was pregnant, and along with pregnancies during that time came joy and fear. There was joy that the mother was fulfilling what could be described in the eighteenth century as a female's most important task in life—that of motherhood. The ever-present and not uncommon fear was that the mother could die during childbirth.

Chapter Three

"Come Pappa Come Home"

1765–1769

uman nature has always had a part to play in history since time began. Even in Puritan Massachusetts, an estimated thirty percent of new brides were pregnant at marriage.[1] If one does the math, it seems the newly pronounced Mrs. Adams wasn't "with child" at her marriage. However, the newlyweds seemingly lost no time in consummating their alliance once arriving inside their new home. Perhaps that very night.

A fine daughter, "Abigail the second," was born just two weeks short of exactly nine months from their marriage. As in today's world when a baby son is given the father's name and the surname of "junior" or "the second," it wasn't unusual back then that daughters received the same naming convention. As was also customary, the female was assigned a nickname. This time, Abigail the second received the same nickname her mother had used—"Nabby." It was expected that the young girl would retain the juvenile nickname until she was wed, in which case social norms dictated that the married woman's new formal surname would be substituted, almost immediately. For instance, by marrying

John Adams, Abigail "Nabby" Smith became "Mrs. Adams." When Abigail the second married William Stephens Smith in 1786, even Abigail, the mother, almost immediately started referring to her daughter in the formal style as "Mrs. Smith."

The first year of married life flew by under a canopy of busy work for Abigail. The promised visit to her sister Mary in Salem was delayed by eighteen months due to pregnancy, home duties, and politics. For even though Abigail had a household servant to help her with an unrelenting list of necessity chores, she still would have performed, at one time or another, every indoor or outdoor household task called for. Like nearly all women of her time, Abigail had been schooled in these domestic skills since childhood. Taking up most of her newlywed time would have been sewing since, with rare exceptions, all their clothes were homemade. In these early days, Abigail probably could frequently have been seen at her spinning wheel downstairs. Another ongoing process was food planning, preparation, and cooking day after day, with the center point being the large roaring fire in the kitchen. Usually, potatoes and puddings were simmering on the coals in the fireplace with some form of veal or pork rotated by hand above the fire itself.

In the early years, John and Abigail's livestock consisted of sheep, chickens, hogs, oxen, and horses. Horses served as the family's transportation as well as the power for field plowing. The Adams' farm also produced oats, wheat, potatoes, rye, and barley—but corn was their most important crop for its varied uses. Water from wells and streams was notoriously dangerous to drink owing to many forms of natural pollution; so, cider from apples had to be pressed for liquid consumption. Being close to the ocean had advantages for Abigail as well. Fresh lobster and fish could often be substituted for meats in some daily meals; the remaining would be smoked or salted for preservation. Seaweed that had been blown up onshore by the wind and waves could be harvested and used as an important source of fertilizer for the crops in the fields. Even after years of marriage, Abigail would still be managing the farm duties in John's absence when she wrote to him: "your Farm wants manure. I shall endeavour to have Sea weed carted every Leasure moment that can be had. That will not be many. Help is so scarce and so expensive I can not Hire a days mowing under 6 shillings."[2]

Despite her many duties, Abigail found a "Leasure moment" or two of isolation with John being gone so much "riding Circuits"[3]—travelling within a judicial circuit—early in their first years of marriage. Luckily, before they moved to Salem, Mary and Richard Cranch lived in the Germantown cove area of Braintree out on Shed's Neck, and Abigail visited them every chance she could. The Quincys, Abigail's maternal grandparents, were close as well at Mount Wollaston. Abigail's many pressing duties were equally magnified during that first year of marriage owing to the delicate condition of her pregnancy.

Abigail had reflected that during that hot summer of mid-July 1765, she had known that "birthing" time was near. With John being gone on his circuit duties sometimes for weeks, Abigail went home to Weymouth for support in giving birth.[4] Childbirth in Abigail's time was a semi-public affair with the mothers' female relatives and friends having been called to the bedside and often assisting the trained female midwife with delivery. No males, fathers, or doctors were present in the same room. The bulk of the delivery work was just waiting for the baby to appear while saying supportive things, fanning, and applying cold water cloths to the mother's forehead. Mothers sometimes used "birthing chairs," wooden chairs with a hole cut in the seat. Sometimes they stood leaning back-to-back against another woman for labor traction, until finally the midwife could "catch the baby." The whole unpleasant process could result in the death of the mother from infection, hemorrhaging, dehydration, or sheer exhaustion, during or after delivery. Abigail, ever the folk medicine woman, wrote Mary about the postpartum problems of a neighbor: "a poultice of Camomile flowers is also very good, but I hope she is relieved before this time. painfull experience would teach me upon the very first chill, to apply a white Bread poultice because those cold fits are always succeeded by a fever and complaints of the Breast always follow."[5]

While Abigail was adapting to her increased responsibilities, John was busier than ever traveling the "eastern circuit" of the Superior Court of Judicature, which today is in southern Maine. Maine was considered part of the Massachusetts Bay Colony and exemplified the vast territory John Adams would travel on his legal duties, as far east as Martha's Vineyard and as far west as Worcester. Although he had a law office in Boston on Queen Street, John kept a desk and library inside their home as his backup legal home base. But whenever John was back in Braintree, he found himself caught up in the growing protests of local Boston citizens. They were objecting to what they saw as violations of their rights as freeborn English citizens by the British Parliament some three thousand miles away. John's second cousin, Samuel Adams, was one of the most vocal of the early Boston protestors. John wrote in his diary: "[Sam] Adams I believe has the most thourough Understanding of Liberty, and her Resources, in the Temper and Character of the People. . . . [but] he is too attentive to the Public and not enough so, to himself and his family."[6]

For nearly one hundred years Parliament had passed many laws or "acts" having to do with trade.[7] But when the French and Indian War, called the Seven Years' War in Europe, ended in 1763, Great Britain found itself the victor over its enemy France, but enormously in debt from the war. Members of Parliament perhaps reasonably assumed that the American colonists would also want to chip in by paying some new taxes to help offset the war debt. Parliament tried to sell the concept that the war was fought for the Americans to free them from the French scourge in North America. But some vocal troublemakers in Boston didn't buy it. They declared that the taxes were illegal since no Americans, who were also natural-born British citizens, voted to approve the taxes, according to their rights spelled out in the Magna Carta and the British Constitution. This gave way to the colonist's phrase "Taxation without representation," but Parliament disagreed with the Americans' interpretation. Parliament insisted that the colonists were "virtually" represented by both Parliament and King George III, who looked out for all his subjects. The king couldn't levy taxes upon subjects since that right was taken away from him in 1215 by the Magna Carta. So, this public argument over taxes was strictly between Parliament and American colonists.

The Boston troublemakers finally had enough when in March 1765, four months before Nabby was born, Parliament passed the first revenue-producing act whether the colonists liked it or not—the Stamp Act. It was a tax on any paper product used in creating newspapers, almanacs, pamphlets, playing cards, and most legal documents. John even noted in his diary the enormity of the event: "This Year 1765 was the Epocha of the Stamp Act."[8] John had joined the Sons of Liberty,[9] a secret underground organization, and he even wrote anonymous articles against the Stamp Act in the *Boston Gazette*. John wrote in his diary: "So tryumphant is the Spirit of Liberty, every where.—Such an Union was never before known in America."[10]

But the activism came at a cost to John and Abigail. The Stamp Act greatly disrupted colonial business and by so doing, cut down on the demand for John's legal skills. Therefore, he had much less income coming in for his family. The Stamp Act had made "a large Chasm in my affairs,"[11] he wrote and added that he and Abigail could only survive by "reducing my Accounts into better order, and by diminishing my Expences."[12]

John's new reputation that he gained during the dark days of the Stamp Act controversy paid dividends in the following year of 1766. Parliament had given in and repealed the Stamp Act in March 1766,[13] which meant that John had a large legal workload again. But he listened to Abigail and her request that they take some time and visit Richard and Mary Cranch. Abigail had missed her sister, with her calm, sisterly advice about childrearing. Richard's watchmaking business in Germantown had failed, so he was giving it another try in Salem, a much more populated, upscale area. In a July letter to Mary, an excited Abigail wrote of their imminent trip to visit them. Unfortunately, she added, Nabby wouldn't be coming with them to visit with her cousin Betsy because "her cough is too bad, then it is too hot weather. . . . Poor Rogue She has been very poorly these 3 or 4 Days, cutting teeth I believe."[14] Abigail ended the letter by mentioning she would also be bringing work for Mary's husband: "I have a little business for him, haveing broke the Spring of our timepiece."[15] In the same letter, Abigail acknowledged the conditions of their sister Betsy, living at home under the strict control of their mother. Abigail proclaimed, "I desire to be very thankful that I can do as I please now!!!"[16]

On August 5 or 12, 1766, Abigail and John set out for Salem in an open chaise, spending the night at "Mr. Bishops"[17] near Medford. They finally arrived at "Brother Cranches at 12 o Clock"[18] the next day, just in time to dine and drink tea. "Thursday" was a day for John, Abigail, and Mary to see the sights while Richard was working. The three toured Marblehead. Then after lunch back in Salem, they "walked to Witchcraft Hill—An Hill about 1/2 Mile from Cranchs where the famous Persons formerly executed for Witches were buried. Somebody within a few Years has planted a Number of Locust Trees over the Graves."[19] It's unclear how long the Adamses spent visiting the Cranches in August; however, they returned for another visit three months later in November. It was during one of those two visits, probably in August when John had more free time, that John and Abigail sat for their earliest pastel portraits. Certainly, the portrait of Abigail is the most seen of her likenesses, looking out at us as a young twenty-two-year-old, a self-assured wife and mother. John's portrait, on the other hand, is one of the most rarely seen of his many images. He appears in a roly-poly wig, like judicial wigs of the time. They sat for Benjamin Blyth, a relatively unknown artist in Salem Village.

By October 1766, Abigail was planning another quick trip to Salem. She had already sent notice to Mary of their intended visit. But because of the poor postal system of the day, Abigail's letter had come back to her "like a bad penny."[20] In an accompanying letter, she asked if Mary could lend her "that quilted contrivance Mrs. Fuller made for Betsy." This may have been a quilted helmet for toddlers, as Abigail added, "Nabby Bruses her forehead sadly she is fat as a porpouse and falls heavey."[21]

Since the Adamses had returned from Salem in August, John's busy court schedule had him appearing in superior courts in Boston, Worcester, Plymouth, and Taunton. John himself jotted down the hecticness of his schedule in his diary: "now at Pownalborough, then at Marthas Vineyard, next at Boston, then at Taunton, presently at Bamstable, then at Concord, now at Salem, then at Cambridge, and afterwards at Worcester."[22]

The next letter to Mary from Abigail would arrive over three months later in the new year of 1767. Abigail packed so much news into it that she admitted that instead of the nicely organized document that she had intended, "My Letter will be a mess medly" and added at the bottom, "P.S. You must burn this for it is most dismal writing."[23]

Two years following the July 14, 1765, birth of Abigail "Nabby" Adams came the July 11, 1767, birth of son John Quincy Adams. He was "at the request of his Grandmother Smith christened by the Name of her Father John Quincy on the day of the Death of his Great Grandfather, John Quincy of Mount Wollaston."[24] John was barely home long enough to enjoy his growing family. It seemed he was always working. Abigail, in a letter to her sister Mary, lamented, "He is such an Itinerant, to speak. . . that I have but little of his company."[25] And still Abigail wrote in a heart-rending letter to John about their fourteen-month-old Nabby and their two-month-old "Johnny"—"our Daughter rock's him to Sleep, with the Song of 'Come pappa come home' to Brother Johnny."[26] John wasn't ignorant of the toll that his work was taking on his family and his own happiness and peace of mind. He knew he was drawn to the legal challenges that such a career demanded—in the varied cities and small-town hamlets in which he found himself almost daily.

The additional problem was that even when John was back in Boston, the political center of a very important colony, he savored the rich evening discussions of his like-minded friends, and it often came at the expense of less time with his family. Abigail's feelings for John's involvement in the evening meetings are not specifically known. Most likely she had mixed feelings on the issue. There was no doubt, however, that John was an important contributor, while pushing the Sons of Liberty members further on to the cause. For example, he wrote that he "Dined with 350 Sons of Liberty at Robinsons, the Sign of Liberty Tree in Dorchester."[27] Adams may have been stretching the truth when he added, "To the Honour of the Sons, I did not see one Person intoxicated, or near it."[28] It has been suggested that there had been fourteen toasts drunk at the Liberty Tree, and forty-five more at the dinner, which almost certainly caused a good many participants to become intoxicated.[29]

For John and Abigail, the decision to relocate into Boston was clear. Even though John would be temporarily leaving his Braintree farm and pastures, and Abigail her nearby friends and relatives, there seemed to be more advantages for the family in Boston.[30] The family would be together more, while helping John with his career and commute time. In April 1768, in what would the first of four moves to and within Boston, they rented a residence where John wrote that he moved "with my Family into the White House as it was called in Brattle Square."[31] Brattle Street[32] was nearly in the center of colonial Boston; their house was just a few blocks from the Town House, the seat of government, and the Brattle Street Church was a short distance to the north. Reverend Samuel Cooper was the minister at the progressive Congregationalist church, which had several revolutionary attendees: Dr. Joseph Warren, Samuel Adams, and now John and Abigail Adams. One other church member, John Hancock, a shipping merchant and one of the wealthiest persons in the colony, almost immediately hired John to defend him against British charges of smuggling. Adams defended Hancock in two different trials in 1768 and got him acquitted both times.

With John back out riding the court circuit in what would be today's southern Maine, adjusting to city life alone was difficult at first for Abigail. Although she had regularly visited Boston and stayed at the house of her uncle Isaac Smith, Sr., she mustered her fortitude toward living with her children within the third largest city in the thirteen colonies. Boston was noisy and dirty with a population of about 16,000 people packed into tall houses on each side of the winding and meandering streets and alleys. The air was stinkingly foul and unhealthy from the rotting fish and dead animals lying uncollected in the streets. At some residences, human waste from the day before was dumped into the street gutters.

Adding to the urban tension, the population had recently been increased by nearly 10,000 when the British government, still smarting after the Stamp Act failure, stationed British soldiers in Boston to intimidate Bostonians into submission and gain support for Parliament's newest measure: the Townshend Acts. One part of the Townshend Acts imposed taxes upon imported items such as paper, lead, paint, glass, and tea. Abigail ran into these cost increases frequently while she was shopping for goods in Boston. She saw the unrest and anger the new duties caused in citizens who had no say in the passing of the acts. The sight and sound of soldiers in their bright red uniforms and gleaming bayonets couldn't be far from Abigail's mind even if she had tried to ignore them. Daily, the military units were put through their drills in Brattle Square, as John noted, "directly in Front of my house."[33]

That summer of 1768, Abigail was pregnant with their third child. It was a girl, Susanna, nicknamed "Suky," who was named after John's mother, Susanna Boylston Adams. Suky was born on the frigid day of December 28, 1768, and quickly baptized on January 1, 1769, by Reverend Cooper at Brattle Street Church. It was immediately obvious that the little newborn was not healthy. She continued to struggle throughout the winter, until by spring and with the approval of Dr. Joseph Warren, the Adams's family physician, Suky was sent to the Braintree house to live and to escape the polluted Bostonian air. She would be watched over by servants and by the baby's namesake, John's mother living next door. Spring brought some relief from the biting snow and wind in Boston, and the Adams family moved for the second time. This time the move was from busy Brattle Street north to quieter Cold Lane[34] up near the Mill Pond, renting "Mr. Fayerweathers House."[35]

During the summer of 1769, John was still ensnared in the Maine territory handling a growing list of legal proceedings in Falmouth, now Portland, at Cumberland County Superior Court. He was so buried in work that he needed someone intelligent back in Boston whom he could trust to be on standby to register his upcoming cases onto the Suffolk County Court's docket. That person of course was Abigail. "I hope to be in Boston before July C[our]t," John wrote to her. "If I should not, you will see that my Actions are entered."[36] When back home in Boston, John often hosted a "Political Clubb" of liberty-loving friends in their Cold Lane home, and Abigail sat in on nearly all the political conversations. John Hancock was a frequent guest at the Adams home, as was Dr. Joseph Warren and John's second cousin Samuel Adams. Sometimes Samuel brought his wife, Elizabeth Wells Adams, "Betsey," whom he had recently married following the death of his first wife, also named Elizabeth, during childbirth. Abigail reported that Elizabeth Adams did not exhibit much interest in listening to the political chatter, while Abigail was intensely drawn to it.

Abigail, like most women of her day, was aware of the dangers of pregnancy and death to herself, and possibly to the infant at any step in that process. By early fall 1769, Abigail knew that she was pregnant once again. It must have been an uneasy time in her life to know another pregnancy was looming, while the life of her poor little one, Suky, was hanging by a thread out in the countryside.

Chapter Four

"I Should Certainly Have Been a Rover"

1770–1773

D*eath for little thirteen-month-old* Susanna "Suky" Adams sadly came on February 4, 1770, despite the best efforts of Boston doctors and of Abigail's famous folk medicines. Both parents were devastated by the death. According to the late author David Mc-Cullough, "[John] Adams was so upset by the loss that he could not speak of it for years."[1] Abigail never did talk about it. Many years later, Elizabeth, Abigail's sister and Susanna's aunt, told Thomas Adams, the Adams's third son, "Your most affectionate Mother, was bereaved of Sons,[2] & my Sister, of a sweet little Daughter, at the most interesting age of thirteen months, just as Reason was budding, & when her playful Innocence was most engaging, & 'that Heaven an Infants Smile' enchanted."[3]

In late spring 1770, the tenseness between Boston residents and British soldiers finally erupted into bloodshed. A little more than one month after Susanna's burial at Braintree, John penned into his diary this historic occurrence: "We were informed that the British Soldiers had fired on the Inhabitants, killed some and wounded others near the Town house."[4]

First, John recorded, he rushed up to his home on Cold Lane to check on Abigail: "Mrs. Adams was in Circumstances [pregnancy], and I was apprehensive of the Effect of the Surprise upon her, who [was] alone, excepting her Maids and a Boy in the House. . . . [so] I went directly home to Cold Lane. My Wife having heard that the Town was still and likely to continue so, had recovered from her first Apprehensions, and We had nothing but our Reflections to interrupt our Repose."[5]

But all was not still; in fact, the earth-shaking event that John called "the Massacre in Kings Street"[6] was almost immediately titled "The Massacre" in popular accounts.[7] Bloody rebellion was just beginning and with it, more bloodshed would come. It would sweep up John and Abigail in its wake.

The infamous event called the Boston Massacre that would give John Adams some international prominence had started off low-key during the cold, gray day of March 5, 1770.[8] John had volunteered as defense attorney for Captain Preston and his six British soldiers who had been arrested and accused of murder. No one else in Boston would even take the case: "I accepted the Choice. Many Congratulations were offered, which I received civilly, but they gave no Joy to me. I considered the Step as a devotion of my family to ruin and myself to death. . . . My health was feeble: I was throwing away as bright prospects [as] any Man ever had before him."[9]

Abigail, still weak from childbirth, was devastated by John's decision. But she was outwardly supportive of John, who had said executing the soldiers would have been no better than "the Executions of the Quakers or Witches."[10] She warned that John's decision could ruin his reputation and his business and might even bring physical harm to him and his family: "In the Evening I expressed to Mrs. Adams all my Apprehensions: That excellent Lady, who has always encouraged me, burst into a flood of Tears, but said she was very sensible of all the Danger to her and to our Children as well as to me, but she thought I had done as I ought, she was very willing to share in all that was to come and place her trust in Providence."[11]

It's unknown if Abigail was present for the hearing, as she was shown in the television miniseries *John Adams*. The series also portrayed that in the evenings John practiced his oratory for the defense in front of Abigail. Although he occasionally did that in other cases, again, there's no written evidence that John and Abigail did that with this trial.

In his defense summation, John uttered his most famous phrase—
"Facts are stubborn things; and whatever may be our wishes, our incli-
nations, or the dictates of our passions, they cannot alter the state of
facts and evidence."[12]

John's hard work for almost no fee at the trials of the Boston Massacre
soldiers made him somewhat of a respected celebrity in and around
Boston. But it came at a price to his health. To continue earning an income, he was still circuit-riding as far away as the Maine territory. He
had also been elected to the Massachusetts Legislature and General
Court. The election was his first real political commitment, on June 6,
1770. This was just a week after the May 29 birth of their third child
and second son, Charles, who was born just four months after Susanna's
death. To add to the stressful year of 1770, the Adamses were evicted
from their Cold Lane townhouse by their landlord. John and Abigail
relocated back to Brattle Square to a smaller house which Reverend
Cooper had found for them. For most of that year John had been almost
constantly away from home.

The close of 1770 was additionally a stressful time for both John and
Abigail, who was pregnant again with Thomas, soon after delivering
Charles. With John away, Abigail was juggling family finances and raising three children. Somehow Abigail dealt with the stress, but the pressure seems to have caught up with John when in early 1771, he had
what we would call a nervous breakdown. Aside from the work pressures
he was also dealing psychologically with the domestic stress of Abigail
giving birth to Charles after the death of baby Susanna. John moved his
family back to Braintree, writing in his diary: "the constant Obligation
to speak in public almost every day for many hours, had exhausted my
health, brought on a Pain in my Breast and a complaint in my Lungs,
which seriously threatened my Life, and compelled me, to throw off a
great part of the Load of Business both public and private, and return
to my farm in the Country. Early in the Spring of 1771 I removed my
family to Braintree, still holding however an office in Boston."[13]

John got away to some rural, tranquil mineral springs and recovered:
"I was advised to take a Journey to the Stafford Springs in Connecticutt,
then in as much Vogue as any mineral Springs have been since. I spent
a few days in drinking the Waters and made an Excursion, through
Somers and Windsor down to Hartford and the Journey was of Use to
me, whether the Waters were or not. On my Return I had my Annual
Journey to make on the Eastern Circuit at Ipswich, York and Falmouth,
now Portland, and this Exercise continued to improve my health."[14]

With John now returned from his health restorative retreat by mid-April and Abigail with her three children safely back to Braintree, John started commuting to his Boston law office. This arrangement lowered his stress level even more by giving him guilt-free time in the days and evenings, "attended my Office till near two, then dined and went over the ferry to Cambridge, attended the House the whole Afternoon, returned, and spent the whole Evening in my Office, alone."[15]

Isaac Smith, Jr., was Abigail's wealthy Bostonian cousin and had been Abigail's pen pal earlier in her life. During the Adamses' stressful year Isaac had been in Charleston, South Carolina, visiting relatives from 1770 to 1771. In a letter to Abigail, Isaac told her of his decision to visit England after he left Charleston. Abigail, now at age twenty-six and a mother of three children ages five and under and with a fourth child on the way, had written Isaac of her enthusiasm for his decision to "visit . . . our (cruel) Mother Country, [but] shall I say. I highly approve your design. Now is the best Season of Life for you to travel; Ere you have formed connections which would bind you to your own little Spot." She suggested that Isaac "keep a dayly journal."[16]

True to his word to write, Isaac sent a letter back to Abigail from England on February 21, 1771, but with no mention of politics. He had written a separate letter back to John also dated February 21, describing the political mood in London.[17] His letter to Abigail relayed all the wonders of England and London. He had created an exciting mental picture to Abigail of Dover Castle, Canterbury, the English countryside, "the Tower, the Cathedral of St Paul, the bank of England, the Theatres, and the Opera"[18] and shared tantalizing details about each one. But the single detail that might have seemed the most exotic to Abigail was that of an exclusive all-female club in Britain: "You have heard, perhaps, of the Female Coterie. . . . It is a Club, (the leaders of which are the fair sex,) calculated for the very genteel purposes of gaming and extravagance, gallantry and intrigue."[19]

Abigail's long, wishful, and notable reply to Isaac on April 20, 1771, stands as the first solid indication that Abigail had grown to be not only a confident mother and wife, but someone who was looking past the limitations imposed on her own sex. It shows that Abigail was pondering what could be, in terms of women's rights and equality. This was the first time she put pen to paper to confirm the independent spirit that was forming within her. She began the letter to her younger, London-based cousin by announcing that she was not writing "from the Noisy Buisy Town [Boston], but from my humble Cottage in Braintree"

and begged forgiveness for snatching him from, "all the Hurry and tu-
mult of London . . . that I may ask you ten thousand Questions."[20]

Abigail began by proclaiming her equal share of curiosity as that of a
man: "From my Infancy I have always felt a great inclination to visit
the Mother Country as tis call'd and had nature formed me of the other
Sex, I should certainly have been a rover. . . . Women you know Sir are
considerd as Domestick Beings, and altho they inherit an Eaquel Share
of curiosity with the other Sex, yet but few are hardy eno' to venture
abroad, and explore the amaizing variety of distant Lands. . . . it almost
imposible for a Single Lady to travel without injury to her character."[21]

Then Abigail, for possibly the first time in her thoughtful writing,
began to express a contemporary angle of the American-British conflict:
"it were better never to have known the blessings of Liberty than to have
enjoyed it, and then to have it ravished from us."[22]

In Isaac's February 21, 1771, reply to John, he wrote of having met
the acclaimed British historian Catharine Sawbridge Macaulay[23] during
his trip. In a male chauvinistic slap, Smith implied Macaulay's physical
looks were secondary to her writing talents: "She is not so much distinguished in company by the beauties of her person, as the accomplishments of her mind."[24]

The idea of a female writer being publicly acknowledged as an eminent author and historian piqued Abigail's interest. It was fascinating,
and her "curiosity" begged Isaac for more information on Macaulay as
she drew her letter to a close: "I have a great desire to be made acquainted with Mrs. Maccaulays own history. One of my own Sex so eminent in a tract so uncommon naturally raises my curiosity and all I
could ever learn relative to her. . . . I have a curiosity to know her Education, and what first prompted her to engage in a Study never before
Exibited to the publick by one of her own Sex and Country, tho now to
the honour of both so admirably performed by her."[25]

For the time being, Abigail probably took pride just in the fact that
John was corresponding with a female historian scholar of such fame.
Abigail, of course, read every one of Macaulay's replies to letters to John,
perhaps absorbing her letter writing style and context. As a youngster,
Abigail had begun reading books on topics out of her age bracket from
the libraries of her father and Bostonian uncle Isaac Smith, Sr. Throughout her married life, she perused the vast home library of her husband—
first for herself, then to help in the children's education.

In August 1772, finally tired of the long commute from Braintree,
John and Abigail agreed that the family would once again move back

to Boston. John and Abigail wanted to buy a house instead of renting and being at the whims of a landlord, "Having found it very troublesome to hire houses and be often obliged to remove."[26]

Adams wrote in his diary on September 22, 1772, of the purchase of a house and the promise to himself to stick to his prosperous law practice[27] and quit public politics: "I am now writing in my own House in Queen Street, to which I am pretty well determined to bring my Family, this Fall. If I do, I shall come with a fixed Resolution, to meddle not with public Affairs of Town or Province. I am determined, my own Life, and the Welfare of my whole Family, which is much dearer to me, are too great Sacrifices for me to make."[28] John had decided to settle into a non-political, lucrative life and "hope to lay a Foundation for better Fortune to my Children."[29]

John and Abigail purchased on August 21, 1772, a "brick house and lot in South Queen Street from Shrimpton Hunt for the amount of £533 6s. 8d."[30] John noted it was, "near the Scaene of my Business, opposite the Court House."[31] He moved his family to the Queen Street house in November where they would live until summer 1774. The move was delayed because of Abigail's pregnancy. Accordingly on September 15, their fourth child (their third son) was born in Braintree and named Thomas Boylston in honor of John's maternal grandfather.

Along with his Boston law practice, John continued to ride the exhausting legal circuit. However, an unusual lull in British-American hostilities took place in 1771–1772 which resulted in less work again for John. He wrote to Abigail hoping "of a speedy revival of the suing Spirit."[32]

The lull would soon be ending. Tranquility would not be returned until the end of the Revolutionary War. John may have been sensing the change in revolutionary unrest. In 1772, he was asked to give an oration in Braintree. His words were a warning to citizens about government and men: "There is Danger from all Men. The only Maxim of a free Government, ought to be to trust no Man living, with Power to endanger the public Liberty." And "If K[ing], Lords and Commons, can make Laws to bind Us in all Cases whatsoever, The People here will have no Influence, no Check, no Power, no Controul, no Negative."[33]

That observation by John Adams applied to the unfair and illegal tax on tea, as well. The five Townshend Acts that Parliament had passed in 1767 and 1768 had been repealed in 1770 because of widespread boycotts and protests. But the tax on tea continued. The tax brought in revenue for Britain. But more so, it was symbolic for Parliament in that though the Townshend Acts had been repealed, Parliament flexed its muscle, showing that it still retained the power to tax Americans "in all Cases whatsoever."[34] The different points of view over tea and taxes were clashing, all pointing to the upcoming 1773 Tea Act, followed by the Boston Tea Party and the outbreak of war.

The year 1773 also brought anxiety of a different kind to Abigail. She worried about the education of "prattling" eight-year-old "Nabby" and six-year-old "Johnny," aside from that of the two toddlers "Charly" and "Tommy."[35] Social rules of the day dictated that the mother was responsible for the early education of children. Of course Abigail took her task very seriously to "the tender twigs alloted to my care"; "I am sensible I have an important trust committed to me; and tho I feel my self very uneaquel to it, tis still incumbent upon me to discharge it in the best manner I am capable of."[36] However, she considered herself at age twenty-eight as still "a young and almost inexperienced Mother in this Arduous Buisness."[37]

Early in 1773, John had begun writing and publishing political articles under his own name in the *Boston Gazette*. British governor Thomas Hutchinson, whom John called a "Shoelicker,"[38] was taking names. When John was voted a seat in the upper house of the Massachusetts Legislature, Hutchinson was quick to veto the move. John was starting to get a reputation as one of Boston's troublemakers. During a July trip to Plymouth County court, John was planning on visiting his acquaintance and "Sons of Liberty" political heavyweight James Warren,[39] who lived in Plymouth. Abigail went with him to be introduced to Mercy Otis Warren, sister to the earlier firebrand patriot James Otis, Jr. Mercy, nearly sixteen years older than Abigail, had just anonymously published a popular satirical play the year before called *The Adulateur*, making fun of Governor Hutchinson. When Abigail met Mercy, she was working on her next anti-Hutchinson piece, *The Defeat*. Abigail may have been taken with Mercy's literary talent, but even more so, with Mercy's courage to buck the socially enforced "gentler sex" label placed upon females. Abigail also bowed to Mercy's childrearing knowledge, as Mercy was the mother to five sons.

Mercy, taken with Abigail's curious spirit, invited a mentor correspondence with Abigail, who eagerly accepted it. Abigail had barely returned to her Boston home when she penned her first letter to Mercy: "The kind reception I met with at your House, and the Hospitality with which you entertained me, demands my gratefull acknowledgment. By requesting a correspondence you have kindly given me an opportunity to thank you for the happy Hours I enjoyed whilst at your House. Thus imbolden'd I venture to stretch my pinions, and tho like the timorous Bird I fail in the attempt and tumble to the ground yet sure the Effort is laudable."[40] Abigail also expressed admiration of Mercy as a role model parent, "in which you have so happily succeeded. . . . When I saw the happy fruits of your attention in your well ordered family, I felt a Sort of Emulation glowing in my Bosom."[41]

Societal gender rules were clear. Married women were to silently support their husbands, educate the children, and keep an orderly home. Mercy Otis Warren broke those rules and was known to have had a critical, prickly personality, perfect for writing her scathing critical poems and plays attacking royal abuses. Underscoring societal expectations of women, her works were published anonymously until 1790.

Mercy may have reinforced to Abigail the idea that a woman was capable of critically thinking in the same capacity as a man, and of expressing her own thoughts. That same summer Abigail forwarded to Mercy her coveted childrearing pamphlet "On the Management and Education of Children." Mercy read it and sent it back to Abigail. She was less than impressed with the piece and said so. Mercy's tepid enthusiasm for a pamphlet that Abigail loved may have also played a part in Abigail's ongoing lessons. Foremost of societal rules pushed upon colonial wives was to be silent, or at the least not critical of political reviews of which women would not understand anyway. But that model was not suitable for Mercy and now—Abigail.

At the very end of 1773, Abigail, in her late twenties and a mother of four, had found her voice. And as political unrest mounted, she was determined to use it. It is ironic that the uproar would also involve a commodity that Abigail was very fond of: tea.

Chapter Five

"The Tea That Bainfull Weed Is Arrived"

1774

In addition to the subject of child rearing, Abigail Adams and Mercy Otis Warren were already kindred spirits on one other subject even before they had met. They both protested attempts by "the oppressor" Great Britain to curtail "the American patriots"[1] rights as natural-born British citizens.

By early 1774, when Mercy wrote those "oppressor" and "patriots" words to Abigail, things had come to a head. In May 1773, Parliament had passed the Tea Act to cut down on the smuggling of Dutch tea into the colonies. It also gave the nearly bankrupt British East India Company a virtual monopoly on the colonial tea trade. The act removed middlemen tea brokers in London from the supply chain, opening tea shipments to sail directly from India to America. Ironically, the Tea Act reduced the price of tea in North America by 50 percent, making legally imported tea cheaper than smuggled tea. But Americans were enraged, claiming that hidden in the lower price was still a Parliamentary tax on tea.

In late November 1773, three British ships filled with tea sailed into Boston Harbor and into port. From there they sat motionless and moored to the dock until mid-December due to a standoff with American patriots. Many of the patriots were members of the Sons of Liberty who blocked the unloading of the tea. Their actions were countered by Governor Thomas Hutchinson who blocked the ships from leaving port still loaded with the tea. According to the law, the ships had to leave port empty, but the Sons of Liberty would not allow them to be unloaded.

John was on his circuit-riding duties. But Abigail, who was just recovering from an illness, was nervous and right in the thick of turmoil as she wrote, "My Heart beats at every Whistle I hear."[2] On December 5, 1773, she wrote to Mercy with fire in her quill and in her heart. "The Tea that bainfull weed is arrived. Great and I hope Effectual opposition has been made to the landing of it. To the publick papers I must refer you for perticuliars. You will there find that the proceedings of our Citizens have been United, Spirited and firm. The flame is kindled and like Lightning it catches from Soul to Soul."[3]

Abigail wrote to Mercy of the civil war she foresaw between Americans and their British brethren, "Altho the mind is shocked at the Thought of sheding Humane Blood, more Especially the Blood of our Countrymen, and a civil War is of all Wars, the most dreadfull."[4] Being familiar with Joseph Addison's *Cato, A Tragedy*, Abigail ended her paragraph with a soon-to-be-famous phrase from that play. Those compelling words (or similar words) would be recited by captured American spy Nathan Hale. Abigail wrote, "Such is the present Spirit that prevails, that if once they are made desperate Many, very Many of our Heroes will spend their lives in the cause, With the Speach of Cato in their Mouths, 'What a pitty it is, that we can dye but once to save our Country.'"[5]

Abigail was caught up in the news of the day, eagerly seeking the latest from the streets where conflict brewed. "Such is the present Situation of affairs that I tremble when I think what may be the direfull concequences—and in this Town must the Scene of action lay."[6] She closed her letter of December 5 to Mercy suggesting, "There was a Report prevaild that to morrow there will be an attempt to Land this weed of Slavery."[7]

The Boston radicals waited until the night deadline of December 16 before they, dressed somewhat haphazardly as Mohawk Indians, converged on Boston Harbor. Nearly silently, they dumped 342 chests of tea overboard from the three ships. When John heard of the "Destruction of the Tea," he was ecstatic. "This is the most magnificent Movement of all. There is a Dignity, a Majesty, a Sublimity, in this last Effort of the Patriots, that I greatly admire. . . . This Destruction of the Tea is so bold, so daring, so firm, intrepid and inflexible, and it must have so important Consequences, and so lasting, that I cant but consider it as an Epocha in History."[8]

Although he deemed the action "absolutely and indispensably . . . Necessary,"[9] John expressed fears in his diary about the expected British vengeance that would come down upon the heads of Bostonians. And vengeance it was. When the tea destruction news arrived at Parliament in early 1774, enraged ministers passed new laws to punish the rebels by completely crippling Boston, the cradle of insurrection.

The last days of 1773 would find Abigail visiting her family in Weymouth, but without her four young children. Because John's court calendar had a holiday pause in it, he stayed home watching the kids while Abigail was visiting her parents and her sister Betsy, who was still living at home. By December 30, she wrote to John, "the Roads at present are impassible" and that she was being prevented from returning to Boston by "snow banks" in Weymouth. She confessed that she was "home sick" and was writing to John to kiss the children for her, adding that she would be bringing some knitted "mittins" to "Johnny" that "his Grand mama has sent him. . . and [tell] Charlly that I shall bring his when I come home."[10]

As this was just two weeks after the tea dumping in Boston, Abigail closed her letter asking for any news that John could send her, writing, "We have not heard one Word respecting the Tea at the Cape or else where." But most of all, Abigail wrote that the warm thought of the children with John was very satisfying to her: "I feel gratified with the immagination at the close of the Day in seeing the little flock round you inquiring when Mamma will come home—as they often do for thee in thy absence."[11]

International matters were of growing interest to Abigail during this time. However, family matters would nearly always override world problems. A Smith family crisis arose in the months following the Boston Tea Party. It was a sisterly intervention to thwart Betsy's infatuation with a male boarder at their parents' Weymouth house.[12] Betsy was twenty-three years old and still unmarried. Apparently, she had been courted by a few young, eligible bachelors, but nothing ever came of it.

However, boarding at Reverend Smith's house was John Shaw, Jr., a twenty-six-year-old Weymouth teacher. Shaw was a divinity school graduate and was waiting for a position to open in a local church. Word got out that Betsy had taken a strong liking to him. Abigail got wind of it and was fit to be tied: "you will find me a little up in arms as they say."[13] She wrote to Mary, the eldest sister, making an unkind reflection upon her younger sister, "the urchin is deaf as well as blind."[14] Abigail wouldn't have Betsy's reputation ruined by fawning over some itinerant, jobless minister, and a strict Calvinist no less, who happened to be living under the same roof.

Meanwhile a storm of incredible scale was forming in the halls of the British Parliament. In the first half of 1774, as expected Parliament came down hard on Bostonians in retaliation for the destruction of the tea. Parliament passed, with King George III's approval, a sweeping number of retribution laws designed to punish and strangle Boston into submission. Parliament referred to them as the "Coercive Acts," while the colonists later called them the "Intolerable Acts." John warned Abigail, "We live my dear Soul, in an Age of Tryal. What will be the Consequence I know not."[15]

The first of the Coercive Acts closed the port of Boston, which put nearly everyone out of work. Following that punishment came the edict that trial juries would now be chosen by a British official and not by a local sheriff. In addition, the 1691 royal charter authorizing self-rule by Massachusetts was revoked. It was also decreed that the New England towns were now restricted to just one town meeting per year. Also, British troops would be housed in any empty building in Boston. The building owners would be paid—but the money would come from the colonial legislature, not the Crown—which meant the people of Massachusetts would pay for the housing of the troops.

A new colonial governor, General Thomas Gage, was appointed by the king. Gage's duties included those of governor as well as military commander-in-chief of all British troops in America. General Gage was ordered to bring the rebellious Massachusetts citizens under control through any means necessary, even in bloodshed. There was no longer any doubt that Boston was at the rebellious epicenter of the colonies.

It was obvious to colonists that the Crown was setting a course to deny them of their rights as free-born English citizens. To respond to the threat, the twelve American colonies (Georgia wasn't included yet) called for delegates from each colony to meet in a Continental Congress and discuss this common danger. The date was set for September 1774 in Philadelphia. Massachusetts elected to send four delegates. John Adams was one.[16]

At first Abigail was proud that her husband had been chosen as a delegate. He was finally recognized as a mover and shaker of the colony. However, with every honor, there was a price to be paid. On Abigail's part, it was to tolerate what would become many months, even years, without John's presence. She was expected to keep the homelife going, raising and educating the children, supervising the hiring and firing of field help, managing tenants, paying taxes, and so many more tasks normally delegated to the male figure of the house.

In early 1774, before reporting to Congress, John had bought his father's house in Braintree from his brother. This was the house where John had grown up and where his mother continued to live; it was next to John and Abigail's current house. John was now the owner of two houses in Braintree sitting on a combined fifty-five acres. Although he kept his law office on Queen Street, Boston was too dangerous for a family to reside. "To prepare myself as well as I could, for the Storm that was coming on, I removed my Family to Braintree."[17] But because of the chaos in Boston, John's income from legal work there had shriveled to a trickle. "I dont receive a shilling a Week. We must contrive as many Ways as we can, to save Expences."[18] Abigail once more found herself in the additional difficult position of household money manager.

At least John's circuit court work in Maine continued, although greatly reduced, yet it kept him away from Abigail and his family for extended periods of time. Income from the Braintree property was somehow going to have to become more of a revenue source for the family. Letters to John from Abigail during this period were sparse as she and John didn't know where he would be from one day to the next. However, John writing to Abigail was effective one-way communication.

His letters show he was already delegating to Abigail the direction of the hired field hands and tenants on the property, "I wish you would converse with Brackett, and Mr. Hayden and Mr. Belcher about a proper Time to get me a few freights of Marsh Mud, Flatts, or Creek Mudd. I must have some If I pay the Cash for getting it, at almost any Price."[19] Living so close to the Atlantic Ocean had its rewards. Excellent field fertilizer came from items such as seaweed and "Marsh Mud" or "Creek Mudd." John reminded Abigail, "You must take Care my Dear, to get as much Work out of our Tenants as possible."[20]

But even with little legal work, John knew that being a delegate to the new, distant First Continental Congress would take him away from his family for an unknown period and much farther away than he'd ever been. The family income would also suffer. Although delegates were to be (barely) reimbursed for their incurred expenses by the new Congress, that reimbursement pay system hadn't been established yet. Delegates received no salary. Income worries were never far from John or Abigail's thoughts during this uneasy time. "I shall not get enough at York Court to pay my Expences for the Week."[21]

John possibly sensed that this most recent circuit trip to York and Falmouth might be his last, and it indeed it was "for the tenth and last time on the Eastern Circuit."[22] The world that he and Abigail had known was changing very quickly and there would be no security in whatever the future held. John mounted his horse and headed south to Boston and to Abigail and his family at Braintree; then soon after that for Philadelphia.

John arrived back home in mid-July and started preparing for his extended absence in Congress. In the days before he left, the hours were taken up directing field work to be done by the tenants or field hands, or by doing the work himself. John spent time studying in his home law library, the legal precedence for colonial claims that their rights were being violated. John assumed that he would be encountering learned scholars in Philadelphia and didn't want to look like a rank country lawyer, nor have it reflect badly on the three other Massachusetts delegates: "I might be furbishing up my old Reading in Law and History, that I might appear with less Indecency before a Variety of Gentlemen, whose Educations, Travel, Experience, Family, Fortune, and every Thing will give them a vast Superiority to me, and I fear to some of my Companions."[23]

At other times, John, seeing both sides of a situation as he often did, worried that he and even the other well-read American academics could never stand up to the considerable weight of well-bred British intellectuals and royal ministers. "We have not Men, fit for the Times. We are deficient in Genius, in Education, in Travel, in Fortune—in every Thing. I feel unutterable Anxiety."[24]

Anxiety and caution were the bywords of the day in and around Boston in late summer 1774. Abigail's sister and brother-in-law Mary and Richard Cranch had moved back to Boston from Tory-heavy Salem and were caught up in the nervousness that permeated every action everywhere. The Cranches had moved to Hanover Street in Boston's North End into an artisans' area where silversmith and Sons of Liberty courier Paul Revere was a neighbor. The North End living arrangement conveniently worked out for secure mail delivery between John and Abigail. It was arranged that letters from John would be picked up by Revere in Philadelphia and brought to Revere's house in North Boston. Richard Cranch would pick up the letters and under instructions from John, "Break open my Letters to my Wife, and then send them as soon as possible"[25] to Braintree.

John, with Abigail's invaluable help, was used to packing and then commuting long distances to work. As during his circuit riding duties, John and Abigail were used to long, lonely stretches of time without the other. When she had time, Abigail had built up the loneliness defense of burying herself in books. She had already selected a new book to start when John left for the First Continental Congress. Abigail would mention the title in her second letter to John.

On Tuesday, August 9, 1774, Abigail accompanied John as far as Boston on the first leg of his journey to Philadelphia. They went to the handsome home of Thomas Cushing, one of the Massachusetts delegates. There the four delegates assembled: John and Samuel Adams, Thomas Cushing, and Robert Treat Paine. It's also where Abigail met the other delegates to the Continental Congress who were preparing to head out the next morning. According to Paine, "At 11 o'clock the honble. Thos. Cushing Esq. and the other Commission[ers] of Congress for this Province sat out in a Coach and four and four Servants."[26]

As the delegates left Boston, Abigail joined the cheering crowds giving them a hearty farewell as they drove off down the dusty post road from Boston to Philadelphia. Just a few days later and not knowing if the correspondence could even be delivered, Abigail sent John her first letter to him as a congressman: "I know not where this will find you whether upon the road, or at Phylidelphia, but where-ever it is I hope it will find you in good Health and Spirits. Your Journey I immagine must have been very tedious from the extreem heat of the weather and the dustiness of the road's. . . . Your task is difficult and important. Heaven direct and prosper you."[27]

She soon followed with a second letter expressing her patriotic anxiety over the growing storm between America and Great Britain. She also told John of the book she had started "since you left me"—it was *Rollins' Ancient History*, a popular book on both sides of the Atlantic. She added the comforting message to John, who was constantly worried about "Johnny's" education, that she had introduced young John Quincy to the book as well: "The great distance between us, makes the time appear very long to me. It seems already a month since you left me. The great anxiety I feel for my Country, for you and for our family renders the day tedious, and the night unpleasent. The Rocks and quick Sands appear upon every Side. . . . I find great pleasure and entertainment from it, and I have perswaided Johnny to read me a page or two every day, and hope he will from his desire to oblige me entertain a fondness for it."[28] Abigail pensively ended the letter, "I want much to hear from you. I long impatiently to have you upon the Stage of action."[29]

Nearly three weeks later, well into September, she still had no reply from John. Abigail was ignoring all the gossip told to her by well-meaning friends or jealous, ill-speaking individuals. The overwhelming rumor was that the British Army had stormed the congressional building housing the treasonous delegates, took most captive, and executed some on the spot.

Chapter Six

"If the Sword Be Drawn"

1774

A *bigail was having trouble sleeping again.* Although insomnia plagued her for her entire life, this time it was different. The rumors of John's capture were always in the forefront of her mind day and night. She had no way of knowing that John was, although uncomfortable, quite safe on his journey with the other delegates.

John's late summer trip by horseback[1] from Boston to Philadelphia was arduous, dusty, and hot. But to John, the trip was also invigorating and worked wonders for his ego. At last, he was finally seen as a recognizable public figure in the colonies as the cheering villagers and townsfolk affirmed his new status when he rolled into each town. As the delegates entered New Haven, Connecticut, sumptuous celebratory meals were offered, and many rounds of toasts were given to the illustrious folks from Boston. John started a diary of his experience which he intended one day to share with Abigail: "As We came into the Town all the Bells in Town were sett to ringing, and the People Men, Women and Children, were crouding at the Doors and Windows as if it was to see a Coronation. At Nine O Clock the Cannon were fired, about a Dozen Guns I think. Bells and cannons sounded out everywhere."[2] Fellow congressional delegates Roger Sherman and Silas Deane, both of Connecticut, met and paid their respects to the Massachusetts delegation.

Throughout the whole upcoming War for Independence and even during the years spent in Europe, the Adamses preferred to have their precious and confidential letters delivered through a trusted acquaintance or personal messenger. Rebel courier Paul Revere sometimes brought letters to and from John in Philadelphia and Abigail in Braintree. The infant postal system was still not secure and more than once, John warned Abigail to not write anything of an incriminating nature in her letters for fear of interception.[3] Later they started using assumed names for secrecy. Letters sent and received were accumulated in a haphazard order by the sender and reader, and one was never sure to which letter the writer was replying to. Sometimes John would write numbers on the outside cover to hint at which order to open them. Often, the entire first paragraph of a reply letter was entirely taken up with housekeeping tasks of establishing to which letter the letter in hand was replying to. During the time it took to receive a reply letter, any question that had been asked by the writer in a previous letter might be invalid or out of date. Letters between Abigail and John weren't just for communication of family incidents. They were also to help with emotional reinforcement for the other or to tell news of a personal nature or point of view.

Additionally, Abigail was keeping John updated on a timely basis about events that she knew he would be interested in. In a very short time, she had mastered an understanding of the whole imperial crisis and the implications for Americans. Abigail's ability to see the big picture —both nationally and locally—would provide John with his chief source of unbiased information until they both left the "President's Mansion" in 1801.

Three days after the opening of Congress, when all the introductory hoopla was over, John wrote Abigail his first letter from Philadelphia on September 8, 1774. He addressed the outside cover as "For Mrs. Abigail Adams att Braintree Massachusetts Bay" and added "C 1 No 2." The "C" may have stood for "Congress" and "No 2" was the second letter sent that had to do with John's trip to Congress. It may have been a way for Abigail to read the letters in chronological order or to tell if one was missing. John's first letter of August 28 was addressed: "To Mrs. Abigail Adams Braintree Massachusetts Bay To be left at Mr. Adams's Office in Queen Street Boston favoured by. . . C 1 No 1." The reason the second letter made no mention of dropping the letter at John's Boston law office was probably because of the very dangerous environment Boston had become. Security of letters was probably paramount in John's mind as well as the physical security of his young law clerks, "Mr. Thaxter and Mr. Rice"[4] at that time. John added a "P.S." to his latest letter asking Abigail to ascertain the security risk of the office and decide whether to abandon Boston: "P.S. You will judge how Things are like to be in Boston, and whether it will not be best to remove the Office entirely to Braintree."[5]

John apologized to Abigail for not writing more often. He said he didn't know when he'd be home but tried to convey the magnificent patriotic spirit of his fellow delegates gathered from the other colonies: "When or where this Letter will find you, I know not. . . . It is a great Affliction to me that I cannot write to you oftener than I do. . . . It would fill Volumes, to give you an Idea of the scenes I behold and the Characters I converse with. We have so much Business, so much Ceremony, so much Company, so many Visits to recive and return, that I have not Time to write. And the Times are such, as render it imprudent to write freely. . . . When I shall be at home I cant say. There is in the Congress a Collection of the greatest Men upon this Continent."[6]

But almost one week later, September 14, Abigail had heard no additional word from John. Abigail inquired, "Five Weeks have past and not one line have I received. I had rather give a dollar for a letter by the post, tho the consequence should be that I Eat but one meal a day for these 3 weeks to come. . . . but I hope now you have arrived at Philidelphia you will find means to convey me some inteligance."[7] Abigail mentioned the postal cost of a dollar for a C.O.D. (collect on delivery) letter. Two days later, John's letter to Abigail dated August 28 from New Jersey successfully made it to John's Boston law office. John Thaxter, Jr.,[8] brought it down to the Braintree house, to Abigail's great relief: "It really gave me such a flow of Spirits that I was not composed eno to sleep till one oclock."[9] She then gave John a detailed update on a false alarm in Somerville near Boston, which had turned out minutemen and armed citizens alike. History would later name this prequel to the Lexington alarm the "Powder Alarm."[10] Abigail ended with "I have lived a very recluse life since your absence" and reminded John, "You will burn all these Letters least they should fall from your pocket."[11] But of course, John didn't do that.

As with the Powder Alarm, sometimes the news items that Abigail shared with John turned out to be false. Such was the case when she wrote John, "There has been in Town a conspiracy of the Negroes." Abigail had heard that slaves inside Boston had created a petition to British General Gage, "telling him they would fight for him provided he would arm them and engage to liberate them if he conquerd." By 1774, Abigail had grown from being ambivalent about slavery when she was a small girl to vocalizing antislavery feelings as a grown woman. The sentiments she added to this letter sum up her feelings on slavery and the glaring illogic in fighting for freedom while keeping others in bondage: "There is but little said, and what Steps they will take in consequence of it I know not. I wish most sincerely there was not a Slave in the province. It allways appeard a most iniquitious Scheme to me—fight ourselfs for what we are daily robbing and plundering from those who have as good a right to freedom as we have. You know my mind upon this Subject."[12]

Abigail also occasionally needed to go into Boston, "this much injured Town," for supplies they could not produce themselves on the farm. She also picked up mail at John's law office, checked on his law clerks, or visited relatives. She wrote to John about the distress she felt when seeing their once beloved city now in full war preparation: "I view it with much the same sensations that I should the body of a departed Friend, only put of its present Glory, for to rise finally to a more happy State. I will not despair, but will believe that our cause being good we shall finally prevail. The Maxim in time of peace prepair for war, (if this may be call'd a time of peace) resounds throughout the Country."[13] She also replied to a statement John had written a couple of weeks earlier that the local militias should begin training for battle. Abigail confirmed that their hometown Braintree militia had been called up for arms drilling: "Next tuesday they are warned at Braintree all above 15 and under 60 to attend with their arms, and to train once a fortnight from that time."[14]

Sometime during September, Abigail replied to a letter to John from the renowned British historian Catharine Sawbridge Macaulay, who had indirectly expressed "a Desire to become acquainted with our American Ladies."[15] Abigail felt that if Macaulay really wanted to know about "American Ladies," Abigail would be well suited to tell her . . . and tell her she did. This, the only letter Abigail sent to Macaulay, contained quite possibly the first full political summary that Abigail ever composed and sent to a person. It showed how much Abigail had learned about the imperial crisis that was unfolding around her every day. Abigail developed a unique perspective of the dispute not only from reading newspapers but speaking to eyewitnesses and rebel leaders. This was coupled with listening to John when he had been at home, along with reading his letters from Congress. Abigail wrote to Macaulay, a fellow woman but also a British citizen: "we shall obtain a release from our present bondage by an ample redress of our Grieveances—or a redress by the Sword. The only alternative which every american thinks of is Liberty or Death.[16] . . . Suffice it to say, that we are invaded with fleets and Armies, our commerce not only obstructed, but totally ruined, the courts of Justice shut, many driven out from the Metropolis, thousands reduced to want, or dependant upon the charity of their neighbours for a daily supply of food, all the Horrours of a civil war threatning us on one hand, and the chains of Slavery ready forged for us on the other."[17]

Abigail hoped to connect with Macaulay based on a mutual platform—female-to-female: "Yet connected as we are by Blood, by commerce, by one common language, by one common religion as protestants, and as good and loyal subjects of the same king."[18]

Taken as a stand-alone statement, Abigail had penned a beautifully written letter to Macaulay. It was full of sweeping, magnificent statements about grievances and patriotism. Abigail likely wrote drafts of the letter before sending the final version to Macaulay . . . from whom she never received a reply.

With Congress still in session, John wrote to Abigail on September 8 asking her if she had decided on whether to close his Boston law office and move everything to his smaller law office inside their Braintree house. Abigail hadn't sent back her thoughts on the idea because she had a full understanding of the local picture, and she thought John did not. She realized that closing the office would necessitate crating and moving to Braintree the law books and files, which would be difficult to store at the house. In addition, there were the two law students who lived with their families in Boston.[19] The move ten miles south would impose a sizable hardship on both. John hadn't considered those deeper circumstances—which Abigail saw.

Silently stalling, Abigail didn't acknowledge the subject to John. Then she received another letter from John dated nearly three weeks later, and embedded in it was John restating the need for the move: "I submit it to you, my Dear, whether it would not be best to remove all the Books and Papers and Furniture in the Office at Boston up to Braintree. There will be no Business there nor any where, I suppose, and my young Friends can study there better than in Boston at present."[20] At this time, the beginning of October, John was more than ever convinced that war would be breaking out with Boston being ground zero. He was firmer in his instructions to Abigail, "I have advised you before to remove my Office from Boston to Braintree. It is now, I think absolutely necessary. Let the best Care be taken of all Books and Papers."[21]

Abigail replied to John's concerns, in a letter written with a very soothing tone, "You mention the removal of our Books &c. from Boston. I believe they are safe there, and it would incommode the Gentlemen to remove them, as they would not then have a place to repair to for study. I suppose they would not chuse to be at the expence of bording out."[22]

Apparently satisfied, John dropped the subject. Instead, he focused on his growing frustration with Congress and the grandiose posturing of delegates that he had been forced to work with for over a month. "In Congress, nibbling and quibbling—as usual."[23] "I am wearied to Death with the Life I lead. The Business of the Congress is tedious, beyond Expression. . . . I believe if it was moved and seconded that We should come to a Resolution that Three and two make five We should be entertained with Logick and Rhetorick, Law, History, Politicks and Mathematicks, concerning the Subject for two whole Days, and then We should pass the Resolution unanimously in the Affirmative."[24] This letter was brought to Abigail in Braintree by Paul Revere.[25]

As Congress was at last ready to adjourn at the end of October, John was advocating to the assembly the idea of peace through strength. More than half of the delegates favored a peaceful resolution to the conflict, supported by the local Quakers whom John called the "Broadbrims."[26] John wrote to Abigail that it was vital that local militias begin serious training, to not be caught unprepared if the peace initiatives failed. "Let them exercise every day in the Week, if they Will, the more the better. Let them furnish themselves with Artillery, Arms and Ammunition. Let them follow the Maxim, which you say they have adopted 'In Times of Peace, prepare for War.' But let them avoid War, if possible, I say."[27]

On October 26, Congress voted to adjourn its session. Some of the delegates had already left to get home for the harvest. Adams stayed to the end. The main accomplishment of the First Continental Congress was signing a compact to begin a colonial boycott of all British goods starting December 1, 1774, unless Parliament rescinded the Coercive Acts. John saddled up his horse and left for Braintree, somewhat satisfied that the Congress had at least agreed on some fundamental demands to Parliament.

It was a common misconception, even among congressional members, that during this period the dangerous path leading to war was being carved out by a corrupt British Parliament and the equally corrupt Parliamentary leader—Prime Minister Lord Frederick North. But few believed that the path to war was being directed by George III. Many colonists and delegates believed His Majesty was just naively unaware of the growing turmoil between the mother country and the colonies.

In accordance with that premise, during Congress's final days, a resolution was sent to George III proclaiming colonial allegiance to His Majesty rather than to Parliament and asking for his help in the colonies' grievances against unjust ministers and Parliament. The document to the king was signed by the members of Congress as "loyal and happy subjects" which probably rankled John, but it was done in the spirit of compromise. With the very slow communication routes, Congress was not aware that two months prior, on August 23, 1774, George III had proclaimed that the colonies were in open rebellion—nearly a declaration of war. Congress voted to meet again in May 1775 if the conditions offered to Parliament had not been met.[28]

Abigail's last letter to John in Philadelphia was written from the point of view of a lonely spouse, who was dreading a possible upcoming "civil war" between Americans and British: "My Much Loved Friend, I dare not express to you at 300 hundred miles distance how ardently I long for your return. . . . I greatly fear that the arm of treachery and voilence is lifted over us as a Scourge and heavy punishment from heaven for our numerous offences.[29] . . . if the Sword be drawn I bid adieu to all domestick felicity. . . . We have too many high sounding words, and too few actions that correspond with them."[30]

Abigail inserted into her letter some personal news for John, "Some folks say I grow very fat.—I venture to write most any thing in this Letter, because I know the care of the Bearer. . . I almost envy him, that he should see you, before I can."[31] The letter carrier was William Tudor, one of John's former law clerks.

George III replied to Congress's appeal for the sovereign's help when he addressed both houses of Parliament on November 30, 1774. In his speech, the king led off with a condemnation of the "criminal nature" of the recent actions of Massachusetts and declared that "a most daring spirit of resistance, and disobedience to the law still unhappily prevails in the Province of the Massachusetts Bay, and has in divers parts of it broke forth in violences of a very criminal nature."[32] News of the king's address was received in Braintree the first week of February 1775. Abigail wrote to Mercy Otis Warren that "The die is cast. . . . The reply of the house of commons and the house of Lords shew us the most wicked and hostile measures will be persued against us—even without giving us an opportunity to be heard in our defence."[33]

War was imminent. John had been back from Philadelphia a few weeks when the Massachusetts Provincial Congress voted for him to be a delegate to the Second Continental Congress in May. John agreed and would be returning to Philadelphia. In the interim, John and Abigail expressed concern over their children's education. Even in the depths of debates during the First Continental Congress, John had written to Abigail that "The Education of our Children is never out of my Mind."[34] Owing to John's absences, the responsibility for the children's education, and mostly that of John Quincy, the eldest son, fell on Abigail's shoulders.

Abigail bore that new accountibility well. Even though the headmaster at Braintree's public school was now Nathan Rice, one of John's former law clerks, Abigail informed John: "I have not sent Johnny. He goes very steadily to Mr. Thaxter who I believe takes very good care of him, and as they seem to have a liking to each other believe it will be best to continue him with him. . . . I have always thought it of very great importance that children should in the early part of life be unaccustomed to such examples as would tend to corrupt the purity of their words and actions."[35] In other words, Abigail thought it important for young children not to be exposed to bad influences at school and an occasional "obscene expression." Bullying of boys by some tough boys was not uncommon. Grammar schools of the time were often one room with many ages of children in it, so Abigail assumed that John Quincy's learning would be minimal or amount to nothing in that distracting environment. Abigail had made the decision to keep Johnny with in-home tutoring, although adding, "However when you return we can then consult what will be best." When John returned from Congress, John Quincy remained in home tutoring with John Thaxter, Jr.

The education of Nabby was a different story. Abigail was torn on teaching Nabby a liberal variety of school subjects, but she concentrated on mostly householding skills such as cooking, cleaning, planting, sewing, and candle making. These would at least ensure her being able to attract a suitable husband and prepare her for motherhood. Although Abigail felt strongly about females also being schooled in a classical education, she was not going to rebel against the existing social system that had been established for women and their role in it. Nabby's future security for marriage and a family was at stake.

The three Smith sisters regretted not having a more advanced education. Recalling her young thirst for knowledge, Abigail now had to decide how far to pursue Nabby's mental stimulation and education past the standard school subjects for females. Society dictated that the reason for allowing any female to gain a cursory level of such subjects as literature was so that she could engage in suitable conversation with a male. But she should not have too much knowledge, as most men found very educated women undesirable. It was also believed that if females thought too much and pondered weighty subjects it affected their reproductive cycles, like a natural form of birth control. Since the purpose of eighteenth-century womanhood was the successful birthing and raising of virtuous children, with each sex specializing in their gender-determined societal role, any form of birth control was greatly frowned upon, at least by the men.

Abigail spoke out against eighteenth-century society regarding the lack of education for females in this hard-hitting paragraph to John Thaxter, Jr.: "It is really mortifying Sir, when a woman possessd of a common share of understanding considers the difference of Education between the male and female Sex. . . . Every assistance and advantage which can be procured is afforded to the sons, whilst the daughters are totally neglected in point of Literature. Writing and Arithmetick comprise all their Learning. Why should children of the same parents be thus distinguished? Pardon me Sir if I cannot help sometimes suspecting that this Neglect arises in some measure from an ungenerous jealosy of rivals near the Throne."[36]

Abigail was exposing society at large for its reluctance to offer an equal liberal education for girls while lavishing it on boys. John completely agreed and implored Abigail to keep speaking out for what society could not or would not contemplate—a deep and diverse education for girls. John replied to Abigail: "I have seen the Utility of Geometry, Geography, and the Art of drawing so much of late, that I must intreat you, my dear, to teach the Elements of those Sciences to my little Girl and Boys. It is as pretty an Amusement, as Dancing or Skaiting, or Fencing, after they have once acquired a [t]aste for them. No doubt you are well qualified for a school Mistress in these Studies."[37] Abigail and John were in complete agreement on how their children should be educated.

John was discovering that Abigail, when given decision-making power on matters of the house, farm, property, and children, could be counted on to make informed decisions. This flew in the eyes of contemporary social rules, along with civil common law, where the husband was absolute lord and master over his domain, keeping power to himself. The ten-year anniversary of John and Abigail's marriage arrived while

John was in the First Continental Congress. They both may have realized that their love and companionship had evolved into a trusted partnership that would last into the next century.

Part II

Revolution

Chapter Seven

"I Want Some Sentimental Effusions of the Heart"

1775–1776

Abigail occasionally expressed that she was a naturally optimistic person. She almost felt guilty about it: "Tis true I enjoy a good flow of spirits for the most part. I sometimes wonder at myself, and fear least a degree of stupidity or insensibility should possess my mind in these calamitous times."[1]

But the year 1775 would even test Abigail's optimism. It was a very difficult year for Abigail and John, and for most Americans. On February 9, the king and Parliament declared the colony of Massachusetts-Bay in open rebellion. John knew that some of the colonies were strongly backing Massachusetts, believing that if Parliament could strip one colony of its charter and rights, it could happen to any of them. But other colonies felt that Massachusetts was just a rebellious colony that would drag the others into a war.

Legal work in Massachusetts had all but dried up for John. Therefore, he was spending much of his time from January through April at home writing argumentative replies to letters printed in the *Massachusetts Gazette*. It became a back-and-forth duel of different points of view on the crisis, both authors writing anonymously. Adams wrote as "Novanglus" ("New Englander") from the Whig (Patriot) point of view. The other author, who turned out to be Daniel Leonard, a friend of John's, wrote as "Massachusettensis" and as a Tory. Whigs and Tories were political party terms. A Whig or Patriot was someone who disagreed with the harsh policies of George III, Lord North, and his Parliament. But a Tory or Loyalist backed the British ruling party and its more aggressive actions against treasonous Americans. John called the Torys "The little, dirty, ministerial Party."[2]

Abigail wanted to be part of the political world that was denied to nearly all women of her time. She was struggling with the social restraints that prevented a female from expressing a point of view on the traditionally male subject of politics. However, the intellectual awakening that Abigail experienced in 1774, mostly through necessity, had created a hunger which only more discussion and correspondence could satisfy.

Abigail reached out to her elder mentor, Mercy Otis Warren. Just days into the new year of 1775, she asked Mercy if she would send the letters that British historian Catharine Macaulay and Warren had exchanged. Abigail said she would like to read them. Mercy made a deal with her, a subtly worded quid pro quo. She would send the letters "provided I may be indulged in Return with the sight of Mr. and Mrs. Adams's Correspondence with the Lady Refered to."[3] In early February, Abigail was following up on their agreement, "My Friend assures me that she will comply with my request and gratify my curiosity,"[4] with Mercy likewise asking later in the month, "Do let me know if the Letters to Mrs. Macauley are gone, and by whom."[5]

In a January 28, 1775, reply letter, Mercy proposed the possible tragedy of having both their husbands, John Adams, and James Warren, "Marked out as Early Victems to successful Tyrany"[6]—in other words, labeled as traitors by the Crown and executed. Mercy added, "And Which of us should have the Courage of an Aria or a Portia in a Day of trial like theirs."[7] Roman heroes and heroines were very much in vogue in the romantic literary styles that Abigail, her sisters, and Mercy used. Mercy had reminded Abigail of two such wives, Portia and Aria, of slain Roman warriors who had died fighting the tyranny of Julius Caesar. Mercy's phrase about "Courage" refers to the fact that both Portia and Aria committed suicide when hearing of their husbands' deaths. The example of ultimate female courage was not lost on Abigail. Less than three months later, John would be leaving for the Second Continental Congress and Abigail would be alone once more. He cautioned her about signing her letters with her real name in case of interception.

The whole world changed the morning of April 19, 1775. British General Thomas Gage had sent seven hundred Redcoat soldiers from Boston westward into the dark countryside to confiscate rebel military supplies hidden at Concord.[8] As the soldiers marched through Lexington near daybreak, they found eighty American militiamen on the Lexington common. The citizen-soldiers stood at alert, but did not block the road. An unknown person fired an opening shot. British soldiers opened fire and charged the Americans with bayonets, killing eight.

The Redcoats marched on to Concord where they found and destroyed some war materiel but were confronted by American militiamen at the Old North Bridge. A bloody skirmish ensued there. The British had accomplished their mission, so they formed up and started their long march back to Boston. During the long trek to the safety of Boston, the British troops were repeatedly sniped at and ambushed by civilian colonists and militiamen. That day about 250 Redcoats were killed or wounded and about ninety Americans were killed or wounded. The British retreated into Boston where they would stay surrounded by Americans until early 1776.

News of the bloodshed traveled extremely fast thanks to a well-defined and practiced network of courier riders who galloped out on paths of concentric circles. John Adams was at his Braintree farm the next morning, Thursday, April 20, when a courier brought news of the battle. Saturday morning, John rode to Lexington and Concord to see the scene of battle and to talk to residents: "I rode from thence to Lexington and along the Scene of Action for many miles and enquired of the Inhabitants, the Circumstances. They . . . convinced me that the Die was cast, the Rubicon passed, and . . . if We did not defend ourselves they would kill Us." John decided that "the Battle of Lexington on the 19th of April, changed the Instruments of Warfare from the Penn to the Sword."[9]

But no sooner had John returned home and was ready to leave for the Second Continental Congress, than he fell very sick. "On my Return home I was seized with a fever, attended with allarming Symptoms: but the time was come to repair to Philadelphia to Congress which was to meet on the fifth of May. I was determined to go as far as I could, and instead [of] venturing on horseback as I had intended, I got into a Sulkey attended by a Servant on horseback and proceeded on the Journey."[10] Since John was still weak from his illness, Abigail had arranged with her father the use of his "Sulky," a two-wheeled cart pulled by a horse for John's trip to Philadelphia. John preferred riding a horse in his travels, but in this case, he gave in to Abigail's offer. She also hired Joseph Bass, a trustworthy son of a neighbor, to accompany John on the trip and to assist him while Congress was in session.

The entourage passed through Hartford, Connecticut. From there John asked Abigail to keep him updated through the mail. He knew he could trust her to give him unfiltered news: "Pray write to me, and get all my Friends to write and let me be informed of every Thing that occurs."[11] This started the custom of Abigail sending John political news whenever they were separated. And Abigail seemed to enjoy the role of news correspondent to John: "I say there is a degree of pleasure in being able to tell new's—especially any which so nearly concerns us as all your proceedings do."[12]

However, more important and with danger always near, John had written to Abigail on what to do if she and the family were accosted by British troops: "In Case of real Danger. . . . fly to the Woods with our Children."[13] The warning for Abigail wasn't an idle one. Open warfare was now all around Boston and Braintree, as Abigail confirmed in her first letter to John, hoping it would catch up to him in Philadelphia: "Our House has been upon this alarm in the same Scene of confusion that it was upon the first—Soldiers comeing in for lodging, for Breakfast, for Supper, for Drink &c. &c. Sometimes refugees from Boston tierd and fatigued, seek an assilum for a Day or Night, a week—you can hardly imagine how we live."[14] She added that "Isaac talks of leaving you, and going into the Army. I believe he will."[15] Isaac Copeland was their hired field hand. Abigail also mentioned they might be losing Nathan Rice, one of John's law clerks living at their Braintree house: "Mr. Rice has a prospect of an adjutant place in the Army. I believe he will not be a very hardy Soldier. He has been sick of a fever above this week, and has not been out of his chamber. He is upon the recovery now."[16]

The war was now on Abigail's doorstep. John reminded her to not panic if fighting started near her in Braintree: "I hope you will maintain your philosophical Composure."[17] Her letter to John dated May 4, 1775, was the first time she signed off with her security code name, "Portia."[18]

The Massachusetts delegation rolled into Philadelphia on May 10 for the start of the Second Continental Congress, which included some new faces that hadn't been there in 1775. John Hancock had been added to the Massachusetts delegation. Thomas Jefferson represented Virginia. From New York, John Jay had been added. Benjamin Franklin was a chief delegate for Pennsylvania. Although the entire colony of Georgia was still not represented, two revolutionary delegates from that wayward colony, Archibald Bulloch and Lyman Hall, were in attendance. Colonel George Washington was again sent from Virginia. As John wrote to Abigail, "Coll. Washington appears at Congress in his Uniform and, by his great Experience and Abilities in military Matters, is of much service to Us."[19] Congress moved from the cramped Carpenter's Hall up the street to the larger and more impressive Pennsylvania State House (today better known as Independence Hall).

Two weeks into the busy congressional session, John wrote Abigail the good news: "The Congress will support the Massachusetts. There is a good Spirit here."[20] As Congress worked through the delicate business at hand, John found himself listening to and deliberating with men who tested his self-control and patience: "But America is a great, unwieldy Body. Its Progress must be slow. It is like a large Fleet sailing under Convoy. The fleetest Sailors must wait for the dullest and slowest. Like a Coach and six—the swiftest Horses must be slackened and the slowest quickened, that all may keep an even Pace."[21]

John was anxious to gain congressional adoption of the four militia groups surrounding Boston: those of Massachusetts, Connecticut, New Hampshire, and Rhode Island. They would constitute the formation of a future and larger Continental Army composed of troops from all thirteen colonies. However, John had to skillfully choose his words and timing as to not alienate more conservative members: "Our Debates and Deliberations are tedious, from Nine to four, five, and once near Six. Our Determinations very slow—I hope sure. The Congress will support Us, but in their own Way. Not precisely in that Way which I could wish, but in a better Way than We could well expect, considering what an heterogeneous Body it is."[22]

Congress had separated into three blocks. The first group was the conservatives, who continued to seek a peaceful resolution to the crisis between the colonies and Parliament. Their leader was Pennsylvania's John Dickinson. The middle and largest group was anti-Parliament, but pro-king. They contended that George III and not ministerial Parliament held the true allegiance of the colonists. They proclaimed that Parliament had no constitutional right to "exercise authority over us."[23] A third faction, for whom John Adams became spokesman, advocated a complete split with the mother country. This meant independence, although that "I" word wasn't uttered yet by delegates, being too radical and divisive at the time.

During this session of the Second Continental Congress, May through August 1775, John made minimal entries in his diary. We know what was going on with him mostly from entries in the *Journal of the Continental Congress* or through his letters to Abigail. We know his health was bad, probably partly from the stress and workload. He complained to Abigail about "smarting Eyes" more than once. "My Eyes depress my Spirits and my Health is quite infirm. Yet I keep about and attend Congress very constantly."[24] John continued, "Dr. Church[25] has given me a Lotion, which has helped my Eyes so much that I hope you will hear from me oftener than you have done. When I shall come home I know not. We have Business enough before Us to detain us, untill the 31. of next December."[26]

Shortly after John wrote and sent that letter, Abigail replied with a marked request that showed the glint of the merchandising savviness that she would develop: "It is that you would send out Mr. Bass and purchase me a bundle of pins and put in your trunk for me. The cry for pins is so great that what we used to Buy for 7.6 are now 20 Shillings and not to be had for that. A bundle contains 6 thousand for which I used to give a Dollor, but if you can procure them for 50 shillings or 3 pound, pray let me have them."[27] Since nearly all clothes were handmade, pins were important in the eighteenth century for fastening, sewing, and mending clothes.

At the close of a late June letter to John, Abigail included the folksy, warm image of the antics of their four children, "Nabby Johny Charly Tommy," to lighten up her war-heavy "We live in continual Expectation of Hostilities" letter. "Tom says I wish I could see par. You would laugh to see them all run upon the sight of a Letter—like chickens for a crum, when the Hen clucks. Charls says mar What is it any good news? and who is for us and who against us, is the continual inquiry."[28]

June 15, 1775, was a momentous day. John had nominated George Washington for the Continental Army's commander-in-chief position over John Hancock of Massachusetts. Before any delegate could raise an objection, John's nomination was quickly seconded by his cousin Samuel Adams. Coupled with that event, on the day before (June 14), Congress had adopted "the New England Army investing Boston"[29] as its own army. Two days later, John wrote Abigail of what would become one of the most fortuitous events coming from the Second Continental Congress: "I can now inform you that the Congress have made Choice of the modest and virtuous, the amiable, generous and brave George Washington Esqr., to be the General of the American Army, and that he is to repair as soon as possible to the Camp before Boston. This Appointment will have a great Effect, in cementing and securing the Union of these Colonies."[30]

The morning of June 17, 1775, when John wrote to Abigail about those positive developments in Congress, the sound of cannon shelling woke Abigail and her four children at 3:00 a.m. They went outside to investigate, and the noise appeared to be coming from the north, from Boston. Abigail sent Nabby, Charley, and Tommy back inside and told them to bar the door. She and John Quincy went up to the top of Penn's Hill[31] above their house to see what was going on. From their vantage point ten miles away, they saw the British ships shelling Charlestown and Breed's Hill, erroneously identified in history as Bunker Hill. It was a major battle; cannon fire briefly illuminated the dark morning light and volumes of smoke clouds billowing upward. Soon afterward Abigail gathered more news on the battle and wrote to John, "our enimies were cut down like the Grass before the Sythe. . . . We had some Heroes that day who fought with amazing intrepidity, and courage. . . . I hear that General How should say the Battle upon the plains of Abram was but a Bauble to this."[32]

The day after the battle Abigail received confirmation that Doctor Joseph Warren, their beloved friend, family doctor, and brother-in-law to Mercy Otis Warren, had been killed in the final moments of the battle. Abigail broke the tragic news to John:

> My bursting Heart must find vent at my pen. I have just heard that our dear Friend Dr. Warren is no more but fell gloriously fighting for his Country—saying better to die honourably in the field than ignominiously hang upon the Gallows. Great is our Loss. . . . the constant roar of the cannon is so [distre]ssing that we can not Eat, Drink or Sleep. . . . I shall tarry here till tis thought unsafe by my Friends, and then I have secured myself a retreat at your Brothers who has kindly offerd me part of his house.[33] . . . Charlstown is laid in ashes. The Battle began upon our intrenchments upon Bunkers Hill, a Saturday morning about 3 o clock and has not ceased yet and tis now 3 o'clock Sabbeth afternoon.[34]

As late as July and even with the bloodshed at Bunker Hill, a faction of Congress still wanted to negotiate yet another peace deal with George III.

It seemed ludicrous to John Adams that a second Olive Branch Petition should be sent by Congress to His Majesty. "This Measure of Imbecility, the second Petition to the King [that] embarrassed every Exertion of Congress."[35] But for the sake of unity, John went along with it.

Following the Battle of Bunker Hill, patriot families began the wholesale evacuation of enemy-controlled Boston. The evacuees fled to the countryside, looking for safety and shelter farther inland away from the coastline and the threat of British warships. Sometimes refuge was found with friends and relatives if they were lucky. Other times, they begged the kindness of strangers. Abigail mentioned this forlorn situation to John, "In this Day of distress for our Boston Friends when every one does what in them lyes to serve them."[36]

The Cranches, living on Hanover Street in Boston's north side, obtained an exit visa from officers of British-held Boston. The visas were needed to screen citizens who were being allowed to leave the town, providing that they left their guns behind. This limited the number of weapons which could in turn be used against the British. Richard Cranch had found a house in Braintree to move his family. It was next to Christ Church on School Street. For a short time, war had brought Abigail and her children again close to her sister Mary and her children.

Now with Boston and the port being a closed, garrisoned town, commodity shortages were becoming common. "We shall very soon have no coffee nor sugar nor pepper here,"[37] Abigail wrote John. But the one commodity that was in her ability to procure was pins, thanks to John's temporary residence in Philadelphia. "Pray dont let Bass forget my pins. Hardwick has applied to me for Mr. Bass to get him a 100 of needles no. 6 to carry on his stocking weaving. He says they in Phyladelphia will know the proper needle."[38]

Yet Abigail continued in her letter of the plight of John's evacuee Boston friend, "G[e]orge Trott and family."[39] Trott had been a jeweler by trade and was an active member of the Sons of Liberty. He had married John's cousin, Ann Boylston Cunningham. But Trott and his family, including his pregnant wife, were now homeless. They stayed for a very short time in the already-crowded home of John's brother, Peter Boylston Adams. But that wasn't going to work. George Trott asked Abigail about the house next door to her. John's mother had remarried and had moved out, allowing the house to be rented to tenant farmers . . . in this case to a rather nasty old man named Hayden: "he [Trott] with all his family were obliged to shelter themselves in your Brothers house till he could seek further. . . . it was impossible for them to tarry there, Mrs.

Trots circumstances requiring more rooms than one. In this extremity he applied to me to see if I would not accommodate him with the next house, every other spot in Town being full. I sent for Mr. Hayden and handsomely asked him, he said he would try, but he took no pains to procure himself a place. There were several in the other parish which were to be let, but my Gentleman did not chuse to go there."[40]

Hayden (his first name is unknown) had been hired as a tenant field hand. However, Hayden made it very clear to Abigail that he wasn't about to be shoved out of the house or even made to share the house with anyone, especially with those "Boston folks."[41] During the entire spring of 1775 Hayden hadn't paid any rent nor performed any work on the property. He was a squatter who refused to budge. Abigail countered with a firm, equitable demand which was met dismissively by Hayden. Abigail explained,

I then sent and asked Mr. Hayden to be so kind as to remove his things into the other part of the house and told him he might improve the kitchen and back chamber, the bed room and the Dairy room in which he already had a bed. He would not tell me whether he would or not, but said I was turning him out of Door to oblige Boston folks, and he could not be stired up, and if you was at home you would not once ask him to go out, but was more of a Gentleman. (You must know that both his Sons are in the army, not but one Days Work has been done by any of them this Spring.) I removed my dairy things, and once more requested the old Man to move into the other part of the house, but he positively tells me he will not and all the art of Man shall not stir him, even dares me to put any article out of one room into an other. Says Mr. Trot shall not come in—he has got possession and he will keep it . . . that obstinate Wretch will not remove his few things into the other part of that house, but live there paying no rent upon the distresses of others.[42]

Uncharacteristically Abigail could barely control her anger, writing to John, "Let it suffice to say it moved me so much that I had hard Work to suppress my temper. . . . I feel too angry to make this any thing further than a Letter of Buisness."[43] Then, knowing that legal and social laws in any conflict gave Abigail, a married woman, very little if any clout. Abigail ended with a strong message to John, "I shall be much mortified if you do not support me."[44]

John sent Abigail an immediate reply. He was incensed about "the ill Usage you have received from Hayden [which] gave me great Pain and the utmost Indignation." Along with Abigail's letter, he sent an accompanying warning and eviction notice. Abigail was to have the notice witnessed and then formally handed to Hayden. John wrote: "Your generous Solicitude for our unfortunate Friends from Boston, is very amiable and commendable, and you may depend upon my Justification of all that you have done or said to Hayden. His sawcy, insolent Tongue is well known to me, but I had rather he should indulge it to me than to you. I will not endure the least disrespectfull Expression to you. In my Absence and in your Situation, it is brutal. I send you a Warning to him to go out of the House immediately. You may send it to him, if you see fit. If you do, let two or three Witnesses see it, before you send it, and let it be sent by a good Hand."[45]

Eventually Hayden received the eviction notice. However, three months later he was still firmly entrenched in the house. Abigail complained to John: "Hayden does not stir. Says he will not go out of the parish unless he is carried out—and here nobody will let him come in. I have offerd him part of the House that Field is in if he will but go out, but no where suits, and it is not to be wonderd at as he has wood at free cost and has plunderd pretty well from the family they live with many articles. I have a great mind to send a sheriff and put him out."[46]

It is unknown if the sheriff was notified, or if any other action was taken against Hayden. In the meantime, Abigail observed with frustration: "Had that house been empty I could have had an 100 a year for it."[47] Nearly three years later Abigail was finally successful in removing Hayden from the house, although it cost her. On April 9, 1778, Abigail wrote to John Thaxter, "I know you will give me joy when I tell you that I have wrought almost a miracle. I have removed H[ayde]n out of the house, or rather hired him to remove."[48] A week later, she updated husband John, "I sit about removeing the Tenants from the House, which with much difficulty I effected, but not till I had paid a Quarters Rent in an other House for them."[49]

Aside from having issued an ignored eviction notice to help Abigail dispose of an unwanted squatter, John's other initiative had brought better results. George Washington had been unanimously voted for his commander-in-chief commission by Congress on June 15–16, 1775. Now General George Washington left Philadelphia on June 24 to assume his command at Cambridge, Massachusetts, across the Charles River from the Boston neck blocking the entrance and exit of that besieged city. Washington and his entourage rode hard for nearly eight days, arriving at Cambridge on July 2. The following day, Washington officially took command of the "Army" and began a dizzying checklist to determine the state of the troops and supplies. What he found was distressing to say the least: rowdy, undisciplined, and untrained soldiers, poor officers, disease, low morale, rampant drunkenness, few supplies and munitions, and inadequate fortifications.

However, during those hectic days, General Washington and General Charles Lee found time to travel from Cambridge to Braintree to make a courtesy call on Abigail Adams. Abigail wrote to John: "I had the pleasure of seeing both the Generals and their Aid de camps soon after their arrival and of being personally made known to them. They very politely express their regard for you. Major Miflin said he had orders from you to visit me at Braintree. . . . General Lee looks like a careless hardy Veteran and from his appearence brought to my mind his name-sake Charls the 12, king of Sweeden." It seems meeting third-in-line General Charles Lee[50] had minimal impact on Abigail. But there's no doubt that meeting George Washington in person made a monumental impression: "I was struck with General Washington. You had prepaired me to entertain a favorable opinion of him, but I thought the one half was not told me. Dignity with ease, and complacency, the Gentleman and Soldier look agreably blended in him. Modesty marks every line and feture of his face."[51]

Abigail's July 16 letter in which she describes meeting George Washington also covered other various topics including the personal condition of friends, also some "intelegance" from Boston ("A poor Milch cow was last week kill'd in Town and sold for a shilling stearling per pound"), the status of the Roxbury military camp, more Boston Bay island skirmishes; and as always in Abigail's letter structure style, the condition of the children came toward the end: "Our little ones send Duty to pappa. You would smile to see them all gather round mamma upon the reception of a letter to hear from pappa, and Charls with open mouth, What does par say—did not he write no more. And little Tom says I wish I could see par."[52]

John had previously asked if Abigail could prod their friends into writing to him more often, as he always wanted a variety of reliable intelligence. Perhaps John was lonely. Abigail addressed his request in her July 16 letter: "You have made often and frequent complaints that your Friends do not write to you. I have stired up some of them. Dr. Tufts, Col. Quincy, Mr. Tudor, Mr. Thaxter all have wrote you now, and a Lady [Mercy Otis Warren] whom I am willing you should value preferable to all others save one."[53] Abigail voiced her own complaint about John's writing habits to her since his letters had gotten short and dry: "May not I in my turn make complaints? All the Letters I receive from you seem to be wrote in so much haste, that they scarcely leave room for a social feeling. They let me know that you exist, but some of them contain scarcely six lines. I want some sentimental Effusions of the Heart. I am sure you are not destitute of them or are they all absorbed in the great publick. Much is due to that I know, but being part of the whole I lay claim to a Larger Share than I have had. You used to be more communicative a Sundays. I always loved a Sabeth days letter, for then you had a greater command of your time—but hush to all complaints."[54]

Abigail was clearly lonely for John, and during those chaotic days she was asking for a little more attention than he'd been giving. But in a different letter, Abigail wrote of her understanding of John's situation and why he had such little time to write to her: "I have received a good deal of paper from you; I wish it had been more coverd; the writing is very scant but I must not grumble. I know your time is not yours, nor mine."[55] Most of the time, Abigail tried to put on a brave face to counter her lonely, private face toward John. In other areas, wartime played havoc with supply chains that kept families, mothers, and children (without the husband present) barely surviving. Abigail voiced the complaints of all Bostonian women who were suffering from wartime shortages. However, now added to Abigail's earlier list of shortages to John were flour and tobacco.[56] But Abigail still elaborated upon her earlier request. In letters of June 16 and July 5, she had requested that John's servant in Philadelphia, Joseph Bass, procure her "pins" while he was there because of the local Boston shortage; adding that "Bass may make a fine profit if he layes in a stock for himself." Abigail realized that money could be made from products in short supply. The germ of her entrepreneurial spirit was born at that time: "You can hardly immagine how much we want many common small articles which are not manufactured amongst ourselves, but we will have them in time. Not one pin is to be purchased for love nor money. I wish you could convey me a thousand by any Friend travelling this way."[57] But she was quick to add that lately Bostonians only wanted sales credits instead of paying cold cash, and that arrangement went against her own personal philosophy, "No person thinks of paying any thing, and I do not chuse to run in debt. I endeavour to live in the most frugal manner possible."[58]

In a portion of the same letter written a day earlier, Abigail also passed along rumored intelligence to John, which turned out to be false. It was about the alleged dishonor that British officers had inflicted upon the body of John and Abigail's friend, Doctor Joseph Warren, after he was killed at the Battle of Bunker Hill: "We learn from one of these Deserters that our ever valued Friend Warren, dear to us even in Death; was [not] treated with any more respect than a common soldier, but the [sav]age wretches call'd officers consulted together and agreed to sever his Head from his body, and carry it in triumph to Gage."[59] Another dishonor by a high-ranking British officer, General John Burgoyne, though this time only to property, had also been told secondhand to Abigail: "General Burgoine lives in Mr. Samll. Quincys House. A Lady who lived opposite says she saw raw meat cut and hacked upon her Mahogona Tables, and her superb damask curtain and cushings exposed to the rain as if they were of no value."[60]

A July 30 letter from John to Abigail gave her the good news that "my Friend Mr. William Barrell"[61] would be bringing to their Braintree home "your Present of Pins." He also added that "Congress has determined to adjourn to sometime in September" because of the tremendous summer heat in Philadelphia which usually brought illnesses and diseases. John wrote that "in this exhausting debilitating Climate . . . our Lives are more exposed than they would be in [military] Camp."[62]

John didn't know that he would be riding back into a deadly outbreak of dysentery, one that would strike his own family.

Chapter Eight

"The Sin of Slavery"

1775–1776

J ohn Adams had barely been home from the short congressional break
when he learned that Elihu, his "youngest Brother [was taken] to the
Grave. He had commanded a Company of Militia all Summer at
Cambridge, and there taken a fatal Dissentary then epidemic in the Camp
of which he died leaving a young Widow and three Young Children."[1]

This summertime epidemic of dysentery, also called the "bloody flux,"
in the Boston/Middlesex area was a killer. Dysentery is a contagious in-
testinal infection caused by parasites or bacteria. It has symptoms of
bloody diarrhea, causing dangerous dehydration accompanied with severe stomach cramps, vomiting, and a high fever. It was easily transmitted in military camps, where rancid water mixed with feces due to
poor sanitation. It was spread by contaminated food or water or by the
organisms being present on an infected person spread by touch. Dysentery could have been partially controlled by vigorous hand washing, a
practice nearly unknown in the eighteenth century.

Abigail wrote to Mercy Otis Warren on August 27 that John was leaving for Congress the next morning, just before the deadly dysentery epi-

demic would move into Braintree itself: "My Friend will leave me to morrow morning, and will have a much more agreable journey for the rain. I find I am obliged to summons all my patriotism to feel willing to part with him again. You will readily believe me when I say that I make no small sacrifice to the publick."[2]

As dysentery fell upon Braintree, it soon hit the Adams household. Isaac Copeland, a hired or "bound" field hand, was the first to be taken ill; "there was no resting place in the House for his terible Groans" and the stench of uncontrolled "puke" and diseased diarrhea. Abigail, too, fell ill: "I was seaz'd with the same disorder in a voilent manner," but "After 3 day[s] an abatement of my disease" occurred. There was no time for rest or full recovery. "The next person in the same week was Susy. She we carried home." Suzy was one of two servants or "bound girls" whom the Adamses had employed.[3] "Our Little Tommy was the next, and he lies very ill now—there is no abatement at present of his disorder. I hope he is not dangerous. Yesterday Patty[4] was seazd and took a puke. Our House is an hospital in every part, and what with my own weakness and distress of mind for my family I have been unhappy enough."[5]

In close-knit New England towns, a sick person knew that local help could be called in for assistance. But during this epidemic it was different. Everyone was sick. Abigail wrote, "And such is the distress of the neighbourhood that I can scarcly find a well person to assist me in looking after the sick. . . . So sickly and so Mortal a time the oldest Man does not remember. . . . The small pox in the natural way was never more mortal than this Distemper has proved in this and many neighbouring Towns. 18 have been buried since you left us." Once more, Abigail implored John to destroy the letter. It was too sad to keep. "Distroy this. Such a doleful tale it contains can give no pleasure to any one."[6]

Three weeks after John had left for Congress, Abigail, assisted by her mother coming daily from Weymouth to help, was still mustering all her post-illness strength to care for Patty, the servant girl, and the Adamses' three-year-old Tommy. Both were near death as Abigail wrote to John: "we live in daily Expectation that Patty will not continue many hours. A general putrefaction seems to have taken place, and we can not bear the House only as we are constantly clensing it with hot vinegar . . . Tommy is better, but intirely striped of the hardy robust countanance as well as of all the flesh he had, save what remains for to keep his bones together. . . . his fever has abated, his Bowels are better. . . .

but was you to look in upon him you would not know him, from a hearty hale corn fed[7] Boy. . . . I know of eight this week who have been buried in this Town. . . . The dread upon the minds of people of catching the distemper is almost as great as if it was the small pox."[8]

Abigail may have wondered why she received no reply to these accounts of serious illness: "Tomorrow will be 3 weeks since you left home in all which time I have not heard one word from you. . . . You will think me melancholy. Tis true I am much affected with the distress'd Scenes around me but I have some Anxietyes upon my mind which I do not think it prudent to mention at present to any one. Perhaps when I hear from you, I may in my next Letter tell you."[9]

It appeared that Abigail's letters to John weren't getting through for some reason. During an era when the cause of dysentery was unknown, letters were sometimes suspected of carrying the disease. Consequently, they were "smoked" (held over an open flame and smoke) or delayed and not handled. Therefore, John had no idea of the crisis unfolding in his town. The only information he had received was from Mercy Otis Warren. John wrote to Abigail that he had not "received one Scratch of a Pen from any Body [in Braintree], till the last Evening, when the Post brought me a Line from Mrs. Warren, in which she informs me that you had been ill, but was better."[10]

A September 25 letter from Abigail told John of even more sorrow brought upon the Adams home: "Woe follows Woe and one affliction treads upon the heal of an other."[11] Abigail's mother was near death in her Weymouth home from the same "disorder" which she had treated in others: "the distress of my dear Mother. Her kindness brought her to see me every day when I was ill and our little Tommy. She has taken the disorder and lies so bad that we have little hopes of her Recovery. She is possess'd with the Idea that she shall not recover, and I fear it will prove but too true."[12]

By September 29, Abigail and her sisters were on death watch for their fifty-three-year-old mother. Abigail spent twelve-hour shifts at her mother's house, "and then am obliged to return home to the most gastly object my Eyes ever beheld"—little Patty, who was also barely clinging to life, "who is continually desirous of my being with her the little While she expects to live, and who is now become such a putrid mass as scarcely to be able for any one to do their Duty towards her."[13] Abigail paused the letter and left for her mother's bedside. "I go . . . to give a respit to my sisters."[14] Abigail was near exhaustion. "At times I almost am ready to faint under this severe and heavy Stroke."[15]

The morning of October 1, 1775, brought the death of Elizabeth Smith, Abigail's mother, as described to John in these tearful and unguarded words: "That morning I rose and went into my Mothers room, not apprehending her so near her Exit, went to her Bed with a cup of tea in my hand, raised her head to give it to her, she swallowed a few drops, gaspd and fell back upon her pillow, opend her Eyes with a look that pirced my Heart and which I never shall forget. It was the eagerness of a last look—I know I wound your Heart. Why should I? Ought I to give relief to my own by paining yours? . . . My pen is always freer than my tongue. I have wrote many things to you that I suppose I never could have talk'd. . . . My Heart is made tender by repeated affliction. It never was a hard Heart."[16]

Eight days later, young Patty also died: "I have just returnd from attending Patty to the Grave. No doubt long before this will reach you, you have received a melancholy train of Letters in some of which I mention her as dangerously sick. She has lain 5 weeks wanting a few days so bad as that we had little hopes of her Recovery; the latter part of the Time she was the most shocking object my Eyes ever beheld, and so loathsome that it was with the utmost dificulty we could bear the House. A mortification took place a week before she dyed . . . and renderd her a most pityable object."[17] Abigail told John how much Patty's death affected her: "The death of Patty came very near me, having lived four years with me, under my care."[18]

However, it was the death of her mother that shook Abigail to her soul: "I have been like a nun in a cloister ever since you went away. . . . My Evenings are lonesome and Melancholy . . . [and] are spent with my departed parent. I then ruminate upon all her care and tenderness."[19] Long gone were the "giddy" restless days of her youth when Abigail chafed at the controls her mother had placed upon her which were later coupled with adolescent resentment. The adult Abigail now fully understood and appreciated the "care and tenderness" her mother had offered as "the best of Parents." "I cannot overcome my too selfish sorrow, all her tenderness towards me, her care and anxiety for my welfare at all times, her watchfulness over my infant years, her advice and instruction in maturer age; all, all indear her memory to me, and highten my sorrow for her loss."[20]

It pained John that he could not be there to comfort Abigail. However, his presence in Congress and sitting on or chairing twenty-five of its committees was sorely needed. He worked long hours and could not have helped much at Braintree had he been there other than offering consolation.

On October 13, the United States Navy was established (much by John's efforts), but that week had also brought to light a spy operating within the uppermost ranks of the Continental Army, surgeon-general Doctor Benjamin Church. He had been arrested for espionage and Congress was in shock. But, knowing that words sent to Abigail about a spy found embedded within their upper ranks would pale next to Abigail's loss, John tailored his words to Abigail and her mother exclusively: "I bewail more than I can express, the Loss of your excellent Mother. I mourn the Loss of so much Purity, and unaffected Piety and Virtue to the World. I know of no better Character left in it. I grieve for you." Still, some of John's resiliency as a New Englander surfaced within the same letter, "It is the Constitution under which We are born that if We live long ourselves We must bury our Parents."[21]

As 1775 was ending, so too was the immediate pain of the death of Abigail's mother. Their son Tommy had recovered, and the two servants Isaac and Susy had also returned to the Adams homestead. Abigail's subsequent letters to John began to feed him the valuable intelligence he craved once again. "There is a Lady at the Foot of Pens Hill, who obliges me, from Time to Time with clearer and fuller Intelligence, than I can get from a whole Committee of Gentlemen."[22] John wrote that phrase describing his wife to Mary "Polly" Palmer, a young admirer from Germantown, Massachusetts, who had written to Mr. Adams offering some intelligence from various fronts.

Abigail was learning to cull the wheat from the chaff in the news stories which came her way and to send John an unbiased news report of events and people. Abigail had a much better sense of people and politics than John, and by late 1775 her talents were sharpening.

On October 24 Abigail was invited to a dinner party at the Mount Wollaston home of her uncle, Colonel John Quincy, in honor of Benjamin Franklin, who would be present. "I have an invitation to dine to morrow with Dr. Franklin, Mr. Bodwin [Bowdoin], Dr. Cooper and Lady at Coll. Quincys. If my Sister is better believe I shall accept of it, as I have a great desire to see Dr. Franklin who I design to ask the favour of taking this."[23]

From her letter, Abigail was less concerned about meeting Franklin and more concerned about the apparent health of sisters Betsy and Mary.[24] However, both sisters were doing better and therefore did not require nursing. That offered Abigail the rare opportunity of meeting the most famous American of that time and perhaps one of the most eminent people in the world. From early childhood, Abigail had revered the stories told to her of the legendary Benjamin Franklin. He was the author of *Poor Richard's Almanac,* inventor of the Franklin stove and bifocal glasses, and the "man who tamed lightning" which directly led to the invention of the lightning rod. Franklin also had declined any patent royalties the lightning rod would have paid. The rod saved countless buildings and people from frequent and deadly fires. Franklin was the quintessential self-made American.

In 1775, Franklin had just returned from his decade-long stay in England where he had been acting as trade agent for numerous American colonies. But he had recently been implicated in shady dealings by officials in the English court and then kicked out of that country by those who declared Franklin an instigator of rebellion and even a spy.[25] Franklin immediately joined the Second Continental Congress in Philadelphia. In October 1775, he was sent on a congressional fact-finding mission to the encampment of the ragged American army at Cambridge, Massachusetts. Franklin and two other committee members met for a week with General George Washington discussing urgent problems such as lack of money and discipline.

John Adams had invited Franklin to meet Abigail while Franklin was in the Boston area. Abigail would introduce Franklin to local notables including Abigail's uncle, Colonel John Quincy. John felt completely comfortable with having Abigail meet and interact with notables. Weekly, Abigail was becoming more and more knowledgeable about the events of the time. John wondered how the meeting with Franklin went. "How do you like Dr. Franklyn? He tells me he called at the House and saw you, and that he had the Pleasure of dining with you at his Friend Coll. Quincys."[26]

Abigail reported on the dinner party for,"Dr. Frankling. . . whom I had the pleasure of dining with, and of admiring him whose character from my Infancy I had been taught to venerate. I found him social, but not talkative, and when he spoke something usefull droped from his Tongue; he was grave, yet pleasant, and affable." Abigail then reminded John of her interest in "physiognomy," the pseudoscience of the time which judged someone's character from studying their face. In the "Age of Sensibility," in which Abigail was fully immersed, judging a book by its cover was just part of the acute awareness that sensibility brought to one's delicate emotions: "You know I make some pretensions to physiognomy and I thought I could read in his countanance the Virtues of his Heart, among which patriotism shined in its full Lusture."[27]

One week after sending John the letter about Franklin, she must have remembered an important detail of their meeting: "Dr. Frankling invited me to spend the winter in Philidelphia. I shall wish to be there, unless you return."[28] One wonders if Abigail sent that invitation in a bid to make John jealous?

Abigail was also starting to harden her attitude about America's struggle that was still raging against the British Empire. Privately and for no one's eyes but John's, she expressed a religious viewpoint about the conflict—that perhaps the bloodshed and strife was retribution for the "Sin of Slavery"; "We have done Evil or our Enimies would be at peace with us. The Sin of Slavery as well as many others is not washed away."[29] Privately she also doubted the resolve of southern Patriots because of their obvious moral defect: "I have sometimes been ready to think that the passion for Liberty cannot be Eaquelly Strong in the Breasts of those who have been accustomed to deprive their fellow Creatures of theirs."[30]

Publicly however, Abigail proclaimed a clear and direct path of action toward the British, "Let us seperate, they are unworthy to be our Breathren."[31] Abigail was now able to distill the multifaceted areas of the conflict. She was equally able to select the best and most candid words to deliver them to any audience. John knew it and rather than being threatened by her growing awareness, he savored each example of Abigail's intelligence. John wrote Abigail of something Stephen Collins, a fellow Massachusetts patriot, recently told John: "Stephen Collins tells me the English Gentleman, in Company with him, when he visited Braintree, pronounced you the most accomplished Lady, he had seen since he left England."[32]

Along with her modesty about being so "accomplished," Abigail ended her letter with a practical request: "Mr. Hardwick desires Mr. Bass would not forget his needles, and I would make the same request to you. . . . I would not croud you with articles, but hope you will remember my other bundle of pins, the price of one paper [for writing] now amounts to what we used to give for a whole Bundle [of pins]."[33]

As the wife of a key congressional delegate, Abigail was expected to occasionally greet and entertain important domestic and international guests whenever the visitors were in Boston. Thus far she had met Benjamin Franklin, George Washington, and Charles Lee, of whom she had observed, "General Lee looks like a careless hardy Veteran."[34] So it was with mixed feelings of duty and much anxiety when in early December 1775, she received a request to attend a large "coffe" reception in Boston with many important people, including Major General Lee again. He was the source of her nervous apprehension because of an embarrassing interception of a letter about five months earlier involving Charles Lee and John Adams.

Back in July, John had written an unsigned letter to James Warren, Mercy Otis Warren's husband, in which he wrote critically about his fellow delegates in Congress. Without saying the exact name of his primary target, John Dickinson of Pennsylvania, John called Dickinson a "piddling Genius" and made other derogatory remarks. John also indirectly criticized Major General Charles Lee, replying to something Warren had written about Lee: "You observe in your Letter the Oddity of a great Man—He is a queer Creature—But you must love his Dogs if you love him."[35] Boston lawyer Colonel Benjamin Hichborn, who was in Philadelphia, offered to hand carry three letters back to Massachusetts: the infamous letter by Adams to Warren, a letter from John to Abigail, and one from congressional delegate Benjamin Harrison to General George Washington.

The letters were seized by the British on Narragansett Bay in route to Boston.[36] Copies of the letters were sent to England by British General Thomas Gage and Admiral Samuel Graves. The British didn't know exactly who wrote the damning unsigned letter about Lee and his dogs, but deduced it was John Adams by the handwriting. The following was written in an unknown British hand: "This Letter was Anonymous, but wrote in the same Hand with that addressed to Abigail Adams."[37] The compromising contents were then published in British newspapers and, within a month, in the *Massachusetts Gazette*, among other Tory newspapers. This touched off a temporary firestorm within the Continental Congress which resulted in Dickinson shunning Adams for a short time on the street. The furor over the intercepted letters seems to have blown over quickly, however.

Lee wrote to John soon afterward saying that if he thought the inflammatory comments made about him in John's intercepted letters made him mad, John should think again. Lee said he took no offense at what was written: "I think it necessary to assure You that it is quite the reverse." And that, "my love of Dogs passes with me as a still higher complement. . . . Consequently when once I can be convincd that Men are as worthy objects as Dogs I shall transfer my benevolence." Lee signed off his letter with a P.S. from Spada, his lead Pomeranian dog: "Spada sends his love to you and declares in very intellegible language that He has far'd much better since your allusion to him for He is caress'd now by all ranks sexes and Ages."[38] Abigail would soon find out that John had made Spada famous.

When Abigail met Major General Charles Lee at the coffee party, she was unaware that John had already received Lee's own blessings for the wayward comments made about Lee and his dogs, and feared the worst.

It was Saturday afternoon, December 9, 1775, when Abigail, accompanied by her father, arrived at the reception at Quartermaster General Thomas Mifflin's temporary quarters near Harvard Yard. She knew some of the guests such as "Gen. [Horatio] Gates [and] a Dr. McHenery [Doctor James McHenry]," and "many others who were strangers to me." And of course, there was Major General Charles Lee accompanied by Spada. To Abigail's relief, Lee was cordial to her and in fact insistent that Abigail meet Spada, in this encounter humorously captured by Abigail: "I was very politely entertaind and noticed by the Generals, more especially General Lee, who was very urgent with me to tarry in Town and dine with him and the Laidies present, at Hob Goblin Hall, but I excused my self. The General was determined that I should not only be acquainted with him, but with his companions too, and therefore placed a chair before me into which he orderd Mr. Sparder[39] to mount and present his paw to me for a better acquaintance. I could not do otherways than accept it.—That Madam says he is the Dog which Mr. . . . [Abigail did not identify the person] . . . has renderd famous." Of course, it was the dog which Mr. John Adams had rendered famous.

Throughout time, farmers in New England had dealt with the ravages of the weather: snow and ice storms, nor'easter blizzards, great droughts, fires, floods, and windstorms. Abigail had been experiencing the "great and incessant rains" of fall 1775 which had "spoild many hundreds of Bushels of Apples, which were designd for cider, and which the great rains had prevented people from making up. Suppose we have lost 5 Barrels by it," Abigail wrote to John. She also included a list of her recent cold weather illnesses, and those of other people she knew: "I have been confined with the Jaundice, Rhumatism and a most voilent cold; I yesterday took a puke which has releived me, and I feel much better to day. Many, very many people who have had the dysentery, are now afflicted both with the Jaundice and Rhumatisim, some it has left in Hecticks, some in dropsies." But she hoped that the ice-cold November wind, "will purify the air of some of the noxious vapours."[40]

Abigail also started thinking about the future government to be established by Congress, and "if we seperate from Brittain, what Code of Laws will be established?" She had doubts about power-hungry men in places of authority in the new country: "I wish I knew what mighty things were fabricating. If a form of Goverment is to be established here what one will be assumed? Will it be left to our assemblies to chuse one. . . . I am more and more convinced that Man is a dangerous creature, and that power whether vested in many or a few is ever grasping, and like the grave cries give, give. The great fish swallow up the small." She wasn't even sure if the country would end up with a "Monarchy or Democracy?" But in her usual optimistic way, Abigail summarized, "Great difficulties may be surmounted, by patience and perseverance." Abigail repeated her familiar message about doing her patriotic duty without the help of a husband and that once again, "I hope the publick will reap what I sacrifice."[41]

Christmas 1775 was approaching, and Congress showed no signs of adjourning. Rather than wait, John made an uncharacteristic move and left for home. He arrived in Braintree on December 21 quite unexpectedly, and found the mood at home was happy, despite the defeats on the military front. Boston was still in British hands and the recent defeat of an American force at Quebec City was another blow. The year 1775 passed with great uncertainty and hushed feelings with most American patriots.

John left early on the morning of January 24, 1776, for a short ride to the Continental Army encampment in Cambridge before his long return trip to Philadelphia. He had been invited to a diplomatic dinner with four American generals—Washington, Mifflin, Gates, and John Thomas, along with "six or seven Sachems and Warriours, of the French Cagnawaga[42] Indians, with several of their Wives and Children." The Indians were there to pledge their allegiance to the American cause, which greatly boosted John's spirits. John also likely hoped that Abigail would be proud of her husband when he wrote her how Washington introduced John to the Indians: "I was introduced to them by the General as one of the grand Council Fire at Philadelphia which made them prick up their Ears, they came and shook Hands with me, and made me low Bows, and scrapes &c. In short I was much pleased with this Days entertainment."

John ended his letter to Abigail with loving family sentiments: "Tomorrow We[43] mount, for the grand Council Fire—Where I shall think often of my little Brood at the Foot of Pens Hill. Remember me particularly to Nabby, Johnny, Charly and Tommy. Tell them I charge them to be good, honest, active and industrious for their own sakes, as well as ours."[44] It was a recurring theme with Abigail: John returned home, stayed a short amount of time, and then left again all too soon for vital congressional work. Abigail would stay behind to educate the children and run the house and farm.

The one simple weakness she had was that she craved letters from John. He never sent enough to satisfy her, even though she knew he was busy doing important work. But when she did hear from him through letters, she thrived on his words. In March 1776 she had jumped for joy when a weighty package was delivered to her, only to open it and discover he had sent her four newspapers. Just newspapers. She wrote to John in reply to his request that she would help the war effort by making saltpeter,[45] the main element in gunpowder. She smartly answered that it was all she could do to sew and mend clothes so that the Adams family would not be naked: "I want to hear much oftener from you than I do. March 8 was the last date of any that I have yet had.—You inquire of whether I am making Salt peter. I have not yet attempted it. . . . I find as much as I can do to manufacture cloathing for my family which would else be Naked."[46]

By mid-February 1776 the disposition in the Continental Congress was gloomy, as the full story of the failed Canadian venture and subsequent tragic death of Major General Richard Montgomery arrived in Philadelphia. Congress sent a delegation to meet with the remnants of the American army in Montreal and to judge the willingness of Canadians to join the United States as the fourteenth colony. "Dr. Franklin, Mr. Chase, and Mr. Charles Carroll of Carrollton in Maryland, are chosen a Committee to go into Canada." John wrote to Abigail: "I wish I understood French as well as you. I would have gone to Canada, if I had. I feel the Want of Education every Day—particularly of that Language. I pray My dear, that you would not suffer your Sons or your Daughter, ever to feel a similar Pain. It is in your Power to teach them French, and I every day see more and more that it will become a necessary Accomplishment of an American Gentleman and Lady." It was at this point when John realized that Abigail's aptitude for grasping a foreign language exceeded some of John's own skills. From this point, Adams would advocate for an advanced level of education for both boys and girls.

In the same letter, John paraphrased a line that Abigail herself might have also known. It was from Joseph Addison's popular play *Cato, a Tragedy*. John wrote to Abigail, "The Events of War are uncertain: We cannot insure Success, but We can deserve it."[47] However, John must have felt at times in early 1776 that insuring success for victory against the British Empire seemed nearly impossible. What the American side needed was help, something to rally the cause of the patriots. John couldn't imagine what that help would look like.

Ironically in this very same letter, John wrote to Abigail, "I sent you from New York a Pamphlet intituled *Common Sense*."[48] Without realizing it, John had touched upon the very help that he had been looking for. It was a short, unassuming pamphlet—appearing at the right time and right place—that would help save the Revolution.

Chapter Nine

"Remember the Ladies"

1776

A*bigail loved* the *Common Sense* pamphlet that John had sent her, as did large numbers of average Americans. John saw that the best part of the popularity of *Common Sense* was that it helped to speed up the public's yearning for independence.

John knew that Congress was moving slowly and that the most conservative of its factions seemed to not be able to come to terms with being "wholly divorced from that Accursed Kingdom calld Great Britain."[1] However, as impatient as John was, he realized that the decision to separate from Britain must be unanimous as that was where the strength of the declaration statement would be.

Since 1774 with each failed peace overture, a small minority group within Congress had slowly shifted to the side of independence, although almost no one used the taboo word of "independence" in committees or on the floor. The "body of the people," the average American citizens, had been slowly moving toward independence regardless. The arrival of *Common Sense* brought more support for the popular viewpoint.

The anonymous forty-seven-page pamphlet had become an instant sensation. In just three months *Common Sense: Addressed to the Inhabitants of America* sold an astounding 120,000 copies, with untold thousands borrowing it and passing it along to many others. In that short time, its author, an obscure British immigrant named Thomas Paine, had done what Congress could never do with its flowery, official legal statements. The pamphlet had galvanized the common American to the cause of independence with its simple, easy-to-understand language.[2]

But John was not caught up in the patriotic fire lit by the pamphlet. Although initially John admitted to Abigail that he couldn't have written a document with "the Strength and Brevity of his style, nor his elegant Symplicity," he greatly criticized Paine for erroneously continuing beyond where he should have stopped. Paine had also designed a new haphazard government in his pamphlet. John wrote of Paine's work, "The Attempt to frame a Continental Constitution, is feeble indeed. It is poor, and despicable," yet John introduced a positive note: "Yet this is a very meritorious Production." Finally, he just couldn't resist adding about Paine's ideas: "In Point of Argument there is nothing new. I believe every one that is in it, had been hackneyd in every Conversation public and private, before that Pamphlet was written."[3]

John told Abigail that Paine's suggestions for a proposed "popular" government were ill-conceived and would never work. Paine had set forth a government design with no separation of powers and no checks and balances, within a proposed one-chamber legislature. John considered the whole concept as folly. He duly wrote that "Indeed this Writer has a better Hand at pulling down than building."[4] Decades later, John would clarify to Thomas Jefferson his true feelings about the popular pamphlet: "What a poor ignorant, malicious, short-sighted, Crapulous Mass, is Tom Pains Common Sense."[5]

Still, Abigail saw the good in the pamphlet. She was "charmed with the Sentiments of Common Sense; and wonder how an honest Heart, one who wishes the welfare of their country, and the happiness of posterity can hesitate one moment at adopting them."[6] She reaffirmed that in the Braintree area the booklet was "highly prized here and carries conviction whereever it is read. I have spread it as much as it lay in my power, every one assents to the weighty truths it contains."[7]

Her letter began, however, by recounting the scare she had just had: rumors had spread "in this and the neighbouring Towns . . . that you and your President [John Hancock, the Continental Congress president] had gone on board a Man of War from N—y and sailed for England."[8] But

Abigail had long ago learned to listen to rumors with only one ear, as nearly all of them would turn out to be false.

While *Common Sense* was surging in popularity, the Revolution among the general population was in full swing, ahead of anything the slow-moving Continental Congress was advocating. The town of Worcester in middle Massachusetts had already overthrown the royal courts in that district and had instituted civilian control. It was a classic insurrection. "We are hastening rapidly to great Events. Governments will be up every where before Midsummer, and an End to Royal style, Titles and Authority," John wrote to Abigail, adding, "It requires more Serenity of Temper, a deeper Understanding and . . . Courage . . . to ride in this Whirlwind."[9]

Before it was printed, however, John sent an advance copy of his own *Thoughts on Government* to Abigail for her consideration and editorial comments, modestly writing that it was a "hasty hurried Thing and of no great Consequence . . . If it has done no good, it will do no harm."[10]

Abigail replied, appreciating John's document in contrast to Paine's. She first offered an affectionate aside, "Upon reading it I some how or other felt an uncommon affection for it; I could not help thinking it was a near relation of a very intimate Friend of mine." She then wrote an excellent summary, "I know it has a near affinity to the Sentiments of that person, and tho I cannot pretend to be an adept in the art of Goverment; yet it looks rational that a Goverment of Good Laws well administerd should carry with them the fairest prospect of happiness to a community, as well as to individuals."[11]

With that reply John realized that Abigail not only could successfully manage a large farm while educating children but was becoming a political intellect of the first caliber, "I think you shine as a Stateswoman, of late as well as a Farmeress. Pray where do you get your Maxims of State, they are very apropos."[12]

On Saturday night, March 2, 1776, Abigail was writing a letter to her "dear Friend" John. She recorded, "but hark! the House this instant shakes with the roar of Cannon.—I have been to the door and find tis a cannonade from our Army. . . . No Sleep for me to Night."[13] The next day brought an uneasy quiet, "I went to Bed after 12 but got no rest, the Cannon continued firing and my Heart Beat pace with them all night. We have had a pretty quiet day, but what to morrow will bring forth God only knows."[14]

Two nights later, Abigail still wasn't sure what was going on, other than the fact that cannons were still firing and on that present night, the firing was even more intense. Abagail saw militia troops marching past her house; she only used the town name's first letter for mail security "W[eymouth], H[ingham] or B[raintree] or M[ilton]." She closed her letter: "I have just returnd from P[enn']s Hill where I have been sitting to hear the amazing roar of cannon and from whence I could see every shell which was thrown. The sound I think is one of the Grandest in Nature and is of the true Speicies of the Sublime. Tis now an incessant Roar."[15]

The "ratling of the windows, the jar of the house and the continual roar of 24 pounders, the Bursting of shells"[16] that Abigail had been describing on those nights was General George Washington's diversion designed to deceive the British who were still occupying Boston. The fierce cannonade from the American batteries surrounding Boston was cover for the Americans who, within one night, pulled seventy artillery pieces to the frozen hilltop of Dorchester Heights. Colonel Henry Knox's bold maneuver, to move the artillery from Fort Ticonderoga to Dorchester Heights by dragging them over the snow-covered Berkshires, had paid off. The mounted cannons were now able to strike Boston and its moored fleet of British ships below. Abigail repeated to John a rumor of what British General William Howe, who had taken over command from General Gage, supposedly uttered when he saw the cannon early Tuesday morning. "I hear that General How said upon going upon some Eminence in Town to view our Troops who had taken Dorchester Hill unperceived by them till sun rise, 'My God these fellows have done more work in one night than I could make my Army do in three months.'"[17]

General Howe was faced with either surrender or a costly Bunker Hill type of assault on Dorchester Heights. Instead, Howe offered, through a third party,[18] an informal gentleman's agreement where the Americans would not attack the British while they abandoned Boston. If the British were attacked, Howe threatened to burn Boston. Since the British did not acknowledge Washington's position as general, they did not formally make the offer to Washington. Regardless a truce of sorts went into effect and the British were allowed to evacuate Boston. British troop ships were loaded with soldiers, loyalist civilians, weapons, and supplies and set sail. The American militia troops were deactivated and sent home. For the first time in eight years, Boston was free of British troops. Boston had been a closed, smallpox-infested city under siege for eleven months. Many locals were jubilant over the change in fortune. Those Tories who were unable to flee with the British were terrified that the returning Whigs would take revenge upon them. Abigail hoped that the evacuating British troops would be issued orders not to loot and destroy Boston, and she fully expected military justice to prevail. Abigail was wrong.

She was also sick, which didn't help her mood any. As Abigail described in her March 17 letter to John, "Being quite sick with a voilent cold."

She wrote of reports that the British troops decamped from Boston to their transport ships. But Abigail had also heard rumors that the "Enemy" first went on a vandalism spree: "they have carried of [every] thing they could [po]ssibly take, and what they could not they have [burnt, broke, or hove into the water. This] is I [believe, fact] that many articles of good Household furniture having in the course of the week come on shore at Great Hill, both upon this and Weymouth Side, Lids of Desks, mahogona chairs, tables &c."[19] Abigail rejoiced as "From Pens Hill we have a view of the largest Fleet ever seen in America. You may count upwards of 100 & 70 Sail. They look like a Forrest."[20]

But the ships didn't sail away; they anchored in the outer Boston Harbor for more than a week waiting for favorable winds. Consequently, many Boston residents assumed they'd been duped by General Howe. Finally, the ships, with over 11,000 soldiers and civilians, set course for the open Atlantic Ocean. Their destination was the British naval base at Halifax, Nova Scotia.

The momentary exhilaration of the enemy leaving Boston was fleeting, while Abigail's work at managing the household and farm was never ending. It was hard for her to find and keep hired hands. They would either take ill or be mustered into military service. She reported the fact in this awkwardly constructed sentence to John: "As to all your own private affair[s] I take the best care I am capable of them. I have found some difficulty attending the only Man I have upon the place, being so often taking of." (She added the postscript, "PS Pray convey me a little paper. I have but enough for one Letter more.")[21]

A few weeks later, the hired hand shortage hadn't improved, and the farm demands upon Abigail hadn't let up: "I find it necessary to be the directress of our Husbandery and farming. . . . I hope in time to have the Reputation of being as good a Farmeress as my partner has of being a good Statesmen."[22]

As spring 1776 came into full bloom and the dirty snow had started to melt away, the melancholy mood that had borne down upon Abigail seemed to have also melted. On March 31 when Abigail began a new letter to John, arguably Abigail's most well known, the effects of spring fever possibly exhibited themselves in a declaration of happy exuberance for the change of seasons: "I feel a *gaieti de Coar* [Abigail meant the French phrase: "gaieté de coeur" or "lightheartedness," a gaiety in the heart] to which before I was a stranger. I think the Sun looks brighter, the Birds sing more melodiously, and Nature puts on a more chearfull countanance. We feel a temporary peace, and the poor fugitives are returning to their deserted habitations."[23]

However shortly after composing her statement about spring, Abigail entered a new writing realm that she had never ventured into before— political petitioning. She knew from John's letters that Congress was very near a declaration of independence. "I long to hear that you have declared an independency," she wrote. She also understood that a new Constitution ("Code of Laws") would also be created to govern the new country. Abigail resolved to seize this moment to see if she could help effect change on behalf of women. She appealed to John and so to the Continental Congress for a legal petition—not for women's voting rights, but for social and legal rights for married women.

In her famous March 31 letter to John she implied that women would not obey laws they had no voice or vote in creating: "[We] will not hold ourselves bound by any Laws in which we have no voice, or Representation."[24] Abigail's "sausy"[25] statement about women's "voice, or Representation" was a half-humorous attempt to equate the cause of the Americans' revolt against Britain to the cause of women's revolt against husbands.

However, her initiative was never about voting rights. Abigail, a woman who loved social order and security, wasn't out to create a major social revolution. She just wanted new legislation which would protect married women from abusive husbands. People might think Abigail was an early feminist, but that was not her intent.

Abigail knew, as certainly did all married women of the period, that women were the unquestioned property of the husband to be treated as the men wished.[26] Some men of decency were kind, understanding, and helpful, as was John to Abigail. But many men were not. Some were drunk and cruel husbands who commonly (and legally) abused their wives with no penalty. Abigail had written to John six months earlier of this scenario for not being able to hold abusive men responsible: "you may as well hope to bind up a hungry tiger with a cobweb as to hold such debauched patriots in the visionary chains of Decency." Abigail believed that unless enforceable laws were created which prevented men from abusing women, no change would happen: "yet as there is a natural

propensity in Humane Nature to domination, I thought the most generous plan was to put it out of the power of the Arbitary and tyranick
to injure us with impunity by Establishing some Laws in our favour
upon just and Liberal principals."[27]

Abigail explained her appeal to Mercy Otis Warren in early 1776: "I
thought it was very probable our wise Statesmen would erect a New Goverment and form a new code of Laws. I ventured to speak a word in behalf
of our Sex, who are rather hardly dealt with by the Laws of England
which gives such unlimitted power to the Husband to use his wife Ill."[28]

On March 31, 1776, Abigail composed her famous "Remember the
Ladies" statement in a letter to John. She tied the "Remember the
Ladies" request to the cause for the current American Revolution. In
her case, women have no voice in laws which govern their lives. The
laws in both of those comparisons were dictated by either Parliament
or husbands. In her letter she issued the same lighthearted threat of rebellion by women for a similar reason as the American Revolution: "and
by the way in the new Code of Laws which I suppose it will be necessary
for you to make I desire you would Remember the Ladies, and be more
generous and favourable to them than your ancestors. Do not put such
unlimited power into the hands of the Husbands. Remember all Men
would be tyrants if they could.[29] If perticuliar care and attention is not
paid to the Laidies we are determined to foment a Rebelion, and will
not hold ourselves bound by any Laws in which we have no voice, or
Representation." Abigail appealed to the better aspects of men's nature:
"That your Sex are Naturally Tyrannical is a Truth so thoroughly established as to admit of no dispute, but such of you as wish to be happy
willingly give up the harsh title of Master for the more tender and en-
dearing one of Friend.[30] Why then, not put it out of the power of the
vicious and the Lawless to use us with cruelty and indignity with impunity. Men of Sense in all Ages abhor those customs which treat us
only as the vassals of your Sex. Regard us then as Beings placed by providence under your protection and in immitation of the Supreem Being
make use of that power only for our happiness."[31]

John's controversial reply to Abigail's "Remember the Ladies" letter
has not been well received in history. Critics claim that John's response
exposed his male chauvinism for the times, and some of those allegations
may be true. But his mind also worked in levels of priority, no matter
the subject. Not only was Congress negotiating treaties with foreign
countries but it was also trying to deal with the crashing economy, sup-
plying the army, establishing courts, conducting and winning the war,

and handling dozens of other critical issues. It's entirely possible that John, and therefore Congress, felt that they had other (more important) issues to confront, and women's rights were not paramount.

However, in today's world, John's comments to Abigail are judged singularly and not against any other moderating situations. Without those other factors, John's words play badly in the twenty-first century. But the reader should also remember that his letter replied to Abigail in a joking manner, the way that Abigail had written to John about her serious points using humor and sarcasm. In their letters each understood what the other meant. Both Abigail and John had been bantering back and forth in letters since their dating days, and there's reason to believe these two letters were also such a form of a spirited and witty exchange between them.

In his reply, John good-naturedly fired back to Abigail's "sausy" (jokingly flippant) letter. He said that he had been firmly warned by others of Congress that declaring independence would cut the threads of social law and order by casting off the existing form of secure government, and therefore, any form of social stability. And now, Abigail was warning him that there's a new "Tribe" in town to contend with. John replied to Abigail: "As to Declarations of Independency, be patient. . . . As to your extraordinary Code of Laws, I cannot but laugh. We have been told that our Struggle has loosened the bands of Government every where. That Children and Apprentices were disobedient—that schools and Colledges were grown turbulent—that Indians slighted their Guardians and Negroes grew insolent to their Masters. But your Letter was the first Intimation that another Tribe more numerous and powerfull than all the rest were grown discontented.—This is rather too coarse a Compliment but you are so saucy, I wont blot it out."[32]

John made a humorous point to Abigail that although the law granted men ultimate authority over wives, in real life many or most families did not operate that way. He half-jokingly announced that men, if they knew what was good for them, wouldn't rule their wives with an iron hand . . . because they knew the wife was the boss. But to give up the symbolic "Name of Masters" would make men subservient to female despots: "Depend upon it, We know better than to repeal our Masculine systems. Altho they are in full Force, you know they are little more than Theory. We dare not exert our Power in its full Latitude. We are obliged to go fair, and softly, and in Practice you know We are the subjects. We have only the Name of Masters, and rather than give up this, which would compleatly subject Us to the Despotism of the Peticoat."[33]

John joked that the British Parliament and ministerial troublemakers had stirred up discontent among various pro-British factions; and now he saw that a brand-new group has been added to the rebellious mix: "I begin to think the Ministry as deep as they are wicked. After stirring up Tories, Landjobbers, Trimmers, Bigots, Canadians, Indians, Negroes, Hanoverians, Hessians, Russians, Irish Roman Catholicks, Scotch Renegadoes, at last they have stimulated the [words left blank here, but John probably meant "women"] to demand new Priviledges and threaten to rebell."[34]

About one week after receiving John's reply, Abigail blew off some steam in a letter to Mercy Otis Warren: "He is very sausy to me in return for a List of Female Grievances which I transmitted to him. I think I will get you to join me in a petition to Congress. . . . I ventured to speak a word in behalf of our Sex . . . [but] there is a natural propensity in Humane Nature to domination. . . . I believe I even threatned fomenting a Rebellion."[35] Abigail and Mercy never sent Congress a petition.

By May 7, 1776, Abigail closed out her campaign for the "new Code of Laws" that she had first submitted to John on March 31. Her May 7 message to John was the final word on the subject. Abigail ceased the debate, but not John. Abigail made one more quick statement of biting irony in the situation, and then she issued a reminder to John that women still held power over the male sex. But instead of legislative legal power, it was emotional "charm" power. Abigail quoted Alexander Pope and then rarely raised the issue again, at least not in writing: "I can not say that I think you very generous to the Ladies, for whilst you are proclaiming peace and good will to Men, Emancipating all Nations, you insist upon retaining an absolute power over Wives. But you must remember that Arbitary power is like most other things which are very hard, very liable to be broken—and notwithstanding all your wise Laws and Maxims we have it in our power not only to free ourselves but to subdue our Masters, and without voilence throw both your natural and legal authority at our feet—'Charm by accepting, by submitting sway / Yet have our Humour most when we obey.'"[36]

Abigail's "Remember the Ladies" statement was directed toward creating laws which would protect married women from husbandly abuse. In a different vein, it has been wondered in the twenty-first century that if the initiative was instead to give women the right to vote—would Abigail have exercised that right? Her answer was "yes" as she stated many years after 1776: "if our state constitution had been equally liberal with that of New jersey and admitted the females to a Vote, I should certainly have exercised it in his behalf."[37] For a while New Jersey's state constitution allowed eligible single, adult women to vote. "The 1776 New Jersey Constitution contained a franchise clause that defined eligible voters as those who had been residents for a year and owned property worth at least £50, thus allowing single adult women who met these criteria to participate in state elections. The law was changed in 1807 when the ranks of eligible voters were limited to male citizens."[38]

Smallpox had been raging in Boston. When the British evacuated Boston, General George Washington sent in 1,000 Continental Army soldiers who had already had smallpox to secure the city. Abigail was anxious to enter Boston to check on the condition of their Queen Street house. She wrote John, "The small pox prevents my going to Town; several have broke out with it in the Army since they went into Boston. I cannot help wishing that it would spread."[39] The reason Abigail wished smallpox inside Boston would spread was because of the outdated law at that time. Inoculations were still suspect then, and it was felt that it was better to catch the disease the "natural" way rather than risking a self-started epidemic through mass inoculations. A disease such as smallpox would have to already be spreading out of control before city officials permitted variolation.[40] Abigail didn't have to wait long. In late spring 1776, a smallpox epidemic in Boston was spreading, and the same city officials who had been holding back inoculation permission went ahead and authorized smallpox inoculations within the Boston city limits on July 3, 1776.

Abigail had wanted to get inoculated in 1764 along with her fiancé John, who was having the procedure done. But her mother, her legal guardian, prohibited it. However, in 1776 Abigail need not have asked permission of anyone, despite the rules of coverture which dictated getting John's permission for the procedure. Abigail's wealthy Boston uncle Isaac Smith, Sr., had invited her, her children, and any others to stay at his house on Court Street for the procedure and quarantine. So, when the opportunity for inoculation for herself, Nabby, John, Charles, and Thomas presented itself along with a secure place for them all to stay in Boston during the quarantine stage, she could not turn it down. Abigail's entire entourage numbering between twelve and seventeen[41] people arrived at her uncle's house in Boston on Friday, July 12. Abigail reported that her four children[42] were inoculated the same day. There wasn't time to ask or even forewarn John of the inoculation. Abigail, while in quarantine, updated John on everything that had already quickly happened:

Boston July 13 1776

I must begin with apoligising to you for not writing since the 17 of June. I have really had so many cares upon my Hands and Mind, with a bad inflamation in my Eyes that I have not been able to write. I now date from Boston where I yesterday arrived and was with all 4 of our Little ones innoculated for the small pox. . . . The House was furnished with almost every article (except Beds) which we have free use of, and think ourselves much obliged by the fine accommodations and kind offer of our Friends. . . . Our Little ones stood the opperation Manfully. Dr. Bulfinch is our Physician. Such a Spirit of innoculation never before took place; the Town and every House in it, are as full as they can hold. . . . I knew your mind so perfectly upon the subject that I thought nothing, but our recovery would give you eaquel pleasure, and as to safety there was none. . . . I immediately determined to set myself about it, and get ready with my children. I wish it was so you could have been with us, but I submit.[43]

Though surrounded by family, relatives, and friends during quarantine, Abigail wrote tenderly to John, "I shall write you now very often. Pray inform me constantly of every important transaction. Every expression of tenderness is a cordial to my Heart. Unimportant as they are to the rest of the world, to me they are every Thing."[44]

Abigail had estimated that the entire inoculation and quarantine procedure would last three to four weeks. It would turn out to be nearly eight weeks and to be much more serious than she had anticipated. Abigail and John constantly worried about each other's health. Their letters, especially during this crucial time, were filled with questions about the other's wellbeing. Their crisscrossing letters conveying news of health were sometimes delayed and at any given time, both were equally in the dark about the other's health. John was near frantic that he'd received no word about Abigail. Worrying about the health of Abigail and his children was in the forefront of John's mind as he and Congress debated and declared independence from Great Britain.

Chapter Ten

"I Am Not Apt to Be Indimidated You Know"

1776

*I*ronically, *during the final days* before the independence vote by Congress, Abigail was unaware of John's precise activities as their letters lately had been lost or damaged. She was busy in Boston taking care of herself, her children, friends, and relatives during the smallpox epidemic. However, she would soon be brought up to date on the historic happenings of which she was proud that her "Dearest Friend" played an important part.

As the June 1776 calendar page turned over to July, the question of separation from Great Britain had become the unavoidable subject in the halls of the Second Continental Congress. It had been the focus for John for well over a year, and Congress' deliberations over the independence decision were coming swiftly to a conclusion. The question of independence had also been the reason John couldn't be with the family that he adored during their trials of the previous year.

In Philadelphia on July 2, Congress voted for independence by a vote of 12-0, with New York abstaining until they received updated instructions. (New York's instructions to vote for independence came one week later, making the total vote unanimous.) July 3 was spent editing the Declaration of Independence, the legal document explaining to the British government, and indeed the world, why the separation from Great Britain was necessary. After the day-long editing session, an exuberant John wrote two letters to Abigail. The first letter announced to her that their goal of declaring independence was finally a reality: "Yesterday the greatest Question was decided, which ever was debated in America, and a greater perhaps, never was or will be decided among Men. A Resolution was passed without one dissenting Colony 'that these united Colonies, are, and of right ought to be free and independent States.' . . . You will see in a few days a Declaration setting forth the Causes, which have impell'd Us to this mighty Revolution, and the Reasons which will justify it, in the Sight of God and Man."[1]

The second letter speaks to John's vision for the future of Independence Day: "The Second Day of July 1776, will be the most memorable Epocha, in the History of America.—I am apt to believe that it will be celebrated, by succeeding Generations, as the great anniversary Festival. It ought to be commemorated, as the Day of Deliverance by solemn Acts of Devotion to God Almighty. It ought to be solemnized with Pomp and Parade, with Shews [Shows], Games, Sports, Guns, Bells, Bonfires and Illuminations from one End of this Continent to the other from this Time forward forever more."[2]

John reminded Abigail, who needed no reminding, of the upcoming sacrifices and blood that the independence vote would bring: "I am well aware of the Toil and Blood and Treasure, that it will cost Us to maintain this Declaration, and support and defend these States.—Yet through all the Gloom I can see the Rays of ravishing Light and Glory. I can see that the End is more than worth all the Means. And that Posterity will tryumph in that Days Transaction, even altho We should rue it, which I trust in God We shall not."[3]

Abigail recorded that she cheerfully received both of John's July 3 letters on July 12; although she apparently mistook one of the two letters as having been written on July 4.[4] "By yesterdays post I received two Letters dated 3 and 4 of July and tho your Letters never fail to give me pleasure, be the subject what it will, yet it was greatly heightned by the prospect of the future happiness and glory of our Country; nor am I a little Gratified when I reflect that a person so nearly connected with me has had the Honour of being a principal actor, in laying a foundation for its future Greatness. May the foundation of our new constitution, be justice, Truth and Righteousness. Like the wise Mans house may it be founded upon those Rocks and then neither storms or temptests will overthrow it."[5]

July 4, traditionally the day independence is still celebrated in the United States, was just a housekeeping day in Congress. On July 3, the delegates had finished editing the Declaration of Independence and sent it off to an overnight printer. On July 4, they heard it read back, and with no printing errors "adopted" it. The thirteen colonies were now thirteen independent states.

Two weeks later, on July 18, Abigail was present in front of the Boston State House when the Declaration of Independence was read from the balcony to the assembled crowd below. Following those words, as she described to John, a spirited uproar marked the occasion and later the golden unicorn and golden lion—emblems of the British Empire—were torn from the building's front facade and tumbled to King Street below:

Last Thursday after hearing a very Good Sermon I went with the Multitude into Kings Street to hear the proclamation for independance read and proclamed. Some Field peices with the Train were brought there, the troops appeard under Arms and all the inhabitants assembled there (the small pox prevented many thousand from the Country). When Col. Crafts read from the Belcona [Balcony] of the State House the Proclamation, great attention was given to every word. As soon as he ended, the cry from the Belcona, was God Save our American States and then 3 cheers which rended the air, the Bells rang, the privateers fired, the forts and Batteries, the cannon were discharged, the platoons followed and every face appeard joyfull. Mr. Bowdoin then gave a Sentiment, Stability and perpetuity to American independance. After dinner the kings arms were taken down from the State House and every vestage of him from every place in which it appeard and burnt in King Street. Thus ends royall Authority in this State, and all the people shall say Amen.[6]

Abigail and her children had little to celebrate though. By mid-July the family's smallpox inoculations overseen by Abigail were not producing the desired results. The procedure was a very hit-or-miss prospect, and there was an outbreak of confusing noninfections in Boston among individuals who had been inoculated. This meant many people possibly became ill but did not show smallpox pustules, which would have visually confirmed that they had the milder form of the virus and therefore were on the road to immunity. Instead, many people were left not knowing if they had immunity or not.

The confusion stemmed from the newer generation of doctors who only made small perforations in the skin. It was called "the Suttonian"[7] method, which called for smaller cuts, rather than making the larger gashes as practiced a decade before, a process that John had undergone. However, it was felt that the less invasive holes didn't transfer the pus in sufficient volume to initiate the virus. Others blamed the summertime heat, for sweating the virus out of the subject before it could start immunization or trigger an immune response. Regardless of the perceived cause of the failures, there was plenty of blame to go around. Doctor Thomas Bulfinch, the physician to the Adamses in Boston, was stumped by the erratic effectiveness. It was becoming common in Boston to undergo a second inoculation, sometimes even more.

John, writing to Abigail from Philadelphia, knew exactly what the problem was and wasn't shy about writing so. He wasn't enthusiastic about Doctor Bulfinch: "The Drs. cannot account for the numerous Failures of Inocculation. I can. No Phisician has either Head or Hands enough to attend a Thousand Patients. He can neither see that the Matter is good, nor that the Thread is properly covered with it, nor that the Incision is properly made, nor any Thing else. I wish you had taken Dr. Tufts for your Phisician and no other. I never liked your Man, and I like him now less than ever."[8]

Since the Boston city officials had allowed inoculations in June, the city became overrun with fearful people who had received the inoculation treatment inside the city limits but were wandering the streets waiting for their own pustule outbreak.[9] Each person was potentially contagious. Just as bad, a person could be walking around thinking that they were immune when they were not. Then the person could accidentally catch smallpox the "natural" and more dangerous way. As in any epidemic, rumors ran rampant. Abigail suspected that "the paper curency spread it everywhere."[10]

Abigail finally began to show "many dissagreable Sensations" on July 21, nine days after her inoculation. She felt she had successfully caught the smallpox virus. She also updated John on the children's health: "Nabby has been very ill, but the Eruption begins to make its appearence upon her, and upon Johnny. Tommy is so well that the Dr. innoculated him again to day fearing it had not taken. Charlly has no complaints yet, tho his arm has been very soar."[11] Nabby had needed a second inoculation. Following Abigail's requested second inoculation for Tommy, she had to give approval for Charles's second inoculation as well. None of the three had shown any actual signs of the virus. The following day, July 22, Abigail herself was so ill she had to cut her letter short, "My own infirmities prevents my writing. A most Excruciating pain in my head and every Limb and joint I hope portends a speedy Eruption and prevents my saying more than that I am forever Yours. The children are not yet broke out. Tis the Eleventh Day with us."[12]

On July 29, seventeen days after first receiving inoculations, Abigail could report to John of her own slow recovery: "I write you now, thanks be to Heaven, free from paine, in Good Spirits, but weak and feeble. All my Sufferings produced but one Eruption. . . . The small pox acts very oddly this Season, there are Seven out of our Number that have not yet had it, 3 out of our 4 children have been twice innoculated, two of them Charles and Tommy have not had one Symptom. . . . When I came into Town I was in great hopes that if we did well we should be able to return in about 3 weeks, and we should have been able to have effected it, if it had opperated as formerly. Now I fear it will be 5 weeks before we shall all get through." Abigail cautioned herself about complaining. She wrote of an unfortunate young girl, also staying at her uncle Isaac Smith's house, named Becky Peck, who "has it to such a degree as to be blind with one Eye, swell'd prodigiously, I believe she has ten Thousand [pustules]. She is really an object to look at. . . . When I cast my eye upon Becky . . . and see what an object she is I am silenced."[13]

It would turn out that Charles had developed mild symptoms of smallpox after his second inoculation, but still no pustules, therefore no physical indication that he was now immune to smallpox. Tommy, on the other hand, started showing twelve pustules on August 1. But along with Charles, Nabby was still a mystery. She became ill after her second inoculation, "was cold and shivery, then a voilent Heat insued but never developed pustules."[14] The doctors guessed that Nabby had developed immunity. But they weren't certain; she could still be susceptible to catching smallpox the natural way. Rather than take a chance on Nabby's life, Abigail asked for a third inoculation for her. Abigail also had Doctor Bulfinch inoculate Charles a third time. The smallpox pus was taken "the 3 time from some fresh matter taken from Becky Peck who has enough for all the House beside."[15]

It turned out that Abigail was right. By August 12, Nabby developed "small pox in plenty, she can reckon 500 allready."[16] On August 17 a weary Abigail wrote John, "Nabby has not been out of her chamber these 3 Days, neither can she stand or sit her foot to the floor. She has above a thousand pussels as larg as a great Green Pea. She is the Dr. says in a good way tho tis hard to make her think so. Charles complains some to day. I hope tis the Symptoms. I have had a Seige of it, I long for the compaign to be over."[17] Abigail was rightfully able to couch the family struggles in military terms because despite Nabby's successful inoculation, Charles still showed no absolute signs of smallpox. The siege of smallpox for the Adams children was not over yet.

On August 19 Abigail wrote to John the worrisome news that not only was Charles now showing signs of smallpox, but it had also been determined that he had caught it the more dangerous natural way:

At present all my attention is taken up with the care of our Little Charles who has been very bad. The Symptoms rose to a burning fever, a stupifaction and delirium ensued for 48 hours. The Doctor attended him as tho he had been his own child. He has the Distemper in the natural way. A most plentifull Eruption has taken place. Tho every thing has been done to lessen it that could, his face will be quite coverd, many if not all will run together. He is yet a very ill child, tho his Symptoms are lessend. I would not have allarmed you. I hope he is not dangerous, but we cannot tell the Event. Heaven grant it may be favorable. I will write you by wedensday Post. I shall see then how he is like to be, and can form a better judgment of Him.[18]

When John received Abigail's letter on Charles's situation, he hurriedly sent her an acknowledgment: "I have only Time before the Post goes out again to thank you for it, and to express my Resignation to the Will of Heaven whatever it may be respecting my dear Charles. I think his Fate is very uncertain. I will hope the best, but Symptoms so terrible indicate the Utmost danger."[19] John added that Abigail's notice about Charles's condition "fixed an Arrow in my Heart, which will not be drawn out, untill the next Post arrives, and then, perhaps, instead of being withdrawn, it will be driven deeper. My sweet Babe, Charles, is never out of my Thoughts.—Gracious Heaven preserve him!—The Symptoms you describe, are so formidable, that I am afraid almost to flatter myself with Hope."[20]

Despite the imminent threat of a formidable British army and navy attack against General Washington and the Continental Army at New

York, John was most worried about Charles's condition: "Amidst all my Concern for the Army, my dear Charles is continually present to my Mind. I dont know what to think. A Load of variolous Matter, sufficient to stupify him for forty Eight Hours, and then to break out so thick, as to threaten a Confluence, I fear will be more than his delicate[21] frame can support. Children of his Age, however, are often seen to bear a great deal."[22]

To add some lightness to the letter, John included happy reflections about the three other children, who had successfully weathered the smallpox outbreak: "Give my Love to my little Speckeled Beauty, Nabby. Tell her I am glad she is like to have a few Pitts. She will not look the worse for them. If she does, she will learn to prize looks less, and Ingenuity more. The best Way to prevent the Pitts from being lasting and conspicuous, is to keep her out of the sun for some time to prevent her from tanning. John[23] and Tom, hardy fellows! I have hardly had occasion to feel at all anxious about them."[24]

By the end of August, Nabby had recovered, and Charles looked like he was recovering. Though not entirely safe from the smallpox danger yet, Abigail and John began to write about other subjects in their letters.

John had been a temporary resident of Philadelphia, a much newer and in many ways a better city than Boston. But John had seen with his own eyes the frustration he shared with Abigail regarding the easier access to higher education that Philadelphia offered when compared to Boston. Even more troubling to him were the provincial and clumsy traits he'd noticed that his fellow New Englanders engaged in when standing alongside more refined gentlemen from other states. He also attributed the "Deficiencies" in New Englanders from their being isolated from the rest of the world. Rambling on paper to Abigail, John touched upon the subject of calling for better education by New Englanders: "Our N. England People are Aukward and bashfull; yet they are pert, ostentatious and vain, a Mixture which excites Ridicule and gives Disgust. They have not the faculty of shewing themselves to the best Advantage, nor the Art of concealing this faculty. . . . Our Deficiencies in these Respects, are owing wholly to the little Intercourse We have had with strangers, and to our Inexperience in the World. These Imperfections must be remedied, for New England must produce the Heroes, the statesmen, the Philosophers, or America will make no great Figure for some Time."[25]

That's just what Abigail wanted to hear. For even though deep into a dangerous family smallpox crisis, Abigail seized the chance to make her passionate thoughts on female education known to John again. . . but even more forcefully and specifically. She expounded that since women were children's first teachers in life, national "Heroes, Statesmen and Philosophers" must first come forth from "learned women." "You remark upon the deficiency of Education in your Countrymen. . . . In this Town I never saw so great a neglect of Education. . . . If you complain of neglect of Education in sons, What shall I say with regard to daughters, who every day experience the want of it. With regard to the Education of my own children, I find myself soon out of my debth, and destitute and deficient in every part of Education. . . . If we mean to have Heroes, Statesmen and Philosophers, we should have learned women. . . . If much depends as is allowed upon the early Education of youth and the first principals which are instilld take the deepest root, great benifit must arise from litirary accomplishments in women."[26]

By September 2, the Adamses' seven-week-long smallpox crisis was over. Abigail and Charles were the last of the family to return to Braintree; the others had already departed. Showing her typical humility and thankfulness, Abigail closed that chapter out for John: "This is a Beautifull Morning. I see it with joy, and I hope thankfullness. I came here with all my treasure of children, have passd thro one of the most terible Diseases to which humane Nature is subject, and not one of us is wanting."[27]

Although the prospect of safely returning to one's own home was pleasurable, the Braintree house was small and cramped compared to the large rooms where the Adams children stayed in their uncle's stately Boston house. As she was leaving, Abigail had a moment of inner reflection. She dreamily told John about how much she enjoyed the small joy of using her aunt's window closet as her own little writing nook: "I have possession of my Aunts chamber in which you know is a very conveniant pretty closet with a window which looks into her flower Garden. In this closet are a number of Book Shelves, which are but poorly furnished, however I have a pretty little desk or cabinet here where I write all my Letters and keep my papers unmollested by any one. . . . I always had a fancy for a closet with a window which I could more peculiarly call my own."[28]

Abigail included the mention of another scurrilous rumor she'd heard about John, one more of the many she had to tolerate until the truth could be confirmed. This time her "P.S." carried the news that a "very odd report has been propagated in Braintree viz. that you were poisond upon your return at N.Y."[29] She made no other mention of it, apparently choosing to ignore it as she had all the "Malicious" rumors that "un-feeling" people seemed to delight in telling her. A few weeks later, John advised her to continue disregarding rumors: "Lyes by the Million will be told you. Dont believe any of them."[30]

Abigail responded to John: "I am not apt to be intimidated you know. I have given as little heed to that and a thousand other Bug Bear[31] re-ports as posible. I have slept as soundly since my return not withstand-ing all the Ghosts and hobgoblings, as ever I did in my life. . . . Sometimes I have been told so by those who really wish'd it might be so, with Malicious pleasure. . . . How unfealing are the world! They tell me they Heard you was dead with as little sensibility as a stock or a stone, and I have now got to be provoked at it, and can hardly help snubing the person who tells me so."[32]

However, the subject of the actual danger of serving in Congress was never far from Abigail's and John's minds. By signing the Declaration of Independence each traitorous delegate was in effect signing their own death warrant if captured. John Adams, as the well-known ringleader of the illegal congressional governmental body, speculated that he would be imprisoned in the notoriously cruel and unsanitary Newgate Prison in London. There he would await trial and possible execution as an ex-ample to other rebels and traitors. Or perhaps, rather than creating a martyr of Adams, he would be held for ransom by the British to end the war. John speculated in his diary his own thoughts on his prison treat-ment by the British: "The Consequence of a Capture would be a Lodging in New Gate. For the Spirit of Contempt as well as indignation and vin-dictive rage, with which the British Government had to that time con-ducted both the Controversy and the War forbade me to hope for the honor of an Appartment in the Tower as a State Prisoner. As their Act of Parliament would authorise them to try me in England for Treason, and proceed to execution too, I had no doubt they would go to the extent of their power, and practice upon me all the Cruelties of their punishment of Treason."[33] John noted that at least in the Tower of London, he could be held as a state prisoner and afforded some dignity.[34] Throughout the entire war, Abigail knew the risks her husband braved every day.

Those state delegates who put their signatures on the Declaration of Independence were men whom George III had labeled as "dangerous and ill designing"[35] in his "Proclamation, For suppressing Rebellion and Sedition."[36]

For months before the agreement to separate from Britain, the follow-ing phrase had made the rounds through the Philadelphia State House:

"It is a true saying of a Wit—We must hang together or seperately."[37] Carter Braxton, a Continental Congress delegate from Virginia, had written it to his uncle Landon Carter on April 14, 1776. The phrase has also been attributed to Benjamin Franklin. It underscored the constant danger the delegates faced due to their traitorous work. The thought was ever present to Abigail, as well.

Chapter Eleven

"A Sacrifice to My Country"
1776–1777

It *was late September* 1776 and the smallpox epidemic in Massachu-setts had come to an end. Abigail, like so many other residents of the Boston area, stumbled out of the infectious world that they had known for months. After Abigail had "underwent the operation of a smoking at the lines"[1] she finally reached home. "I think I never felt greater pleasure at comeing Home after an absence in my Life."[2] People had to pick up where their lives had left off. That included Abigail's management of John's assets which had been ignored during the out-break. She wearily updated John: "I know the weight of publick cares lye so heavy upon you that I have been loth to mention your own pri-vate ones." But she had to warn John about their house in Boston and other assets: "unless you return [,] what little property you possess will be lost. In the first place the House at Boston is going to ruin. When I was there I hired a Girl to clean it, it had a cart load of Dirt in it. . . . One of the chambers was used to keep poultry in, an other sea coal, and an other salt. You may conceive How it look'd. The House is so exceed-ing damp being shut up, that the floors are mildewd, the sealing falling down, and the paper mouldy and falling from the walls. I took care to have it often opened and aird whilst I tarried in Town. I put it into the best state I could."[3]

Abigail later wrote another letter to John with further details: "In the next place, the Lighter[4] of which you are or should be part owner is lying rotting at the wharf. One year more without any care and she is worth nothing. You have no Bill of Sale, no right to convey any part of her should any person appear to purchase her. . . . The Pew I let, after having paid a tax for the repairs of the meeting House. As to what is here under my more immediate inspection I do the best I can with it, but it will not at the high price Labour is, pay its way."[5]

To add more thoughts to her melancholy letter, Abigail was struggling with the one-year anniversary of her mother's death. "The Image of my Dear Mother seems ever before me, and fresh to my memory. I felt more than common depression of spirits the other day when I enterd the House, nor could I enjoy myself whilst I stay'd, a Train of melancholly Ideas forced themselves upon me and made me very unhappy."[6] Along with those "depression of spirits," she had found out that her sister Mary and husband Richard Cranch were in dire financial straits. "Ever since the Removal of the army and the opening of Boston he has not had half Buisness enough to employ him."[7] The sound defeat of the Continental Army at the Battle of Long Island on August 27 had brought worse news. John captured the defeat in a clever sentence he had written to Abigail: "In general, our Generals were out generalled on Long Island."[8] Abigail was determined to at least put a brave spin on the event: "The Best accounts we can collect from New York assure us that our Men fought valiantly. We are no ways dispiritted here, we possess a Spirit that will not be conquerd."[9]

For many months in 1776, John had been writing to Abigail that he would soon be home, either by taking leave of his post in Congress or by permanently resigning. Abigail just wanted him home regardless. As early as July 1776, John notified Abigail, "I design to write to the General Court, requesting a Dismission, or at least a Furlow."[10]

However, each time John was planning on taking a congressional leave, a new crisis would arise requiring him to stay. He had just been appointed the president of the Board of War and Ordinance—the critical duty of which was to raise supplies and men for the Continental Army, an important and frustrating job. He was also leading debates on the Articles of Confederation, drafting instructions for Silas Deane and Benjamin Franklin as the first ambassadors to France, and drafting the model treaty so that America could reach out to foreign powers for assistance. Despite the numbing levels of responsibility, John was still trying to take leave of Congress, permanently or temporarily. But to be excused from duty, John had to appeal to the Massachusetts General Court who selected and sent state delegates. "The Court will not accept your Resignation, they will appoint Mr. Dalton and Dana to releave you,"[11] Abigail wrote reassuringly to John. In a postscript to her letter Abigail also proudly announced, "Master John has become post rider from Boston to B[raintree]."[12]

In mid-September Massachusetts General Court Speaker James Warren, husband to Mercy Otis Warren, wrote John, "We have not yet made an addition to our Delegates . . . so it is procrastinated and left to the next setting."[13] John was very angry; he fired off a letter to the General Court and likely didn't hold back with his blistering temper. However, it was a rare example of John using a self-directed calming action. Rather than heeding a warning from Abigail, John wrote at the bottom of the letter, which he had decided not to send, "not sent, nor fit to be sent."[14]

Finally tired of the whole thing, by mid-October John boldly left Philadelphia on a self-appointed absence from Congress. It left a hole in the Massachusetts delegates list. By early November, John was back at his home in Braintree with his four children and a thankful Abigail.

As usual during the times when Abigail and John lived together—right after marriage, residing in Europe, while he was vice president and president—their letters to each other became scarce or nonexistent. There was no reason to write letters when you physically interacted every day. But sometime in November 1776, the procrastinating Massachusetts General Court reconvened and not surprisingly elected John again as a delegate to the Continental Congress. Word was delivered to the Adamses' Braintree house, and most assuredly another debate began within the house of weighing private life versus public duty. As always with John and Abigail, public duty won out. As Abigail wrote Mercy Otis Warren: "I had it in my Heart to disswade him from going and I know I could have prevaild, but our publick affairs at that time wore so gloomy an aspect that I thought if ever his assistance was wanted, it must be at such a time. I therefore resignd my self to suffer much anxiety and many Melancholy hours for this year to come."[15] Abigail again was sacrificing personal happiness for the public good, something she had gotten used to. It was during this time that Abigail wrote another memorable sentence. In it she hoped the adversities that were endured by early Americans for the betterment of future generations would not be forgotten: "Posterity who are to reap the Blessings, will scarcly be able to conceive the Hardships and Sufferings of their Ancesstors."[16]

The year 1777 dawned, and with it the "gloomy"[17] time that Abigail had endured eased up a bit. Over Christmas 1776, General Washington had executed a bold, complicated, and almost reckless "Victory or Death"[18] plan to attack the Hessian forces encamped at Trenton, New Jersey. Its exuberant victory sparked another American victory at Princeton, New Jersey, on January 3, 1777. But when John left Braintree for Congress on January 9, it would be to make the longer ride to Baltimore, Maryland, instead of to Philadelphia. Congress had decided to temporarily move out of its home of Philadelphia because of an expected imminent attack by the British.[19] Again, the fear of John being captured or killed was a daily thought that Abigail had to handle.

John and his fellow Massachusetts traveler Congressman James Lovell[20] arrived safely in Baltimore on February 1. He wrote Abigail that he was very impressed with Maryland, except for the "worst Roads and the worst Weather": "I think I have never been better pleased with any of our American States than with Maryland. We saw most excellent Farms all along the Road, and what was very striking to me, I saw more sheep and more flax in Maryland than I ever saw in riding a like Distance in any other State. We scarce passed a Farm without seeing a fine flock of sheep, and scarce an House without seeing Men or Women, dressing Flax. Several Times We saw Women, breaking and swingling this necessary Article."[21]

The new year of 1777 also brought news from Abigail's youngest sister, Elizabeth (Betsy) of her engagement to John Shaw, the thirty-year-old pastor of the First Congregational Church of Haverhill, Massachusetts, some fifty miles frim Braintree. He was the same man Abigail had suspected of impure motives toward Betsy in 1773, as he boarded in their father's rectory. Abigail heavily insinuated to John that Betsy was marrying out of desperation to avoid being an "old maid."[22] Even though Betsy was now twenty-seven, Abigail had rounded her age up when she wrote John, "An Idea of 30 years and unmarried is sufficent to make people do very unacountable things." However, Abigail would never sanction the marriage, "since the mortification I endure at the mention of it is so great that I have never changd a word with her upon the subject, altho preparations are making for house keeping. . . . I would not make an exchange with her for the mountains of Mexico and Peru. She has forfeited all her character with me and the world for taste &c."[23]

Abigail also disliked John Shaw's strict Calvinistic leanings about such doctrines as original sin. Even more so, the Adamses' Congregationalist church was more lenient about certain rigid beliefs like original sin and predestination. And having "nothing to do with it" pertained to Abigail and the upcoming marriage of Betsy and John Shaw. Abigail was glad she never wavered in her dislike for their union: "Thank Heaven my Heart was early fix'd and never deviated."[24]

In the spring, Abigail was dealing with a severe rash and eye infection. Tommy was suffering from worms. Abigail asked John to find and send worm medicine: "If you should have an opportunity pray purchase me a Box of Dr. Ryans Wafers for worms, and send them. T[omm]y is much troubled with them, has lost most all his flesh, you would scarcly know him."[25]

She also noted the unpleasant news of the capture of General Charles Lee by the British. But even more heartbreaking for Abigail was the news that at the point of capture, Lee's Pomeranian dog Spado had bolted away, never to be seen again. "I see by the news papers you sent me that Spado is lost. I mourn for him."[26]

Quietly through the spring of 1777 Abigail harbored her own secret. She was pregnant again. She was carrying their sixth child[27] after having conceived in November, almost immediately upon John's return home. By April and in her fifth month of pregnancy, Abigail used vague language in case of interception, in a letter to John to describe her situation of "perticuliar circumstances." She further alluded to a vague promise made by John to be home for the baby's delivery as he had been for their other children: "As the Summer advances I have many anxieties, some of which I should not feel or at least should find them greatly alleviated if you could be with me. But as that is a Satisfaction I know I must not look for, (tho I have a good mind to hold You to your promise since some perticuliar circumstances were really upon that condition) I must summon all the Phylosophy I am mistress of since what cannot be help'd must be endured."[28] Abigail was bracing herself for John's expected reply that he would not be able to leave Congress for the baby's birth. She sensed it. But in living day to day, she linked her pregnancy to the happy thought of it as "a constant remembrancer of an absent Friend, and excites sensations of tenderness which are better felt than expressd."[29]

The summer of 1777 in Braintree was unusually hot, a circumstance that Abigail, even in perfect health, normally disliked. The heat made sleeping at night very hard for her, aside from the further discomfort of being eight months pregnant: "We have had very Hot weather which you know never agrees well with me, and greatly distresses me under my present circumstances. I loose my rest a nights, which makes me more unable to bear the Heat of the day. I look forward to the middle of july with more anxiety than I can describe."[30]

Near to the ninth month, a very uncomfortable Abigail reported to John (who obviously by then knew of her pregnancy), "I can but poorly walk about [the] House."[31] And with rumors also resurfacing of a British attack upon Boston, Abigail wistfully stated, "I do not feel very apprehensive of an attack upon Boston. I hope we shall be quiet. I should make a misirable hand of running now."[32] Eleven-year-old Nabby was turning out to be a wonderful helpmate to Abigail in her awkward condition, "I am happy in a daughter who is both a companion and an assistant in my Family affairs and who I think has a prudence and steadiness beyond her years."[33]

Heartbreak would arise on July 9. Abigail explained to John that "I was last night taken with a shaking fit, and am very apprehensive that a life was lost. As I have no reason to day to think otherways; what may be the consequences to me, Heaven only knows. I know not of any injury to myself, nor any thing which could occasion what I fear. I would not Have you too much allarmd. I keep up some Spirits yet, tho I would have you prepaird for any Event that may happen."[34] She had felt her miscarriage and instinctively knew what had happened. The baby wasn't moving. A doctor came to see Abigail the next day and gave her the prescription to "hope" that all was well with the baby. But Abigail, who was now experiencing contractions, knew differently: "The Dr. encourages me to Hope that my apprehensions are groundless respecting what I wrote you yesterday, tho I cannot say I have had any reason to allter my mind."[35]

Abigail even wrote to John during a contraction that night. "Slow, lingering and troublesome is the present situation. I pray Heaven that it may be soon or it seems to me I shall be worn out." Abigail had to stop writing the letter as she felt another painful contraction coming on: "I must lay my pen down this moment, to bear what I cannot fly from." Then, post-contraction, she started again, "and now I have endured it I reassume my pen."[36] She continued writing the letter, filling John in on scarcity and prices of "Hogsheads of rum," "Sugar," "Lamb," "Corn," "Hay," and "manure."

The next morning, July 11, Abigail noted that it was the birthday of ten-year-old Johnny and she hoped that it would continue to be a good day to be born: "I got more rest last night than I expected, this morning am rather more ill than I was yesterday. This day ten years ago master John came into this world. May I have reason again to recollect it with peculiar gratitude."[37]

But in a touching letter to John dated Wednesday, July 16, Abigail gave him the heartbreaking news that although she had survived,[38] their "dear Infant is numberd with its ancestors. My apprehensions with regard to it were well founded. Tho my Friends would have fain perswaded me that the Spleen [or] the Vapours[39] had taken hold of me I was as perfectly sensible of its discease as I ever before was of its existance. I was also aware of the danger which awaited me; and which tho my suffering[s] were great thanks be to Heaven I have been supported through, and would silently submit to its dispensations in the loss of a sweet daughter."[40]

Elizabeth Adams, the name they had decided on, had been a stillborn baby. Adams family historians surmise that the umbilical cord had gotten twisted around the baby's neck, gathered from the coded description which Abigail wrote in her very sad observation: "it appeard to be a very fine Babe, and as it never opened its Eyes in this world it lookd as tho they were only closed for sleep. The circumstance which put an end to its existence, was evident upon its birth, but at this distance and in a Letter which may possibly fall into the Hands of some unfealing Ruffian I must omit particuliars. Suffice it to say that it was not oweing to any injury which I had sustaind, nor could any care of mine have prevented it. . . . My Heart was much set upon a Daughter. . . . No one was so much affected with the loss of it as its Sister who mournd in tears for Hours. . . . I have so much cause for thankfullness amidst my sorrow."[41]

John was heartbroken when he received four of Abigail's letters on the same day describing the forlorn events. But with a considerable percentage of colonial mothers dying during childbirth, the first thing John wrote was that he thanked God for sparing Abigail's life:

> My dearest Friend, Never in my whole Life, was my Heart affected with such Emotions and Sensations, as were this Day occasioned by your Letters of the 9. 10. 11. and 16 of July. . . . Is it not unaccountable, that one should feel so strong an Affection for an Infant, that one has never seen, nor shall see? Yet I must confess to you, the Loss of this sweet little Girl, has most tenderly and sensibly affected me. I feel a Grief and Mortification that is heightened tho it is not wholly occasioned, by my Sympathy with the Mother. My dear little

Nabbys Tears are sweetly becoming her generous Tenderness and sensibility of Nature.[42]

The year 1777 was called the "Year of the Hangman" because the three sevens looked like three gallows, which was a form of "gallows humour" by tired Americans. It was also the year when the Continental Congress learned an important lesson about creating money. Congress had no way to coin or print money. Congress also did not have the power to tax so it could not raise money. It had been the duty of the thirteen states to produce and supply money to Congress. But the question was how the states were going to raise the money. The problem was left to the states, most of which were broke and devastated from years of war.

To fight the war, money was needed. The solution seemed to be to print paper money. When more money was needed, more money was printed. However, there was nothing backing the currency. Even though it was near worthless from the start, the states had started printing money in 1775 with the outbreak of hostilities. Soon Congress itself started printing money and war bonds.

By 1777, it had become obvious that as more paper notes and bills were printed, the face value of the currency was becoming worth less and less. For the consumer, simple goods required more and more money to buy, as the money came closer to having no value at all. This uncontrolled inflation, coupled with speculation, hoarding, and profiteering, made it almost impossible for the soldiers to be paid or supplies to be purchased. The efforts of price controls by Congress were useless. Counterfeiting was also becoming a major problem.[43] All these combined factors were ruining the entire colonial economy. Only secret foreign loans by France were temporally keeping the United States afloat, but that arrangement couldn't go on forever. A British naval blockade of American ports kept many goods unavailable and created devastating shortages of nearly everything that was imported.

Abigail was finding it more and more difficult to find and hire farmhands for almost any rate of pay. The farm hands would soon enlist in the army. "I endeavour to live with as great frugality as posible. I am obliged to pay higher wages this year than last; Prince was offerd 8 dollors a month and left me. I found upon trial that I must give 12, and put to great difficulty to hire a Hand even at that price," Abigail complained.[44]

In many letters, Abigail and John raged about the "Avarice, venality, Animosity, contention, pride, weakness and dissipation" and an "evil spirit"[45] of materialism among American citizens. It seemed that amid war, many people had become ravenous and sought to take advantage of the unusual wartime demands. It was not uncommon for a store owner to hoard popular items and then sell them at incredibly high prices. On July 24, 1777, in what would become known as the "Boston Coffee Riot," an angry group of Bostonian women took matters into their own hands as described by Abigail to John:

> You must know that there is a great Scarcity of Sugar and Coffe, articles which the Female part of the State are very loth to give up, expecially whilst they consider the Scarcity occasiond by the merchants having secreted a large Quantity. . . . It was rumourd that an eminent, wealthy, stingy Merchant[46] (who is a Batchelor) had a Hogshead of Coffe in his Store which he refused to sell to the committee under 6 shillings per pound. A Number of Females some say a hundred, some say more assembled with a cart and trucks, marchd down to the Ware House and demanded the keys, which he refused to deliver, upon which one of them seazd him by his Neck and tossd him into the cart. Upon his finding no Quarter he deliverd the keys, when they tipd up the cart and dischargd him, then opend the Warehouse, Hoisted out the Coffe themselves, put it into the trucks and drove off. . . . A large concourse of Men stood amazd silent Spectators of the whole transaction.[47]

Besides trying to hire farmhands at high wages, Abigail tried to recover money owned to John; some legal debts were many years old. In 1777 with deflated Massachusetts state currency now worth one-third of its face value that it had in 1775, debtors could pay off John with currency worth much less than they owed him. It was an economic system spiraling downward and bringing bankruptcy and chaos to many colonists.

Abigail became aware of a way for her family to survive the crippling inflation and to even make a profit. She never revealed in her letters who the economics teacher was, but it almost assuredly was Doctor Cotton Tufts, her uncle on her mother's side and the Adamses' physician. Doctor Tufts dabbled in stocks and securities as well as practicing medicine.

Abigail appeared to be a very quick student on the complex subject of securities and investments. She soon wrote to John "this week I propose to send in to the continental Loan office a hundred pound LM [Lawful Money]."[48] Congress had started printing IOU's in October 1776 called

"Loan Office certificates," which paid the bearer 4 percent interest. In February 1777, the interest rate was raised to 6 percent. At that time Abigail became aware of this opportunity to exchange her near-worthless paper currency for loan office certificates. The certificates also slowly lost value over time, however they did not lose value as fast as continental currency. The loan office certificates were an excellent hedge against inflation and Abigail, as a risk taker, deserves more praise for her bravery in trying a new venture.

After buying the loan office certificates, Abigail added to her letter to John, "I have done the best in my power with what I received."[49] She also had made the final payment to John's brother for the purchase of John's birth house: "have also paid your Brother 5 hundred & 50 dollors which with what you paid when at Home and the small sums that were paid before, amount to the whole of the principal and part of the interest."[50]

Part of the hundred pounds that she had converted to federal bonds came from the sale of John's old barge, the "lighter" which had been rotting away in Boston Harbor: "24 pounds which I received for the Sale of a Lighter!"[51] For a person never trained in accounting, Abigail's sense of money matters became one of her greatest assets and would serve the Adamses well. Abigail observed: "Tis almost 14 years since we were united, but not more than half that time have we had the happiness of living together. The unfealing world may consider it in what light they please."[52] Abigail considered it a personal sacrifice.

Chapter Twelve

"A Very Dangerous Man"

1777–1778

H ad *John Adams been captured or killed*, there was no formal procedure set in place to notify Abigail, his next of kin. As John was a high-ranking member of Congress, notification may have come from a personal visit or a letter from a congressman. In wartime, receiving such an ominous visit or letter was never far from Abigail's awareness. However, to be able to function every day she most certainly had to banish such thoughts from her mind.

Then, in September 1777 Abigail received a letter franked[1] by a member of Congress. However, the letter wasn't from John. It was from James Lovell, another Massachusetts delegate. Abigail had briefly met Lovell in January 1777 when her husband and Lovell set off for Baltimore together from the Adamses' Braintree home.[2] Abigail froze in fear and could not open the letter, thinking it was bad news. She later wrote to John of her experience:

> there is no reward this side the grave that would be a temptation to
> me to undergo the agitation and distress I was thrown into by re-

ceiving a Letter in his Handwriting franked by him [James Lovell]. It seems almost imposible that the Humane mind could take in, in so small a space of time, so many Ideas as rushd upon mine in the space of a moment, I cannot describe to you what I felt. The sickness or death of the dearest of Friends with ten thousand horrours seazd my immagination. I took up the Letter, then laid it down, then gave it out of my Hand unable to open it, then collected resolution enough to unseal it, but dared not read it, begun at the bottom, read a line, then attempted to begin it, but could not. A paper was enclosed, I venturd upon that, and finding it a plan [map], recoverd enough to read the Letter——but I pray Heaven I may never realize such a nother moment of distress.[3]

It turned out that Lovell's reason for contacting her was simple but strange. His polite cover letter explained that he was sending a self-drawn map of an area between Philadelphia and Baltimore where he indicated the location of the next big battle. He drew and sent it because he knew she liked to keep up with military campaigns.[4] Lovell explained in the short letter that rather than give the map to John to forward to Abigail, he decided to send it directly to Abigail: "This knowledge is only part of the foundation of my affectionate esteem of you. . . . I could, it is true, have delivered it to your Husband. But, I could not with delicacy have told him, to his face. . . . I shall rather apologize for what there is already of Gallantry in my manner of conveying this little Present to your hand."[5]

"Affectionate esteem" and "Gallantry" were awkward words to send to the wife of a colleague. Abigail explained later that she'd only casually met Lovell twice, and she barely knew him. She could not explain why he had taken this uncomfortable, improper action with her. Lovell sent the first letter to Abigail on August 29, 1777. She in turn, after the shock of receiving it wore off, replied to Lovell on September 17[6]—first chastising him for scaring her: "I esteem myself much obliged for the enclosed plan [map], but I cannot describe to you the distress and agitation which the reception of your Letter threw me into. It was some time before I could get resolution to open it, and when I had opend it I dared not read it. Ten thousand horrid Ideas rushd upon my Soul. I thought it would announce to me the sickness or death of all my earthly happiness. As I could not read the Letter I opened the paper enclosed and upon finding it a plan, was releaved from my distress."

Then she wrote one shorter paragraph in which she acknowledged the flattery toward her, "Your professions of esteem Sir are very flattering to me,"[7] and gave him the standard brushoff from afar. She ended with a complimentary allusion to his heroic, patriotic sufferings. She was referring to his prison time in Boston and Halifax at the hands of the British.

James Lovell was a "schoolteacher, prisoner, and patriot"[8] and much more. Born in Boston in 1737, he was seven years older than Abigail. He earned a scholarship to Harvard, where he first met John Adams. When British taxing policies became front and center news in Boston, James broke with his Tory father, John Lovell, who was a widely respected teacher at Boston Latin School. In 1760, James Lovell had married Mary Middleton and they went on to have nine children.[9] Soon Lovell became affiliated with the Sons of Liberty, and after the Battle of Bunker Hill he was charged as a spy by the British. The guilty evidence was the discovery of an incriminating note with Lovell's name on it in the pocket of the slain Doctor Joseph Warren. Lovell was arrested and thrown into the Boston Stone Jail on Queen Street and stayed there throughout the winter of 1775–1776. With the evacuation of Boston, the British took Lovell with them to their naval base in Halifax, Nova Scotia. Lovell was later exchanged for Colonel Philip Skene. Lovell, "emaciated and weak,"[10] returned to Boston. He became a Massachusetts delegate and an already proven American patriot and hero. Lovell served as a French translator in Congress and was chairman of the important Committee on Foreign Affairs.

The James Lovell/Abigail Adams letters number 94 in total[11] with Abigail writing thirty-four and Lovell writing sixty over the course of twelve years (1777–1789). Some of the letters seem to be charged with innuendo-filled, double-entendré sexual themes initiated by Lovell, then batted away by Abigail or skillfully turned back on Lovell.

Above all, Abigail kept the tone of her letters courteous, which was the standard behavior expected between two near strangers. Abigail had written her short reply to Lovell using much of the verbiage that she used in John's letter which she wrote to both on September 17, 1777. Abigail was very aware that letters were routinely captured in transit and their contents published. She could never compromise her integrity or risk the shame that would fall upon John for writing phrases which could be deemed dangerous or unfaithful.

Lovell delayed two months in replying to Abigail because Congress had to flee Philadelphia for fear of a British attack. This time the scare was real, as the British under General William Howe captured Philadelphia on September 26. Congress had fled to Lancaster, Pennsylvania, and later fled farther west to York, Pennsylvania. Abigail received the good news in October of the surrender of British General John Burgoyne and his army of 6,000 soldiers at Saratoga, New York, on October 17.[12] The American victory led to a treaty of alliance being signed with France at Versailles on February 6, 1778. From that single event France publicly entered the war on the side of America.

However, France had been secretly assisting America prior to that time with munitions, uniforms, and money. The primary goal of France was never to support Americans and their fight against a monarchy. It was to weaken Great Britain as a world power and to regain some of France's lost territory given up during the French and Indian War.

Abigail mentioned the big news of Burgoyne's surrender at Saratoga in a letter to John: "I believe I may venture to congratulate my Love upon the completion of his wishes with regard to Burgoin."[13] In the same letter, Abigail ungraciously buried the matrimonial news of her sister, Betsy: "Among the late mariages which have taken place and are like to, Miss B[ets]y S[mit]h to Mr. S[ha]w last Thursday."[14]

Abigail also received word that would strongly affect the Adamses' finances. She had gotten in on the ground floor of buying government securities, exchanging near-worthless Continental currency for loan office certificates. To raise much-needed money, Congress had sold investment interests in the American government, much like savings bonds during World War II. However, purchases had fallen off as of recently. In the fall of 1777, Congress needed to make purchasers happier with the investing terms. Instead of backing the depreciating loan office certificates with worthless congressional promises, actual French bills of exchange would now be used as backing of Continental currency. That was huge. France was a major power on the world stage and their bills of exchange[15] were backed by gold. Specifically, now the source of the future payments would not come from Congress's assurances, but directly from the financial support of France's King Louis XVI. To Abigail this now meant that a 6 percent annual interest rate would be accumulated through the bills of exchange.

The best news of all, however, for Abigail was that John was departing from Congress on November 7 on an official leave of absence. John wasn't sure if he would ever be returning. "When I asked Leave of Congress to make a Visit to my Constituents and my Family in November 1777, it was my intention to decline the next Election, and return to my practice at the Bar. . . . I was loosing a fortune every Year by my Absence."[16] The prospect of returning to a law practice in Massachusetts was appealing to him for many reasons, particularly for family and finances. On November 27, John arrived at his home in Braintree. A few days later, he rode to Portsmouth, New Hampshire, to prepare for a legal case about the captured enemy merchant vessel *Lusanna*. In his absence Abigail opened his mail as John had always requested.

In one of the mail packets was Congress' appointment of John as United States envoy to France. He was to replace Silas Deane who was being recalled. John would be working with Benjamin Franklin and Arthur Lee, who were already in France, to negotiate a written alliance. Abigail must have reacted solemnly when reading this life-changing appointment.

However, waiting for John when he returned from Portsmouth were "Large Packetts from Congress, containing a new Commission to Franklin, Lee and me as Plenipotentiaries to the King of France, with our instructions and other papers, had been left at my House, and waited my Arrival. A Letter from the President of Congress informed me of my Appointment, and that the Navy Board in Boston was ordered to fit the Frigate *Boston*, as soon as possible to carry me to France."[17]

John struggled with the decision to accept the new position, which would take him away from home for a long, dangerous, and unknown period. Abigail hoped he wouldn't accept, but in the deepest part of her soul she knew that the answer would be "yes." John wrote in his diary: "On the other hand my Country was in deep distress and in great danger. Her dearest Interest would be involved in the relations she might form with foreign nations. . . . My Wife who had always encouraged and animated me, in all antecedent dangers and perplexities, did not fail me on this Occasion. . . . I resolved to devote my family and my Life to the Cause, accepted the Appointment and made preparation for the Voyage."[18]

John accepted the assignment and would make the treacherous midwinter voyage across the Atlantic Ocean. Abigail apparently pleaded with him to let her go along on the trip, but John declined. He was concerned that their farm and home would deteriorate in Abigail's absence, as well as worried about the well-known dangers involved in a winter crossing. During such a crossing, ships had been known to ice over, capsize, and sink with no trace of the passengers or crew. Coupled with Abigail's fear of deep water was the chance of capture by the British. "The Dangers from Enemies was so great, and their treatment to prisoners so inhumane and Brutal, that in case of a Capture my sufferings would enhance his misiry, and perhaps I might be subjected to worse treatment on account of my connection with him."[19] Abigail described her plea to John: "Most willingly would I have hazarded the danger of the Sea to have accompanied him, but the dangers from Enemies was so great that I could not obtain his consent."[20]

Abigail and John did decide, however, to allow ten-year-old John Quincy to travel with his father on the trip. This fateful decision by Abigail and John is the definitive example of how valuable they thought a superior European education would be for their young son. It would be a once in a lifetime learning opportunity beyond any experience John Quincy could obtain in Braintree. Abigail was also aware of the "snares and temptations" that Europe would expose Johnny to: "there are many very many which may stain his morals even at this early period of life. But to exclude him from temptation would be to exclude him from the World in which he is to live, and the only method which can be persued with advantage is to fix the padlock upon the mind."[21] It was set. The Adamses, father and son, would set sail for France on February 14, 1778.

Although congressional records show that Elbridge Gerry nominated John for the position of French minister, all its ambassadorial proceedings were under the authority of the Committee on Foreign Affairs. And by a strange coincidence the chairman of the Committee on Foreign Affairs was James Lovell. In fact, by 1779 Lovell was the entire Committee on Foreign Affairs, a fact that wasn't lost on Abigail. Could it be that Lovell arranged to have Abigail's husband conveniently out of the way? As the appointment became accepted and official, Abigail lashed out in writing at Lovell: "O Sir you who are possessd of Sensibility, and a tender Heart, how could you contrive to rob me of all my happiness? . . . I know Sir by this appointment you mean the publick good, or you would not thus call upon me to sacrifice my tranquility and happiness. . . . And can I Sir consent to be seperated from him whom my Heart esteems above all earthly things, and for an unlimited time? My life will be one continued scene of anxiety and apprehension, and must I cheerfully comply with the Demand of my Country?"[22] Then Abigail stepped back for a moment realizing the forwardness of pouring out angry words, "I beg your Excuse Sir for writing thus freely, it has been a relief to my mind to drop some of my sorrows through my pen."[23]

Abigail's anxiousness wasn't helped when she read in the February 23, 1778, edition of the *Boston Gazette*: "A Letter from Bourdeaux of December 12, mentions, That the illustrious Patriot Dr. Benjamin Franklin has been assassinated in his Bed-Chamber, at the Instance of Lord Stormont. The Villain left him for dead; but one of the Doctor's Ribs prevented the Stab from being instantly fatal, and he lay in a languishing Condition when the Vessel sail'd that brings this Account."[24] It wasn't until a month later when Lovell assured Abigail that the Franklin assassination rumor was false. "I tell you that no Credit is to be given to the late Report of an attempted Assassination of Doctor Franklin."[25] But, strangely, in the same letter Lovell admitted that he liked Abigail's "Allarms and Distress." "Call me not a Savage, when I inform you that your 'Allarms and Distress' have afforded me Delight."[26] Abigail's "Distress" gave Lowell "Delight"?

Abigail was at the start of a tug-of-war involving overt sexual advances by a powerful near stranger versus her own need for information as the wife of an important political figure. John had stopped writing to her for over four months after he had sailed to France. Abigail did not know if her husband and son were alive or dead. There simply were no letters. Lovell, in contrast, received secret periodic congressional business and news updates. Abigail needed those to stay informed and wasn't shy in asking for copies of them: "Am I entitled to the journals of Congress, if you think so I should be much obliged to you if you would convey them to me."[27] Lowell began to send Abigail a trickle of confidential updates.

Lovell also passed along privileged financial insider information in reply to Abigail's question about continental currency. She asked: "I want to be resolved in an other question, what shall we do with our currency? I fear it will be a Hurculean labour to extricate it out of its present forlorn condition. There is a universal uneasiness with regard to it and some are speculating one project, some another."[28] (Even two years earlier she had written to John, "Our money will soon be as useless as blank paper.")[29] Lovell replied, "It is recommended to redeem the continental Currency at 40 for 1 and to model the Tender Laws equitably."[30]

Abigail believed that Lovell could help with John's infrequent pay vouchers from Congress. Money for farm labor was spotty coupled with the drastic lack of farmhands. It was clear that Abigail needed James Lovell. The problem was how to ask for help in such a way as to keep him interested, but not to convey any other interest. Abigail played the coquette angle expertly: "Will you forgive my so often troubling you with my fears and anxieties; Groundless as some of them have been they were real to me for a time, and had all the force of truth upon me. . . .

Tis full time if he was safe to hear from him. My anxiety daily increases, and I write to you Sir who have been acquainted with sorrow and affliction in various shapes, enduring with unshaken fortitude the Horrours of Capitivity and chains, in hopes that you will communicate to me some share of that hidden strength."[31]

Abigail began a flirtatious epistolary cat-and-mouse game with Lovell for years, teasing him lightly but never going over the line. "I know not whether I ought to reply to your favour of April the first, for inded Sir I begin to look upon you as a very dangerous Man."[32] She started to sign her letters to Lovell using her secret and very personal code name of "Portia." Lovell picked up on that and tested his limits by calling Abigail "lovely Portia" and included a line from the Scottish painter-poet Allan Ramsay, "gin ye were mine ain Thing how dearly I would *love* thee!"[33]

By January 1779, Lovell went so far as to imply that at least John had not left her pregnant: "You say 'tis near 11 months since he left Braintree. I find myself relieved by that period from a certain anxiety, which was founded on my tenderness towards your dear Sex that Mr. A's *rigid patriotism* had overcome."[34]

For five years Abigail tolerated Lovell's cloaked but brazen advances, in exchange for help or information about John and John Quincy in Europe. Here is a sampling of a few typical bold lines from James Lovell which he had embedded in his letters to Abigail:

"I would close here by telling you how affectionately I esteem you."[35]

"Very platonically to be sure but, very, very affectionately your humb. Servt."[36]

"Do I love the natural Sentiments of the Heart?—Yes, Amiable Correspondent, I truly love them; and your little Story was far, very far from non-natural. You was betrayed, it seems, by a Combination of Circumstances such as a tender Sensibility and the Dusk of the Evening, to make a Pressure to your lovely palpitating Bosom which soon after cost you a crying Spell."[37]

"How do you do, Lovely Portia, these very cold Days? Mistake me not willfully; I said Days. I will strive however to refrain from coveting my Neighbour's Blankets. I shall find that not difficult. But really I doubt whether I shall be able to keep myself void of all Coveteousness. I suspect I shall covet to be in the Arms of Portia's Friend and Admirer." Lovell wrote the non-possessive name "Portia" by itself at the bottom of the page, and then on the next page added the possessive 's. The separation of letters was not a mistake, but clearly written as, "I shall covet to be in the Arms of Portia's" to shock Abigail.[38]

"Eccles: IV. 11." In the above letter, Lovell quoted a scripture to the very religious Abigail, Ecclesiastes 4:11: "Again, if two lie together, then they have heat; but how can one be warm alone?"[39]

Abigail occasionally shot back some well-sighted barbs of her own to Lovell. In a third-person context, she quoted a reply between "Portia" (Abigail) and "Cornelia" (possibly Mercy Otis Warren): "Cornelia. No, only as the world will naturally believe that a Gentleman possessing domestick attachments would visit his family in the course of 4 years, when only 3 hundred miles distant."[40] Abigail was making reference to Lovell's absence from his family in Boston for many years and that he had never even visited them. When challenged on that fact by Abigail, Lovell's pretenses collapsed. "I must now be very serious," Lovell wrote to her. He said he was broke and financially couldn't afford to go home. All his income came from "my Pay for Time and Service as a Delegate, which ceases the day I arrive in Boston."[41]

By 1781 the correspondence between Abigail and Lovell became more truthful now that Abigail knew Lovell posed no danger to her or her marriage. "In truth Friend thou art a Queer Being. . . . I do not recollect that I ever had that opportunity with my correspondent, twice only in my life do I remember to have seen him, and then my harp was so hung upon the willows that I cared not whose face was sweet or sour."[42] She added that her husband John "used to say I was a physiognomist."[43] "But I did not study the Eye that best Index to the mind to find out how much of Rogury there was in the Heart, so here I have been these four years obtaining by peacemeal what I could have learnt in half an hour."[44]

After 1782, James Lovell took the post of "continential Receiver of taxes"[45] in Boston. It was given as a gift from Congress' Superintendent of Finance, Robert Morris. Abigail and Lovell exchanged letters only three times after their 1782 cluster of letters; one in 1784 when Lovell had been appointed as the port of Boston naval officer, and two letters in 1789 after a five-year pause in their correspondence. Lovell's final letter to Abigail mentioned that he had just sent Abigail's husband, John (and now vice president), a request seeking a naval office position in the new federal government:

In Abigail's final reply letter to Lovell, she wrote a positive but vague response: "I presume the enquiry will be in the appointment of offices. Who now holds them? Are they qualified? Have they discharged the office with fidelity? Why displace a man worthy of his trust? I know Mr A is sufficiently sensible of the importance of having the naval office filled by a gentleman of firmness and integrity."[46] But nothing ever came of Lovell's request. Abigail closed her final letter to Lovell with, "My best regards attend Mrs Lovell."[47]

On February 14, 1778, the 24-gun frigate *Boston* was waiting to set sail to France. John and John Quincy were up and dressed in near darkness with only fire embers lighting the parlor. Abigail had compiled a check-list of every item that needed to be packed in the travel cases. She hadn't gotten much sleep either that night, and was choking on words that wouldn't come out. Abigail didn't accompany John and John Quincy that dark, freezing morning. She would stay at home, "seated by my fire side Bereft of my better Half."[48]

The two Adamses landed safely in Bordeaux, France, on April 1.[49] As John recorded in his diary, the first of the French officials to welcome him were disappointed to find that John was not the famous Samuel Adams. As John sarcastically wrote, "When I arrived in France, the French Nation had a great many Questions to settle. The first was— Whether I was the famous Adams, Le fameux Adams?—Ah, le fameux Adams?"[50]

To add to John's bruised ego, a popular edition of *Common Sense* written by Thomas Paine had been printed in France, minus the parts which criticized monarchies. The anonymous authorship had been attributed to Sam Adams. John decided not to try to correct everyone he met, mostly because of his deficiency in speaking French.

Unfortunately, upon arrival in Paris John quickly learned that the Franco-American alliance circumstances had radically changed. John's congressional mission had been twofold: to replace former minister Silas Deane and to assist in agreement on the terms for a Franco-American alliance. But John discovered at Bordeaux that the treaty agreement had already been accomplished even before he left Braintree. The compact of friendship and commerce with the French government had been se-cured by Benjamin Franklin. Unfortunately, news traveled very slowly, and John was never notified. John Adams was in France with no mission to accomplish. It would be an uncomfortable dilemma for the worka-holic Adams.

The first ship which could securely carry a letter to Abigail from France was leaving the very same day that John had been notified, April 25. John hurriedly composed a letter to his wife, but he had to keep his letter short to make the departure. He included the letter that John

Quincy had written as "a few Lines from Johnny." John wrote a few initial sentiments which he may have regretted later.

John and Abigail had been apart, physically and by written word, for two months. It would be another two months, June 30, before Abigail would receive John's first letter. The letter must have been disappointing to Abigail. John wrote no words of affection, but instead it featured compliments on French women: "My venerable Colleague [Benjamin Franklin] enjoys a Priviledge here, that is much to be envyd. Being seventy Years of Age, the Ladies not only allow him to [kiss[51] and] embrace them as often as he pleases, but they are perpetually embracing him. . . . To tell you the Truth, I admire the Ladies here. Dont be jealous. They are handsome, and very well educated. Their Accomplishments are exceedingly brilliant. And their Knowledge of Letters and Arts, exceeds that of the English Ladies much, I believe."[52]

John innocently didn't know how his quickly written words would be taken by Abigail. It's doubtful he intended to provoke jealousy on Abigail's part, but assuredly it could be taken that way. Abigail's two-part reply letter is a model of self-control, and an example of how she cleverly turned the irony back upon John: "Dearest of Friends, Shall I tell my dearest that tears of joy filld my Eyes this morning at the sight of his well known hand, the first line which has bless[ed] my Sight since his four months absence. . . . I have lived a life of fear and anxiety ever since you left me. . . . I know not how you fared upon your Voiage, what reception you have met with, (not even from the Ladies, tho you profess yourself an admirer of them)." Abigail skillfully used the obvious paradox John stated that the French women "are handsome, and very well educated." "I can hear of the Brilliant accomplishment[s] of any of my Sex with pleasure and rejoice in that Liberality of Sentiment which acknowledges them. fashonable it has been to ridicule Female learning."[53]

Even though Abigail successfully reversed John's jealousy-inducing words to those championing education for women, she still entertained the chance to make John jealous somehow. She saw her chance. It involved French Admiral Comte d'Estaing and his flagship filled with young French officers.

Chapter Thirteen

"Labour and Rates Devour the Proffets"

1778–1780

Abigail's lengthy separations from John were "the hardest conflict[s] I ever endured."[1] "Danger and hazard, fear and anxiety will ever be uppermost in my mind."[2] Furthermore Abigail confessed to her friend Hannah Quincy Lincoln Storer the additional effect of the absence of her eldest son, John Quincy: "after the departure of my Son when I found a larger portion of my Heart gone than I was aware of."[3] Those representative quotes are by Abigail written in 1777 and 1778, two of the hardest years, along with 1779, that she had to endure with John being nearly constantly gone.

It didn't help when John, after writing no letters to Abigail for months from France, sent only a short letter to her praising the French women. Abigail saw an opportunity to innocently return the volley and possibly to make John a little jealous. It involved French Admiral Jean Baptiste Charles Henri Hector, Comte d'Estaing and a boatload of his young sailors.

As a first visible sign of the defense treaty that America and France signed, the French fleet had sailed across the Atlantic Ocean. However just before a battle off Newport, Rhode Island, the fleet had suffered damage in a storm. The French anchored in Boston Harbor for repairs. During that repair time, Boston dignitaries were invited onboard *Le Languedoc*, the flagship of the French admiral, Comte d'Estaing.

Abigail Adams was one of the honored guests. She was rowed out to the admiral's ship. Not missing a tantalizing word, Abigail wrote to John of the exciting party which ran into the night: "The French Ships are still in the Harbour of Boston. I have received great civility and every mark of Respect that it has been in the power of their officers to shew me. Count dEstaing has been exceeding polite to me. . . . I according waited upon his Excellency who very politely received me, insisted upon my Dineing on board his Ship. . . . An entertainment fit for a princiss was prepared, we spent a most agreable day. The Count is a most agreable Man, Sedate, polite, affible with a dignity that is lost in Ease yet his brow at times would be overclouded with cares and anxieties."[4]

She described the evening in detail: "We . . . were sumptuously entertaind with every delicacy that this country produces and the addition of every foreign article that could render our feast Splendid. Musick and dancing for the young folks closed the day. Not one officer has been seen the least disguised with Liquour [drunk] since their arrival."[5]

When John and John Quincy arrived in Paris on April 8, 1778, they were housed in the Hôtel de Valentinois in Passy where Benjamin Franklin also lived. At first John was on cordial terms with Franklin, a condition that would deteriorate in the ten months he spent there. In the early stages of his time in Paris, John was intrigued with the French way of life. Once established with housing, John enrolled John Quincy in M. Le Coeur's private boarding school also in Passy. John, and on weekends with John Quincy, explored the Parisian buildings and streets, the food and drink, and the rich culture which were all so foreign and magnificent to John, the frugal Yankee. Keeping his correspondence more innocent, he wrote Abigail: "The Delights of France are innumerable. The Politeness, the Elegance, the Softness, the Delicacy, is extreme. In short stern and hauty Republican as I am, I cannot help loving these People, for their earnest Desire, and Assiduity to please."[6]

But Abigail was in an uncommonly depressed mood, "Some part of the time my mind has sufferd a distress which cannot be described . . . and gave me a much Deeper wound than it seems,"[7] she wrote to her cousin John Thaxter, Jr.[8] It is here where Abigail injected some happy, satisfying news: "I know you will give me joy when I tell you that I have wrought almost a miracle. I have removed H[ayde]n out of the house, or rather hired him to remove."[9] The curmudgeonly tenant who had been illegally squatting since 1775 in John and Abigail's oldest house had finally left, or according to Abigail—was paid to leave.

During John's stay in Paris during 1778–1779, Abigail had learned to become a farm manager by necessity. Indeed, she competently handled each situation, planned or unplanned. Her primary problem was something she had little control over—that of retaining hired hands. They were still being lured away by the Continental Army's ability to offer a higher pay rate even though the payment was in near-worthless American currency. She had explained the problem to her cousin John Thaxter, Jr., a congressional clerk, and repeated her intention to always be able to pay her debts: "Labour is much more exorbitant than it was when you left us. . . . The Farm remains but the Labour and Rates devour the proffets, and the Money is all annihilated, or very little better. . . . I mean that I might always have it in my power, to answer the first demand of a Creditor, a Dun was always my abhorance; nor will I ever involve my partner if oeconomy and frugality will prevent it."[10]

Abigail decided to abandon the idea of employing a field manager. Instead, she hired two recently married brothers and contracted an arrangement called sharecropping of the crops and livestock. At harvest, the two "Industerous young Fellows" would split the yield 50/50 with Abigail: "I have put in a couple of Industerous young Fellows, to whom I let the Farm to the Halves. This I found absolutely necessary to do as I could see no way for me to get through the Labour and Rates so that I have reduced my Family from 13 or 14 to 7. You know my situation, and that a ridged oeconomy is necessary for me to preserve that independancy which has always been my ambition."[11]

By June 1778, Abigail knew every step needed to keep her fields growing oats, corn, and wheat—her "grains,"[12] as she called them. The Adamses' 180 acres had to yield enough profit for Abigail to stay solvent season after season, which was always unpredictable. Aside from surviving bad weather, the ability to pay numerous taxes was a task always looming at year end. Abigail shared that reality with John, telling him that it was difficult to make a profit from the farm after paying taxes. She asked him for advice: "We have a prospect of a fine Season again. If you are safe in France direct me into some way to pay taxes. Besides the tax of 47 pounds 18 & 6 pence there is a continental and town tax which

"The house of Rev. William Smith and the birthplace of Abigail (Smith) Adams, Weymouth, Massachusetts." The only portion which remains is the center structure that has a door and four windows. Watercolor rendered in approximately 1765. (*Massachusetts Historical Society*)

The house where Abigail Smith (Adams) was born in 1744 in Weymouth Landing, Massachusetts. (*Author*)

Pastel portrait of John Adams by Benjamin Blyth, August 1766, a companion to the Abigail Smith Adams portrait facing the title page of this book. John Adams is wearing his "rolly polly" legal wig. (*Massachusetts Historical Society*)

Portraits of Abigail and John's four children who survived infancy. Top left, a 1785 oil portrait of Nabby painted in London by Mather Brown. It is labeled "Portrait of Abigail (Nabby) Adams Smith (daughter of John and Abigail Adams.)" Top right, a 1795 miniature portrait of John Quincy Adams painted at The Hague, 1795, by English artist John Parker. (*US Department of State*) Bottom left, Charles Adams, Abigail and John's troubled second son. The date of this rendering and the name of the artist are not known. Bottom right, Thomas Boylston Adams, the Adams's third son, a miniature watercolor portrait on ivory by Charles Knight, 1815. (*Massachusetts Historical Society*)

Detail from J. De Costa and Charles Hall, "A Plan of the Town and Harbour of Boston," 1775, showing the area from Boston down to Braintree and Weymouth at the very bottom margin. Buildings and tree growth had not yet blocked the sight of Charlestown/Bunker Hill from the top of Penn's Hill in Weymouth. It is from that hill where Abigail and John Quincy witnessed the Battle of Bunker Hill. (*Library of Congress*)

Law left to use us with cruelty & iniquity with impunity. Men of Sense in all Ages abhor those customs which treat us only as the vassals of your Sex regard us then as Beings placed by providence under your protection & in immitation of the Supreem Being make use of that power only for our happiness —

April 5

Not having an opportunity of sending this I shall add a few lines more; tho not with a heart so gay. I have been attending the sick chamber of our neighbour Trott whose affliction I most sensibly feel but cannot discribe. Striped of two lovely children in one week. Gorge the Eldest died on wedensday & Billy the youngest on Friday — with the Canker fever a terible disorder so much like the throat distemper, that it differs but little from it — Betsy Cranch has been very bad, but upon the recovery. Becky Peck they do not expect will live out the Day — Many Grown persons are now Sick with it, in this Street 5 — It rages much in other Towns. the Mumps too are very frequent. Isaac is now confined with it — our own little flock are yet well. My Heart trembles with anxiety for them, God preserve them,

I want to hear much ofter from you than I do. march & was the last date of any that I have yet Had — you inquire of whether I am making Salt peter. I have not yet attempted it, but after Soap making believe I shall make the experiment, I find as much as I can do to manufacture cloathing for my family which woud else be Naked — I know of but one person in this part of the Town who has made any, that is mr Tertias Bass as he is calld who has got very near an Hundred weight which has been found to be very good. I have heard of some others in the other parishes. Mr Reed of weymouth has been applied to, to go to Andover to the mills which are now at work, & has gone — I have lately Seen a small Manuscrip decribing the proportions for the various Sorts of powder, fitt for cannon small arms & pistols — if it would be of any Service your way I will get it transcribed & send it to you — every one of your Friends Send their regards. and all the little ones. your Brothers youngest child lies bad with convulsion fitts — adieu I need not Say how much I am your ever faithfull friend —
[A A]

The cream-painted saltbox house where John Quincy Adams was born. Abigail and the children spent most of the Revolutionary War in this house. (*Author*)

The Old State House in the center of Boston. Abigail stood approximately where this photo was taken to hear the Declaration of Independence read on July 18, 1776, from the small elevated porch. The Boston population was mostly in a lockdown during the smallpox epidemic occurring at the same time, but throngs of patriots turned out for the reading. (*Author*)

Westminster Abbey, 1780. This is approximately how Westminster Abbey would have looked when Abigail, unescorted, went to hear Handel's *Messiah* performed. She called it, "Sublime beyond description." (*New York Public Library*)

Left, portrait of John Adams painted in London by John Singleton Copley soon after the Treaty of Paris was signed in 1783. (*Harvard University Portrait Collection*) Right, A scene from *Psyché* in 1785. Abigail attended performances by the Paris Opéra. At first the lack of modesty by the dancers made Abigail uncomfortable, but she later admitted that she had gotten used to it. (*New York Public Library*)

Richmond Hill house was located along Varick Street, between Charlton and Vandam Streets in present-day Greenwich Village, Manhattan. It was the official vice-presidential residence and Abigail's favorite abode. Even though she was wed to the vice president, she did not have the clout to prohibit hunting on her property and from killing her many songbirds. (*New York Public Library*)

The earliest known illustration of the White House appears on the cover of *The Stranger In America* by Charles William Janson Esq., published by James Cundee in London in 1807. President John Adams and Abigail Adams were the first to occupy the house in 1800 toward the end of its original construction. (*The White House/The White House Historical Association*)

"Peacefield" or "The Old House," Quincy, Massachusetts, built in 1731 and purchased by John and Abigail Adams in 1788. Abigail remodeled the house with European styles. The Adams lived here until their deaths. (*National Park Service*)

Abigail Adams's First Lady portrait by Gilbert Stuart, painted somewhere between 1810–1815, and delivered much later than anticipated. The paired portrait of President John Adams was also not delivered until the same period of 1810-1815. Son John Quincy Adams labeled Stuart's procrastination, "Mr. Stuart thinks it the prerogative of genius to disdain the performance of his engagements." (*National Gallery of Art*)

amounts to about 50 pounds more for this year. The price of Labour, I think I formerly mentiond. Least you did not get the Letter I will mention that tis 12 pounds per month—I make no comments—you can make calculations."[13]

A month later, in July 1778, bad weather threatened their crops. Abigail would mention it in her mid-July letter to John. She also wrote in very poetic terms of how much she missed her "dearest Friend": "In vain do I strive to divert my attention, my Heart, like a poor bird hunted from her nest, is still returning to the place of its affections."[14] Abigail had found that the only thing that suppressed her loneliness was to "quit it at the midnight hour, and rise in the morning suppressing these too tender sensibilities."[15]

Abigail continued writing her letter: "The Season has been fine for grass but for about 3 weeks past we have had a sharp and severe Drouth which has greatly injured our grain. . . . Debts are my abhorrence. I never will borrow if any other method can be devised."[16] The "other method" to make needed extra money, Abigail recalled, was when she bought and sold pins and made a profit.

During John's absence in the summer of 1778, Abigail cautiously broached the idea to him of becoming an import merchant to help bring in some money: "I have thought of this which I wish you to assent to, to order some saleable articles which I will mention to be sent to the care of my unkle S[mit]h a small trunk at a time, containing ten or 15 pounds Sterling, from which I may supply my family with such things as I need, and the rest place in the hands of Dr. T[uft]s Son who has lately come into Trade, and would sell them for me."[17]

Abigail may have thought of this merchandizing plan variation on her own or taken the idea from her Weymouth cousin, Cotton Tufts Jr., who was actively engaged in it. But Abigail saw the opportunity of using John as her transatlantic supplier, just as he had sent pins from Philadelphia. She reminded John to stick to her shopping list for the "Goods" that he should send because she knew what would command the highest prices in Boston. To avoid potential disclosure and a profiteering scandal that might stain John, Abigail employed Cotton Tufts Jr. to work on commission and make the sales for her: "There is no remittances you can make me which will turn to a better account than Goods, more especially such articles as I enclose a list of but I believe a ship of war is the safest conveyance for them. Doctor Tufts son has lately sit up in Trade, whatever I receive more than is necessary for family use I can put into his hands which will serve both him and my-self."[18]

By October 1778 John had shipped to Abigail on American warships a few cargoes of goods she requested. However, John became anxious that a shipment might be captured by British naval vessels or privateering ships. He was concerned that Abigail was only getting a fraction of what he was sending. He was even more concerned that he would be exposed for using government warships for private gain. John's code in his letters to Abigail for merchandising goods was "Articles for the Family."[19]

Still another shipment aboard the *Boston*, the ship which carried John and John Quincy to France, was overdue to Boston. John noted: "By Captain Tucker I sent you the whole of the List you gave me of Articles for the Family. These I hope have arrived safe. But I have been so unlucky, that I feel averse to meddling in this Way. The whole Loss is a Trifle it is true: but to you, in the Convenience of the Family, and to Mr. Cranch in his Business they would have been of Value. If the Boston arrives, the little Chest she carries to you will be of service."[20]

John and Abigail also asked each other about their health, as they always had. They cared and worried about each other's wellbeing for their entire marriage. John noted that the style of French living had made him feel more alive and that his health had improved. Abigail, in contrast, wrote about her depressed mental state: "I have enjoyed a tolerable good state of Health, Depression of spirits I often experience from the state of anxiety in which I live."[21] Every day Abigail reminded herself of her personal heroic sacrifice for liberty and America. Even with that, Abigail still couldn't help ending one letter to John, "the tears have flowed faster than the Ink."[22] Abigail was becoming very depressed. The flint-gray skies and early frost hit her especially hard during late 1778.

For many years Abigail's only break from the stress of home and farm management was to fall under the magical spell of writing letters late at night. There she would compose long letters to her "best friend," husband and love, John.

Sometimes she unrealistically expected a timely reply from John in equal length as hers and expressing his love. Other times she expressed understanding that he couldn't always write. She knew that John was very caught up in the delicate and dangerous affairs of revolution, and Abigail was proud that her husband was leading the Continental charge against British tyranny. She knew and was sympathetic that John's writing time wasn't always available during those days. But Abigail was also human, and occasionally she began her letter to John expressing some frustration with mail delivery: "I have to acknowledg the Recept of a very few lines dated the 12 of April. You make no mention of the whole sheets I have wrote to you, by which I judge you either never Received them, or that they were so lengthy as to be troublesome; and in return you have set me an example of being very concise. I believe I shall not take the Hint, but give as I love to Receive."[23]

Abigail's occasional use of the word "concise" to describe John's letters translated as "too short." More than once, Abigail received a package tied up with twine from John. As she excitedly tore into it, to her great disappointment she found only a few folded newspapers and no letter. In a September 1778 letter to John, Abigail included the usual phrase of "Our publick affairs," since by law everything she owned belonged to John. However, in the very same letter, she inserted her ownership phrase "As to my own affairs,"[24] which was a slight defiance of the law.

With John and John Quincy still in France as winter approached, from October 1778 through the first half of 1779, Abigail was lonely and frustrated enough to launch a serious written spat with John over the irregularity and shortness of his letters. Also, as with his letters of late, they were devoid of any sentiment. Abigail sent a terse letter, "I determine very soon to coppy and adopt the very concise method of my Friend—and as I wish to do every thing agreable to him, send him Billits [short letters] containing not more than a dozen lines at the utmost Especially as paper has grown so dear, which will afford some coulour of an excuse to his most affectionate Portia."[25]

This seven-month-long snit between Abigail and John was born out of each other's frustrations relative to their own situation. It was political frustration for John. It was winter loneliness for Abigail: "How lonely are my days? How solitary are my Nights? Secluded from all Society. . . by the Mountains of snow which surround me I could almost fancy myself in Greenland. We have had four of the coldest Days I ever knew, and they were followed by the severest snow storm I ever remember, the wind blowing like a Hurricane for 15 or 20 hours renderd it imposible for Man or Beast to live abroad, and has blocked up the roads so that they are impassible."[26]

Before John sailed for home, Abigail had spent the very cold fall and winter of 1778–1779 uncharacteristically lashing out in letters to him in Paris. Her weariness over her situation rose to the surface as it never had before. One of the excuses John had for the unexplained letter shortage from him to Abigail was the naval process of throwing overboard a weighted diplomatic pouch containing any confidential documents that the ship was carrying if captured by a belligerent adversary. John mentioned that possibility in letters to Abigail many times. Abigail reasonably wondered if John was using that scenario so often as an excuse for not writing.

In December 1778 and deep into their spat, John sent Abigail his own account of the number of letters he had sent: "I know not how often you receive Letters from me, so many are taken, or sunk: but I write as often as I can. . . . It is impossible for me to write as I did in America. What should I write? It is not safe to write any Thing, that one is not willing should go into all the Newspapers of the World.—I know not by whom to write. Notwithstanding this, I have written to you, not much less I believe than fifty Letters."[27]

Some of John and Abigail's squabbling rhetoric hit low accusations judging by these exchanges:

Abigail: "I have never let an opportunity slip without writing to you since we parted, tho you make no mention of having received a line from me; if they are become of so little importance as not to be worth noticeing with your own Hand, be so kind as to direct your Secretary."[28]

John: "It is now my Turn to complain. Last night We had great Packetts from the [Massachusetts] Council, but no Line from you." "I suppose I must write every day, in order to keep or rather to restore good Humour, whether I have any thing to say or not."[29]

By February 1779, the finger-pointing and accusations began to lessen with Abigail taking the first initiative to tone things down. John followed her lead, but even allowing for the long delay in the transatlantic letter delivery, it was late spring before both sides realized that the spat was over.

By that time John was already on his way back home. On February 20, 1779, John had written to Abigail that he and John Quincy were leaving France, coming back to America, and that he was quitting politics altogether. "I am reduced to the Condition of a private Citizen. . . . [Congress] never so much as bid me come home, bid me stay, or told me I had done well or done ill. . . . I will draw Writs and Deeds, and harrangue Jurys and be happy."[30]

One good feature which came out of John's stay in France was John and Abigail's importation and sales of European goods, which were impossible to find in Boston. It was a trade consignment arrangement that John, Abigail, and her cousin, Cotton Tufts Jr., had put into motion during 1778–1779. Abigail had estimated that 66 percent of the goods being sent back to Boston for sale were being captured. John, whose political intellect didn't transfer over to business expertise, considered his sending goods to Abigail as a failure. Abigail, in contrast, had the accounting figures to know the profits of the business. She answered back to John: "This is our present situation. It is a risk to send me any thing across the water I know, yet if one in 3 arrives I should be a gainer."[31] Abigail shrewdly knew that if the remaining 33 percent of goods arrived safely, she came out ahead. And bringing up a subject that had recently been retired by the couple, the same theory applied to her letters to John. As Abigail stated in the very same letter, "Yet I will not be discouraged, I will persist in writing tho but one in ten should reach you."[32]

Writing from the French ship *L'Orient* on May 14, 1779, John tried to explain the delays to Abigail, not knowing if she would ever get the letter: "I left Paris on the Eighth of March, expecting to find the Alliance, at Nantes and embark immediately for home, but when I arrived there I found the Alliance was still at Brest. . . . Dont think hard of me for not writing. I have wrote as often as I could. But there are Letters of mine still in the Ports of this Kingdom, which were written I believe 9 Months ago—many many others are in the Sea. When you come to know how few Letters I have received from America, you will be surprized."[33]

On June 8, 1779, Abigail wrote a letter to John, but she assumed it would be futile. His location was unknown, and so many of her numerous previous letters had been seemingly undelivered: "Six Months have already elapsed since I heard a syllable from you or my dear Son, and five since I have had one single opportunity of conveying a line to you. Letters of various dates have lain months at the Navy Board, and a packet and Frigate both ready to sail at an hours warning have been months waiting the orders of Congress." If Abigail had any good news to tell in her letter; it was about one person, her brother-in-law Richard Cranch. "Our Brother Cranch is immersd in publick Buisness—and so cumbered with it that he fears He shall not be able to write you a line."[34]

Abigail mentioned James Lovell to John as an "attentive friend" who sent her news of her "dearest friend": "C[ongre]ss have not yet made any appointment of you to any other court. There appears a dilatoryness, an indisicion in their proceedings. I have in Mr. L[ovel]l an attentive Friend who kindly informs me of every thing which passes relative to you and your situation, gives me extracts of your Letters both to himself and others."[35]

On March 3, 1779, John took leave of the French ministry at Versailles. Then without telling Abigail or Congress, John and John Quincy sailed for home, although there would be mix-ups in the attempt to book passage. On March 11 after arriving in Nantes they discovered that no ship was available for the Adamses until the *Alliance* sailed April 22 from St. Nazaire. While John and John Quincy were stuck in Nantes, John met American expatriate and Maryland merchant Joshua Johnson at a dinner party. Ironically many years later, John Quincy Adams would marry Joshua Johnson's daughter Louisa Catherine in London.

Another dinner party guest John was introduced to was Captain John Paul Jones. Jones was waiting in France for the French to finish fitting out a ship for him which Jones had named the *Bonhomme Richard* or "Poor Richard" in honor of Doctor Benjamin Franklin. Jones would soon put to sea and become world famous for his naval exploits. John entered into his diary: "I like Captain Jones very well. . . . the Captain who is as cool a Man as ever I saw."[36]

Finally, early in the fog-covered morning of June 17, 1779, John and John Quincy boarded the French frigate *La Sensible*, bound for Boston. They had an uneventful crossing owing to the mid-summer weather and catching the western direction of the Gulf Stream, a fast-moving current only recently discovered. On or about August 3, 1779, John and John Quincy were rowed to shore at Nantasket Roads, from where they had departed. There were no welcoming crowds. Abigail wasn't waiting on the shore waving a handkerchief at them. No one knew they had sailed or had landed. There had been no time to properly notify anyone. Abigail, not expecting them, was likely very confused, but overjoyed when she saw them both arrive at their house.

John had been home all of one week in August 1779 when the state of Massachusetts elected him as a delegate to the Massachusetts Constitutional Convention. This was unexpected for John and Abigail, but for both the burden was slight in comparison to what they'd just gone through. John and John Quincy were home safe. John was working from home and Abigail was enjoying every day that the family was together again.

It was a time in America's young history when there was no strong central government or national constitution. Each state was independent and accountable to only the terms of a weak confederation of states. John was appointed to a state constitution committee of three delegates, including his second cousin, Samuel Adams. John effectively became a committee of one and wrote nearly the entire state constitution by himself. The major components of John's signature constitution work include designing the familiar balance of power between the three branches of government: executive, legislative, and an independent judiciary. John also suggested that the Massachusetts Supreme Judicial Court justices be appointed rather than elected. He also suggested inserting the condition that the justices' term was permanent "as long as they behave themselves well."[37] Also unique to the Massachusetts Constitution is the section "The Encouragement of Literature, Etc."[38] It states that it is the duty of the state to provide education to every child without regard to gender. Abigail must have been thrilled.

The Constitution of the Commonwealth of Massachusetts was written by John, Samuel Adams, and James Bowdoin in the Adamses' downstairs parlor. The desk where it was written is still on display in its same spot. The document remains in effect today and is the longest-lived written constitution in the world.[39]

Congress had first sent John to Paris in 1778 to help the American ministers convince the French government to publicly come to the aid of the United States against their mutual enemy Great Britain. By the time John had arrived in France the stated purpose of that task was finished. Four months after John had been home from his disappointing journey to Paris, he again received official notification that Congress had commissioned John as the sole American minister stationed in France. His mission was to negotiate peace with Great Britain when the time came.

Once again, Abigail and John agreed that Abigail would stay home, and that John Quincy would again travel to Europe.[40] This time, nine-year-old Charles would be accompanying his brother and father. Also, along on the trip would be Francis Dana, a congressional aide, and Abigail's cousin, John Thaxter, Jr. as John's private secretary and tutor to both John Quincy and Charles. Rounding out the Adams entourage was assistant Joseph Stevens.[41] With John's prodding, John Quincy began keeping a personal diary of the trip. This habit would be engrained in John Quincy for nearly seven decades to come.

La Sensible weighed anchor in Boston Harbor on November 13, 1779. Abigail and Nabby had seen the men off the night before. John Quincy would not see his mother and sister again for over four and a half years, until July 30, 1784, following the war's end. He would meet up with all of them in London as they were en route to France.

The voyage to France aboard *La Sensible* was horrendous. The ship sprung a leak halfway across the Atlantic which required round-the-clock pumping by the crew and passengers. It barely made it to the coast of Spain at El Ferrol, where it sunk at the dock. It would be months before either it was fixed or another vessel would be available to take the Adams party to Bordeaux, France. John decided they would take some mules and carts, and the Adams party would walk and ride the near-thousand miles to Paris.[42] "Whether I can get Carriages, Horses, Mules &c. What Accommodations I can get upon the Road. . . are all Questions that I cannot answer. . . . The Passage of the Pyrenees is represented as very difficult."[43]

Abigail wrote a letter to John Quincy on January 19, 1780, hoping it would reach him in Paris. She had no way of knowing that her written expressions that night would become some of her most treasured wisdom. As his "Mamma," Abigail had been the person who coaxed him into making a second winter crossing of the Atlantic Ocean—a treacherous endeavor at that. However, she wanted to remind Johnny that the payoff was very much worth it at that time in history:

> My dear Son,
> I hope you have had no occasion either from Enemies or the Dangers of the Sea to repent your second voyage to France. If I had thought your reluctance arose from proper deliberation, or that you was capable of judgeing what was most for your own benifit, I should not have urged you to have accompanied your Father and Brother when you appeared so averse to the voyage. You however readily submitted to my advice, and I hope will never have occasion yourself, nor give me reason to Lament it.
> These are times in which a Genious would wish to live. It is not in the still calm of life, or the repose of a pacific station, that great characters are formed. . . . Great necessities call out great virtues.[44]

Chapter Fourteen

"A Few Necessaries for the Family"

1780–1782

T he second trek across the Atlantic Ocean in wintertime for John and John Quincy was worse than the first sailing, but at least they both had known what to expect. However, it was young Charles Adams's first trip. John knew that Abigail would be wondering how he had tolerated the trip. To counter some of Abigail's apprehension, John added into a letter, "Your delicate Charles is as hardy as a flynt. He sustains every thing better than any of Us, even than the hardy Sailor his Brother. He is a delightful little fellow. I love him too much."[1] It was the first time that anyone including his father characterized Charles as "delicate," but not the last time.

With a painful "very soar hand," Abigail signed her first combined letter to John Quincy and Charles as "Mother." She introduced the new family dog, "Lady Trips," and told Charles that his "favorite Songster is alive, has been well nourished and carefully attended through the winter, and now repays all his care by the Melody of her voice."[2]

Once in Paris, John took up residence in the Hôtel de Valois rue de Richelieu and again enrolled his sons in M. Le Coeur's boarding school. He wrote to make sure Abigail knew he had sent her four other letters written while he was en route to France. That opened the door for him to inform Abigail about the shipment sent from Bilbao to her, and again he used their secret merchandizing phrase: "These are a few necessaries for the Family."[3]

However, as John was sending the assorted goods, Abigail faced an obstacle to receiving "a few necessaries for the Family." Massachusetts was frozen over in a historic ice storm that had seemingly brought life in the Northeast to a standstill: "You left this coast in the best time that could have been chosen. Winter set in with all its horrors in a week after you saild, and has continued with all its rigours ever since. Such mountains of snow have not been known for 60 years. No passing for this fortnight, only for foot travellers, [and] no prospect of any as one Storm succeeds another so soon that the roads are filld before a path can be made."[4] Abigail added: "In the latter part of December and beginning of Janry. there fell the highest snow known since the year 1740, and from that time to this day the Bay has been froze so hard that people have walked, road, and sleded, over it to Boston; it was froze across Nantasket road, so that no vessel could come in or go out; for a month."[5]

With the French winter climate more hospitable compared to the wicked snowstorms in Braintree, John continued his part in the mercantile arrangement which Abigail had made with him: that of shipping scarce goods, as determined by Abigail, from Paris to Boston. In June 1780 John used an expanded secret phrase that only Abigail would know. However, Abigail was struggling to pay an increased tax burden coupled with out-of-control inflation. The message from John—"I will send you Things in the family Way which will defray your Expences better"[6]—translated to "From the retail sale of these items, you will be able to pay taxes and offset inflation."

John added that he'd also thought of a way to diversify their shipments. His idea was to stop sending everything in a single crate which could be easily targeted by thieves. Since most of the items didn't take up much bulk (handkerchiefs, linen, fabric, pins, tea and tea cups, etc.), he would request that guests and dignitaries traveling to Boston hand carry the "gifts" to Abigail in person. The first courier turned out to be none other than Gilbert du Motier, Marquis de Lafayette. Abigail covertly acknowledged to John receiving the gift from Lafayette: "Last week arrived at Boston the Marquis de la Fayette to the universal joy of all who know the Merit and Worth of that Nobleman. He was received with the ringing of Bells, fireing of cannon, bon fires." And, incidentally, Abigail hid in the middle of the letter "Received the present by the Marquis."[7]

In summer 1780 Abigail again put her entrepreneurial spirit and business savvy to good use. She had been receiving through John a large assortment of "small articles" of saleable goods. These items included gauze, ribbon, lace, feathers, and linen handkerchiefs. Abigail supervised her two new sales agents, Cotton Tufts Jr. and George Warren, son of Mercy Otis Warren. She watched over stock orders, prices, and fickle fashion trends, all of which could change with little advance warning. In this letter to John, Abigail acknowledged receiving the "present" (imported goods) carried to her by Colonel François-Louis Teissèdre de Fleury, a decorated French engineer. Then she reminded John that the small articles that were sent in a letter need not be counted as an import because Congress had instituted franked letters with free postage. "Franking" was started in 1775 as an inexpensive way for congressmen to send official correspondence. In her letter to John, Abigail again displayed her astute business sense: "Should you send any thing of the kind in the same way, be so good as to let it be blew, white or red. Silk Gloves or mittins, black or white lace, Muslin or a Bandano hankerchief, and even a few yard of Ribbon might be conveyed in the same manner. I mention these things as they are small articles, and easily contained in a Letter, all of which by Resolve of congress are orderd to come Free."[8]

Abigail's shrewdness at balancing business with family issues came up again during this time. Though John was willing to fill Abigail's wholesale purchasing lists from European vendors, John, the New England Puritan, had always considered such goods as "Frippery."[9] Abigail knew this. So, when fourteen-year-old Nabby, the Adamses' daughter, sheepishly had asked for some French ribbon, gauze, and lace so she could dress like her friends, Abigail softened the request to John: "as a little of what you call frippery is very necessary towards looking like the rest of the world, Nabby would have me add, a few yard of Black or White Gauze, low priced black or white lace or a few yards of Ribbon but would have Mamma write to Pappa at the same time that she has no passion for dress further than he would approve of or to appear when she goes from home a little like those of her own age."[10]

By late 1780, John was having difficulties purchasing requested small articles in sufficient quantities to make a profit for Abigail. In some situations, he found himself buying items at retail prices, leaving Abigail with little if any profit. Soon John decided that Abigail should purchase her goods directly from European vendors. Abigail was not timid about dealing with suppliers on her own. In 1781 an apparently disappointed Abigail sent a letter of stern disapproval to the Dutch company Jean de Neufville & Son. Their reply letter shows their consequent mortification: "We are honor'd with your Ladyship's letter of the 15th Jany. last, and deem ourselves peculiarly unfortunate, not to have been more happy in the choice of the Color of Silk we sent you. Tis the more painful to us, as we can make no amends but by redoubling our attention and Vigilance, In the execution of your future Commands which we set so high a value on that we consider your Continuance of them, Notwithstanding the egregious mistake comitted, as a mark of distinguish'd favour. We flatter ourselves we shall not Incur your Ladyships reprehension in the execution of your last order."[11]

One of the obvious tests that the Revolution was having some degree of success was the ability of the states to pass laws and elect their own leaders without fear of British retaliation. The autumn of 1780 brought the first statewide election as stipulated in the new Massachusetts state constitution. Abigail was a vote counter, which was as much as she, as a woman, could legally be involved. "What a politician[12] you have made me? If I cannot be a voter upon this occasion, I will be a writer of votes. I can do some thing in that way but fear I shall have the mortification of a defeat."[13] Abigail was writing John that unfortunately it appeared that the most popular candidate, John Hancock, would become governor. The Adamses didn't care for Hancock, whom they considered a wealthy and pompous "tinkleling cymbal."[14] Instead, they both backed the man who "ought to be our Chief [but] is not popular,"[15] James Bowdoin. Hancock won the election with 90 percent of the vote.

It was good that Abigail and John decided that all the mercantile business be conducted by Abigail alone, as John no longer had the time to help. He had been appointed by Congress as minister plenipotentiary to negotiate treaties of peace and commerce with Great Britain, which he was eager to do. But this assignment would only take effect when Great Britain agreed to give up the war. While waiting for surrender talks, most of the letters Abigail received from John involved John gushing about the beauty of Paris such as in May 1780: "The public Walks, Gardens, &c. are extreamly beautifull. The Gardens of the Palais Royal, the Gardens of the Tuilleries, are very fine. . . . To take a Walk in the Gardens of the Palace of the Tuilleries, and describe the Statues there, all in marble. . . . another Walk in the Gardens of Versailles. . . . I could fill Volumes with Descriptions of Temples and Palaces, Paintings, Sculptures, Tapestry, Porcelaine, &c. &c. &c.—if I could have time."

John jokingly reminded Abigail that he also was on an "artistic" mission in Paris for his government: "the Art of Legislation and Administration and Negotiation." Then John optimistically looked to the future in the letter to Abigail. He foresaw that because of founders such as himself sacrificing their most productive parts of life, the way of future generations could be more refined and artistic. It was one of John's most timeless thoughts about self-sacrifice for the betterment of those who came after: "I must study Politicks and War that my sons may have liberty to study Mathematicks and Philosophy. My sons ought to study Mathematicks and Philosophy, Geography, natural History, Naval Architecture, navigation, Commerce and Agriculture, in order to give their Children a right to study Painting, Poetry, Musick, Architecture, Statuary, Tapestry and Porcelaine."[16]

In the autumn of 1780 and into the spring of 1781, correspondence between John and Abigail became sketchy. Abigail did learn however that John became extremely frustrated with trying to work with Charles Gravier, comte de Vergennes, minister of foreign affairs and chief minister of the French monarch. The two did not like each other at all. John offended Vergennes with his bluntness and unwelcome advice on other matters. Furthermore, John suggested that Vergennes was trying to control future peace negotiations while also implying that Vergennes was insincere: "he means to keep us down if he can.—to keep his Hand under our Chin, to prevent Us, from drowning, but not to lift our Heads out of Water."[17]

Adams's commission would only take effect when there was a peace proposal to negotiate, and it seemed that Great Britain was dragging its feet. Benjamin Franklin remained the only certified minister in Paris representing the United States. Once again John found himself in France with no mission.

Frustrated, in July 1780 Adams decided on his own as a private citizen to travel to Amsterdam "to try whether something might not be done to render us less dependent on France."[18] John brought along John Quincy and Charles and enrolled them at the University of Leyden. Then, without being formally received as an official envoy to the Netherlands, John wrote and delivered to the States General documents urging Dutch recognition of American independence. John's official capacity changed for the better a few months later. At the very end of the year, December 29, 1780, the Continental Congress empowered John

to seek a treaty of friendship, "amity," and commerce with the Netherlands. With those instructions, John was happy and busy—too busy to
write Abigail.

In April 1781 Abigail wrote a letter to John, hoping it would reach
him wherever he was. At the closing of the letter, she wrote about the
crippling state taxes and their effect on her neighbors: "Poor Mrs. D[an]a
says she is taxed to death and she shall be ruined if he stays any longer."
It was Abigail's successful merchandising initiative which kept the
Adams family from facing a similar fate. But in her latest letter Abigail
introduced a new idea to help hedge inflation and taxes. In today's language, Abigail was already speculating in Vermont real estate. "I have
ventured to make some improvements in Husbandry and have a desire
to become a purchaser in the State of Vermont. I may possibly run you
in debt a hundred dollors for that purpose. Many people are removeing
from this Town, and others. Land is sold at a low price, what do you
think of a few thousand acres there? I know you would like it, so shall
venture the first opportunity a hundred and 20 or 30 dollors will Buy
a thousand acres."[19] There was no reply on this subject by John.

Summer 1782 was the deadline for purchasing the Vermont land for
retirement that Abigail had long been hinting to John that she could
buy. Hints like "My favorite Virmont is a delightfull Grain Country"[20]
were injected into occasional letters to John during the next year. On
July 18, 1782, "Col. Davis of Woster" and others met with Abigail and
brought the sales proposals and the congressional statehood documents,
even though Vermont was an independent republic at this time. The
tracts of land for sale were in Vermont's Salem Township, Orleans
County, near the Canadian border. Abigail wanted to buy five lots for a
total of 1,620 acres, costing her £55. She paid £44 and signed a promissory note for the remaining £11. Her motivation seemed to be that it
would yield a quick profit, and at the very least the land could potentially be a nice retirement investment for her and John. It is worth noting during early pre-Constitution years, money was used from many
different origins—ranging from British currency, to dollars printed by
individual states, to Spanish "pieces of eight." Bartering was also still
in vogue. A currency was as valuable as the two persons trading deemed
it to be.

But there was one obvious problem. Abigail was a married woman
and bound to the law of coverture,[21] which meant that she could not
buy or own property in her name. To get around that constraint, in July
1782 Abigail purchased the five lots in the names of John and their four

children. John didn't know anything about it until Abigail wrote him that she had already made the purchases: "Nothing venture nothing have; and I took all the Lots 5 in number 4 of which I paid him for, and the other obligated myself to discharge in a few months."[22] She emphasized the angle that it could become a retirement refuge for John: "Two years my dearest Friend have passd away since you left your Native land. Will you not return e'er the close of an other year? I will purchase you a retreat in the woods of Virmont and retire with you from the vexations, toils and hazards of publick Life. Do you not sometimes sigh for such a Seclusion—publick peace and domestick happiness[?]."[23]

After Abigail made the purchases, John ordered Abigail: "dont meddle any more with Vermont."[24] He never told her why. The reason probably was what John wrote James Warren a few months later: "Roving among these and the Quails Partridges squirrells &c that inhabit them shall be the amusement of my declining Years God willing. I wont go to Vermont. I must be within the Scent of the sea."[25] Abigail's enthusiasm for the parcels also cooled off after 1782 due to Congress's hesitation to recognize the Vermont Republic's claim for legitimacy and statehood. Vermont didn't become a state until 1791.

The unimproved Vermont land that Abigail had bought continued to decline in value over the next few decades. Existing records show Thomas Boylston Adams, their youngest child, tried to sell his parcel but was unsuccessful. The land was listed and included with his estate in 1833. The tract that belonged to John Quincy Adams was sold in 1825 for an unknown amount.

Abigail had received a few letters from John and John Quincy when the group had safely landed in Spain in early 1780. Throughout the year, the correspondence with Abigail tapered off. In the first eight months of 1781, Abigail received no letters from John. It was agonizing for her: "not a line had reachd me from you, not a syllable from my children—and whether living or dead I could not hear."[26] By December she had barely heard from him: "I do not hear from you. A few lines only dated in April and May, have come to hand for 15 Months."[27]

She did not know that in July 1781, fourteen-year-old John Quincy was sent to St. Petersburg, Russia, to accompany Francis Dana as America's first envoy to Russia. John Quincy would serve as French interpreter and secretary to Dana. To top it off, Abigail never knew that John had been deathly ill, likely from malaria or typhus, for seven weeks while in Amsterdam from August to October 1781.[28] A few years later, John described the illness: "The Fever which I had at Amsterdam, which held me for five Days hickouping and Senseless over the Grave, eshausted me in such a Manner that I never have been able to recover it entirely."[29]

It was only through other sources that Abigail discovered young Charles had become terribly homesick and had left to return to Braintree in August 1781. But he wouldn't arrive home until late January 1782. Oddly enough, during that time no one knew where Charles was. For four months Abigail lived with the belief that Charles and his ship had sunk. John had written of the original sailing plans to Abigail in July 1781: "My dear Charles will go home with Maj. Jackson. Put him to school and keep him steady.—He is a delightfull Child, but has too exquisite sensibility for Europe."[30] John wrote a more detailed account twenty-nine years later: "My second son, after the departure of his brother, found himself so much alone, that he grew uneasy, and importuned me so tenderly to let him return to America to his mother, that I consented to that, and thus deprived myself of the greatest pleasure I had in life, the society of my children."[31]

The mystery of young Charles' whereabouts reflects the uncertainty of transatlantic crossings during a war. On August 12, 1781, the frigate *South Carolina* left Amsterdam with Charles and some other passengers on board. One passenger was Major William Jackson[32] of the Continental Army, to whom John had assigned care and custody of Charles. Instead of sailing to Beverly, Massachusetts, the destination port, however, the *South Carolina* docked at La Caruña on the Spanish coast. Its captain, Commodore Alexander Gillon, had decided to change the itinerary and plunder some British shipping before sailing for America. The passengers were rightfully angry and got off the ship.[33] Major Jackson and Charles made their way back to Bilbao, where they waited for three months for another vessel sailing to America.

As fall arrived, it was apparent that instead of crossing the Atlantic in the good weather of summer Major Jackson and Charles would now be traveling during the treacherous month of December. The two booked December passage on the *Cicero* anyway. In early winter Abigail had learned of ships that had left Bilbao after the *Cicero* and had landed safely in Massachusetts, so she expected Charles any day. But days rolled into weeks with no word. Finally, the *Cicero* docked in Beverly on January 21, 1782. Charles made his way back home to Braintree and to his mother on January 29, five months after he had left Amsterdam.

The year 1782 brought with it stunning changes. On October 19, 1781, General Charles Cornwallis surrendered his army of 7,000 soldiers to General George Washington at Yorktown, Virginia.[34] Since some battles and skirmishes took place after the Yorktown surrender, most American, British, and French military officials did not expect that Yorktown would be the defining final clash for America, Great Britain, and France. Many, including John, expected the war to continue: "If We make Peace, you will see me next summer. But I have very little faith as yet. I am most inclind to think there will be another Campaign."[35]

John's mission to negotiate peace terms with Britain was delayed. But John, still in the Netherlands, was more than elated with what he had accomplished with the Dutch. In early spring 1782, the States General of the United Provinces of the Netherlands formally recognized the United States of America's independence. Recognition was a gigantic step, one that John would doggedly hold out for in any surrender terms from Britain. But for the time being, the Dutch had recognized American independence. That important point put John on an equal basis with other nations' diplomats at The Hague.

Additionally, on June 11, 1782, John negotiated a five-million-guilder loan by the Dutch to the United States with a very low interest rate. With America flat broke, John considered that the two accomplishments of Dutch recognition and an initial loan were some of his proudest life achievements. John would go on to negotiate three additional loans from the Dutch in 1784, 1787, and 1788.

But the war with Britain was still not officially over, it was just stalled. Life and debts still had to go on. Abigail sent John in June 1782 a list of Dutch materials which she knew would sell for a premium in Boston: "Black and white Gauzes and Gauze hankerchiefs (the best articles imported), tapes Quality bindings Shoe binding, Low priced linen, Black caliminco red tammies, fine threads low priced calicos Ribbons."[36]

In addition to her order, and on the dawn of a British surrender and a new "code of laws" (the US Constitution) to be written, Abigail had included a statement about women's overlooked patriotism, writing that males should acknowledge and appreciate women's contributions toward victory during the war.

Patriotism in the female Sex is the most disinterested [unselfish] of all virtues. . . . Deprived of a voice in Legislation, obliged to submit to those Laws which are imposed upon us, is it not sufficient to make us indifferent to the publick Welfare? Yet all History and every age exhibit Instances of patriotick virtue in the female Sex; which considering our situation equals the most Heroick of yours. A late writer observes that as Citizens we are calld upon to exhibit our fortitude, for when you offer your Blood to the State, it is ours. In giving it our Sons and Husbands we give more than ourselves.[37]

She ended with the stark reminder to all male wartime soldiers, "You can only die on the field of Battle, but we have the misfortune to survive those whom we Love most."[38] Abigail rightfully included herself into that self-sacrificing legion: "I will take praise to myself. I feel that it is my due, for having sacrificed so large a portion of my peace and happiness to promote the welfare of my country which I hope for many years to come will reap the benefit."[39]

Many of Abigail's letters during this time included a wish that John would return to her. "I never receive a packet from your mamma without a fit of melancholy that I cannot get over for many days,"[40] John wrote daughter Nabby. But Abigail knew he wouldn't come back until his public work and duty was finished. The situation was immovable. She expressed her sadness, but John was unable to alleviate Abigail's gloominess by promising something he couldn't make happen—that of returning to her very soon.

Part III

Europe

Chapter Fifteen

"To Hazard the Watery Element"

1782–1784

A *bigail was worried* about seventeen-year-old Nabby. She didn't act "giddy" and outgoing, as Abigail had been at the same age. Nabby also seemed to have little "sensibility."[1] "Not [that] she is like her Mamma. She has a Stat[l]iness in her manners which some misconstrue into pride and haughtiness. . . . [but] she has prudence and discretion beyond her years. She is in her person tall large and Majestick. . . . Her sensibility is not yet sufficiently a wakend to give her Manners that pleasing softness which attracts whilst it is attracted. Her Manners rather forbid all kinds of Intimacy."[2]

Along with her undeveloped sensibility, Abigail thought Nabby was also "rather too silent."[3] Nabby seemed to be living in a shell of her own making. Nothing was working to coax her out of it, "nor could repeated invitations nor the solicitation of Friends joined to the consent of her Mamma, prevail with her to appear at commencement this year."[4]

Nabby didn't particularly like books, either. John asked her what books she would like, and he would send them to her from Europe.

Nabby's answer probably astonished John: "Whatever Books my Dear Sir you think proper to recommend to me, I shall receive with particular pleasure, those of your choice, cannot fail, to gratify your Daughter. I have not that taste for history which I wish and which might be greatly advantagous, but I hope it is yet to be acquired."[5]

Instead, Nabby discussed the subject of boys with her cousins and friends in a pen pal club where she had adopted the pen name of "Amelia." Nabby's cousin who was two years older, Elizabeth Cranch ("Betsy," pen name "Eliza") returned from a stay in Boston; Betsy hinted to Nabby in a letter of seeing a boy there. The uplifting letter Betsy wrote Nabby elicited this mundane reply, "Your late excursion [to Boston] has given you spirits. . . . Your Amelia is the same cold indifferent Girl she ever was. . . . I long to be in Love, it must be a strang feeling, seems to me."[6]

Then, on one midsummer day in 1782, Nabby proposed to her mother that she be allowed to travel to Europe, unescorted, to become the housekeeper for her father. Abigail asked John his opinion: "What think you of your daughters comeing to keep House for you? She proposes it."[7] Predictably John vetoed that idea in its infancy because of the sailing dangers faced by an unescorted female.

But John expressed his parental caution to Abigail just a few months later about another aspect of Nabby. John had started a letter to Abigail on January 22, 1783, proclaiming in the first paragraph the long-awaited news that, "The Preliminaries of Peace and an Armistice, were Signed at Versailles on the 20 and on the 21. We went again to pay our Respects to the King and Royal Family upon the Occasion."[8] Then John wrote that he had just finished writing the first paragraph when Abigail's letter "of 23 decr. was brought in. Its Contents have awakened all my sensibility."[9] The alarming news was that Nabby possibly had a law student boyfriend.

Abigail disclosed: "And we have in the little circle an other gentleman who has opend an office in Town, for about nine months past, and boarded in Mr. Cranch['s] family. His Father you knew. His Name is Tyler, he studied Law upon his comeing out of colledge with Mr. Dana."[10] The young man's name was Royall Tyler.

John angrily replied, "I confess I dont like the Subject at all. My Child is too young for such Thoughts."[11] He spent the next eight paragraphs in his letter explaining why he and Abigail could not let this courting continue. John put into writing every piece of gossip he'd heard about the Tyler family and of Royall Tyler's questionable reputation.

Abigail wrote of the pleasant occasion where one evening during his legal studies at the Cranch's house, Royall came over to the Adamses's house to return John's bookcase key. He "had a difficult writ to draw. He requested the favour of looking into your Book of forms, which I readily granted; in the Evening when he returned me the key he put in to my hands a paper which I could not tell what to make of; untill he exclaimed 'O! Madam Madam, I have new hopes that I shall one day become worthy your regard.'"[12]

Abigail may have been charmed by Royall, but John saw right through the ploy, writing that "I dont like this method of Courting Mothers." John used descriptive words like "Rascall" and "reformed Rake"[13] to further make his thoughts known about that young lawyer. Then Abigail may have seen the opportunity to get John back home again. She wrote to him, "I wish most sincerely wish you was at Home to judge for yourself. I shall never feel safe or happy untill you are. I had rather you should inquire into his conduct and behaviour, his success in Buisness and his attention to it, from the family where he lives, than Say any thing upon the subject myself. I can say with real Truth that no Courtship subsists between them, and that I believe it is in your power to put a final period to every Idea of the kind, if upon your return you think best."[14]

Royall Tyler, twenty-five years old, was a handsome lawyer with a charming personality and a sizable family inheritance, of which Royall by his own admission had wantonly wasted nearly half. When he established a law office in Braintree in 1782, he apparently set his eyes upon seventeen-year-old Abigail "Nabby" Adams as a good prospect for an advantageous wife. But Nabby was also wise to Royall, at least for a while. In the summer of 1782, she warned her cousin Betsy of the rumors she'd heard about "the gentleman that lately has resided in your family. . . . [He] is the essence and quintessence of artfulness. . . . I was told the other day that I could not see him and not become acquainted with him."[15] But those feelings and warnings would fall upon deaf ears as the Adams–Tyler courtship would take a more serious turn.

By late summer 1782, after a three-year separation, John was starting to hint that following the signing of the final peace treaty, he would not be returning home. He would like to be named the very first ambassador to the British Court of St. James's. As a reaction, Abigail was also starting to vaguely introduce the proposal of her traveling to Europe, be it the Netherlands or France, to be with John. She was feeling that the process of sending letters to each other had grown stale. "You so seldom acknowledge the recept of any Letters from me, that but for many of the vessels arriveing safe, I should suppose they never reach you."[16] Abigail also realized that she could bring Nabby with her to Europe. The trip would be a fix for Abigail's loneliness for John but could also serve to smother the bothersome flames between Nabby and Royall Tyler. A double benefit like that "would have prevaild over my aversion to the Sea."[17]

Dr. Benjamin Waterhouse, a renowned physician,[18] visited Abigail on August 4, 1782. He had just returned from the Netherlands, rooming with John Adams while he was there. He told Abigail that he sensed a melancholy within John which, Waterhouse presumed, could only be alleviated by a visit from Abigail. She informed John: "Dr. Waterhouse yesterday made me a visit. . . . He wished me exceedingly to go to you. He was sure it was necessary to your happiness."[19] One month later, with John's silence on the subject, Abigail came out and said that if John wanted her there in Europe with him, he had to clearly state it or she would stay home: "it is that I may come to you, with our daughter, in the Spring, provided You are like to continue abroad. . . . Remember that to render your situation more agreable I fear neither the Enemy or old Neptune, but then you must give me full assureance of your intire approbation of my request. I cannot accept a half way invitation. . . . To say I am happy here, I cannot, but it is not an idle curiosity that make me wish to hazard the Watery Element."[20] No word from John.

Abigail had been separated from John for three years now. A Christmastime letter of December 23, 1782, written by Abigail to John, described her feelings of her personal sacrifice in exchange for the elusive benefit of establishing a new country: "If you had known said a person to me the other day; that Mr. A[dam]s would have remained so long abroad; would you have consented that he should have gone? I recollected myself a moment, and then spoke the real dictates of my Heart. If I had known Sir that Mr. A. could have affected what he has done; I would not only have submitted to the absence I have endured; painfull as it has been; but I would not have opposed it, even tho 3 years more should be added to the Number, which Heaven avert! I feel a pleasure in being able to sacrifice my selfish passions to the general good, and in imitating the example which has taught me to consider myself and family, but as the small dust of the balance when compaired with the great community."[21]

In the meantime, it seemed that an agreement for peace was near. Two months prior to the signing of the final peace treaty, surprisingly, it appeared that all the parties agreed on all the issues of the treaty. On November 30, 1782, John and other dignitaries signed the preliminary Anglo-French and Anglo-Spanish peace treaties at Versailles. The peace treaty process was a two-step affair. First the preliminary treaties were signed which outlined certain large agreements and conditions. Then while each country ratified their part of the agreement, discussion went on about the minor points, all of which would culminate in a final or "definitive" treaty.

With the war ended, the value of Abigail's imported merchandise fell drastically in value. Her principle of supply and demand was turned on its head—the supply increased since there was no more danger posed by enemy ships, and in consequence, demand fell off. The prices set for goods plummeted. Abigail characterized the peacetime irony: "I enclose a list of a few articles in the family way. I have done with any thing more. My last adventure from Holland was most unfortunate. The Length of the passage was such, that the News of peace arrived a few days before; Goods fell and are now sold much below the sterling cost; many are lower than ever I knew them; Some persons are obliged to sell, and I believe the peace, will ruin more merchants and traders than the War. Many solem faces you see in concequence of it. No such rapid fortunes to be acquired now. Taxes heavy, very heavey—trade stagnated, money scarce. . . . I expect to close my mercantle affairs with this Letter."[22]

In early 1783 John found himself in another anxious situation. If his commission in Europe wasn't to be extended by Congress, he would hurry home to be with Abigail and his family and friends. If he was selected to continue to do Congress's work in France, the Netherlands, or Great Britain, then he would send for Abigail and Nabby to join him. However, he still received no word from Congress. "If therefore Congress should renew my Commission to make a Treaty of Commerce with G. B., come to me, with your Daughter."[23] Finally on May 1, 1783, John got the answer that he'd been waiting for. The Continental Congress had reissued commissions for John and Benjamin Franklin. John Jay would soon be replaced by Thomas Jefferson. After watching over the final peace treaty, the three were commissioned to negotiate a commercial treaty with Great Britain.[24] That provided the needed answer— John would be staying in Europe, so Abigail and Nabby would come to him in Europe as soon as it was possible. He explained to Abigail: "In these Circumstances I must stay another Winter. I cannot justify going home. But what Shall I do for Want of my Family. By what I hear, I think Congress will give Us all Leave to come home in the

Spring. Will you come to me this fall and go home with me in the Spring? If you will, come with my dear Nabby, leaving the two Boys at Mr. Shaws, and the House and Place under the Care of your Father Uncle Quincy or Dr. Tufts, or Mr. Cranch."[25]

Nabby promised her hand in marriage to Royall Tyler upon her return, whenever that might be. John and Abigail had finally given in, and both gave their approval for the union just as Nabby and her mother were going aboard the ship. Although Nabby might not have agreed, Abigail privately thought a separation might be good as a test of affection.

Even before the European trip was planned, Abigail had been in a quandary about schooling for Tommy and Charles. They were already at a point which challenged Abigail and her knowledge of subjects. "I know not what to do with my Children. We have no Grammer School in the Town, nor have we had for 5 years."[26] The random male tutors hired by Abigail always eventually left for better prospects. Finally, Abigail had to swallow her dislike for Reverend John Shaw, her sister Elizabeth's husband, and enroll Charles and Tommy into the Shaw-run Haverhill Academy. Abigail had taken this step prior to John suggesting it. The school had a good reputation for preparing boys for admittance into Harvard: "our two Sons go on Monday with Billy Cranch to Haverhill; there to be under the care and tuition of Mr. Shaw who has one in his family which he offers for colledge in july. I have done the best I could with them. They have been without a school ever since janry. . . . Andover was full and so is every other private School."[27]

Regarding the Paris Peace Treaty, the Continental Congress had issued orders to the American peace ministers—John Adams, Benjamin Franklin, and John Jay—to take their instructions from Charles Gravier, comte de Vergennes. But Adams reflected in his diary that Congress had "surrendered their own Sovereignty into the Hands of a French Minister." "It has basely prostituted its own honour by sacrificing mine."[28] In the meantime Adams and Franklin had come together again as friendly co-workers and it was left to Franklin to inform Vergennes that the Americans had settled a separate peace with the British despite what Congress had ordered. Vergennes was predictably enraged, but Franklin smoothed it over with him claiming that it was just a "little Misunderstanding."[29] Then, amazingly, silver-tongued Ben Franklin asked Vergennes for another loan for the nearly bankrupt United States. This time it was for six million livres, and Vergennes gave it.

The preliminary treaties were being ratified by the governments of the United States of America, Great Britain, France, and Spain, a time-consuming process. Adams had little to do during most of 1783 and he fell into a depression. He was also affected by unnamed aches and pains. He poured his weariness, anxiety, and illnesses out in letters to Abigail: "Day after day, Week after Week, Month after Month, roll away and bring Us no News. I am So weary of this idle useless Time, that I dont know what to do with myself. . . . My [leg] Swelling has never been So violent, but it is not yet cured. If I increase my Exercise, beyond the usual degree, it returns in [same] degree. I . . . have never done any Thing for it but Walk every day. But this Weakness in the Ankles is not all. I am vexed with other Relicks of that [Dutch] fever, which are very troublesome. They appear in sharp fiery humours which break out in the back of my Neck and in other Parts of me and plague me, as much as the Uncertainty in which I am in of my future destination."[30]

Franklin was aware of John's anxiety, aches, and pains. While writing to Robert R. Livingston, the first United States Secretary of Foreign Affairs, in midsummer 1783 Franklin suggested that John's illnesses were chiefly due to mental instability: "I am persuaded however that he means well for his Country, is always an honest Man, often a Wise One, but sometimes and in some things, absolutely out of his Senses."[31]

The final Treaty of Paris was signed on September 3, 1783, at the Hôtel d'York in Paris by the three American ministers and David Hartley, Great Britain's representative. The Revolutionary War was over. The first condition of the peace treaty was that America receive its independence. It was the last condition Great Britain grudgingly recognized.

Two weeks following the final treaty signing, Abigail likely didn't know the ceremony had taken place. She was focused on her father's suddenly declining health. Her father, Reverend William Smith, died September 17, 1783. He was seventy-seven years old and was considered to have led a long life and, "a Life well Spent."[32] Abigail reported that he died from a "strangery"[33] after fifteen days.[34] His will and its redistribution of his wealth would create fundamental changes in the lives of the Smith survivors. He left practically nothing to his son: "To William Smith Jr., who had abandoned his family: only his apparel, valued at £21.13.4, and the forgiveness of all debts."[35] The law of coverture prevented William Smith, Jr.'s wife from inheriting their Lincoln, Massachusetts, farm where they lived or their separate Concord property. The property was put into a trust to support William Jr.'s wife, Catharine "Kitty" Louisa Salmon Smith, and their six children. The trust's administrators were Doctor Cotton Tufts and William Sr.'s son-in-law Richard Cranch.

Reverend Smith had distributed assets according with the neediest of his children receiving the most. Mary Cranch, through Richard Cranch, received the parsonage and its eighteen acres. Elizabeth Shaw, through Reverend John Shaw, received forty-six acres in Hingham, and half-parcels, split equally with Abigail in a Medford farm, as well as equally divided ownership of a "Salt marsh in Malden."[36] Aside from Abigail's half-ownerships of acreage, through John Adams, she was bequeathed her father's "Silver Tankard."[37] Reverend Smith also bequeathed money to various family members.

The most curious aspect of his will involved his only remaining slave, "my Negro Woman Phoebe."[38] Reverend Smith offered Phoebe her freedom. However, he stipulated that if she didn't want freedom, then to "either of my Daughters Mary Cranch, Abigail Adams or Elisabeth Shaw" Phoebe would become a charge, complete with annual support expenses. "And it is my will that one hundred pounds be retained out of my estate, and that to such my daughter with whom the said Phoebe shall live, the annual interest thereof shall be paid so long as she shall live with her."[39] Phoebe chose freedom.

One of the main reasons Abigail hadn't already gone to be with John in Paris was because she worried about the health of her father in Weymouth. Now upon his death she felt freed up to make travel plans. However, she realized as the fall months of 1783 waned that getting away from her responsibilities in Braintree was complicated. Of course, a large consideration of the trip would be the season she sailed. If possible, a dangerous winter crossing should be avoided.

Abigail also had another ongoing project. She, with John's approval this time, was buying up nearby land and property. One of the pieces of property they eventually purchased was the house and farm of the Veasey family, very near their own house. It would be called "the Old House" or "Peacefield."[40] After the sale of their Boston house, the Adamses would own four additional houses in "Braintree together with the Farms belonging to them."[41] The Adamses would receive rent from all four properties during their retirement—all stemming primarily from Abigail's business savvy.

Owning land and property (tangible assets) was John's favorite form of investment.[42] That didn't apply to Abigail, however. She felt most comfortable investing in government securities, as she first had in 1777. In explaining government securities to John, Abigail showcased her ability to understand and work with finances:

There is a method of laying out money to more advantage than by the purchase of land's, which a Friend of mine advised me to, for it is now become a regular merchandize. Dr. T[uft]s has sold a Farm with a design of vesting it in this manner, viz in State Notes. Provision is now made for the anual payment of Interest, and the Notes have all been consolidated. Foreigners and monied Men have, and are purchaseing them at 7 shillings upon the pound, 6 and 8 pence they have been sold at. I have mentiond to you that I have a hundred pounds sterling in the hands of a Friend, I was thinking of adding the 50 you sent me, and purchaseing 600 pounds LM[43] in state Notes provided I can get them at 7 shillings or 6 and 8 pence. This would yeald me an anual interest of 36 pounds subject to no taxes.[44]

It would take the entire winter of 1783 for Abigail to arrange to leave Braintree and travel to Paris in the spring, "to cross the ocean, coward as I am."[45] She informed John, "I have already arranged all my family affairs in such a way that I hope nothing will suffer by my absence."[46] A logical choice to manage the Adams's finances, "Estate and affairs"[47] was Doctor Cotton Tufts, Abigail's uncle and financial mentor. On June 18, 1784, Abigail left him extremely detailed instructions about keeping the Adamses' interests going, including payments of debts and collecting income. Her level of detail in the document was striking. It included paying her charity "pensioners,"[48] her poor widowed neighbors. She also stipulated, "The Library to be under the care of Mr. Cranch. No Books to be Lent out unless to him and Mr. Tyler without your permission."[49]

Her Boston uncle who was active in shipping, Isaac Smith, Sr., booked passage for Abigail, Nabby, and two assistants—John Briesler and Esther Field.[50] The Adams farm would be leased. The Adams home itself was placed in the care of Abigail's father's recently freed slave, Phoebe, "to whom my Father gave freedom, by his Will, and the income of a hundred a year during her Life."[51] Phoebe and her new husband, William Abdee, had recently married at the Adamses home; since there was no "setled minister in Weymouth I gave them the liberty of celebrating their nuptials here, which they did much to their satisfaction."[52] They also would be allowed to live in the Adams home, free of charge, until Abigail and John returned from Europe. As to the "the dwelling house, Garden and furniture to be left in the care of Pheby and Abdee,"[53] Abigail commented, "I have no doubt of their care and faithfullness, and prefer them to any other family."[54]

On June 18, 1784, Abigail received "my Friends and Neighbours" at the Adamses' house. The tear-filled send-off was sprinkled with phrases said to Abigail such as "Fatal day! I take my last leave; I shall never see you again." Later, Abigail wrote in her diary, "I had possessd myself with calmness, but this was too much for me, so I shook them by the hand mingling my tears with theirs, and left them."[55]

The next day, June 19, was the day where she "had recoverd some from my fatigue and employed the day in writing to several of my Friends and in getting my baggage on Board." She would sail the following day on the ship *Active* to London, England, capital of the former enemy empire. For the first time in over three and a half years, Abigail would see John. The plan was for John to meet Abigail, Nabby, and their traveling companions in London. Then they would all sail together across the English Channel to France. Abigail had started a diary, to be given to Mary upon Abigail's return: "Sund[ay] at 12 oclock Mr. Foster sent his carriage for myself and daughter. We bid adieu to our Friends and were drove to Rows Wharf, from whence we allighted amidst an 100 Gentlemen who were upon the Wharf, to receive us. Mr. Smith handed me from the Carriage and I hastned into the ship from amidst the throng. The ship was soon under sail and we went of with a fine wind."[56]

However just two hours into the passage, Captain Nathaniel Lyde[57] warned "all the Ladies to put on their Sea cloaths and prepare for sickness. We had only time to follow his directions before we found ourselves all sick. . . . the Nausia arising from the smell of the Ship, the continual rolling, tossing and tumbling contribute to keep up this Disorder."[58] The uncomfortable cruise would last slightly over one month. Abigail moaned, "I can bear every thing I meet with better than the Nausias Smells: it is utterly impossible to keep nice and clean."

Chapter Sixteen

"In a Land of Enchantment"

1784

Abigail *recorded that her* seasickness lasted for "ten days; with some intermissions. We crawled upon deck when ever we were able, but it was so cold and damp that we could not remain long upon it, and the confinement of the Air below, the constant rolling of the vessel and the Nausea of the Ship which was much too tight, contributed to keep up our disease."[1]

The ship stunk from sloshed-out barrels of spermaceti oil and potash, along with human puke all mixed by the rocking of the boat: "the oil leaks the potash smoaks and ferments, all adds to the flavour."[2] The cargo was stored down inside the hold, very near the makeshift sleeping and changing quarters of Abigail, Nabby, and the eleven other passengers. All but one of the others were "Male companions." But at least, Abigail noted, they were "well behaved, decent." The male companions assisted whenever the wobbly-legged, seasick women tried to move about, as "it is not once in the 24 hours that we can even Cross the cabbin; without being held, or assisted. Nor can we go upon deck without the assistance of 2 Gentlemen; and when there, we are allways bound into our Chairs . . . with his Arm fastned into ours; and his feet braced against a table or chair that was lashed down with Ropes, Bottles, Mugs, plates crasshing to peices, first on one side; and then on the other. The Sea running mountain high, and knocking against the sides of the vessel as tho it would burst the sides."[3]

Aside from the side-to-side pitching, the ship was filthy and coated with a stinky, oily residue caked onto nearly every sunbaked surface. An inexperienced walker onboard would slip as much from the deck scum as from the rolling of the waves. As soon as Abigail had recovered from prolonged seasickness and rheumatism from the dampness, she decided to put everyone to work cleaning, with full approval of Captain Lyde. "No sooner was I able to move; than I found it necessary to . . . demand a Cleaner abode. I soon exerted my Authority with scrapers mops Brushes, infusions of viniger; &c. and in a few hours you would have thought yourself in a different Ship."[4]

The inedible food onboard, Abigail also recorded, was inexcusable. She noted that men could eat the slop that was served "and if they can get enough to eat five times a day all goes well."[5] The ladies, however, stayed hungry for nearly the whole trip. In an uncharacteristic racial slur, Abigail blamed the disgusting food on the cook who "is a great dirty lazy Negro; with no more knowledge of cookery than a savage."[6] In a short letter to her sister, Elizabeth Shaw, Abigail added, "[I] taught the cook to dress his victuals, and have made several puddir gs with my own hands."[7]

On the evening of July 8, Abigail was called up onto the deck to behold a brilliant natural phenomenon. "I went last evening upon deck. . . . to view that phenomenon of Nature; a blaizing ocean. A light flame Spreads over the ocean in appearence; with thousands of thousands Sparkling Gems, resembling our fire flies in a dark Night. It has a most Beautifull appearence."[8] As the ship was cutting through the water, Abigail was amazed by the brilliant glow of the water streaming out of both sides of the bow. It was "bioluminescence, caused by the slow oxidation of material found in certain marine organisms."[9] But Abigail, a very religious woman, saw the handiwork of "God Almighty" in many things, including "a blaizing ocean."[10]

The *Active* was just four days out of port. It was July 16 and Abigail was closing out her diary journal for her sister Mary. But she had to describe a verbal match she had just had with a fellow passenger, "Mr. Green," whom nobody onboard liked. He was a "haughty Scotchman" who criticized the French and Americans alike, especially General

George Washington. Abigail could read in him that the only reason he was civil to her was due to her "connection" to John Adams: "We have but one passenger which we should have been willing to have been without. . . . I have felt a Disposition to quarrel with him several times; but have restraind myself; and only observed to him mildly, that merit; not tittles, gave a man preeminence in our Country. . . . All our passengers enjoyed this conversation, and the Gentleman was civil enough to drop the Subject, but the venom Spits out very often." She closed the subject of Mr. Green with a philosophical statement: "Such men have no musick in their Souls."[11]

Though English land and the cliffs of Dover had been sighted, it took the *Active* over three days to sail through the English Channel. A fierce gale had sprung up, tossing the ship from side to side along with the passengers and reintroducing seasickness to the travelers. Captain Lyde explained that the *Active* would not sail west up the Thames River to London, adding another week to the schedule. Instead, the passengers would be shuttled over to the small town of Deal on the English southeast corner. From there they would travel by land the "72 miles"[12] to London. The passengers were eager to get off the ship and onto solid ground again. Abigail was also eager to disembark as she had a "violent sick head ack."[13]

But just one more inconvenient occurrence was still in the cards. Men from Deal ran a pilot boat shuttle out to the *Active*. However, once the boat was loaded, the six-foot waves tossed the people around like playthings. "Finally a Wave landed us with the utmost force upon the Beach; the Broad Side of the Boat right against the shore, which was oweing to the bad management of the men, and the high Sea."[14] It was July 20, 1784. Abigail was finally standing on English soil, though completely soaked. The passengers made their way up the beach to dry off, to enjoy some edible food at a tavern, and to sleep overnight there. Abigail noted that the obnoxious "Mr. Green" left the party "immediately for London—no body mourn'd."[15]

Abigail and her entourage left for London in four post chaises at six the next morning. One reason for leaving early and reaching London before nightfall was the threat of robbery and highwaymen after dark. Abigail had breakfast near Canterbury Cathedral, and she marveled at its history. She was struck with England's "old Gothick Cathedrals, which are all of stone very heavy, with but few windows which are grated with large Bars of Iron, and look more like jails for criminals, than places designd for the worship of the deity. One would Suppose from the manner in which they are Gaurded, that they apprehended devotion would be stolen. They have a most gloomy appearence and realy made me shudder."[16]

Not far into the trip that day, Abigail witnessed a captured and shackled highwayman. When he saw Abigail, he tried to lift his cap to her. "We saw the poor wretch gastly and horible, brought along on foot, his horse rode by a person who took him; who also had his pistol. He looked like a youth of 20 only, attempted to lift his hat, and looked Dispair." She was shocked to hear the constable teasing the young man telling him that he'd get a quick trial "and then my Lad you Swing."[17]

Finally, Abigail and Nabby made it into London by about eight that evening, and Abigail noted, "As I had no particular direction to any Hotel when I first arrived a Gentleman passenger who had formerly been in London advised me to [L]ows Hotel in Covent Garden." Aghast at the prices there, the next morning Abigail and Nabby, with the assistance of friends,[18] moved their lodgings to the more reasonable "Osbourne's new family Hotel, in the Adelphi Buildings in the Strand,"[19] where John and John Quincy had stayed in fall 1783. Abigail immediately wrote John a letter that she had "landed upon the British Shore"[20] and sent it post haste to his address in The Hague, Netherlands. John received the letter within three days and excitedly wrote back to her, "Your Letter of the 23d. has made me the happiest Man upon Earth. I am twenty Years younger than I was Yesterday."[21] He added that regrettably he couldn't go to her now because of demanding work, but that he would immediately send John Quincy to her. He charged his son with purchasing "a Coach, in which We four must travel to Paris."[22]

Abigail noticed two distinct things as she looked around at the British residents, and specifically the women of London: "The London Ladies walk a vast deal and very fast."[23] More so she was comparing her attire to that of the "London ladies" and "dispiseing the tyranny of fashion."[24] She knew that eventually she would have to upgrade her clothes to reflect the status of being a statesman's wife, but she decided to hold off until she reached Paris, as she would be spending more time there. Still Abigail loved the country simplicity in some English women's casual features: "Tis true you must put a hoop on and have your hair dresst, but a common straw hat, no Cap, with only a ribbon upon the crown, is thought dress sufficient to go into company."[25]

But it was the indoor plumbing, of sorts, inside the hotel that amazed Abigail. "Into a closet by my chamber, water is conveyd by pipes, and as there is not half an inch of Ground unoccupied we have no occasion to go out of our rooms, from one week to an other, for by ringing the bed chamber bell, the Chamber Maid comes; and the drawing room Bell brings up the other waiters; who when you go out attend you from the Stairs to the Carriage, the Land Lady waiting at the foot to recive you, and so again upon your return. This is the stile of the Hotels."[26]

The friends and well-wishers of Abigail in London, Loyalists or not, took up much of her first days in that capital city. But on one of Abigail's first trips outside, she and Nabby went to the London studio in Haymarket of expatriate painter John Singleton Copley. The year before Copley had rendered a full-size portrait of John Adams, and Abigail was eager to see it. "I went yesterday accompanied by Mr. Storer and Smith to Mr. Copelys to see Mr. Adams picture. This I am told was taken at the request of Mr. Copely and belongs to him. It is a full Length picture very large; and a very good likeness. Before him stands the Globe: in his hand a Map of Europe, at a small distance 2 female figures representing peace and Innocence. It is a most Beautifull painting."[27]

The next visit that same day was to the studio of famed sculptor Patience Wright. It turned out to be nowhere near as pleasant as the Copley visit. Patience Wright was an American-born Quaker, then living in London. She had gained international fame as a gifted waxworks artist, sculpting many British notables of the day. It was rumored that during the Revolutionary War she sent coded messages to Benjamin Franklin and John Hancock. But it was her very unconventional behavior and bohemian dress that set her apart from other artists. Abigail wasn't forewarned about Patience Wright's eccentricities ahead of time, which made for an uncomfortable visit by both Abigail and Nabby, along with Mr. Storer and Mr. Smith. Abigail noted the awkward social call: "Upon my entrance (my Name being sent up) she ran to the Door, caught me by the Hand, 'Why is it realy and in truth Mrs. Adams, and that your daughter? Why you dear Soul you, how young you look! Well I am glad to See you, all of you Americans! Well I must kiss you all. . . . I love every body that comes from America,' says she, 'here,' running to her desk, 'is a card I had from Mr. Adams. I am quite proud of it, he came to see and made me a noble present, dear creature I design to have his Head. . . . In this manner She ran on for half an hour." In her letter to sister Mary, Abigail labeled Patience as "the Queen of sluts."[28] (In the eighteenth century, according to English dictionary writer Samuel Johnson, "slut" meant "a dirty woman" in the sense of having poor hygiene.)

The first Sunday spent in London was July 25. The morning was spent attending a religious service at the chapel of the Foundling Hospital, established in 1739. It was built to take in abandoned babies and children left in the streets by poor women or prostitutes. Abigail added a word about stained glass: "I should have mentiond that the chaple windows are painted Glass, the Arms, and Names of the most distinguishd Benefactors are in the Different Squares of the Glass."[29]

After dining with friends, they all attended the early evening service at Magdalene Hospital for the Reception of Penitent Prostitutes, "which is 3 miles from where I dined, for this is a *Monstrous* great city." One service custom at the hospital made Abigail well up with tears: "I observed upon going in; a Gallery before me railed very high and coverd with Green canvas. Here set these unhappy women screened from publick view. You can discern them through the canvas, but not enough to distinguish countenances. I admired the delicacy of this thought. The Singing was all performd by these females accompanied with the organ. The Melancholy melody of their voices, the Solemn Sound of the organ . . . . drew tears from my Eyes."[30]

Abigail, like any tourist, visited "the curiositys of the city"[31] during the following week before the family trip across the English Channel to the Netherlands. Abigail went to the Tower of London, Westminster Abbey, the Royal Botanic Gardens in Kew, and "Pope's Grotto" in Twickenham. Pope's Grotto was part of an underground tunnel that Alexander Pope had built in his gardens to run under a road and connect his two properties. Alexander Pope was one of Abigail's favorite authors.

John had many commerce treaty negotiations going on and preferred if Abigail came to him in The Hague before they all traveled to Paris, "Mr. Adams chuses I should come to the Hague, and travell with him from thence."[32]

Abigail expected John Quincy to arrive on Friday, July 30. She was correct. But Abigail hadn't seen John Quincy in nearly five years, and she hoped she would still recognize him: "Whilst I am writing a servant in the family runs puffing in, as if he was realy interested in the matter. 'Young Mr. Adams is come.' 'Where where is he,' we all cried out? 'In the other house Madam, he stoped to get his Hair dresst.' Impatient enough I was, yet when he enterd, (we have so many Strangers), that I drew back not realy believing my Eyes—till he cried out, 'Oh my Mamma! and my dear Sister.' Nothing but the Eyes at first Sight appeard what he once was. His appearence is that of a Man, and in his countanance the most perfect good humour."[33]

Meanwhile, Abigail received a letter from John written on August 1 updating her on a change of plans. The family would not be going to the Netherlands, as was expected. John wrote that he would "join you in London . . . in Eight Days at farthest, and sooner, if possible." Then they would all travel directly to Paris instead. The reason for the change was simple. Congress had appointed Thomas Jefferson as minister plenipotentiary taking John Jay's position with John and Benjamin Franklin. "I must join my Colleagues in Paris without Loss of Time. . . . Mr. Jeffersons Arrival, a Month sooner than he expected, have indeed changed my Plan."[34]

In a tongue-in-cheek statement, John told Abigail, "Stay where you are, and amuse yourself, by Seeing what you can, untill you See me."[35] The communication from John about imminent reunion plans helped to make both Abigail and Nabby feel better. Both had been ill from colds, and Abigail reported that she "found myself so unwell that I could not venture to day into a crouded assembly. My walk Yesterday gave me a pain in my head, and stiffned me so that I can scarcly move. Nabby too has the London cold, which they say every body experiences who comes here."[36]

Leaving London and England weighed more heavily upon Abigail than she had ever anticipated. For more than a decade she had considered Great Britain an evil empire. But after her positive reception there and seeing the beauty of the gardens and within its people, she felt completely differently in that summer of 1784. She saw living in France as something she would not be thrilled by. She would miss England, she confided to Mary: "I cannot find myself in a strange land. I shall experience this when I get to a country the language of which I cannot speak. I sincerely wish the treaty might have been concerted here. I have a partiality for this Country. . . . [and in] a most Beautifull Garden, to walk. In some of these places; you would think yourself in a land of enchantment."[37]

Nabby had gone out for a walk Saturday morning, August 7. When she arrived back, she noticed things in the rooms thrown all about. She noted in her journal, "every thing around appeared altered, without my knowing in what particular. I went into my own room, the things were moved. . . . Why is all this appearance of strangeness?" She was told that the room's condition was because her father had arrived and was upstairs! "Up I flew, and to his chamber, where he was lying down, he raised himself upon my knocking softly at the door, and received me with all the tenderness of an affectionate parent after so long an absence."[38]

It was early Sunday morning, August 8 when the four Adamses climbed into their recently purchased carriage and left London for Paris.

The onboard entertainment was the book *Lives of the Poets* by Samuel Johnson, which they took turns reading. Their two servants followed in a post chaise. They reached Dover in late afternoon and took an overnight crossing of the English Channel. By dawn, Monday, August 9, they were in Calais, France. But during the two-hundred-mile trip to Paris, Abigail was shocked while passing through the fabled French countryside to see that "the villages look poor and mean the houses all thatchd and rarely a Glass window in them. Their Horses instead of being handsomely harnessed as those in England are, have the appearence of so many old cart horses." There were dirty, poor-looking peasants working in fields everywhere. To her niece, seventeen-year-old Lucy Cranch, Abigail wrote, "You inquire of me how I like Paris?" Abigail reported to Lucy that long before she saw Paris, "I have smelt it." "It is the very dirtyest place I ever saw . . . the streets are narrow, the shops, the houses inelegant, and dirty, the Streets full of Lumber and Stone with which they Build."[39] She acknowledged that she should have seen the two capital cities in reverse order, "To have had Paris tolerable to me; I should not have gone to London."[40]

The Adamses stayed their first few Parisian nights on the Left Bank in the Hôtel d'York, where the Paris Peace Treaty had been signed. It was temporary lodging until John, who hadn't been back in Paris in a year, could locate better housing. During the first few days in Paris, John Quincy gave his mother and sister a tour of the city. Meanwhile John and the new third minister, Thomas Jefferson, met up daily at Benjamin Franklin's house in nearby Passy. They would discuss recent details about establishing commercial treaties with European powers.

Finally, on August 17, the Adamses arrived in the village of Auteuil, four miles west of the city limits, near Passy on the road to Versailles, and a mile from Dr. Franklin's residence. It was a beautiful, rural area which abutted Bois de Boulogne, then a royal hunting ground and pleasure reserve. They moved into the Hôtel de Rouault,[41] "elevated above the River Seine and the low Grounds, and distant from the putrid Streets of Paris, is the best I could wish for."[42]

Abigail was struck with how many rooms were in the three-story house. It took her nearly a month to discover them all, some forty to fifty rooms, she counted. Even by September, as she wrote to her niece Betsy Cranch: "There are appartments [large rooms] of every kind in this House, many of which I have never yet enterd." Beyond the many rooms, the house had "an expence of 30,000 liveres in looking Glasses."[43] However, Abigail didn't particularly care for the Mirror

Room, a small version of the Palace of Versailles attraction, as it made her feel self-conscious: "the room is encompassed with more Glass than the Chamber, the ceiling being intirely glass," the walls were "panneld with looking Glasses. . . . why my dear you cannot turn yourself in it without being multiplied 20 times. Now that I do not like; for being rather clumsy and by no means an elegant figure, I hate to have it so often repeated to me."[44] Abigail couldn't also neglect mentioning the filthy stairs one had to climb many times per day, "the Stairs which you commonly have to assend to get into the family appartments; are so dirty that I have been obliged to hold up my Cloaths as tho I was passing through a cow yard."[45]

Nabby was equally harsh describing the lower-class French people to her cousin Betsy Cranch. "The people are I believe, the dirtiest creatures in the Human race. . . . The streets are very narrow in general, and the buildings amaizing high, all built of stone, and which was once white but by the smoke and dirt they have acquired, a very disagreeable appearance. . . . The appearance of the lower class of people, is of a heavy leaden kind of creatures, whose greatest art and what indeed is most attended to by almost all classes is to cheat you of as much as they possibly can, in which they succeed with strangers, much to their own satisfaction."[46]

In an age when proper politeness hinged on paying social visits to each other, Abigail discovered that the visiting rules in Paris were different than in London. She confessed to her niece Betsy that "I have been in company with but one French Lady since I arrived, for strangers here make the first visit and nobody will know you untill you have waited upon them in form."[47] The distinct problem for Abigail was that while she could read and understand basic French, she did not know how to speak it. "As I cannot speak the language, I think I should make rather an awkward figure."[48] That prevented her from making a first social call, which would allow French acquaintances to then visit her.

The "one French Lady" of whom Abigail wrote was an unfortunate choice as an introduction. At the invitation of Benjamin Franklin, or "Dr. Franklings," as Abigail nearly always referred to him, John, Abigail, and other guests were invited to have dinner with Madame Helvétius on September 1. The sixty-two-year-old Anne-Catherine de Ligniville, Madame Helvétius, was a very wealthy widow who kept a visiting salon of some of the most influential and brilliant people in French society.[49] To the conservative Abigail, the salty language and actions of the bohemian Madame Helvétius were shocking, even scandalous. Abigail wrote to her niece Lucy Cranch of the colorful display: "She enterd the Room with a careless jaunty air. Upon seeing Ladies who were strangers to her, she bawled out ah Mon dieu! where is Frankling?, why did you not tell me there were Ladies here? You must suppose her speaking all this in French. How said she I look? takeing hold of a dressing chimise made of tiffanny which She had on over a blew Lutestring, and which looked as much upon the decay as her Beauty, for she was once a handsome woman. Her Hair was fangled, over it she had a small straw hat with a dirty half gauze hankerchief round it, and a bit of dirtyer gauze. . . . She had a black gauze Skarf thrown over her shoulders."

Abigail continued, "She ran out of the room. When she returnd, the Dr. enterd at one door she at the other, upon which she ran forward to him, caught him by the hand, 'Hélas, Frankling!', then gave him a double kiss one upon each cheek and an other upon his forehead. When we went into the room to dine she was placed between the Dr. and Mr. Adams. She carried on the chief of the conversation at dinner, frequently locking her hand into the Drs. and sometimes spreading her Arms upon the Backs of both the Gentlemans Chairs, then throwing her Arm carelessly upon the Drs. Neck."

Abigail carried on, "I should have been greatly astonished at this conduct, if the good Doctor had not told me that in this Lady I should see a genuine French Woman, wholy free from affectation or stifness of behaviour and one of the best women in the world. For this I must take the Drs. word, but I should have set her down for a very bad one altho Sixty years of age and a widow. I own I was highly disgusted and never wish for an acquaintance with any Ladies of this cast."

Abigail summed up her story describing an appalling incident: "After dinner she threw herself upon a settee where she shew more than her feet. She had a little Lap Dog who was next to the Dr. her favorite. This She kisst and when he wet the floor she wiped it up with her chimise. This is one of the Drs. most intimate Friends, with whom he dines once every week and She with him. She is rich and is my near Neighbour, but I have not yet visited her. Thus my dear you see that Manners differ exceedingly in different Countries. I hope however to find amongst the French Ladies manners more consistant with my Ideas of decency, or I shall be a mere recluse."

As Abigail went through the first few weeks of living in Auteuil, she had to set up the management of the household which she called "the necessary care of organizeing my family, which I find a much more difficult matter than in America."[50] Abigail summarized her new French duties as "I have become Steward and Book keeper."[51]

Abigail's budgeting expertise in this situation was more difficult because of the size of the house, compared to her six-room house in Braintree. But even more so, as she wrote her uncle Doctor Cotton Tufts, it was because of the strange and strict French arrangement of labor specialties, like a caste system for domestic servants: "For Instance your Coiffer de femme, will dress your Hair, and make your bed, but she will not Brush out your Chamber. Your cook will dress your vituals, but she will not wash a dish, or perform any other kind of business. A pack of Lazy wretches, who eat the Bread of Idleness, are Saddled upon you to Support and mantain for the purpose of plundering you, and I add to make one unhappy. . . . We have 8 servants in pay. Both in England and here I find such a disposition to Cheat, that I dare not take a step alone. Almost every person with whom you have to deal, is fully determined to make a prey of you."[52] Abigail humorously added that there was even a servant "Maiter de Hotle" and "his Buisness is to . . . oversee that no body cheats but himself."[53]

Abigail had seen this system of legal robbery for the first time when she and her family landed in Calais: "I was highly diverted. . . . tho provoked, where I first landed. The passengers had brought on shore 7 hand trunks, concequently 7 porters laid hold of them. These were to be carried to the Custom House, only a few Steps, and when they returnd we had 14 of these Rascals to pay, 7 of them for carrying them and 7 more for bringing them back."[54]

It had also become obvious to Abigail of the lack of outhouses in Paris. The reason wasn't because open land was rare, as was the case in London. It was because emptying chamber pots was the express job of yet another specialized servant. "There is an other indispensable Servant who is called a Frotteurer. His buisness is to rub [wax] the floors, and to do a still dirtier peice of Buisness, for it is the fashion of the country, and against that neither reason convenience or any thing else can stand, or prevail, tho there is plenty of land and places sufficiently convenient for Buildings [outhouses]."[55]

Abigail continued to vent in her letter to her uncle Cotton Tufts about the pressure to wear the correct Parisian fashion, "Parissians . . . have established a tyranny of fashion, which is above Law and to which their must be an implicit obedience."[56] "To be out of fashion is more criminal than to be seen in a state of Nature to which the Parissians are not averse."[57]

But Abigail kept the most important message to Doctor Tufts until closing. It was to overrule an instruction from John to Tufts: "Mr. Adams tell[s] me he has written you requesting you to buy him wood land, Salt Marsh or Veseys place. To the two first I do not object, but Veseys place is poverty, and I think we have enough of that already."[58]

Chapter Seventeen

"The Business of Life Here [Is] Pleasure"

1784–1785

hen Abigail was in London, she saw commercial business everywhere. But in Paris she saw very few signs of any business being conducted. How do Parisians earn a living, she wondered? Writing to Mercy Otis Warren, she concluded from observation: "If you ask me what is the Business of Life here? I answer Pleasure."[1] Abigail also compared another obvious difference between London and Paris. "The suicide which is so frequent in London I have heard attributed to the everlasting fogs of that Island. . . [such as] the last ten days of fog and clouds and rain."[2]

Safety was another area where England and France diverged. "In one Country [England] you cannot travel a mile without danger to your person and Property yet Publick executions abound; in the other your person and property are safe; executions are Rare." Abigail found that she could even attend a play in Paris by herself, "with perfect security to your Person, and property; Decency and good order, are preserved, yet are they equally crowded with those of London, but in London, at going in and coming out of the Theatre, you find yourself in a Mob: and are every Moment in Danger of being robbed."[3]

There was another stark difference between the two cities. In Paris, "where vice is Licenced," Abigail was offended by that large number of Parisian prostitutes registered with city officials: "sixty Thousand prostitues in one city, Some of them; the most Beautifull of their Sex!!!"[4] It was different than on "London Streets. . . . where it is suffered to walk at large soliciting the unwary, and unguarded."[5]

Often times in both cities the unplanned and unwanted infants were abandoned on the streets to sometimes freeze to death, while others were taken to a church or an orphanage.[6] As Abigail and Nabby did in London, they visited the Parisian Hôpital des Enfants-Trouvés (Hospital for Foundling Infants). While Abigail praised the compassion and care that the French showed toward "helpless innocence," she wrote "truly it is a painfull pleasing sight." She could not hold back expressing her obvious thoughts after visiting the adjacent "Hôpital de la pitié which joins upon this is the place where they are received when they return from the Country. There they are taught to read and write, the Boys to knit, and the Girls to sew and make lace. . . . Whilst we approve the Charatable disposition, and applaud the wise institution which alleviates the fate of helpless innocence; can we draw a veil over the Guilty Cause, or refrain from comparing a Country grown old in Debauchery and lewdeness with the wise Laws and institutions of one wherein Mariage is considerd as holy and honourable."[7] Regardless, Abigail was also comparing France and America. "My Heart and Soul is more American than ever,"[8] Abigail affirmed to her uncle Cotton Tufts.

By fall 1784, Abigail had started to make a few social acquaintances among a small number of ladies in the Paris area who spoke English. Although most were Americans, one of the women was French and was perhaps Abigail's most valued new friend. Her name was Marie Adrienne Françoise de Noailles, Marquise de Lafayette. She was the wife of General Marquis de Lafayette, America's most valuable ally and an esteemed member of General George Washington's elite military "family."[9] Abigail described Adrienne Lafayette as "a middle siezd Lady Sprightly and agreeable."[10] Abigail noted that in a city as devoted to pleasure as Paris was, most upper-class women were married, but frequently took a lover. In her letter to Mary, her sister, Abigail noted the difference with Madam Lafayette by twice using three exclamation marks: "Madam de la Fayette. . . . I should always take pleasure in her company. She is a good and amiable Lady, exceedingly fond of her Children and attentive to their education, passionatly attached to her Husband!!! A French Lady and fond of her Husband!!!"[11]

Even nineteen-year-old Nabby wrote much the same observations to her cousin, twenty-one-year-old Elizabeth Cranch: "I wish I could give you some idea of the French Ladies, but it is impossible to do it by letter, as I should absolutely be ashaimed to write, what I must if I tell you truths. There is not a subject in Nature that they will not talk upon, in any company, and there is no distinction of sex, after they are Married. I will venture to give you one very small instance of their unreserve in what is called a descent Woman. . . . I sometimes think Myself fortunate in not understanding the Language."[12]

Through it all, Abigail also bemoaned that she was getting fat from getting no exercise in her adopted country, a complaint she never had in Massachusetts: "I suffer through want of excersise, and grow too fat. I cannot persuade my self to walk an hour in the day in a long entry which we have merely for exercise, and as to the Streets they are continually a Quagmire; no walking there without Boots or Wooden Shoes, neither of which are my feet calculated for."[13] The initial evenings in Auteuil just after her arrival were lonely for Abigail, as she confessed to Mary, "our Evenings which are very long, are wholly by ourselves."[14]

However, in late 1784 Abigail discovered the magic of French theater. She had read plays growing up but had never experienced seeing one in person. She discovered that in Paris she could attend plays and the theater in complete safety by herself and without scandal for not being escorted. Abigail became enthralled with the impact of the scene settings, the costumes, and the magnificent music. But she noted that she also paid for it in her health: "I go into Paris sometimes to the plays of which I am very fond, but I So severely pay for it, that I refrain many times upon account of my Health. It never fails giving me a severe Headack, and that in proportion as the House is thin or crowded, one 2 or 3 days after, I suffer."[15] However Abigail had other seemingly contradictory issues which she admittedly struggled with when writing of her experiences to Mary. She wrote of attending operas put on by the Académie Royale de Musique et de Danse, or the Paris Opéra. The lack of modesty by the dancers made Abigail extremely uncomfortable . . . at first. But then things changed for her:

I have found my taste reconciling itself to habits customs and fash-
ions, which at first disgusted me. The first dance which I saw upon
the Stage shoked me, the Dress'es and Beauty of the performers was
enchanting, but no sooner did the Dance commence, than I felt my
delicacy wounded, and I was ashamed to bee seen to look at them.
Girls cloathd in the thinest Silk: and Gauze, with their peticoats
short Springing two foot from the floor poising themselves in the
air, with their feet flying, and as perfectly shewing their Garters and
draws, as tho no peticoat had been worn, was a sight altogether new
to me. Their motions are as light as air and as quick as lightning.
They balance themselves to astonishment. No description can equal
the reality. They are daily trained to it from early infancy, at a Royal
academy instituted for this purpose. You will very often see little
creatures not more than 7 or 8 years old as undauntedly performing
their parts as the eldest amongst them.

Abigail confessed that, now having often attended plays, the shock of
seeing immodest dancers had worn off, leaving beauty in its place.

Shall I speak a Truth and say that repeatedly seeing these Dances
has worn of that disgust which I first felt, and that I see them now
with pleasure. The art of dancing is carried to the highest degree of
perfection that it is capable of; at the opera . . . And O! the Musick
vocal and instrumental, it has a soft persuasive power and a dying
dying Sound. Conceive a highly decorated building filled with
Youth, Beauty, Grace, ease, clad in all the most pleasing and various
ornaments of Dress which fancy can form; these objects. . . . Singing
like Cherubs to the best tuned instruments most skilfully handled,
the softest tenderest Strains, every attitude corresponding with the
musick, full of the God or Goddess whom they celebrate, the female
voices accompanied by an equal number of Adonises.[16]

In contrast, Abigail expressed little fascination with French royalty
who attended shows: "Dukes and Duchesses, Lords and Ladies, bedi-
zened with pomp, and stuck over with titles, are but mere flesh and
Blood, like their fellow worms, and sometimes rather frailer."[17]

French operas and royalty aside, after a few months of social isolation
which stemmed from not being able to speak French, Abigail decided to
concentrate on more important personal matters. Chief among those was
her two sons, Charley and Tommy, at Reverend John Shaw's school in

Haverhill, Massachusetts. Elizabeth Shaw sent Abigail an update on the boys. In the late eighteenth century being a gentleman also meant dancing well.[18] The report on that subject from her sister Betsy most likely made Abigail very proud: "Your Children are still in fine Health, they have been two Quarters to dancing School, and they both dance excellently, but Mr. Charles exquisitely. You know what an Ear he has for Musick, and that has been of Great advantage to him in his movements. He is graceful in all his motions, and attitudes, he, as if his Profile had been faithful to the maternal charge, has held up his head much better than formerly."[19] However, Abigail had been uneasy since Elizabeth's first letter telling her that the Shaws had also taken in sixteen-year-old Nancy Hazen, daughter of the late Captain John Hazen of Haverhill and "adopted daughter" (niece) of General Moses Hazen. After going on and on about Nancy's beauty and intelligence, and therefore a possible attraction to fourteen-year-old Charles, Elizabeth comforted Abigail. "I know a *Mother's* thoughts fly quick. But at present she need not have a fear. Master Charles is yet a School Boy, and Miss Nancy considers him as such, and their behaviour to each other is polite and attentive—Just as I would have it."[20]

Abigail thankfully answered her sister: "How justly did you describe my Ideas; when you said 'a parents thoughts flew quick.'. . . The age of the Young Lady relieved me from some anxiety, especially as I have since heard that she has much older admirers. Charles's disposition, and sensibility will render him more liable to female attachments."[21]

Abigail's information from home also contained some sorrowful news. Her wayward brother afflicted with alcoholism, William Smith, Jr., was sinking into worsening health. His wife, Catharine "Kitty" Louisa Salmon Smith, was doing the best she could raising their six children alone. Kitty wrote Abigail that she tried very hard to smile and keep up a brave face for the children: "I have lived upon hope for many years past. I set and please myself with illusions, with dreams. I cultivate all in my power a Chearful disposition. Tis a duty I owe my Children for how could I otherwise inspire them with a chearful gratitude to him whose sentence governs eternity and whose goodness is over all his Creatures, were they to see anxiety painted on my brows."[22]

Kitty poured her heart out to Abigail about her husband and how much she could help him if he would just come back: "Mr. S[mit]h has not been in this part of the Country for almost two years. I seldom hear from him and when I do the intelegence is not what I could wish. Poor unhappy man! It is yet in his power to add much to the happiness of his famely, and ensure to himself a comfortable evening of Life."[23]

If Abigail was discouraged from visiting other French women because she wasn't fluent in French, that hesitation didn't apply to hosting dinner parties which the Adamses were expected to hold. That duty was required as being one of the wifely obligations to John of international courtesy and diplomacy. But it was getting more difficult to host those events—of which the hosts were expected to bear the costs. The Congress of the Confederation[24] had just recently cut the annual expense amount for foreign ministers by 18 percent, from $11,000 to $9,000. It left a very small amount to entertain dignitaries when compared to the working budgets of most other ministers. Yet it was expected that each foreign minister would accommodate other delegations with lavish parties and food.

Abigail squeezed every franc and livre (French currencies) out of the household budget to plan and execute parties which would still look ostentatious but would not shatter their budget. The guest lists included many American and French celebrities of the time. One such guest was at a December 1784 gala at the Adams residence: Captain John Paul Jones.

Captain Jones had become an American hero and somewhat of a dashing, romantic figure during the Revolutionary War. His daring exploits against British warships and merchant ships became extremely popular reading in the United States. In 1780 King Louis XVI even bestowed upon him the title of "Chevalier."[25] Commanding his vessels, the USS *Ranger* and USS *Bonhomme Richard,* Jones had been the essence of chivalry in battle. Many American women had preconceived ideas of what Jones must have looked like, including Abigail. But when introduced to him in 1784, she was very much taken back, as she described to her niece: "Chevalier Jones you have heard much of. He is a most uncommon Character. I dare Say you would be as much dissapointed in him as I was. From the intrepid Character he justly Supported in the American Navy, I expected to have seen a Rough Stout warlike Roman." But instead, Abigail expressed complete surprise when meeting Captain Jones:

Instead of that, I should sooner think of wraping him up in cotton wool and putting him into my pocket, than sending him to contend with Cannon Ball. He is small of stature, well proportioned, soft in his Speach easy in his address polite in his manners, vastly civil, understands all the Etiquette of a Ladys Toilite as perfectly as he does the Masts Sails and rigging of a Ship. Under all this appearence of softness he is Bold enterprizing ambitious and active. He has been here often, and dined with us several times. He is said to be a Man of Gallantry and a favorite amongst the French Ladies: whom he is frequently commending for the neatness of their persons their easy manners and their taste in dress. He knows how often the Ladies use the Baths, what coulour best suits a Ladys complextion, what Cosmecticks are most favourable to the skin.[26]

Captain Jones and John Adams had met on May 13, 1779, while John was stranded in Lorient, France, trying to book passage back to America. John noted in his diary on that day of his use of Abigail's science of physiognomy (being able to judge a person's inner self by examining facial features), in this case, of Captain Jones: "Excentricities, and Irregularities are to be expected from him—they are in his Character, they are visible in his Eyes. His Voice is soft and still and small, his Eye has keenness, and Wildness and Softness in it."[27]

Abigail's loneliness caused by the absence of female friends in France was eased in spring 1785. Abigail bought a bird whose "melodious Notes"[28] needed no translation. The bird would serve as a pet and a friend to her as she explained to Mary: "I have bought a little Bird lately, and I realy think I feel more attached to that, than to any object out of my own family animate, or inanimate. Yet I do not consider myself in the predicament of a poor fellow who not having a house, in which to put his Head, took up his abode in the stable of a Gentleman; but tho so very poor he kept a Dog, with whom he daily divided the small portion of food which he earnd. Upon being ask'd why when he found it so difficult to live himself, he still kept a Dog, What Says the poor fellow part with my Dog! Why who should I have to Love me then? You can never, the language of it."[29]

Abigail was a dog and songbird lover for her adult life. The Adamses, like all farmers, employed freelance cats to patrol the farm keeping the rodent population in check. But there's no record of Abigail ever having an indoor cat as a pet in America. However, in Auteuil, she cautiously entertained the idea of getting a cat as was so widely done in France: "Tell Lucy I would give a great deal for one of her Cats. I have absolutely had an inclination to buy me some little Images according to the mode of this country that I might have some little creatures to amuse myself with, not that I have turnd worshiper of those things, neither."[30] There is no evidence that Abigail took on the task of adopting a cat in France.

Abigail had met many of the primary characters of the Revolutionary War. But one person she had never had the opportunity to meet until they were introduced in France was Thomas Jefferson. Jefferson, who in 1784 was a Virginia delegate to Congress, had been selected to go to Paris to take a third post as a foreign envoy with John Adams and Benjamin Franklin. Together the three Founders were America's "Ministers Plenipotentiary for Negotiating Treaties of Amity and Commerce," charged with negotiating treaties with Great Britain and nineteen other countries, kingdoms, and territories. As soon as Jefferson arrived in Paris in August 1784, Abigail, John, and Thomas became very close friends. It was a time in all their lives that each would look fondly upon in later years.

Weekends were filled with visiting, eating, drinking, touring, and talking. On Sunday, September 19, 1784, the Adamses, including Nabby, accompanied Jefferson to the Château des Tuileries gardens. They witnessed the scientific marvel of a manned hot air balloon flight. Nabby captured the moment in her journal, "September 19th. To-day we went to see the balloon; it was to ascend from the garden of the Tuilleries; we had tickets at a crown a person to go in. . . . There were eight or ten thousand persons present."[31]

Thomas Jefferson had lost his wife in September 1782, and some of his children had died early as well. Abigail was aware of those losses. Having experienced herself early deaths of children, it seemed to draw her closer to Jefferson. Though Jefferson was very shy around others, he came out of his shyness when talking to the Adamses. Abigail loved Jefferson's intelligence and soft manner of speaking. Most of all she loved the fact that Thomas and John got together so well: "he is one of the choice ones of the Earth."[32]

That same month, September 1784, Abigail overruled a request John had made to Cotton Tufts to purchase Mr. Vesey's property in Braintree, along with two other parcels. Again, in April 1785 John had sent another letter to Tufts acknowledging two of the three purchases that John had requested: "I am glad you purchased the Pasture and Marsh."[33] But John added a second request for Tufts to buy the Vesey house: "You may draw upon me, to the amount of Three hundred Pounds when you please, and also to pay for Veseys Place if he will sell it reasonably."[34]

In a notable move, John showed Abigail his letter for Tufts which contained his request to buy the Vesey house. Abigail must have shut down the idea and John apparently agreed with his wife's opinion. Many men, out of wounded pride, might have rewritten the letter to not look weak or emasculated.[35] Remarkably, John did not. He simply added a new paragraph of different instructions at the bottom of the page, "Shewing what I had written to Madam she has made me sick of purchasing Veseys Place. Instead of that therefore you may draw upon me, for two hundred Pounds at as good an Exchange as you can obtain and lay it out in such Notes as you judge most for my Interest."[36]

Just two days later, Abigail wrote her own letter to Tufts containing two intriguing statements: "By my son I have sent you 50 pounds Lawfull Money, part of which is money which I brought with me, but not passing neither here or in England I thought it best to return it, to America. With this money which I call mine I wish you to purchase the most advantageous Bills and keep them by themselves. If hereafter I should be able to add to it, I may establish a little fund for my pensioners."[37]

Abigail's phrase "With this money which I call mine" is interesting because "the common-law doctrine of coverture prevented married women like herself from owning personal property."[38] But Abigail had no problem with privately disregarding that law or at least not going to extremes to hide the fact that she did own items.

Second, there was a problem with whom she was establishing a fund for. With her phrase "my pensioners," Abigail was taking her own money which she could not legally own—in this case £50 in Massachusetts currency—and was setting up a fund for poor women she knew and some of her female relatives. Those people were discovered only in Abigail's last will, with the key fact that all her female pensioners mentioned in the will would not legally be able to own the money they were bequeathed. For her whole adult life, Abigail believed in aiding her less fortunate relatives and friends—all female—despite the antiquated laws she lived under.

The letter from Paris which contained these instructions for Abigail's "pensioners" and the £50 to Cotton Tufts was to be hand-carried to Tufts by son John Quincy. John Quincy was going back to Massachusetts and preparing to take the Harvard entrance test. He would take a room and study at his aunt Elizabeth Shaw's house and her husband's academy in Haverhill.

It had been rumored both in America and in France that John Adams would be the first American minister to the defeated Great Britain. John did nothing to squash those rumors and he even spread them. The ambassador post to Britain was what John had desired for a long time, yet no official confirmation had ever been sent to him in Paris. But on April 26, 1785, Abigail told her Uncle Tufts, "Mr. Jefferson came in from

Paris and informd us that the March packet had arrived and that he had received some Letters, one of which from Mr. [Elbridge] Gerry informd acquainted him that Congress had appointed Mr. Adams Minister to London."[39] It was true. On May 2, John received his congressional appointment as the United States Minister to the United Kingdom, the Court of St. James's.

Abigail began the methodical directions to the staff for packing up the Adamses' residence. John had wanted to first travel to The Hague to officially resign his ministry position to the Netherlands. But Congress wanted John to assume his duties in London by King George III's birthday on June 4. So, plans were switched to allow for the immediate trip to Great Britain. The nine months of living in Paris left Abigail with mixed emotions about her staff. She expressed her real emotions for what she would miss the most: "I shall have some regret I assure you in quitting Auteuil. . . . the Song of the Nightingale too regales me as I walk under the trees whose thick branches intwin'd, form a shade which secures you from the rays of the Sun. I shall mourn my garden more than any other object which I leave. . . . The fish pond and the fountain is just put in order, the trees are in blossom, and the flowers are comeing on in succession. The forest Trees are new clad in Green, several beautifull rows of which form arched bowers, at the bottom of our Garden, the tops being cut, so that they look like one continued plain."[40]

On May 20, 1785, the Adamses' carriages were all packed. As was custom for welcoming and saying goodbye to the manor hosts, the servants gathered outside the front door in two neat lines. Abigail noted there was not a dry eye to be seen anywhere: "At leaving Auteuil our domesticks surrounded our Carriage and in tears took leave of us, which gave us that painfull kind of pleasure, which arises from a consciousness, that the good will of our dependants is not misplaced."[41]

Abigail requested that the final passenger be loaded into the carriage. It was her songbird. However, the bird went into a panic fluttering inside its cage so much that Abigail decided not to stress the poor bird like that. She sadly bestowed her bird on the spot to her chambermaid, but there was a happy addition to the story. From London, Abigail wrote to her dear friend back in Paris, Thomas Jefferson: "My little Bird I was obliged, after taking it into the Carriage to resign to my Parissian Chamber Maid, or the poor thing would have flutterd itself to death. I mourn'd its loss, but its place was happily supplied by a present of two others which were given me on Board the Dover pacquet, by a young

Gentleman whom we had received on Board with us, and who being excessively sick I admitted into the Cabin, in gratitude for which he insisted upon my accepting a pair of his Birds. As they had been used to travelling, I brought them here in safety, for which they hourly repay me by their melodious Notes."[42]

By May 28, 1785, the tranquility of Auteuil seemed a distant lifetime ago. The Adamses had arrived in London amidst great hustle and bustle. The excitement was over three events that were happening at the same time. The birthday celebration of King George III, the "Sitting"[43] of Parliament, and a Westminster Abbey performance on June 8 of Handel's stirring oratorio *Messiah*. This combined commotion gave Abigail a headache: "I had lived so quietly in that Calm retreat, that the Noise and bustle of this proud city almost turnd my Brain for the first two or three Days."[44] The commotion also resulted in a shortage of available rooms to rent anywhere in London. The Adamses tried to book rooms in Osbourne's Hotel in the Adelphi Buildings in the Strand[45] when they first arrived, but it was full. They were able to temporarily settle in the Bath Hotel in Piccadilly. Finally on June 9, after finding a few good house leads, Abigail wrote, "none realy fit to occupy under 240 £. 250, besides the taxes, which are serious matters here. At last I found one in Grovenor Square which we have engaged."[46]

Previously Abigail had been happy having her own writing nook as she had in Auteuil, and in Boston at her uncle's house during the smallpox epidemic. Now she remarked to John Quincy that in London, she would also be enjoying, "my own little writing room below stairs."[47] John signed a twenty-one-month lease for the house which Abigail had located on the northeast corner of Grosvenor Square. It also became the first American embassy and legation. Abigail was delighted with their townhouse and its location, but was unimpressed with at least one neighbor and cleverly wrote of it: "If I could feel myself elated by my vicinity to Nobility I might boast the greatest share of it, of my square in London, but I am too much of a republican to be charmd with titles alone. We have not taken a side with Lord North but are still opposite to him."[48]

While John was in a conference with Lord George Gordon on June 8, Abigail took it upon herself to go alone, a habit she picked up in Paris, to the production of Handel's *Messiah* at Westminster Abbey. She was thunderstruck with the spectacle. She wrote to Thomas Jefferson of how much she loved it . . . except for the woman sitting behind her, who never stopped talking: "I went last week to hear the Musick in Westminster Abbey. The Messiah was performd, it was Sublime beyond description. I most sincerely wisht for your presence as your favorite passion would have received the highest gratification. I should have sometimes fancied myself amongst a higher order of Beings; if it had not been for a very troublesome female, who was unfortunately seated behind me; and . . . not a person enterd but what she knew and had some observation to make upon their dress or person which she utterd so loud as to disturb every person who sat near her."[49]

Protocol called for John to be presented to King George III upon his arrival in a private audience as the new American ambassador to Great Britain. One week later in a second ceremony, John would be presented separately to Queen Charlotte. A couple weeks after that, a third presentation would be called for when Abigail, John, and Nabby would be presented to both Queen Charlotte and King George III in a crowded reception called a "Levee."

Abigail was to be less than impressed with the king and queen of England.

Chapter Eighteen

"The Tory Venom Has Begun to Spit"

1785–1786

J *ohn's initial reaction* to his appointment as the first American ambassador to Great Britain was excitement. The honor was confirmation that his life of selfless dedication to the cause of Liberty was finally being recognized.

Soon, however, John discovered from his congressional friend Elbridge Gerry that he hadn't been Congress's first choice as British ambassador. In fact, far from it. John was offended and hurt. Criticism had been raised on the floor of Congress that John, when confronted, could be combative, petty, and vain. Ironically confirming those traits, John drafted an angry response to his congressional critics in a long, contentious letter which contained phrases such as "These Criticisms Smell as rank as the Ripeness of a Rabits tail."[1] It's probable that had Abigail proofread the letter, as John often had her do, she would have advised him not to send it. It indeed was never sent.

However, John had undeniably been appointed to a very important post. Almost immediately he started meeting with the Crown advisors,[2] who outlined the diplomatic protocol that John would be expected to know and follow when presented to King George III and the royal family. Subtly John was also advised to include a certain degree of flattery when speaking to the king. Phony adulation wasn't in John's makeup. Nevertheless, he carefully made note of the respectful words that he would say. He memorized the speech and practiced it with Abigail as his audience. He also practiced the very specific bows that he was required to do when approaching and leaving the presence of the king. The whole spectacle was far from what John had really wanted to do: "my first Thought and Inclination had been to deliver my Credentials Silently and retire."[3]

What was unknown was how His Majesty would treat John Adams, a former subject, when they would first meet. As a signer of the Declaration of Independence, indeed he was a framer of that controversial document and longtime rebel leader, John was about to discover his standing with the British sovereign. Abigail did not accompany John on the first meeting, but would later be the first person to hear all about it.

Back at the townhouse, John excitedly and repeatedly told Abigail of each moment in the encounter. Within a week afterwards the biased British press howled with headlines as, "An Ambassador from America!—Good Heavens, what a sound!"[4]

That was one presentation down and a few more to go. "There is a Train of other Ceremonies to go through, in Presentations to the Queen and Visits to and from Ministers and Ambassadors which will take up much time."[5] However that's when John and the Marquis of Carmarthen realized an oversight in their preparation. John had not been supplied a letter of credence from Congress to the queen. Carmarthen said that he'd smooth over the omission, so it didn't appear like a snub, which the Marquis did.

Abigail and Nabby's presentation to King George III, Queen Charlotte, and their royal children was set for 2:00 p.m. on June 24. The Marquis wrote to John on June 22 to describe the proper manner of Abigail's presentation to the Queen at her circle or "drawing room."[6]

However, in the two weeks which followed John's two presentations, the British press printed brutal editorials about John Adams. In a letter to Mary, Abigail seethed at the false reporting, something she would do throughout John's future presidency. "The Tory venom has begun to

spit itself forth in the publick papers as I expected. . . . The News Liars
know nothing of the Matter, they represent it just to answer their purpose."[7] Although false, the June 10 edition of the *Daily Universal Register*
detailed the "cool reception of the American Ambassador."[8] The June
13 issue of the *Morning Post and Daily Advertiser* proclaimed that Mr.
Adams was so tongue-tied when greeting the king that he couldn't "pro-
nounce the compliment prescribed by etiquette."[9]

June 24, 1785, the day of royal introductions had finally arrived. Abigail wrote to her sister, Mary, of the exhaustingly long day of preparation
and royal presentations. She went on at lengths describing the event
which a few short years before would have seemed like a dream: the
Adamses meeting British royalty with mutual respect! Abigail described
in tantalizing detail such things as what she wore to the royal reception,
the "small talk"[10] from King George III, Queen Charlotte, their royal
princesses, Abigail's perception of everybody, and the wastefulness of elegant clothing: "The ceremony of presentation here is considerd as indispensable. One is obliged here to attend the circles of the Queen which
are held in Summer once a fortnight, but once a week the rest of the
year, and what renders it exceedingly expensive is, that you cannot go
twice the same Season in the same dress, and a Court dress you cannot
make use any where else." She navigated these expectations as best she
could: "I directed my Mantua Maker to let my dress be elegant but plain
as I could possibly appear with Decency." When describing her clothing
worn, Abigail called the complete outfit her "rigging,"[11] as if it were
ropes on a ship.

Once arrived at St. James's Palace,[12] Abigail described meeting the
king and queen. In general, during the promenades of the British upper
classes and royalty, Abigail and John had been treated politely, but no
more than that: "The Queen was evidently embarrased when I was presented to her. I had dissagreeable feelings too."[13] However, at least Abigail now had a personal measuring stick to confirm that the British press
was lying. "Scarcly a paper excapes without some scurrility. We bear it
with silent Contempt, having met a polite reception from the Court."[14]
Otherwise, Abigail wrote that she "found the Court like the rest of
Mankind, mere Men and Women, and not of the most personable kind
neither."[15] Her views of the royal family were particularly harsh, as she
told her sister in confidence: "They are pretty rather than Beautifull,
well shaped with fair complexions and a tincture of the kings countanance. The two sisters look much alike. . . . The Queen . . . is not well
shaped or handsome. As [to] the Ladies of the Court, Rank and title

may compensate for want of personal Charms, but they are in general very plain ill shaped and ugly, but dont you tell any body that I say so."[16]

A few days later, when the thrill of the drawing room reception had passed, Abigail realized she had looked ridiculous: "I could not help reflecting with myself during the ceremony, what a fool do I look like to be thus accutored and stand here for 4 hours together, only for to be spoken too, by 'royalty.'"[17] Abigail had always ridiculed the expense involved with having to wear elegant dresses only once to the numerous royal receptions, writing: "It is very tiresome however and one pays dear for the smiles of Royalty."[18]

The Queen's drawing room gathering occurred often and Abigail attended the September event. Being over the nervous pageantry which accompanied Abigail during the first gathering, she now critically noticed attendees and their quirkiness. It all made for some choice comments in a letter to her niece, Lucy Cranch: "But I cannot close without describing to you Lady North and her daughter. She is as large as Captain Clarks wife and much such a made woman, with a much fuller face, of the coulour and complexion of mrs cook who formerly lived with your uncle Palmer, and looks as if Porter and Beaf stood no chance before her. Add to this, that it is coverd with large red pimples over which to help the natural redness, a coat of Rouge is spread, and to assist her shape, she was drest in white sattin trimd with Scarlet ribbon. Miss North is not so large nor quite So red, but a very small Eye with the most impudent face you can possibly form an Idea of."[19]

To Mary, Abigail continued her brutally honest remarks about the Royal Family and gathered royalty: "I attended the Drawing room last week upon the Aniversary of the Coronation of their Majesties. The Company were very Brilliant, and her Majesty was stiff with Diamonds. The three eldest Princesses and the Prince of Wales[20] were present. His Highness [King George III] lookt much better than when I saw him before. He is a stout well made Man, and would look very well; if he had not sacrificed so much to Bacchus. The Princess Elizabeth I never saw before, she is about 15, a short clumsy Miss and would not be thought Handsome if she was not a Princess. The whole family have one complexion; and all inclined to corpulent. . . . Not with standing the English boast so much of their Beauties, I do not think they have really so much of it. . . . Amongst the most celebrated of their Beauties stands the Dutchess of Devonshire, who is Masculine in her appearence. Lady Salsbury is small and geenteel, but her complexion is bad."[21]

September 1785 brought with it the changing autumn leaf colors in London. However, to Abigail, fall usually meant coming down with a seasonal "disorder" as she reminded Mary: "I had about a week since a small attack of the Fall disorder which I hoped I had got the better of. The next seizure was such a swiming in my Head when I laid down in the Bed, as to throw me almost into convulsions. It finally produced a violent puking which relieved me of that, tho I cannot say I feel well. You know I am accustomed to ill turns in the Fall."[22]

In mid-August, Nabby had asked for a mother-daughter talk about a certain "Man of Honour," meaning Royall Tyler. By mid-1785 even Nabby had become aware of Tyler's dishonesty and unfaithfulness toward her. The reference was picked up by Abigail and quickly acted upon: "I thought this the very time to speak. I said if she was conscious of any want of honour on the part of the Gentleman, I and every Friend she had in the world, would rejoice if she could liberate herself."[23] During their talk, as Abigail recounted to Mary, what Nabby had finally decided on her own, "That no state of mind is so painfull as that which admits, of fear, suspicion, doubt, dread and apprehension. 'I have too long' says she 'known them all—and I am determined to know them no longer.'"[24]

One of the reasons the Adamses had taken Nabby to Europe and away from Royall Tyler was to let their overheated attachment simmer down. A good test of the relationship would be, they reasoned, how it fared when the pair were separated. Once in Europe, Nabby still considered herself honor bound to marry Tyler and wrote him many letters. Abigail also frequently wrote to her possible future son-in-law. But Tyler wrote no letters in return. He later claimed all his letters were lost or sunk en route to Nabby.

Much to Abigail's relief, Nabby eventually sent Royall Tyler this breakup letter: "Sir, Herewith you receive your letters and miniature with my desire that you would return mine to my Uncle Cranch, and my hopes that you are well satisfied with the affair as is. A. A."[25]

That was not the end of it, however. It seems that Tyler had moved to Boston and into a boardinghouse run by General Joseph Palmer along with his wife and daughter, Mary Palmer, whom Tyler ended up marrying. But to save face, Tyler started a gossip campaign about the breakup with Nabby. First, he denied the breakup had ever happened. Then he said the whole Adams clan was involved in a conspiracy against him. He denied his earlier admissions of wasting a fortune and not studying. But to no avail; the Tyler-Adams courtship was over, and Tyler was living with the social black eye. One year later, Abigail finished off that episode in her life by writing, "I wish the Gentleman well. He has good qualities, indeed he has, but he ever was his own Enemy."[26]

September 1785, after Nabby sent her breakup letter, brought continued mother-daughter time spent together. Abigail and Nabby frequently left their Grosvenor Square townhouse and explored London's fascinating world of show houses and music hall performances. In Piccadilly Circus, a Charing Cross theater boasted the world's only "learned pig." It had made its London debut early in 1785 and Abigail admitted it was "the Ton of London."[27] The pig fetched printed cards from the audiences and gave the impression it could solve arithmetic problems and could read in several languages. Another favorite venue of the two Adamses was Sadler's Wells playhouse, which headlined "dancing dogs, and the little Hare that Beats the Drum." To Lucy Quincy Tufts (Doctor Cotton Tufts' wife) Abigail recalled the spectacle:

The Tumbling and rope Dancing is worth seeing once or twice, because it gives you an Idea of what skill agility and dexterity the Humane frame is capable of, and of which no person can form an Idea without having seen it. The House where these wonderfull feats are exhibited is calld Sadlers Wells and is accomodated with Boxes and a Stage in the manner of a play House. Dancers mount drest very neat with a Jocky and feathers and a silk Jacket and Breaches, the Jacket very tight to the waist and a sash tied round the Jacket. He bows to the company; upon which a person who stands near him gives him a long pole made thick at each end. With this pole which serves to Balance him, he commences his dance to the Musick which he keeps time with. He will run backwards and forwards poise himself upon one foot, kneel jump across the rope, spring upon it again, and finally throws down the pole and jumps 6 foot into the air repeatedly, every time returning upon the rope with the same steadiness as if it was the floor, and with so much ease, that the spectator is ready to believe he can perform, the same himself.[28]

Once again, as in Paris, Abigail felt an uneasy embarrassment when watching females dance or perform acrobatic feats on a stage with what seemed very little modesty about the performers' dress: "All this is wonderfull for a Man, but what will you say, when I assure you I have seen a most Beautifull Girl perform the same feats! Both in Paris and England.

Why say you what could she do with her peticoats? It is true that she had a short silk skirt, but she was well clad under that, with draws, and so are all the female Dancers upon the stage, and there is even a law in France that no woman Shall dance upon the stage without them; But I can never look upon a woman in such situations, without conceiving all that adorns and Beautifies the female Character, delicacy modesty and diffidence, as wholy laid asside, and nothing of the woman but the Sex left."[29]

Nabby, in a letter to her brother John Quincy, included seeing a "Singing Duck" and described some indignant stage strife, "The Tumblers of Sadlers Wells, have made great objections that the Learned Pig, should be introduced upon the Stage and have I beleive left it."[30]

Abigail wrote the letter about stage shows to her aunt Lucy Quincy Tufts of Weymouth, wife of Doctor Cotton Tufts. Abigail had heard that her aunt was very ill and thought a letter describing the curious attractions of London would lift her spirits. Unfortunately, the letter did not make it into Aunt Lucy's hands before she died on October 30.

Abigail's passion for attending plays hit a bump in the road, however, on September 17, 1785. She had attended the Shakespeare play *Othello* in the Covent Garden theater in Drury Lane. The role of Desdemona was played by the internationally acclaimed stage actress Sarah Siddons, whom Abigail noticed was quite likely pregnant at the time. But that fact didn't offend Abigail's sense of propriety. It was the portrayal of Othello. Shakespeare's character is written as a black Moorish general of the Venetian army. The tragedy of the play is when Othello erroneously believes rumors of Desdemona, his loyal wife, taking a lover and Othello kills her. But it wasn't even that aspect of the tragic story that made Abigail uncomfortable in her seat. Abigail admitted in her letter to her sister, Elizabeth, "I lost much of the pleasure of the play, from the Sooty appearence of the Moor."[31]

What made Abigail uneasy was the aspect of the two characters of different races touching each other. "Perhaps it may be early prejudice, but I could not Seperate the affrican coulour from the man, nor prevent that disgust and horrour which filld my mind every time I saw him touch the Gentle Desdemona." Even though Abigail knew that the role of Othello was played by the brother of Sarah Siddons, John Philip Kemble—who was wearing heavy blackface stage make-up—she admitted, "Othello was represented blacker than any affrican. Whether it arises from the prejudices of Education or from a real natural antipathy I cannot determine, but my whole soul shuderd when ever I saw the sooty heretik More [Moor] touch the fair Desdemona."[32]

This excerpt disappoints fans of Abigail Adams. But it serves to demonstrate that even though she was a lifetime opponent of any form of slavery and was a vocal advocate of black assistance (such as Phoebe's generous living arrangements), she was honest about her innermost feelings. She was admittedly confused by her own "prejudice" against interracial relationships.

Throughout the summer months of 1785, Nabby had come to terms with her less-than-loving treatment by Royall Tyler. That relationship was now over. In contrast, it had become obvious to Abigail that Colonel William Smith, the secretary of the American legation in London and former staff officer to General Washington, had become lovestruck over Nabby. Social dictates of the day, however, prevented a male suitor from even being so forward as to ask the relationship status of the girl he was infatuated with. Without writing names in her letter to Uncle Tufts, Abigail brought him up-to-date about Tyler: "I own I cannot but feel for the situation of a Gentleman who has by his own folly and indiscretion lost all hopes of a connexion where he once lookd for it." However, she couldn't stop praising the prospective, unnamed new beau, Colonel William Stephens Smith:

> I think proper to acquaint you Sir in very explicit terms, that she is now addrest by a Gentleman of unexceptionable Character, both in publick and private Life. In the Army which he enterd at the commencment of the War, he distinguishd himself by his Bravery his intrepidity and his Humanity, of which he has the amplest testimony from General Sullivan and Washington. By the latter and by congress he was appointed to inspect the evacuation of Newyork, and afterwards received a comission of Secretary of Legation to this Court. He possess as high a sense of honour. . . . We have every reason to beleive that his Character will bear the strickest Scrutiny. Against this Gentleman we could have no objection.[33]

To her sister Mary, Abigail concentrated her praising of Colonel Smith in terms of his physical attributes and his sensibility: "he is tall Slender and a good figure, a complextion naturally dark, but made still more so, by seven or 8 years service in the Field, where he reaped laurels more durable than the tincture of a skin. He appears a Gentleman in every thought, word and action, domestick in his attachments, fond in his affections, quick as lightning in his feelings, but softned in an instant."[34]

In the right margin on the last page of the letter, Abigail wrote, "You will keep this letter much to yourself."[35]

Abigail's earlier uncomfortable interracial situation at Sadler's Wells did not stop her from attending other plays in London. In fact, Abigail wrote to her little sister, Elizabeth, "I saw Mrs Siddons a few Evenings ago, in Macbeth a play you recollect, full of horror." However, Abigail explained, the process of obtaining a ticket to see Sarah Siddons in London was very similar to getting any ticket in America, "to get a Box when she plays, as to get a place at Court, and they are usually obtain in the same Way. It would be very difficult to find the thing in this Country which money will not purchase, provided you can bribe high enough."[36]

With the spring of 1786 bursting forth in London, Abigail was concerned with her weight, accompanied by John's own growing girth. Her sense of humor shows again in her letter to Mary: "The Spring is advancing and I begin to walk so that I hope exercise will be of service to me. . . . Tis true I enjoy good Health, but am larger than both my sisters compounded. Mr. Adams too keeps pace with me, and if one Horse had to carry us, I should pity the poor Beast."[37]

Chapter Nineteen

"Ironing Is Very Bad for You"
1786–1787

Q ueen *Charlotte's* forty-second birthday and "Birth day Ball"[1] on February 9, 1786, was cause for much celebration by the British upper class. The king and queen would both be in attendance. For invited guests it involved many hours of negotiating crowds inside St. James's Palace. Abigail and Nabby were expected to be there, of course: "we were told it was essential that we should go to the Ball."[2] They ran into a traffic jam just trying to get to the celebration. The streets were lined with carriages and people. Nabby recorded that from "Piccadilly to the Pallace was so obstructed by Carriages full of People to look at the Ladies who might pass on their Way, that there was no such thing as getting through. So we went through st James park and found no difficulty."[3]

Once there, Abigail and Nabby mapped out a strategy to place themselves in a quick-exit location inside the rooms after meeting both monarchs. As they wedged themselves into the king's waiting room, they noticed a large cluster of well-wishers gathered around a Mohawk chief from the United States, Joseph Brant, clothed in his Indian dress "with that pretty plaything his Tommy Hawk in his hand."[4] He was in Great Britain to gain help from King George III and his government to stop American attacks on the Iroquois confederacy. "There was a feast made for him by, some Persons of distinction at Which the Company all were drunk, except himself."[5]

After being nearly "squeezed to death between the post of the door, and half a dozen great Hoops,"[6] Nabby and Abigail gained access into the king's drawing room. "We at last got into the room, and situated our-selvs, so that the King spoke to us very soon. He has askd me one question for these three Months. . . 'do you get out much in this weather.'"[7]

Finding a sneak-away spot in the queen's room was more difficult, they learned. The mass of people absorbed every inch of the floor; it took two hours just to find the queen. Eventually, however, they were able to greet her and to be seen. "We got home at five,"[8] but it was to be a long day and night culminating with the queen's birthday ball starting at 9:00 p.m., which demanded their presence as well. Nabby and Abigail ate and prepared for the ball that night.

Nabby narrated the spectacle of the royal ball in her letter to her brother, John Quincy. She noted that the Prince Regent, the future King George IV, arrived at the ball extremely drunk and made quite an entry: "A little before Nine the Prince came staggering in. . . . He chatted with the Ladies who were to dance. . . . At the 3d dance the Prince some how, I dont know how, had a fall, and the first that we saw was he Laed flat on his back."[9] Nabby, on the other hand, enjoyed the elegant evening and wrote, "There were many minuets danced, till I was quite tired."[10]

Although Abigail didn't dance, she had her moments to shine in British society. Any form of gambling for money back home in Braintree had been taboo for her given her Puritanical upbringing. But in London, she realized that to get along politically, "you cannot live with any Character or concequence unless you give in some measure into the Ton."[11] The evening of April 5, 1786, the Adamses were invited to a party at the Swedish Minister's residence. Abigail didn't condone gambling for money, "But I never play when I can possibly avoid it, for I have not conquerd the dissagreeable feeling of receiving money for play."[12]

Abigail, however, recounted of how she swept the table: "There were about 2 hundred persons present last evening, three large rooms full of card tables. I went with a determination not to play, but could not get of, so I was Set down to a table with three perfect Strangers, and the Lady who was against me started the Game at half a Guiney a peice. I told her I thought it full high, but I knew she designd to win, so I said no more, but expected to lose. It however happend otherways. I won four Games of her. it was the luck of the cards rather than skill, tho I have usually been fortunate as it is termd."[13]

There was one more curious trait that Abigail learned about the upper class of London which she passed along to sister Elizabeth in a letter: "persons who have no children substitute cats dogs and Birds in their stead."[14] Dogs and (song) birds were Abigail's favorite pets, as well. But cats? She didn't feel the feline connection.

The romantic looks deep into each other's eyes by Nabby and Colonel Smith were unmistakable. Abigail had taken steps to delay the nuptial announcement between Colonel Smith and her daughter until all lingering rumors about Nabby and Royall Tyler were put to rest. But the eager couple, especially Colonel Smith, couldn't wait any longer. Abigail accepted that they would marry regardless of parental approval, so Abigail gave in. She even passed along a humorous reflection of Nabby marrying a military man: "I believe a soldier is always more expeditious in his courtships than other Men, they know better how to Capture the citidal."[15]

The wedding date was set for Sunday, June 12,[16] 1786, at 8:00 p.m. It would take place not in an Anglican church, for the obvious reasons of a still-smoldering anger by the British. The vows were recited in the Adamses' townhouse in Grosvenor Square with only a small number of guests attending. John asked Jonathan Shipley, the Bishop of St. Asaph Diocese, to officiate the ceremony. During the American Revolution, Shipley was the only Anglican bishop to oppose the policies of King George III; he was, John wrote, "well known and respected as a Friend to America."[17]

Abigail was prone to sleeplessness if worrisome thoughts were on her mind late at night. At 4:00 a.m. the night following the wedding she wrote these words to Mary: "Any agitation of mind, either painfull or pleasureable always drives slumber from my Eyes. Such was my Situation last Night; when I gave my only daughter, and your Neice to the man of her choice. . . . In what a World do we live, and how Strange are the visisitudes? Who that had told your Neice two years ago, that an English Bishop should marry her, and that to a Gentleman whom she had then never seen; who of us would have credited it?"[18]

Abigail and Nabby were very close, and her marriage to Colonel Smith meant Abigail would be seeing Nabby less. Abigail wrote to Thomas Jefferson with a whimsical solution to her loneliness for a daughter. It involved one of her three sons and Patsy Jefferson, Thomas's daughter: "I suppose you must have heard the report respecting col Smith—that he has taken my daughter from me, a contrivance between him and the Bishop of St Asaph. It is true he tenderd me a Son as an equivilent and it was no bad offer, but I had three Sons before, and but one Daughter. . . . Now suppose Sir you should give me Miss Jefferson, at least till I return to America. I am for Strengt[hen]ing [the] federal Union. . . . Some future day, perhaps I might tender you a son in exchange for her. I am lonely in concequence of this, Theft I had almost said. I should think myself very happy to have miss Jefferson come and Spend the Summer and winter with me. Next Spring I hope to return to America."[19]

The newlywed couple lived with John and Abigail for a couple of weeks until they found a place for themselves. "Upon the first of this Month [July] they commenced House keepers in Wimpole Street."[20]

Her sister Mary Cranch wrote to Abigail in July 1786, updating her on her two daughters, Abigail's nieces Elizabeth ("Betsy") and Lucy. Between the two, Mary wrote that Lucy was the more scientific, if that interest had been open to girls during that time. "Betsy is in Boston very attentive to her Harpsicord and is in better health than I have known her for many years. Lucy is at home affording her mama all the assistance she is able too, and if her Soul is not tuned to Harmony it is to Science. Had she been a Boy she would have been a Mathamatition."[21] Perhaps it ran in the family. Like Abigail, Mary Smith Cranch was now also advocating for the educational and political equality of women. Richard Cranch, Mary's husband, was by this time a representative of the Massachusetts General Court and would go on to hold many state legislative posts, although they didn't pay much. Mary would use her husband as a sounding board on issues in the same way Abigail used John. Mary wrote: "Ask no excuse my dear Sister for writing Politicks. . . . Let no one say that the Ladies are of no importance in the affairs of the nation. . . . We do not want spirit. We only want to have it properly directed."[22]

The Fourth of July certainly was not celebrated in Great Britain. On that day in 1786, Abigail, still in London, started another letter to Mary. In it she hinted that, after so many years of wishing she could be in Europe with John, Abigail was beginning to miss being back home: "You will have a Buisy time this Month with all the Lads about you. I seem as if I was living here to no purpose, I ought to be at home looking after my Boys."[23]

Very homesick, Abigail laid out the comparison examples between Massachusetts and London to her niece Elizabeth: "Every thing [in Massachusetts] is upon a Grandeur scale, our Summers heats and Winters colds, form a contrast of great Beauty. Nature arising from a temporary death, and bursting into Life with a sudden vegatation yealding a delicious fragrance and verdure which exhilirates the spirits and exalts the imagination, much more than the gradual and slow advance of Spring in the more temperate climates, and where the whole summer has not heat sufficient to sweeten the fruit, as is the case of this, climate. Even our Storms and tempests our thunder and lightning, are horibly Grand. Here nothing appears to leap the Bounds of Mediocrity. Nothing ferocious but Man."[24]

John Quincy had passed his Harvard entrance test in March 1786. In fact, he was so advanced that he would be starting off at Harvard as a junior. Charles would be entering Harvard as a freshman and young Thomas was applying for admission.

Congress had not filled John's position as United States Minister to the Netherlands since he was first appointed in 1782. But now John, still as the sole minister, had to race to The Hague to sign a trade agreement ratification with Prussia. Thomas Jefferson and John had both produced the treaty in July 1785, but the ratification didn't come until May 1786. It was near the treaty's expiration date. Jefferson said he couldn't go. John decided to take Abigail with him.

After returning from her five-week long trip to Holland, Abigail painted a vivid picture for her sister Mary of that mysterious flat land of canals and dikes. First, Abigail was annoyed at how little credit Holland was getting for their invaluable help to the United States throughout "the American War." Abigail observed a feeling of "Holland [being] totally neglected,"[25] everywhere in Europe. But "The Spirit of Liberty appears, to be all alive in them."[26] The Dutch themselves were an admirable people, she witnessed: "They appear to be a well fed, well Cloathed contented happy people, very few objects of wretchedness present themselves to your view. . . . The civil government or police of that Country must be well Regulated, since rapine Murder nor Robery are but very seldom found amongst them."[27] Abigail visited the Dutch stock exchange, the Amsterdam Exchange or "Bourse." While she was sitting up in the "Chamber above the exchange," she noted that, "the Buz from below was like the Swarming of Bees."[28]

"The most important places" Abigail visited "were Roterdam, Delpt the Hague Leyden Harlem Amsterdam and utrech."[29] Abigail had to single out Leiden as "the cleanest City I ever saw, the streets are wide, the Houses brick, all neat even to the meanest building. The River Rhine runs through the City."[30] John and Abigail were invited to dine one day with "Sir James Harris's the British Minister at that Court." His twenty-four-year-old wife, Lady Harris, didn't impress Abigail. Although she "may be ranked with the first of English Beauties," Abigail wrote, "her Ladyship has no dignity in her manners" and "Seems of the good humourd gigling class."[31] When the Adamses were leaving Holland, they were given a gift of many pounds of chocolate. Abigail, back in London, was writing her letter to Mary on September 12, and she noted, "Mr Adams was just mourning over his last pound."[32]

Abigail had scarcely been back in London when she received an alarming letter from Mary Cranch. Mary had been occasionally updating Abigail on local gossip, which Abigail humorously called "domestick intelligence."[33] The news involved Royall Tyler's claims that he had been treated cruelly by Nabby and the whole Adams family. Tyler, who had since moved from Weymouth to Boston, had been boarding in the home of General Joseph Palmer (Richard Cranch's brother-in-law), his wife, Elizabeth Hunt Palmer, and their young daughter, Mary Palmer.

But that wasn't the end of the story. Tyler had converted at least one family over to his side of the story. It was the family of Tyler's own landlords and eventually his in-laws, the Palmers. In fact, Elizabeth Palmer and Mary Cranch had gotten into an argument in Boston and reportedly some unkind words were said by Elizabeth about Abigail, Nabby, and Colonel Smith, as detailed in a letter to Abigail.

However, Elizabeth Palmer spoke too soon. In this sordid tale, it was disclosed that Elizabeth, Royall Tyler's mother-in-law, was pregnant with Royall's baby! Richard Palmer, Elizabeth's husband, refused to say anything about the usual gestation time of nine months which would mean he was not the father. Mary also somehow had come into possession of a letter written by Elizabeth to Tyler. Mary shared some of the contents with Abigail: "What should you think if you should pick up a Letter from a married Lady, whose Husband is absent, directed to a gentleman, with such sentences as these in it, 'I am distress'd, distress'd by many causes, what can we do. I know you would help me if you could. Come to me immediately.'"[34]

When Elizabeth's baby was born, Mary wrote some of the details to Abigail in a sarcastic vein:

We live in an age of discovery. One of our acquaintance has discover'd that a full grown, fine child may be produc'd in less than
five months as well as in nine. . . . You may laugh: but it is true.
The Ladys Husband is so well satisfied of it that he does not seem
to have the least suspicion of its being otherways, but how can it
be? for he left this part of the country the beginning of september
last, and did not return till the Sixth of April, and his wife brought
him this fine Girl the first day of the present Month [September].
Now the only difficulty Seems to be, whether it is the product of a
year, or twenty weeks. . . . The child is perfect large and Strong. I
have seen it my sister: it was better than a week old tis true, but a
finer Baby I never Saw. . . . It was a matter of So much Speculatin
that I was determin'd to see it. I went with trembling Steps, and
could not tell whether I should have courage enough to see it till I
had Knock'd at the Door. I was ask'd to walk up, by, and was follow'd
by her Husband. The Lady was seting by the side of the Bed suckling
her Infant and not far from her [Richard Palmer] with one sliper off,
and one foot just step'd into the other. I had not seen him since last
May. He look'd, I cannot tell you how. He did not rise from his seat,
prehaps he could not. I spoke to him and he answer'd me, but hob-
ble'd off as quick as he could without saying any thing more to me.
There appear'd the most perfect harmony between all three.[35]

In 1794, Royall Tyler and his wife Mary Palmer Tyler moved to Vermont. The baby named Sophia Palmer, who was born to Mary's mother,
was quietly moved up to Vermont in 1798 to live with the Tylers.

Ironically Royall Tyler ended up making a much better name for himself during his later life accomplishments than Nabby's husband,
Colonel William Stephens Smith.[36] Abigail probably quietly mulled
over that uncomfortable thought for a long time.

And yet more troubling news sent by Mary made its way across the
Atlantic Ocean and into a letter received by Abigail. It was about
Phoebe, the freed slave of Abigail's father from three years before. Before
leaving for Europe, Abigail had given Phoebe and Phoebe's husband,
William Abdee, permission to live in their house. It was a mutually
beneficial arrangement—the recently married Abdee couple would have
a secure roof over their heads, and Abigail would have people she knew
living inside the house, protecting it from theft and from the elements.

But because firewood was expensive, Phoebe blocked off certain rooms
in the house so as not to heat them. The inevitable cold, mold, and mois-

ture crept into those unused rooms and Mary reported to Abigail that the wallpaper was peeling. But concerning Mary most of all was that the Abdees were allowing "Stragling Negros lodging and staying in the House sometimes three or four days together. I [Mary] have forbid her doing it, and the Doctor [Doctor Cotton Tufts] did so also, but there have been poor objects who have work'd upon her compassion sometimes."[37]

Royall Tyler (whom Mary calls "Mr T" in her letter) had also sent his pregnant servant to Abigail's house to find a rest spot; he had promised the Abdees firewood and food for taking her in. Mary continued narrating the encounter for Abigail: "Mr Ts negro who I told you was like to have a child, was put there (and wood and provision promiss'd if She would keep her). . . . She was not a good Girl, and I did not think, your things safe."[38] Mary told Tyler that Phoebe had been ordered by Abigail Adams not to take in strangers. Tyler's reply to Mary was, predictably, "keep her conceal'd." Mary confronted Tyler on the situation: "I talk to mr T about sending such creatures thire, for this was not the first he had sent. He deny'd it, but look'd guilty enough."[39] The situation of taking in stragglers would not end until Abigail and John returned home from Europe in June 1788.

For two weeks each October, Harvard celebrated its traditional fall vacation, and the dormitories were closed. But in fall 1786, the scheduled break was extended for a total of eight weeks into 1787 because of the severe snowstorm that struck the area and the fact that students had no firewood for their rooms. Students usually went back home for those traditional breaks. But John Quincy, Charles, and Thomas couldn't return home because the Abdees were housesitting in their parent's absence. They temporarily moved in with their aunt Mary Smith Cranch.

During that same October, Abigail had been very ill for three weeks as she returned from Holland. But back in London and fully recovered, Abigail shared the news of her sickness in a reply to Mary. However, she then expressed alarm that Mary, who was in "ill Health" as well, was reluctant to stop "washing and Ironing" for Mary's own Harvard student son, William, and her three Adams nephews.[40] "I fear the addition to your family cares is too fatiguing for you," Abigail answered. "I know your sisterly kindness leads you to exert yourself for the service of your Nephews, but the washing and Ironing for 3 Lads is too heavy a load for your family. . . . I insist that you Charge it to me, together with their

Board during the vacancy."[41] In a quote which would be very humorous to modern-day people, Abigail reminded Mary, "Ironing is very bad for you."[42]

Recently, John and Abigail had each pursued a different form of investing. Now the situation had changed. Abigail had yielded large profits out of importing European items through the blockades which she had easily sold. However, the peace treaty with Great Britain had dried up opportunities for selling scarce imported items. Instead, Abigail continued with her savvy investments of purchasing federal security bonds.

John, in contrast, had always determined that buying land was the prudent and safe investment. After all, land was a finite commodity and was something tangible. In 1787, however, land had also become a complicated commodity to own. A tax-collecting crisis was developing in the United States, as Abigail and John learned while in London, making land ownership a mixed investment because of the expensive land taxes the postwar states had levied upon homeowners. The tax crisis/revolt in Massachusetts was labeled Shays' Rebellion, named after Captain Daniel Shays, a former Continental Army officer. The defiant farmers had taken over the Massachusetts Supreme Court at Springfield, preventing any tax notices from going out.

Abigail condemned the rebellion's leaders to Jefferson in the strongest of words: "Ignorant, wrestless desperadoes, without conscience or principals, have led a deluded multitude to follow their standard, under pretence of grievances which have no existance but in their immaginations. . . . these mobish insurgents are for sapping the foundation, and distroying the whole fabrick at once."[43]

The next month Jefferson replied to Abigail, nursing a broken right wrist. The letter produced one of the most famous and controversial quotes by Jefferson, still recited by people without knowing the full context of its setting. As was his nature, Jefferson was couching Shays' Rebellion in the framework of positive republican political theory: "The spirit of resistance to government is so valuable on certain occasions, that I wish it to be always kept alive. It will often be exercised when wrong, but better so than not to be exercised at all. I like a little rebellion now and then. It is like a storm in the Atmosphere."[44]

Abigail was incensed at Jefferson's airy answer. Not only was rebellion impractical and dangerous in the early days of the fledgling country, but it also impacted the Adamses' income. Taxes could not be collected, which meant the interest on government bonds that Abigail held could not be paid even as the bond's face value was dropping.

Uncle Cotton Tufts, Abigail's financial advisor, quite likely advised Abigail to take the recent offer by the US government to exchange the near-worthless bonds for tracts of land in rural Maine (then part of Massachusetts). But like the modern investing mantra of "Buy the Dip," Abigail replied to Tufts that now would not be the time to sell; now would be the time to buy. She put in her "buy" order using her husband's name so that the transaction was legal: "We request you upon the receit of this Letter to purchase two hundred Guineys worth of congress Paper. We are told that it is sold at 2 and 6 pence pr pound. Do not be affraid, as the little he [John] has is in publick Securities, it is as safe in one kind as an other, and if one sinks all must Sink, which God forbid. . . . it will never be at a lower ebb than at present unless actual war takes place."[45]

There was one last important point in Abigail's January 24 letter to Cotton Tufts. Her awkwardly constructed last sentence, just above the closing salutation, read: "Will that House be to be sold do you imagine which he owns?"[46]

The "House" Abigail referred to was commonly called, "Borland's Place in Braintree"[47] or the "Vassall-Borland house." Both John and Abigail knew of the grand house and property close to their own "cottage" and had their eyes on it for some time. However, Abigail deemed that the property would be a just and fitting retirement abode to celebrate John's long public service life. It had been, according to the editors of the *Adams Papers*, "built by Leonard Vassall about 1730, and the garden and farm surrounding it on the old coast road from Boston to Plymouth. With the house enlarged and outbuildings added, but with the farm property greatly reduced, it is today the Adams National Historic Site, having been in the possession of the Adams family from 1787 to 1946 and usually referred to by the family itself as 'the Old House.'"[48]

The stately home, gardens, carriage house, and eighty-three acres of land had gone through a variety of owners, renters, leasers, and squatters since 1775 when John Borland died after falling off the roof, allowing it to become abandoned loyalist property. By 1783 when the war was nearly over, Mrs. Borland successfully reclaimed possession of the house and property and sold it to her son Leonard Vassall Borland. Borland then turned around and sold it to Abigail's young nemesis—Royall Tyler, who bought it "at a thousand pounds Lawfull Money."[49] He seemingly had bought it on credit with "but one object in view"[50]—that of marrying Nabby Adams. When that plan fell through, Tyler quit making payments and walked away. Abigail saw the golden opportunity and made an offer to buy the property. The purchase would called "Peace-field," John's name for the family generational estate and retirement habitat—but informally known as "the Old House." She successfully completed the buy "through Cotton Tufts, on 26 Sept. 1787, at a cost of £600."[51]

The year 1787 brought only increased frustration to John. He was posi-tioned in London primarily as the trade representative to Great Britain to guide the creation of a trade agreement with America. Yet John and his diplomatic mission as the first United States Minister to the United Kingdom were fundamentally ignored by the British government and the people. The relationship between the two countries was still an ex-posed raw nerve. Both John and Abigail saw it in every British engage-ment they attended. The Adamses were ignored, or at best, treated indifferently.

Abigail, never at a loss for words, described her feelings of the British in general: "I shall never have much society with these kind of people, for they would not like me, any more than I do them. . . . We tremble not, neither at the sight or Name of Majesty. I own that I never felt my-self in a more contemptable situation than when I stood four hours to-gether for a gracious smile from Majesty."[52]

To Thomas Jefferson, she wrote, "They affect to despise the French, and to hate the Americans, of the latter they are very liberal in their proofs. So great is their pride that they cannot endure to view us as in-dependant, and they fear our growing greatness."[53] Besides, Abigail had noted, "I believe they have as many Spies here as the Police of France."[54]

On January 24, 1787, John drafted his resignation notice to Congress. "I Shall compleat, with submission to Providence, my ten Years in Eu-rope, and then go home," he wrote.[55] Because Abigail and John were living together and not writing letters to each other, we don't know how Abigail felt about it. But we can guess that she was happy about the decision. Abigail had been homesick for Braintree and everyone there for nearly a year. However, she also didn't know it would be another year and a half before the Adamses would sail back home.

Chapter Twenty

"A Beautifull Country"

1787–1789

J ohn's *January 1787 resignation* from Congress wasn't the only news
that Abigail wrote to her sister Mary. She added "in April tis probable your Sister may be a Grandmama. New Relatives create new
anxieties."[1] It was the April 2 birth of Abigail's first grandson—William
Steuben Smith, born in London to Nabby and the namesake husband.
But the new baby's father, Colonel William Stephens Smith, had "already obliged to leave him, & yesterday morning very reluctantly set
off on a journey to portugal, in his way to which he takes France & Spain,
& will be absent we expect near four Months."[2]

To her niece Lucy, daughter of Mary Cranch, Abigail felt she had to
not only answer a recent letter but also introduce Lucy to the rewarding
world of female education that Europe offered. Lucy would only be able
to envision this educational freedom, but probably never experience it.
Abigail added that "we are quite alone"[3] since John had left "set of[f]
for portsmouth in order to hear the examination of a set of villians who
have been counterfeiting the paper money of the American States."[4]

"Aunt A. Adams," as she lovingly signed this letter, informed Lucy of her unfortunate recent and prolonged illness of six weeks. But she added, "I hope will reestablish my Health. My disorder has been long accumulating, & arises from a Billious state of my Blood. it has afflicted me spring & fall for several years, and has at last produced a slow intemitting fever."

But then Aunt Abigail informed Lucy that she had just attended five scientific lectures, which she never would have been allowed to attend in America—just because of her gender. She described learning deeply scientific subjects as a "Beautifull Country."

> Some days I am able to go out, others not, but it has wholy prevented my attendance upon. . . . Seven Lectures out of 12 to which I Subsribed,[5] and which I fear I shall never have the opportunity of attending. they would have afforded me much matter for future recollection & amusement from a retrospect of the Beauties of Nature, and her various opperations manifested in the Works of creation, an assemblage of Ideas entirely new, is presented to the mind. the five Lectures which I attended were experiments in Electricity, Magnetism Hydrostatics optics pemematicks [pneumatics] . . . it was like going into a Beautifull Country, which I never saw before, a Country which our American Females are not permitted to visit or inspect.[6]

Although Abigail's letters describe that she was nearly always suffering from some affliction of some sort, they above all showed that she cared deeply about the health of John and her children. In the winter of 1787, she worried about John Quincy working in the arctic-like climate of Russia as the American ambassador. Her anxiety grew from the idea that he would not be active enough and stressed the idea of exercise to him, "I fear you will grew too Indolent," she wrote. "Your Blood will grew thick & you will be sick. your Pappa is sure of it. he is always preaching up excercise to me and it would be a very usefull doctrine if I sufficiently attended to it."[7] She did not exempt herself. "As you and I both are inclined to corpulence we should be attentive to excercise. Without this a Sedantary Life will infallibly destroy your Health. . . . I would advise you upon the approach of Spring to lose some Blood, the Headacks and flushing in your face with which you used to be troubled was occasiond by too great a Quantity of Blood in your Head."[8] Signing off one of the letters, Abigail apologized, "I only intended you a line, but how I have spun."[9]

Summer 1787 brought with it the opportunity by Abigail to affect the life of another young, impressionable female. It was a gesture of helping her dear friend Thomas Jefferson, who was buried under diplomatic paperwork in Paris. Three years prior, Jefferson had brought his eldest daughter, Martha, to Paris. Now in 1787, he asked Abigail if his youngest daughter, eight-year-old Mary (nicknamed "Polly"), could board with Abigail in London until Jefferson could cross the Channel to pick her up. Abigail agreed and started planning the many activities and sights that she could offer her. Abigail wrote Jefferson, "I had the Honour of addressing you yesterday and informing you of the safe arrival of your daughter."[10] Polly would be traveling with an enslaved chaperone. Jefferson had requested that "some woman who has had the smallpox must attend her. A careful negro woman, as Isabel, for instance, if she has had the smallpox."[11]

However, Isabel, the chaperone, was ill and not able to make the journey with Polly, so Isabel's sister, fourteen-year-old Sally Hemings, was selected as a substitute. Abigail wrote Jefferson, "The old Nurse whom you expected to have attended her, was sick and unable to come. She has a Girl about 15 or 16 with her, the Sister of the Servant you have with you."[12] Abigail wrote Jefferson, "The Girl who is with her is quite a child, and captain Ramsey is of opinion will be of so little service that he had better carry her back with him, but of this you will be a judge. she seems fond of the child and appears good Naturd."[13]

Abigail welcomed Polly and Sally but was cautioned by Captain Ramsey, who had sailed Polly from Virginia to London. Ramsey whispered that Polly had been quite devastated at her uprooting. She didn't really know her father. Most of her early life she had stayed with "her Aunt Epps."[14] After "5 weeks at sea,"[15] Polly had developed a deep trust in Captain Ramsey. Now it seems her safe reliance on Ramsey was being yanked away. Jefferson wrote that he originally was going to cross the Channel and pick up Polly himself. But now he was too busy and would be sending a French aide, Adrian Petit, who spoke little English. Jefferson had added that once in Paris, he would place Polly in a convent.

Abigail lightly scolded Jefferson: "Tho she says she does not remember you, yet she has been taught to consider you with affection and fondness, and depended upon your comeing for her. . . . I express her own words. . . . I cannot but feel Sir, how many pleasures you must lose; by committing her to a convent, yet situated as you are, you cannot keep her with you."[16]

Jefferson replied, "her distress will be in the moment of parting & I am in hopes Petit will soon be able to lessen it."[17] As Polly was being taken to Paris by a man she did not know and then to her father, whom she also did not know, Abigail confessed, "she clung round me so that I could not help sheding a tear at parting with her."[18]

It seemed that the revolutionary comaraderie which bound most of the major figures together in the Great Cause was becoming frayed. Shays' Rebellion was representative of that conflict in 1786 and 1787. From Europe, Abigail could only speak out, "an unprincipald mob is the worst of all Tyrannies."[19] And writing to Mercy Otis Warren, she could only wonder if unprincipled Americans squandered their victory with laziness: "Success crowned our efforts and gave us Independance, our misfortune is that then we became indolent and intoxicated; Luxery with ten thousand evils in her train, exiled the humble virtues. Industry & frugality, were swallowd up in dissipation."[20]

A bitter feud was erupting between kindred Americans. These political differences essentially created the first two political parties. One of the factions was the Federalist Party of George Washington and Hamilton. The other was the Democratic-Republican Party of Jefferson and Madison. The onetime allies separated into two groups in a power struggle interpreting and ratifying the new United States Constitution. Even the 1787 election for the local political office of Massachusetts governor was fraught with contention. James Bowdoin, friend to the Adamses, was running against John Hancock, who displeased Abigail and John with his arrogance. Despite his crippling gout, Hancock won the seat and would go on to win reelection. Hancock was governor of Massachusetts from 1780–1785 and 1787–1789. The once good relationship between the Adamses and the Warrens was diminishing, as well. James Warren was catering to Hancock because he needed a job. Mercy Warren was trying to associate her five lazy boys with the Adams boys, but to no avail.

It was July 1787 and beautiful summer weather in England. John and Abigail[21] decided to get out of London's dirty air, to take some time and tour the southern and western parts of the country. Abigail had wanted to visit Winchester, where she'd heard that the first Earl of Winchester—the Sieur de Quincy—had lived. She remembered as a small child seeing his coat of arms on the wall inside the Quincys' Mount Wollaston estate. But the parchment proof was not found during Abigail's investigation, and she ceased the effort.

But Abigail apologized in her letter to Mary for mentioning that she wanted to check on her genealogical lineage from the Sieur de Quincy.

It wasn't because suddenly Abigail had begun embracing royalty. It was because the Sieur was one of "the 25 barons who demanded that King John accept the provisions of the Magna Carta in 1215."[22] This historic document for the first time lessened a king's power over lords and barons: the Magna Carta "which I have seen, the original being now in the British Museum with his Hand writing to it."[23] However Abigail wrote that she did "not expect either titles or estate from the Recovery of the Geneoligical Table."[24]

On Sunday, July 22, the Adamses sat in on a mass at Winchester Cathedral, which disappointed Abigail. There was nobody there and the minister gave a very poor sermon. The entourage then rolled down to the seaside resort area of Southampton.

At about this time in the late eighteenth century, bathing in the sea was becoming fashionable, especially for the upper class, although still segregated by gender. Even John went for a dip, as he put to his diary, "for the first time in my Life I tried [it] this morning."[25]

Abigail continued, "from Winchester we proceeded to Southhampton, which is a very pretty sea port Town and much frequented during the summer months as a Bathing place, and here for the first time in my Life I tried the experiment." She continued, "the places are under cover, you have a woman for a Guide, a small dressing room to yourself an oil cloth cap, a flannel Gown and socks for the feet (protection from the hot sand); we tarried only two days at Southhampton, and went ten miles out of our way in order to visit Weymouth merely for its Name."[26]

As Abigail rumbled along the English roads, she saw firsthand what the British land ownership system of lords and peasants resulted in, and it troubled her very much. She observed that "the pesantry are but slaves to the Lord, notwithstanding the mighty boast they make of Liberty . . . the Money earned by the sweat of the Brow must go to feed the pamperd Lord & fatten the Greedy Bishop, whilst the misierble shatterd thatched roof cottage crumbles to the dust for the want of repair. to hundreds & hundreds of these abodes have I been a witness in my late journey."[27]

In late summer of 1787, the Adamses planned for their voyage back to the United States. The American political climate was unsettled; however, John intended to abandon politics and live the life of a gentleman farmer: "If I Serve the Publick, in future, it must be in Retirement and in my own Way."[28] He and Abigail had purchased the Vassall-Borland farm which John called "Peacefield." In a letter to Abigail's uncle Cotton Tufts, John laid out his new life plans: "And now for Retirement among the Rocks and Hills of Old Braintree. The

Plough, the Spade, the Ax and the Hoe, stone wall and fresh Meadow Ditches. . . . To be the Football of Faction, I never was, and never will be. . . . I will be a private Man, and a Brewer of Compost for my Farm."[29]

For quite a while, Abigail had been concerned about her brother William's abandoned wife Catharine "Kitty" Louisa Salmon Smith and her six children struggling on a farm in Lincoln, Massachusetts. The farm and house had been given to William Smith, Jr. by their father, but by 1781 it was clear to William Smith, Sr. (Parson Smith—Abigail's father) that his son had abandoned his family. Since William Smith, Sr. could not legally give the property to Catharine due to the law of coverture, he set up a trust for Catharine. He asked Richard Cranch and Cotton Tufts to administer the property for Catharine.

By 1785, the three Smith sisters had given up trying to rehabilitate their alcoholic, ne'er-do-well brother. They weren't even sure of where he was. His wife, Catharine, informed Abigail, "Mr. S[mit]h has not been in this part of the Country for almost two years. I seldom hear from him and when I do the intelegence is not what I could wish. Poor unhappy man!"[30] In letters Abigail, Mary, and Elizabeth rarely if ever used his birth name "William" when writing about him; he was a source of family shame. He was usually referred to in cloaked references. From London on October 20, 1787, Abigail yet innocently queried Mary, "where is our Brother? is he in any buisness I hope he does not suffer for want of the necessaries of Life, tho he has been so underserving."[31] But Abigail's conjecturing was already too late. Word eventually reached Abigail, her sisters, and Catharine Smith that a month before, on September 1, 1787, William Smith, Jr. had died of chronic alcoholism at the age of forty in Lancaster, Pennsylvania. His burial site is still unknown. Even five months after their brother had died, Abigail reasoned to Mary that his life and death were "only as a proof how much the best & worthyest may err, & as some mitigation for the conduct of our deceast Relative."[32]

The Constitutional Convention secretly met from May–September 1787 in Philadelphia. Their purpose was to scrap the weak Articles of Confederation and form a whole new government. Some consider it a Second American Revolution. The irony of the whole convention was that it wasn't attended by arguably the two most influential delegates of the earlier Continental Congress—Thomas Jefferson and John Adams. In 1787, they were both working in Europe as representatives of the new nation to France and Great Britain, respectively. But both ambassadors had contacts at the Constitutional Convention. Jefferson had his neighbor James Madison keeping him informed.

Designing an entirely new and functional government was the ultimate object of the US Constitutional Convention. But many private interests who advocated a strong national administration were also at stake. One such area was the treatment of the various war bonds issued throughout the eight and a half years of war. This directly affected Abigail Adams and, to a lesser extent, John Adams, who had been a late convert to government securities. The question was whether the new stronger government being proposed, which also had the power to tax, would pay off speculators on their investments of depreciated government bonds.

On September 17, 1787, the new Constitution of the United States of America was signed by thirty-eight of the forty-one delegates. Now the work began of convincing the public, "We the People," to approve the document. Voting for the Constitution, called ratification, was put out to all thirteen states. It had been agreed that the Constitution would become law if nine states voted for it. Some delegates and states, such as Rhode Island, refused to vote for the Constitution unless it also had a written Bill of Rights with it.

John Quincy, who was studying law after graduating from Harvard, wrote to his sister, Nabby, that he was convinced that their father should "Spend the remainder of his days in retirement."[33]

In her reply Nabby wrote that she didn't see that happening. Nabby hoped her father would fit into the new country when her mother and father sailed back home in two months. "I have no desire that he should be chosen Governor of the State—let those Possess that station who are ambitiously grasping—at a Shadow . . . but I do hope—upon the establishment of a New Constitution—to see Him in some respectable and usefull Office under it—the Americans in Europe—say he will be Elected Vice President."[34] Nabby, herself now a married woman to Colonel William Stephens Smith and mother to their one-year-old son, was not sailing back to Massachusetts with her parents. Instead, the Smith family would be sailing to Long Island for Colonel Smith to take the position as a United States Marshal in New York. Smith was given that job in 1789 by President George Washington as a "thank you" for faithfully serving as one of Washington's aides-de-camp during the war.

February 1788 found Abigail writing a farewell letter to her beloved friend Thomas Jefferson, "in the midst of the Bustle and fatigue of packing, The parade & ceremony of taking leave at Court."[35] She wrote that she looked forward to "retiring to our own little Farm feeding my poultry & improveing my Garden has more charms for my fancy, than residing at the court of Saint Jame's where I seldom meet with Characters So innofensive as my Hens & chickings, or minds so well improved as my Garden."[36]

Jefferson liked Abigail a great deal. Like John, Thomas was not intimidated by smart women, but attracted to them. Thomas was also possibly jealous of John for having such an intelligent woman at his side—especially one who was financially savvy.[37] Jefferson wrote to Madison, "When he [John Adams] established himself [in European diplomacy], his pecuniary [financial] affairs were under the direction of Mrs. Adams one of the most estimable characters on earth, and the most attentive & honourable œconomists."[38]

Political protocol required John and Abigail to officially take their leave of the British Crown Court and the various dignitaries and wives that they had encountered during their three years in England. John also felt strongly that he should also officially resign his Netherlands minister position, while of course, requesting one more financial advance from the Dutch for the United States. Jefferson met John in The Hague and they both negotiated a final loan from the Dutch, the fourth such transaction over time from the Dutch States General.

On April 20, 1788, John and Abigail sailed for home on the vessel *Lucretia*. They arrived in Boston about eight weeks later, on June 17. Accompanying them were their two servants who had also been with them since 1784—John Briesler and Esther Field (Briesler). The Brieslers had been quickly married in mid-February 1788 in St. Marylebone Parish Church in London, when it was disclosed that Esther was pregnant. "I bring her Home a marri'd woman & perhaps a Mother which I fear will take place at sea,"[39] Abigail wrote Mary. Abigail's math was correct, and Esther gave birth to a little girl, Elizabeth, in May on the voyage.[40] Once again, the journey west was anything but smooth. Squalls set the arrival date back to mid-June, tossing the seasick travelers to and fro during a "very tedious passage of eight weeks and two days."[41]

As the *Lucretia* sailed into Boston Harbor on June 17, 1788, with John and Abigail up on deck, the greeting was nothing like they'd ever seen. "The Pier was crowded—and his Excellency welcomed on shore by three huzzas from several thousand persons."[42] Cannons roared from Castle Island in Boston Harbor. They were welcoming home a national hero, "his Excellency JOHN ADAMS, Esq.—with his lady."[43] read a public

reception ad. Abigail was proud of her hero husband and of the salutation he was being given, recognizing the near decade that he had spent
in Europe on official business for the United States of America. Governor
John Hancock had turned out many thousands of cheering citizens for
the celebratory welcome home. His motive was unknown, but since he
personally welcomed the Adamses at the dock and rode to the governor's
house through the crowds with them, it's not hard to believe that he
was soaking up the glory and political votes, as well. Regardless, the
festive salute was an occurrence both John and Abigail would remember
for the rest of their lives.

Abigail and John traveled to Braintree to temporarily move in with
John's brother. There they would await their furniture delivery from the
hold of the ship and to check out the Borland house in person. Abigail
was extremely disappointed with the condition and size of the house.
"We went to our worthy brother's, where we remained until the next
week, when our furniture came up. But we have come into a house not
half repaired, and I own myself most sadly disappointed. In height and
breadth, it feels like a wren's house."[44] Compared to their previous house
in Braintree, the saltbox cottage, the Borland house was significantly
larger. But Abigail had gotten used to the townhouse and stately mansion they'd lived in while in London and Paris.

Abigail immediately began remodeling the Old House. "Ever since I
came, we have had such a swarm of carpenters, masons,"[45] Abigail wrote
Nabby. A library, another kitchen, and dairy room were being planned
out, as well. To Abigail's additional grief, when the furniture was delivered that had been purchased in Europe for the house, Abigail was
shocked at its condition: "In short, I have been ready to wish I had left
all my furniture behind."[46] The china was cracked or had been reduced
to pieces, and the dampness of the voyage had done irreparable damage
to much of the wood furniture.

But nothing could dampen the cheerful reunions which greeted Abigail and John once they had gotten home to Braintree. Sons Charles and
Thomas excused themselves from their Harvard law classes and arrived
home. John Quincy, himself a recent Harvard graduate, took leave from
his legal studies in Newburyport. The Cranches were there to welcome
their famous relatives. Dr. Tufts added himself to the well-wishers. And
sister Elizabeth and her husband Reverend Shaw rode from Haverhill
to the welcome home celebration.

Early fall 1788 brought the good news that eleven states had ratified
the US Constitution, making it officially the law of the land. The lone

holdouts were North Carolina and Rhode Island. February 4, 1789, was the date chosen to select the presidential electors, who would then elect a president and vice president.

In early elections there was no political "ticket"[47] which would elect two people with the same viewpoint to become the president and vice president. The candidates were the two people with the two highest number of votes. Everyone knew that George Washington would become the first president; he was uniformly respected by nearly all Americans for his honor and integrity. The only question was: who would be vice president? John Adams's name was routinely overheard in conversations. Even to himself, John had decided he couldn't be president, George Washington had that position tied up. Additionally, since the office of a president was a new one in history, it was still unknown if a president was a lifelong appointment, like a king.

With Abigail's full approval, John had decided that the only other two positions he would ever entertain were vice president or Supreme Court justice. They both knew this even before setting foot back in America. But in those early days of the republic, it was considered selfish and suspicious for a candidate to campaign for his own election. For that reason, John Adams purposely laid low and worked on his Braintree farm.

Abigail, on the other hand, was preparing to go to Jamaica, New York, and was leaving late in the season—mid-November 1788. The purpose of her trip was to assist daughter Nabby with the birth of her second child. She would also keep her ears open for any political news coming out of New York City, then the nation's capital. Unfortunately, Abigail was too late for the successful birth on November 9 of her second grandchild, John Adams Smith. But while Abigail was there, she was visited by John Jay, who had just been elected sixth President of the Continental Congress.

Abigail wrote John: "mr Jay came out on Saturday to visit me. . . . He expresst a great desire to see you, and thought you might have come on without subjecting yourself to any observations, tho he knew your Reasons were those of Delicacy."[48] It was too dangerous to be seen. John Adams could have been sighted near New York City and his presence may have been proof of him secretly campaigning. Abigail replied to Jay that John was really enjoying farming, when Jay answered back, "that you must not think of retireing from publick Life."[49] Jay told Abigail that John was very much needed in government and Jay passed along some political intelligence from a new and little-known delegate to the Congress of the Confederation from New York—Alexander Hamilton. Abigail wrote to John: "col Hammilton shew him a Letter from madison in which he 'Says, we consider your Reasons conclusive. the Gentleman you have named will certainly have all our votes & interest for vice President.'"[50]

The first presidential election of the new republic was directed by the new Constitution of the United States of America. Accordingly on February 4, 1789, the 138 presidential electors met in their respective states. They would be voting for the nation's first president and vice president. Of course, George Washington received 69 of the votes, 50 percent of the total number. Washington would become president. The runner-up with 34 votes and therefore vice president was John Adams. (John Jay received 9 votes for vice president; John Hancock received 4 votes. The remaining 22 votes were spread among the remaining 8 other candidates.)

Abigail returned to Braintree in mid-January 1789. But it was March before John received confirmation of his election to vice president. He left for New York, very soon afterward to find a house where he and Abigail could live. The newly elected position did not come with many established privileges like housing. No one even knew the salaries the executives would be receiving. Those details had yet to be determined, but John's workload was already heavy. He realized he couldn't spend much time house hunting. To make matters worse, he found that most of the rentals on the market were also devoid of any furniture. In the meantime, he was rooming at John Jay's large house on Broadway, a temporary solution but one that John disliked. The pressure came from the fact that the federal government needed to start as soon as possible to establish its legitimacy. John sent for Abigail, once again he needed her badly.

Abigail's time at Braintree was being stretched to the limit to put all in order before leaving for an unknown amount of time in New York City. It had been assumed from an earlier agreement that John's brother, Peter Boylston Adams, would take care of the farm. But Peter backed out of the arrangement because he feared he wouldn't be able to farm well enough to produce the good results that his brother would expect. Abigail wrote to John Quincy that "Uncle Peter" thought "your Father has so much higher notions about his Farm than he can possibly answer, that he shall come under Blame."[51]

Abigail also needed to pack up the selected furniture and household items to transport to New York—furniture which had only recently been uncrated from their trip from France and was still dinged up from the rocky cruise. All her other items which would be sent to New York City totaled more than one hundred boxes.[52]

She also needed to start asking for rent from Phoebe Abdee and her husband. The couple had just been relocated from the saltbox cottage they lived in free of charge to another house also owned by the Adamses. Abigail decided rent of four dollars per year was still being very charitable. The growing levels of disobedience by Charles in his senior year at Harvard were also weighing heavily upon her mind. John and Abigail decided to let Charles graduate but asked him to skip the commencement ceremony. "I have many reasons for wishing to avoid comencment, some of them you can Guess at,"[53] Abigail confided to John Quincy. She would require Charles to immediately come to New York City. Arrangements were made for Charles to work in the New York law office of the new political up and comer—Alexander Hamilton. But more importantly, Charles would never be out of his parents' eyes.

John was elected vice president in February 1789 and presided over the United States Senate for the first time on April 21, about one week before George Washington's inauguration at Federal Hall as president. One of the first orders of Senate business was to decide what the official title of the president should be; there had never been a position of an elected president in history, so the senators had nothing to model the salutation by. The senators debated variations of "Your Highness." The Senate even considered the long, legal label, "His Highness the President of the United States and Protector of the Rights of the Same."

John was partial to "His Most Benign Highness" and "His Excellency," possibly after spending so many years near the monarchies of Europe. He felt that the office of president should be revered and honored, almost as a monarch would be. Thus began an aura around John for the next ten years that people pointed to when they accused him of supporting a kingly monarchy and aristocracy. One of the unkind titles for John Adams that was quietly whispered was "His Rotundity."

The final decision for the president's title was voted by the Senate on May 14, after the House of Representatives passed the same recommendation. It turned out to be a very republican title—"the President of the United States" and in conversation, "Mr. President." John's official title would be "the Vice President of the United States" and "Mr. Vice President." John also came to hate the office of the Vice President. He called it "the most insignificant Office that ever the Invention of Man contrived or his Imagination conceived."[54] The US Constitution defined the vice presidential position as having "no vote, unless they be equally divided,"[55] meaning John would only be a tie-breaker in Senate votes. Indeed, during John's eight years as vice president and Senate president, he cast at least twenty-nine tie-breaking votes. Otherwise, he was to just preside over that legislative body, but he would not be able to join in on debates. He couldn't even open his mouth. For someone like John, who never met a debate he didn't like, it was torture. Abigail reminded her frustrated husband, "Arm yourself with patience and forbearence and be not Dismayed."[56]

"This Whirligig of a World"

1789–1790

By mid-May 1789 and in Abigail's absence, John had been able to find a satisfactory house for them: "I have taken an House, and now wish you to come on, as soon as possible."[1] Abigail would come to know the house on Manhattan Island as "Richmond Hill," and it would invoke pleasant memories for the rest of her life.

At the end of May 1789, Abigail, still at Braintree, wrote to John, "I hope to be able to relieve you soon from [all] domestick, cares & anxieties."[2] She knew that having John staying with John Jay and his family was getting irksome—for both parties. Like the long-time married couple that they were, Abigail knew all the small comforts that John loved but couldn't get there—like his daily sniff of Cayenne pepper to get the old body going. "I know you want your own Bed & pillows, your Hot coffe & your full portion of kian where habit has become Natural,"[3] she wrote.

But all was not well with John. Indeed, he was seriously sick. When he wrote to Abigail on June 6, he alluded to his, "disorder of Eight years standing" from his time in Amsterdam with probably malaria or typhus: "I must now most Seriously request you to come on to me as soon as conveniently you can. never did I want your assistance more than at present, as my Physician and my Nurse. my disorder of Eight years standing has encreased to such a degree as to be very troublesome and not a little alarming. . . . You must leave the Furniture to be packed by others and sent after you—We must have it all removed and Sent here, as well as all the Liquers in the Cellar, and many of the Books, for here We must live, and I am determined not to be running backward and forward, till the 4 years are out, unless my Health should oblige me to resign my office of which at present there is some danger."[4]

Abigail sent John a note prescribing specific herbal medicines[5] and departed Braintree for New York City. "I last Evening received your Letter of june 7th I will set of on Wednesday [June 17] for Providence and embark in the first packet for New-york. . . . I will be with you however as soon as possible."[6]

John's mysterious illness vanished just before Abigail arrived in New York on June 24, leaving one to wonder if it was just stress. "I reach'd Richmond Hill on Thursday one oclock to my no small joy I found mr Adams in better Health than I feard."[7] Together Abigail and John traveled to the lower Manhattan estate of Richmond Hill, which John had just rented. It commanded a striking scene on a bluff above the Hudson River. The site where Richmond Hill was is Varick Street at Charlton Street in today's Greenwich Village.

To Thomas Brand Hollis, a British dissenter and dear friend to the Adamses,[8] Abigail wrote describing Richmond Hill, "I have a situation here, which, for natural beauty, may vie with the most delicious spot I ever saw. It is a mile and half distant from the city of New-York. The house is situated upon an eminence; at an agreeable distance. . . . A lovely variety of birds serenade me morning and evening, rejoicing in their liberty and security." Abigail, a lifelong songbird lover, had banned bird hunting on her grounds; however, "my orders have not been sufficiently regarded." That's when she almost "wished for game laws" to stop the armed hunters intruding on her Richmond Hill property. "The partridge, the woodcock, and the pigeon are too great temptations to the sportsmen to withstand."[9]

It was "the morning after my arrival" when Abigail received an invitation to call upon the new First Lady—Martha Washington. Although Abigail had met General Washington in the main room of her Braintree home in June 1776, Mrs. Washington and Abigail had never met. Abigail developed what would become a lifelong fondness for Martha: "[I will] go & pay my respects to mrs Washington mrs Smith accompanied me. She received me with great ease & politeness, she is plain in her dress, but that plainness is the best of every article . . . her Hair is white, her Teeth Beautifull, her person rather short than otherways, hardly so large as my Ladyship, and if I was to speak sincerely, I think she is a much better figure, her manners are modest and unassuming, dignified and femenine, not the Tincture of ha'ture about her."[10] Abigail was supposed to have been also welcomed by President George Washington, but he was very ill; Abigail noted "his majesty was ill & confined to his Room. I had not the pleasure of a presentation to him, but the satisfaction of hearing that he regreeted it equally with myself."[11] According to the editors of *The Papers of George Washington*, "George Washington's illness was more serious than most people realized, with a fever stemming from an infection connected to a tumor in his leg. He had the tumor removed on June 17, 1789. By early July, he was able to conduct government business though he remained weak for some time thereafter."[12]

About two weeks later Abigail again called upon the president and First Lady. President Washington had the dangerous tumor removed from his leg a few weeks prior to Abigail's latest visit. He beckoned from his room for Mrs. Adams to enter his chamber:

the Fever which he had terminated in an absess, so that he cannot sit up. . . . he was laying upon a settee and half raising himself up, beggd me to excuse his receiving me in that posture, congratulated me upon my arrival in New york and askd me how I could realish the simple manners of America after having been accustomed to those of Europe. I replied to him that where I fund simple manners I esteemed them, but that I thought we approachd much nearer to the Luxery and manners of Europe according to our ability, than most persons were sensible of, and that we had our full share of taste and fondness for them. . . .

The President has a Bed put into his Carriage and rides out in that way, allways with six Horses in his Carriage & four attendants mrs Washington accompanies him. I requested him to make Rich-mond Hill his resting place, and the next day he did so, but he found walking up stairs so difficult, that he has done it but once. Mrs Washington is one of those unassuming Characters which Creat Love & Esteem, a most becomeing plasentness sits upon her coun-tanance, & an unaffected deportment which renders her the object of veneration and Respect, with all these feelings and Sensations I found myself much more deeply impressd than I ever did before their Majesties of Britain.[13]

With or without the president, the political show still had to go on in the dizzy "Whirligig of a World,"[14] as Abigail called it. It happened in the form of Martha Washington's levee: on "fryday Evenings mrs washington has a drawing Room which is usually very full. . . . here the company are entertaind with Coffe Tea cake Ice creams Lemonade &c they chat with each other walk about, fine Ladies shew themselves, and as candle Light is a great improver of Beauty."[15]

Meanwhile back in Boston, John Quincy Adams had set up a law office in the Boston Court Street building still owned by his father. But he had been smitten by a local girl. Her name was Mary Frazier, daughter of a Newburyport retailer. Abigail did her best to break up the premature romance, warning John Quincy to wait until he was an established lawyer. "[A]n entanglement of this kind will only tend to depress your spirits should you be any time before you get into Buisness and believe me my dear son a too early marriage will involve you in troubles that may render you & yours unhappy the remainder of Your Life,"[16] she wrote.

Abigail's efforts worked and the romance was smothered. Next Nabby, who had just had another baby, told Abigail that her husband William's erratic employment record from government jobs was resulting in conflict between the couple. He had conjured up a money-making scheme that, he predicted, could not go wrong. His plan was to sail to London to procure a low-cost loan. Then he would return to buy sinking US government securities, pay back the loan money, and make a profit. Gambling plans do not always turn out well. Considering the fluctuations in currency exchange rates with interest, Colonel Smith was even poorer when he returned to America than when he left. The instability of her husband's plans prompted Nabby and her two children to move in with her parents.

Predictably, even before John's official installment as vice president, a throng of federal job seekers came petitioning John or Abigail for jobs. Mercy Otis Warren, though Abigail's friend previously, snubbed her and went right to John. In some assertive language, Mercy asked for an assortment of administration jobs—not only for her husband, James, but also for their five sons. The relationship between the Adamses and Warrens had cooled because of disagreements over issues such as the Warrens' loud support of John Hancock and their refusal to back ratification of the US Constitution.

Mercy's embarrassing groveling in her long letter to John was shocking; he had not even answered her previous letter asking for the same federal jobs. In her new letter to John, Mercy employed persistence and flattery and included such phrases as "I again address you without waiting an answer to my last. . . . You my dear sir . . . are placeed in a situation to do eminent service to your Country to Establish your family & to assist most Esentially your Friends. . . . Yet I do not think it by any means necessary in order to secure your patronage.—I am sure of it."[17]

Two people had petitioned Abigail directly, rather than go to John. The first was James Lovell. Lovell had straightened himself out during the letter writing pause between him and Abigail. He was back with his family and teaching at a school, but he was requesting a federal customs collector job. Abigail replied to him and his wife in veiled terms: "Mr & Mrs L may be assured that an old friend so well qualified for the office he holds will not be forgotten, and that it would be of little consequence whether P: [Portia] is at Braintree or N York. . . . My best regards attend Mrs Lovell who has really flattered me by hinting that it was in my power to serve her or her family."[18] Abigail no doubt passed his name along, but it appears nothing ever came of the action. That ended any further communication between Abigail and James Lovell.

The second person to petition Abigail was her sister and best friend, Mary Cranch. Of course, the situation between Abigail and Mary called for a completely different approach. Abigail had to consider her sisterhood with Mary and a deep lifelong friendship with both Cranches, as well as the Cranches' own personal pride. Richard Cranch had never been a successful businessman and now at the age of sixty-three, it was unlikely that he had the energy or business acumen to succeed at a federal job.

Abigail produced the best and most sensitive solution that she could arrange, given all the constraints. Abigail knew that the Cranches owed John and Abigail a sum of money, so Abigail intended to cancel their debt in return. Rather than repeat the exact amount (Abigail knew it was £10), she asked if Mary and Richard could agree on an amount of money they owed. Then Abigail, also to shield John from knowing what was going on—since he always opened Abigail's mail—asked Mary to enclose the letter of the amount owed inside of an envelope addressed to Nabby. Then, since Nabby had moved back in with her parents, Abigail would receive the envelope with the money amount disclosed inside. She further instructed Mary to leave a stamp off from the outside envelope when she mailed it. When John received the envelope for Abigail, he would sign his name in the upper right corner in a process for incoming and outgoing mail called "franking."[19] John would see the inside envelope for Nabby and give it to Abigail.

Charles was also now living with his parents since his law tutorship with Alexander Hamilton had ended when Hamilton became Secretary of the Treasury. Abigail reported to Mary, "Charls is quite fat. he is very steady and studious. there is no fault to be found with his conduct, he has no company or companions but known & approved ones, nor does he appear to wish for any other."[20]

Congress adjourned for the fall in September 1789 and would reconvene in January 1790. John decided to go home to Braintree to rest from his exhausting work schedule. In a complete twist, Abigail decided to stay at Richmond Hill during the congressional winter recess. It was far enough from New York City to offer Abigail a rare healthy place to stay through the winter, as "it is very sickly in the City."[21] But Abigail learned that in the middle states like New York, unlike in New England, the locals were serious about celebrating the New Year: "the New years day in this State, & particularly in this city is celebrated with every mark of pleasure and satisfaction. the shops and publick offices are Shut."[22]

Her servants who were staying with her, however, presented another story of New Year's Eve rambunctious behavior: "finding two of my servants not alltogether qualified for Buisness, I remonstrated to them, but they excused it saying it was new year, & every body was joyous then."[23] Abigail informed Mary of the traditional New Year's celebratory food and drink, especially "cherry Bounce": "there is a kind of cake in fashion upon this day call'd New years cooky. this & cherry Bounce as it is calld is the old Dutch custom of treating their Friends upon the return of every New Year."[24]

Even in normal times as the vice president's wife, Abigail described her house staff as an assorted mix—some of them were drunks, another was "an indifferent steward,"[25] and one was apparently a sexual free spirit. "I cannot find a cook in the whole city but what will get drunk,"[26] "in short it is next to imposible here to get a servant from the highest to the lowest grade that does not drink male or Female."[27] The downstairs house maid was, "a vixen of a House maid,"[28] but she apparently was trying to keep her libido in check, as Abigail explained, "she has done much better latterly."[29]

The second session of Congress reconvened in January 1790 and John was back presiding over the Senate. Abigail's time was chiefly occupied by greeting the many visitors to her house or returning visits to them if they missed each other. She knew what was expected of her as the wife to a national public figure. However, Abigail, not fond of obligatory visits, discovered a time-saving loophole in that long-established custom. First, Abigail banned all visitors in the morning. The visitations would have to be in the afternoons—which by coincidence was the time that Abigail wasn't often at home. If a person called upon Abigail in the afternoon and missed her, Abigail was required by politeness to return the visit to that missed person. . . . but the courtesy rule said that she didn't necessarily have to see the person. She just had to leave her card to show that she had been there. Then she was officially released from any reciprocal duty.

Considering Abigail's love of Braintree, she had adjusted very well to her days at Richmond Hill. But change was in the air. On July 9, 1790, Congress voted to temporarily move the federal capital from New York City to Philadelphia. The Residence Act stipulated that the relocation should happen following Congress's second term. It was all part of a larger deal: a historic compromise among Hamilton, Jefferson, and Madison. The Residence Act spelled out that a separate location would be designated for the nation's permanent seat of government to be located on the Potomac River. The land wasn't designated as a separate state, but as a federal district carved out at the borders of the southern states of Virginia and Maryland. This was because the slavery proponents in Congress felt less threatened if the national capital was in the south and not in a northern city. In return, the southern members were willing to compromise to the terms of Hamilton's public credit financial "assumption" proposals. The construction deadline of December 1800 was given to the national capital project. In the interim for the next ten years, from December 6, 1790, to May 14, 1800, Congress met at Congress Hall[30] in Philadelphia.

Before Congress adjourned for fall recess in September 1789, it had also confirmed Alexander Hamilton as the new Secretary of the Treasury under the new US Constitution. The first item needed from Hamilton was a comprehensive public credit report. The acceptance or rejection of the report's premise would greatly impact John and Abigail's future lives. The report which Hamilton returned recommended the reorganization of the national debt, estimated at $77 million.[31] He advocated the process through full face-value "redemption" payments to holders of national securities—what Abigail had purchased during the war. The government would call in all federal certificates and substitute new "fully funded" securities in their place.

That's just what Abigail hoped would happen: "I have reason to think that congress will take up the matter and Fund the Debt."[32] Abigail understood that if the federal government did not fund the national debt, America's public credit-worthiness would drop so low that it could never borrow on credit ever again in the worldwide fiscal market. On top of that, rejection of the funding plan could wipe out John and Abigail's speculative investments. The final vote in Congress was set for August 1790. In a letter to Cotton Tufts, Abigail acknowledged that discussing the national debt that spring was taking up nearly all the time of Congress: "the National Debt is a subject of such vast weight and importance as requires the wisest Heads."[33] However, Abigail added an important instruction at the bottom of the letter, "be so good as to buy me a ticket in some of the Lotteries, I care not which."[34]

Included in the national debt was the $25 million in state debt which some states had on their books since the Revolutionary War. Under the part of the public credit report called "assumption," Hamilton recommended that the federal government absorb the states' debts as well. This led to a fairness debate in the House of Representatives since many of the southern states had already paid off their debts, while the northern states still carried a load of liability. James Madison, a House of Representatives member from Virginia, was well known and trusted from his work writing much of the US Constitution and the Bill of Rights, and from his active involvement to get the Constitution ratified.[35] However, in 1790 Madison was leading the charge in the House of Representatives against Hamilton and the Funding Act of 1790.

It was no coincidence that on February 22, 1790, Abigail drove her carriage[36] from Richmond Hill to New York City's Federal Hall, where George Washington had recently taken his inaugural oath of office on the balcony. Abigail sat in the gallery while aspects of the Funding Act were being debated. She and John had a lot to gain or lose from the debate's outcome. Ironically, as long-time securities investors, even the Adamses symbolized the "Speculating stockjobbing Rage"[37] which Hamilton had criticized that year. Abigail defended it, reminding John that "it existed before col Hamilton came into office."[38]

The final congressional voting on the Funding Act of 1790 took place on August 4. To Abigail's delight, Congress voted to fully fund the debts of the individual states and the federal government. The debts covered those that were incurred during the Revolutionary War, the Confederation period, and as part of a single federated union under the US Constitution. But the rules were changed for anyone who was exchanging their old bonds for the new ones—the name of the buyer had to be disclosed and not just veiled behind a "trustee" name. Cotton Tufts wrote Abigail that he now had to divulge her name: "they must either be loaned in my own Name, or as Trustee to Mrs. A. Adams."[39] Abigail had preferred the previous anonymity of not disclosing her name due to any sensitivity of her being married to John. But the generous interest payoff and security of the bonds was well worth revealing her name. For the moment, Abigail was thrilled with the step taken by Congress. She had made huge profits from her speculative investments which were then endorsed by the federal government. Her only regret was that she had not bought more of them.

But bothering her more at that moment was enduring another laborious move for her and John. Abigail had quickly grown to love Richmond Hill and having her children and grandchildren around her. She sent Mary some forlorn thoughts: "at present you have your Family with and near you, but it is my destiny to have mine Scatered, and scarcly to keep one with us."[40]

One final, lavish ceremony in New York City was staged by the federal government in mid-summer 1790. A delegation of Creek Indians accepted the invitation of President George Washington and Secretary of War General Henry Knox to co-sign a treaty to keep Creek land (South Carolina, Georgia, Alabama, and parts of Florida) protected from encroachment by American settlers.[41] Abigail wrote to Mary some of her thoughts on the "Creeck Savages" spectacle which she and John witnessed one night, reflecting common societal views from her era of Native American people as exotic and primitive: "yesterday they signd the Treaty, and last Night they had a great Bond fire dancing round it like so many spirits hooping, singing, yelling, and expressing their pleasure and Satisfaction in the true Savage Stile. these are the first savages I ever saw. mico maco, one of their kings dinned here yesterday and after dinner he confered a Name upon me the meaning of which I do not know, Mammea he took me by the Hand, bowd his Head and bent his knee, calling me Mammea, Mammea."[42] She continued, describing the warriors' physique, "they are very fine looking Men placid contanances & fine shape."[43]

In mid-October 1790, as Abigail was organizing and packing for the unwelcome move to Philadelphia, she was struck down by a devastating mysterious illness. In a letter to her "dear sister" Mary, she explained what happened:

> I retired to my chamber, and was taken with a shaking fit which held me 2 Hours and was succeeded by a fever which lasted till near morning, attended with severe pain in my Head Back &c the next morning I took an Emetick which operated very kindly and proved to me the necessity of it. on tuesday I felt better and went below stairs, but was again Seazd with an other skaking fit which was succeeded as the former by the most voilent fever I ever felt. it quite made me delirious, no rest for 5 Night & days. it setled into a Regular intermitting Fever. the dr after having repeatedly puked me, gave me James's powders, but with very little effect I began upon the Bark the 10th day which I have taken in large Quantities and it has appeard to have put an end to my fever, but I am very low and weak.[44]

On top of the stressful need to recover quickly, Abigail was reminded every day, "I have a jouney before me which appears like a mountain & three Ferries to cross."[45] On September 14, 1790, Abigail updated John Quincy that "Your Father is just returned and has taken Bush Hill. . . . so that matter is decided. I presume we must remove next month."[46] After seventeen months at Richmond Hill in New York, Bush Hill was to become the residence of John and Abigail while the federal government was housed in Philadelphia. Abigail was less than ecstatic at her first glimpse of Bush Hill: "there remains neither bush nor shrub upon it."[47] She added, "the British Troops rob'd this place of its principal Glory by cutting down all the Trees in front of the House and leaving it wholly Naked."[48] The Bush Hill mansion was eventually demolished in the widening project of Spring Hill Street. Today the grounds are where the Community College of Philadelphia stands.

The Adamses arrived at Bush Hill in late November 1790 and found the house freezing cold inside, along with wet paint on the walls which seemed as if it was never going to dry. They left their belongings inside and went into Philadelphia searching for warmth, meals, and overnight accommodation. From his early Continental Congress days, John remembered City Tavern. The owner cleared a spot inside the tavern for such a distinguished and old-time friend and his celebrated wife. "As chance governs many actions of my life," Abigail recalled, "when we arrived in the city, we proceeded to the house. But, as I expected many things of this kind, I was not disappointed nor discomfited. As no wood nor fodder had been provided beforehand, we could only turn about, and go to the City Tavern for the night."[49]

Abigail described returning to Bush Hill the next morning: "The next morning was pleasant, and I ventured to come up and take possession; but what confusion! Boxes, barrels, chairs, tables, trunks, &c.; every thing to be arranged, and few hands to accomplish it."[50]

Once again, Abigail had to find competent house staff to assist in running such a large mansion. Her written remarks about the interviewed candidates echoed her earlier reviews about the sorry domestic labor pool: "not a virtuous woman amongst them all; the most of them drunkards. I recruited with a new one last monday, who brought written recommendations with her, and who to all appearence is very capable of her buisness, but on thursday got so drunk that she was carried to Bed."[51]

Through her experiences, Abigail began to prefer giving the various household duties to blacks: "the chief of the Servants here who are good for any thing are Negros. . . . the white ones are all Foreigners & chiefly vagabonds."[52] She told her sister Mary, "I had rather have black than white help."[53]

Friday evening, December 26, 1790, found Abigail at her first Philadelphia public social appearance. She was at the lavish home of wealthy socialite Anne Willing Bingham. The last time Abigail and Anne had met was in Paris at the same 1784 reception where Abigail had met Captain John Paul Jones. Even then Anne had very strong feelings that American women needed to involve themselves in the politics of the day, and she felt even more strongly now. Anne and Abigail, on such common ground, probably enjoyed each other's company. On this evening, Abigail was completely charmed by the beauty of Anne and her two sisters, as she wrote to Nabby: "The room became full before I left it, and the circle very brilliant. How could it be otherwise, when the dazzling Mrs. Bingham and her beautiful sisters were there. . . . in short, a constellation of beauties."[54]

In the letter to Nabby, Abigail confessed that she would like very much to get to know such women as Mrs. Bingham and her sisters, but it just could not be done without attending the constant social functions in Philadelphia. She shared a perfectly sound reason for not attending such parties, and furthermore stated she was not sorry: "I should like to be acquainted with these people, and there is no other way of coming at many of them, but by joining in their parties; but the roads to and from Bush Hill are all clay, and in open weather, up to the horses' knees; so you may suppose that much of my time must be spent at home; but this, you know, I do not regret."[55]

Part IV

First Lady

Chapter Twenty-Two

"A Devision of the Southern & Northern States"

1791–1795

D r. *Cotton Tufts*, Abigail's uncle and financial advisor, asked in a letter to Abigail about President Washington's levees and drawing rooms that he'd read about. He imagined that they'd be very elegant and glamorous. Abigail replied that indeed they were: "the company are entertaind with Coffe Tea cake Ice creams Lemonade &c they chat with each other walk about, fine Ladies shew themselves, and as candle Light is a great improver of Beauty, they appear to great advantage."[1]

With the new year of 1791 on the horizon in Philadelphia and after Abigail got settled, she once again turned to quietly, even secretly, distributing gifts or money to her "pensioners"[2]—the poor of Braintree among whom she was now including Mary and Richard Cranch. Uncle Cotton Tufts maintained the records of Abigail's gift offerings. Specifically, she requested her uncle to secretly purchase and give "5 cords of wood on my account"[3] to the Cranches. Abigail also asked Tufts to provide an accounting of her "pensioners" financial status, so that she would know her balance. But she further asked Tufts not to send the report through the mail where it would be subject to the prying eyes of John opening the letter. She asked that her uncle wait until it could be sent to her through a more secure system. She included a version of secret cryptography in her letter that Tufts should use: "‡ a mark of that kind in your Letter will inform me that what I request will be Complied with."[4]

As often happened in the summertime in Philadelphia, a portion of that city's population and most of the government left to spend the summer elsewhere. Philadelphia had the bad reputation of sprouting various diseases in the hot and humid environment. Knowing the disease cycle, President Washington planned on leaving the capital in spring and, as he had promised citizens, to finish visiting all parts of the United States during his presidential term.

The trips were to promote unity in the new country, and he had already visited New England and the Middle States. He started the third and final trip, on March 21, 1791; his itinerary was to visit the southern states of Virginia, the Carolinas, and Georgia. Washington would then spend the rest of the summer at his estate, Mount Vernon, in Virginia. It was good timing; the affairs of state were very quiet then. Secretary of State Thomas Jefferson wrote to President Washington while he was on his southern tour, "We are still without any occurrence foreign or domestic worth mentioning to you."[5] Abigail noted to her sister a similar sentiment at that time: "our publick affairs never lookt more prosperious."[6] Even John made a positive statement about the public, with a condition added of course. In a summer 1791 reply letter to Colonel Smith, John wrote, "Never since I was born, was America so happy as at this time, and if the French delirium should not again turn our brains, we shall continue so."[7]

John referred to the French Revolution which was going on at that time. The subject was causing strife among the two American parties which had recently sprung up. The Federalists were mostly northerners who, along with supporting the ratification of the Constitution, opposed the brutalities that the rebelling French were committing on their own citizens. Countering the Federalists were the Democratic-Republicans comprised mainly of southerners. Their party campaigned against constitutional ratification and mostly supported the revolutionary violence by the French citizens as necessary to make the abrupt change from a monarchy. Thomas Jefferson wrote to Lafayette, "we are not to expect to be translated from despotism to liberty, in a feather-bed."[8] The French battle cry of "Liberté, égalité, fraternité" ("liberty, equality, fraternity") was picked up by admiring Americans supporting the French rebellion.

John and Abigail were likewise planning "our passing the summer at Braintree."[9] Abigail had already relocated Phoebe and her husband to another house on their property so the Adamses would be able to move back in, at least for the summer congressional break. As she often did, Phoebe was also providing free room and board in their new house to homeless Blacks, this time to an entire family. Abigail was informed of that fact by Mary before Abigail returned to Braintree so that there would be no surprises. Abigail turned around and offered the errant mother and father paid jobs as servants over the summer, which they accepted. Otherwise, Abigail updated Mary on their departure date, "we proposed Sitting out on our journey on monday or twesday next."[10] Abigail added an estimated time of arrival, "but shall not reach Braintree (Quincy I beg your pardon) till next week."[11] Abigail added the slightly boastful name change correction to correspond to the very recent incorporation of the North Precinct of Braintree into the town of Quincy. The purpose was to honor Colonel John Quincy, Abigail's maternal grandfather. John and Abigail had also given the Quincy name to their eldest son—John Quincy Adams—as another honor.

Abigail informed Mary that she'd be bringing with her from Philadelphia a very capable free young stable boy: "I have a very clever black Boy of 15 who has lived with me a year and is bound to me till he is 21,[12] my coachman will not allow that he is a negro, but he will pass for one with us."[13] The young boy was James.[14]

The coachman named Robert, however, had to be let go for drunkenness. Abigail discharged him in April 1791. She knew that without Robert as coachman and his talent for avoiding the potholes in the long road back, it was going to be a torturous trip. "I am not so perfectly easy on account of travelling Home as I should have been with Robert when he was sober, but he really got to such a pass that I have been obliged to part with him," she wrote.[15]

The remaining part of Abigail's letter to Mary dealt with the recent explosion of political hostility between American party factions that had sprouted up on different sides of issues. The parties were firmly planted in the two regions of the fragile union: the North and the South as was obvious to Abigail: "the North and South appear to be arranged very formidably against each other in politicks."[16] Furthermore, "the Southern Members are determined if possible to Ruin the Secretary of the

Treasury, distroy all his well built systems, if possible and give a Fatal stab to the funding system."[17]

Abigail also gave a chilling prediction about how the future might unfold: "I firmly believe if I live Ten years longer, I shall see a devision of the Southern & Northern states."[18] To Abigail the purpose of the American Revolution was not to change society, which served as the underpinnings of civilization, but to change the government and its effect upon its citizens. By destroying the very society which had provided collective support, she felt the French were undermining their own existence. It's no wonder the French Revolution was turning more violent and brutal. "I pitty those who are blinded by Party,"[19] Abigail wrote.

The cool October weather in Philadelphia traditionally killed off the diseases which had dominated the scene during the hot, humid months. October also ushered Congress's reconvening for another year. Again, John took his seat as vice president sitting in the US Senate for the first session of the Second Congress, October 1791–May 1792. But before John had left for Congress and was still at the summer homestead in Braintree, Abigail and John had agreed that they would seek out a different house than Bush Hill upon their arrival. The commute to the city was just too far, and Bush Hill was too far from markets and social or political gatherings. John wrote to Tench Coxe, Assistant Secretary of the Treasury, in Philadelphia, asking his assistance "in procuring a house in Town."[20] John added, "I have determined in all Events to remove my family into Philadelphia from Bush hill, on Account of the many Inconveniences We experienced last year in passing and repassing."[21] Coxe located a small house at Arch and Fourth Streets which John and Abigail approved upon arrival.

It only took a few weeks of living in Philadelphia to adversely affect Abigail's fragile health. She was severely struck down by "Inflamitory Rhumatism" for over six weeks:

Tis now the sixth week since I have been out of the door of this Chamber, or moved in a larger circle than from my Bed to the chair. I was taken six weeks ago very ill with an Inflamitory Rhumatism and tho it did not totally deprive me of the use of my Limbs, it swelld and inflamed them to a high degree, and the distress I sufferd in my Head was almost intolerable. 3 Times was I let Blood, the state of which was like a person in a high Plurisy. I am now lame in my wrists from the 8th pr of Blisters which I have had. a week after the Rhumatism attackd me the intermitting fever set in, and under that I am still Laboring. it was necessary to quell the inflamitory disease first, & Bark could not be administerd for that. I am now reduced low enough to drive away the Rhumatism, but the old Enemy yet keeps possession. the dr promisses me the Bark in a few days, but my dear sister you would scarcly know me reduced as I am. I have scarcly any flesh left in comparison of what I was.[22]

Although Abigail was now living in Philadelphia, she informed Nabby in January that she had been refusing invitations and that "I have been to one assembly," the reason being "very severe weather for several weeks; I think the coldest I have known since my return from abroad."[23] She added that despite the bitter winter, "I have been to one play . . . 'The School for Scandal.'"[24] One other reason Abigail had for not venturing out too far from home in April 1792 was her long-time rheumatism and a recurrence of the disorder she had caught in New York City—probably malaria, adding that "this everlasting fever still hangs about me & prevents my intire recovery."[25] (To add to her other physical illnesses, she wrote in code to Mary, "a critical period of Life Augments my complaints.")[26]

In closing the letter to Nabby, Abigail painted a humorous picture of her father interacting with their three-year-old grandson, John Adams Smith, by playing horsy: "As to John[ny], we grow every day fonder of him. He has spent an hour this afternoon in driving his grandpapa round the room with a willow stick."[27]

One of the benefits of The Funding Act of 1790 was to make federal securities more attractive which would make them more valuable, therefore stimulating sales. But by late 1791, the bond prices had elevated to a dangerous "bubble" level. In early 1792 wild speculation crashed the securities market, ruining the life savings of many "of the richest people there, and from the Spirit of Speculation which has prevaild & brought to Ruin many industerous Families who lent their Money in hopes of gain."[28] Alexander Hamilton's First Bank of the United States is generally credited with flooding the market with bank notes, then slamming the brakes on the process when the bond bubble was near bursting. The sudden halt in liquidity brought about the securities market crash of 1792. Many speculators, who had used borrowed money to buy bonds, had to sell their stocks for practically nothing.[29] Abigail escaped the worst of the crash; she had invested early and wisely. "Such is the wheel of fortune,"[30] she wrote, adding "the Grumblers will growl."[31]

John was late leaving Quincy for Congress in the fall of 1792. Normally he would have been present in October when Congress reconvened; instead, he didn't arrive in Philadelphia until December 4. In the election of 1792, he did not want to be seen as campaigning for reelection, an unpardonable sin in the early days of the republic. So, he stayed away. It was also decided that Abigail would stay in Quincy and not be with John during his second and last term as vice president. The reasons were twofold: Abigail's health had suffered in Philadelphia, and their own expenses had been over budget during the first term. Living by himself, John could rent a much smaller house and would not be pressured into hosting expensive parties.

For the election of 1792 the electors met on December 5. John sent a short note off to Abigail: "This Day decides whether I shall be a Farmer or a Statesman after next March. They have been flickering in the Newspapers and caballing in Parties: but how the result will be I neither know nor care."[32] In reality, John did care about the result. He, Abigail, and a large portion of the country were looking at the second national election as a sign to "determine whether their Government shall stand four years longer or Not."[33]

Incumbent George Washington did not want to be president for four more years. He was talked into running for a second term by Thomas Jefferson, James Madison, Alexander Hamilton, and Henry Knox. They all centered their plea on the fact that the infant United States still needed the stability that only Washington could offer, giving the country extra time to work out its growth problems. Washington was the only person whom everyone trusted not to make a power play during that time. The president had no biological sons, so that lure of empire building also wasn't a factor. Washington gave into the pressure and to his own high sense of honor and duty. It was no surprise that once again Washington was reelected unanimously, pulling in the full 132 electoral votes. John Adams was also reelected vice president by a solid margin in the next largest group of electors and their 77 total electoral votes.[34]

Smallpox had been the great killer of people in past decades. With improved immunity and inoculations, the feared smallpox epidemics became less commonplace. However, a new, terrible disease—yellow fever—took its place, and Philadelphia became the center point for its transmission during the summer of 1793. Between August and November, the "sickly season," an estimated 5,000 people died of yellow fever, a tenth of Philadelphia's population.

In late fall 1793, John Adams returned to Congress, which was still seated in Philadelphia. He was again presiding over the Senate in the first session of the Third Congress, which ran from December 1793– June 1794. He wrote Abigail that the cold weather had seemingly suspended "the Pestilence"[35] (yellow fever). John mentioned the religious zealots who saw the new disease "Distemper"[36] as retribution for man's sinful ways, "Moral and religious Reflections I shall leave to their own Thoughts."[37]

When John reconvened with the Senate in 1794, the United States had become very polarized over aspects of the French Revolution. Abigail herself had been shocked by the brutality that the French people were still exacting on its citizens, and indeed its former rulers. King Louis XVI had been arrested by the National Convention and guillotined on January 21, 1793. Queen Marie Antoinette received the guillotine nine months later on October 16. Abigail and John had both met the royal couple and found the ruthlessness of their executions very disturbing.

Though the United States was officially neutral, aspects of both France and Britain were pushing Americans into taking one side or the other, thereby tipping the North Hemispheric power scales. The French, declaring the Americans were siding with the British, were seizing American ships in various ports and selling the cargoes. The British, declaring the Americans were siding with the French, stalked and boarded American ships, then they "impressed" (kidnapped) sailors for the British Navy. President Washington refused to budge about America's positioning—declaring it neutral on the seas and in the streets of London and Paris. He was referring to the bloody Jacobin[38] conflict which was playing out all over France during that time. Washington's "Neutrality Proclamation" declared that America was at peace with both Britain (though supported by Hamilton) and France (though supported by Jefferson).

The neutrality position outraged the two American political parties, their followers, and their leaders even seated within Washington's own cabinet. Jefferson soon resigned his Secretary of State position in protest to Washington's neutrality stance. John wrote to Abigail of his response to Jefferson's resignation. It showed the frayed edges of their once happy relationship in Paris: "Jefferson went off Yesterday, and a good riddance of bad ware. I hope his Temper will be more cool and his Principles more reasonable in Retirement than they have been in office. I am almost tempted to wish he may be chosen Vice President at the next Election for there if he could do no good, he could do no harm. He has Talents I know, and Integrity I believe: but his mind is now poisond with Passion Prejudice and Faction."[39]

Reports of the atrocities being committed by the extremist French rioters and their guillotine shocked and hardened Abigail against the French. In a letter to John, she sent this toughened conclusion about the radicalized French whom she thought she knew: "unlesss mankind were universally enlightned, which never can be. they are unfit for freedom."[40] She added this general disillusionment statement, "Some were made for Rule others for submission, and even amongst my own Sex this doctrine holds good."[41] True to her nature, Abigail couldn't end the letter to John with such anger and disheartenment. She closed with a very clever and loving thought, "but as Reigning and Ruling is so much out of fashion at the present day, my ambition will extend no further than Reigning in the Heart of my Husband."[42]

But in 1794, President Washington's recent unpopularity from his neutrality stance among Americans raged on. Ironically it gave a break to John and the usual unrelenting attacks upon him. "The Rascals are now abusing the President as much as ever they abused me," he wrote to Abigail. "I am weary of this eternal Indecision. This is Egotism enough to deserve the Guillotine to be sure."[43] In another letter, he declared "The Hellhounds are now in full cry in the Newspapers against the President, whom they treat as ill—as ever they did me."[44]

Abigail had regretted being stuck in London in 1787 when son John Quincy graduated second in his class at the Harvard commencement. By 1793 as he was establishing his own successful law practice, John Quincy published a series of anonymous newspaper articles attacking Edmond-Charles Genêt, a French envoy who gave his diplomatic name as "Citizen Genêt." As Genêt traveled about in the United States, he urged Americans to ignore President Washington's neutrality decree and to give full support to the French Revolution.[45] John Quincy's essays shed valuable light upon the French ruse, and in 1794 as a thank you, Washington appointed John Quincy Adams as the official United States envoy to the Netherlands. It was an influential post and the same position that his father had held during the Revolution. John Quincy took his younger brother and recent 1790 Harvard graduate, Thomas, with him as secretary.

Even John and Abigail's other son and similar Harvard graduate, Charles Adams, seemed to be doing well during these happy times. On August 29, 1795, Charles was married to Sarah "Sally" Smith, the sister of Nabby's husband, Colonel William Stevens Smith. Charles had the blessings of the family as Abigail approved the marriage with her words, "Heaven Bless them."[46] Even John wasn't opposed to the union, now that Charles was a lawyer and owned the security of future potential income of that profession: "Charles has passed his Examination with honour and is now a Barrister—or Councillor, and if a premature Marriage should not injure him, in a good Way."[47] But John disliked the casual, near modern familiarity that Charles used in referring to his wife as "Sally" and told him so. "I dont approve of your calling her Sally unless to herself in a Family Way. To other People especially in Writing you must call her Mrs Adams."[48] As a father would say to his son, John gave advice to Charles for a reason; "I throw out these broken hints, Charles only to put you upon thinking and reading."[49] Alternately, Nabby and her husband, Colonel William Smith seemed to be thriving upon their return from Europe in 1793. Colonel Smith was bragging about several successful speculation schemes he had designed. Smith was even publicly boasting about his new wealth, which John cautioned his son-in-law not to do.

The breadth of Abigail's farm skills grew every fall through spring, as John returned to Philadelphia during those seasons and Abigail took over managing the houses, farms, and properties. In their letters to each other, Abigail wrote daily an in-depth record of the trials she encountered and how she had solved them. For instance, this snippet from February 1794: "The Animals in the yard have all had the Mumps I believe one of them[50] I thought we should have lost. he was so sweld in his Throat that for a week he never eat a mouthfull and could not lye down. the poor creature set up on his hind legs & slept. I cured him by having his Throat Rubd with Goose oil daily."[51] Abigail and John knew each other so well by this time that they often found themselves exchanging the very same thoughts through the mail, sometimes crisscrossing each other in transit. "You cannot but remark that each of our Thoughts run in the same channel. in many instances we have been expressing the same sentiments at the same time as may be calld the Tellegraph of the Mind."[52]

One more reason Abigail wasn't with John in Philadelphia during that time was that she was caretaking for John's dying mother, Susanna Boylston Adams. Susanna came from the celebrated Boylston New England family. Her paternal grandfather, Doctor Thomas Boylston, discovered and popularized smallpox inoculations. Susanna outlived two husbands, John Adams Sr., and Lieutenant John Hall. There is evidence to suggest that she was illiterate and had a strong temper. Confidentially as Abigail wrote to John, the task of taking care of his mother at her advanced age of eighty-six made Abigail less inclined to live a long life, "as her decay becomes more and more visible . . . my constant attendance upon her has very much lessned my desire of long life."[53]

The world of Abigail's youngest sister, Elizabeth, changed completely in September 1794. Her husband, Reverend John Shaw, had died in his sleep. Obviously, the academy that Shaw ran was soon closed; if that wasn't tragic enough, the house that the family lived in for seventeen years was owned by the town of Haverhill. Shaw's employment contract specified that when a new minister was hired, the Shaw family would be evicted. Four months after Shaw's death, Elizabeth wrote to Abigail, "I attribute a certain depression of Spirits which has troubled me for some time."[54] As fortune would have it, Elizabeth received a marriage proposal later in 1795 from a minister just over the state line in Atkinson, New Hampshire—Reverend Stephen Peabody. They married on December 8, 1795. Peabody also owned and ran a successful academy and was a progressive thinker for his time, advocating education for females. The first girls were admitted to the academy in 1791. "In Mr Peabody I have an attentive Partner, who is one of the warmest advocates for female education,"[55] Elizabeth wrote Abigail. Atkinson Academy was one of the first coeducational preparatory academies in the country and exists to this day.

As the term of John's vice presidency ran out, Abigail was looking forward to fully retiring with John at the "Old House" (or "Peacefield" as John named it). Unknown to either one however was that President Washington had decided not to seek a third term. For his replacement, Washington was to endorse Abigail's husband for president. Abigail and John had already started to secretly write to each other about such an occurrence. The entire nation had idolized George Washington during his first term as president. But the shine had started to wear off in his second term due to political party feuding. Abigail wrote to John, "You write me fully assured that the P[resident] is unalterably determind to retire. this is an event not yet contemplated by the people at large. . . no Successor, can expect such support as the P. has had."[56]

Then Abigail foretold to John that he could well expect a political maelstrom waiting for him as president, "You know what is before You. the whips and Scorpions, the Thorns without Roses, the Dangers anxieties and weight of Empire." Abigail knew she wasn't immune to the political storm, either. She imagined the situation for herself if she should become First Lady, after watching the gracious but quiet Martha Washington invent that role: "I should say that I have been so used to a freedom of sentim[ent] that I know not how to place so many gaurds about me, as will be indispensable, to look at every word before I utter it, and to impose a silence upon my self, when I long to talk." Abigail even had strong doubts that she could ultimately fulfill her role of First Lady in the grand style of Martha Washington, her friend and mentor, "Whether I have patience prudence discretion suffcient to fill a station so unexceptionably as the Worthy Lady who now holds it, I fear I have not."[57]

Chapter Twenty-Three

"In His Wicked Eyes . . . the Very Devil"

1796–1797

bigail's presence near her vice-presidential husband was noted by
politicians and power brokers of her time. Egbert Benson was a
distinguished member of the Continental Congress from New
York City and later served in the US House of Representatives. He was
the first attorney general of the United States and a chief justice of the
New York Supreme Court. As a diehard Federalist, he got to know John
and Abigail very well over the years. When Benson met and worked with
Abigail while they were in New York City, the country's capital, he was
extremely impressed with her political and people skills. In January 1793,
he made a remark to John, who passed it along to Abigail: "Benson says
he is for making Mrs Adams Autocratrix[1] of the United States."[2] Abigail's
reaction to Benson's suggestion was humorously dismissive. However, it
also displayed her growing skill at brushing off a political statement with
a glib reply: "tell Benson I do not know what he means by abusing me
so, I was always for Equality as my Husband can witness."[3]

"Autocratrix" is but one compliment made by acquaintances regarding Abigail's political skills during the eight years of John's vice presidency. Another equally gracious comment was passed along to Abigail by John from a mutual female friend in Philadelphia, Martha Bland Blodget (Corran), "who I dare say is more desirous that you should be Presidante than that I should be Presidant."[4] John picked up on the witty titles thrown out in the political corridors, and even he would kiddingly call Abigail "Presidante," "Madame La Presidante," "Mrs. President," or "Presidentess."[5] But there was some truth in those titles. It was informally known around New York City and Philadelphia that to get an audience with John as vice president and later as president, you had to go through Mrs. Adams. And that was no easy feat. Abigail was politically skillful, and everyone knew it. Author and series editor for *The Papers of John Adams* Sara Georgini wrote that Abigail "exerted serious power of her own"[6] as John's presidential assistant.

The Polish patriot and writer Julian Ursyn Niemcewicz had visited with John Adams in November 1797. He made this notation in his diary: "I passed then into a room opposite and I found there the true counterpart of Mr. Adams. It was his wife. Small, short and squat, she is accused of a horrible crime. It is said she puts on rouge. What is certain is that if her manner is not the most affable, her mind is well balanced and cultivated."[7]

Judith Sargent Stevens Murray was a distinguished essayist and women's educational rights advocate of the eighteenth century. Murray and Abigail had much in common. In a letter to Epes Sargent, Murray passed along a compliment about Abigail Adams that she had overheard. Groups of Bostonian men had agreed that if John Adams was elected president, but was to die suddenly in office, "they should rather see Mrs. Adams in the Presidential chair, than any other character now existing in America."[8]

Vice President John Adams never said out loud that he wanted to be president of the United States, for to do so would cast a shadow of suspicion over him. In the social and political rules of that time, one had to appear "disinterested"[9] in seeking a higher office. Americans were still cautious from past history that any man who appeared overly ambitious would quite likely become a dictatorial and power-hungry king, emperor, or czar. One person was already setting off alarms by advocating himself for president—Aaron Burr of New York. He openly campaigned in New England for six weeks during fall 1796. But inwardly, John felt that his being elected president would be an acknowledgment of the unselfish decades that he had labored for his country, while other men were enjoying their family lives and making considerably more money than John was paid as a public servant.

As the election of 1796 drew closer, it was thought of as the year in which the American democratic experiment would either continue to exist or would collapse in flames. The fuse was lit when President Washington announced that he would not seek a third term. For nearly eight years, Washington had held the title of "Mr. President" and the country had been in his trusted hands. However, during his tenure, two political parties with differing points of view had risen to challenge each other for power and influence. Even before Washington's farewell became public knowledge, the two parties began to coalesce around their own presidential candidates. Thomas Jefferson was supported by the Democratic-Republicans, while John Adams was the choice of the Federalists. The Constitution hadn't foreseen the emergence of opposing political parties. The national election was still a simple procedure which stipulated that the man with the most votes would be president, and the runner-up was vice president, no matter his party. John received word that he was being opposed for nomination within his own Federalist Party by Governor Thomas Pinckney, a patriot South Carolina infantry captain and foreign ambassador. Pinckney was also pro-British, a stance that the Federalists supported in the post-Revolutionary War years.

But behind the scenes there was a dark, shadowy person manipulating the selections, "Secretly cunningly" as Abigail claimed. He was the former aide-de-camp for General Washington and New York lawyer Alexander Hamilton. Hamilton did not like John Adams, and their feud would become legendary in the years to come.

Abigail had briefly met Alexander Hamilton, and from the first time meeting him, she did not trust him. She summed up her feelings toward Hamilton, writing: "O I have read his Heart in his Wicked Eyes many a time the very Devil is in them. they are laciviousness it self, or I have no Skill in Phisiognomy."[10]

The federal election was coming up in autumn 1796. But in early February of that year, Abigail (in Quincy) and John were writing to each other weighing the pros and cons of accepting the presidential nomination. Abigail had heard whispers that John was the logical "heir apparent" to the political office. But in 1796, she cautioned John that President Washington hadn't announced anything yet about seeking a third term. She advanced the possibility that perhaps Washington would run for a third term after all: "You write me fully assured that the P [President] is unalterably determind to retire. this is an event not yet contemplated by the people at large."[11] In her signoff to John, Abigail nevertheless quoted Shakespeare on the subject: "Shakspears says, [']some are born great, some atchive greatness, and some have greatness thrust upon them.[']"[12]

Just one day after discussing politics in her letter, Abigail wrote a new and longer letter to John which demonstrated her expertise in management of their farm: "I believe I must devote this page to. . . . Farming. our people have carried up the Hill all the manure which they suppose will be necessary and which can be spaired from the corn ground."[13] But at the end of the farming letter, Abigail found that she had drifted off into politics again when she hadn't meant to: "but I am running again into politicks When I did not design a word upon the Subject."[14] Abigail herself acknowledged that politics was deeply planted within her very being.

Meanwhile John enjoyed civil politics later that month when he dined with President Washington, noting that "Mr Washington came and civilly enquired after your Health."[15] John also dined with James Madison, Dolley Paine Madison, and her sisters: "I dined Yesterday with Mr Madison. Mrs Madison is a fine Woman and her two sisters are equally so; These Ladies, whose Names were Pain, are of a Quaker Family once of North Carolina."[16]

Late in the campaign, September 1796, George Washington announced his decision not to run for a third term. He established a tradition of each future president only serving the maximum of two terms, until Franklin D. Roosevelt. Also, late in the campaign George Washington endorsed John Adams, which spelled the end of Pinckney's drive coordinated by Adams-hater Hamilton.

As 1796 ended, the national election date of February 7, 1797—the day to count the ballots—crept closer and closer. Abigail wrote to John about the landmark election to come. This would be the first openly contested election between two rival political parties and without the steady presence of George Washington being one of the choices. "[A]t no period has our National interest been in a more Dangerous, or difficult situation than the present. the Struggles of party and faction run very high."[17]

On New Year's Day 1797, Abigail wrote to John, "The new year opens upon us with new Scenes of Life before us. what are to be the trials the troubles and vexations of it, are wisely withheld from our view."[18] She then relayed to John a troubling dream that she had the night before—on New Year's Eve—and she wondered how, "the Sooth sayers [would] interpret this Dream?"[19] "I was riding in my Coach, where I know not, but all at once, I perceived flying in the Air a Number of large black Balls of the Size of a 24 pounder. they appeard to be all directed at me. all of them however burst and fell before they reach'd me, tho I continued going immediatly towards them. I saw them crumble all to Attoms, but During this Scene, two Guns were dischargd at My left Ear the flash of which I saw and heard the report. I still remaind unhurt, but proceedeed undaunted upon My course."[20] Abigail's dream occurred one month before the national election votes were counted; it could be said that she was seeing a premonition of her role as First Lady for the next four years.

The Election of 1796 had been close and contentious. John and Abigail were disappointed that long-time friendships dissolved during the campaign because of belligerent feelings by some of the Adamses' closest friends. There would be no more camaraderie with Thomas Jefferson because of the words written and spoken by both sides about each other as they ran for president. Abigail and John were further shocked that close friends had also thrown their support behind Jefferson. Samuel Adams, John's second cousin, was one of the first dissenters against John. Others included Dr. Benjamin Rush and James and Mercy Otis Warren.[21]

Because of the distances involved in casting a ballot in the election, the polls stayed open from November 4 to December 7, 1796. In addition to the original thirteen states, the new states of Vermont, Kentucky, and Tennessee voted. When the ballots were counted, Adams had won the electoral vote of 71 by a mere three votes more than Jefferson's total of 68. Adams also won the popular vote: 35,726 to 31,115 for Jefferson. Protocol required John to formally resign his vice-presidential duties as Senate president. He sent his resignation rough draft to Abigail for comments; she in turn made many edits and comments—although she added that the severe coldness in Quincy that month "has frozen the ink in My pen."[22] As John read Abigail's notes, he realized he was now receiving excellent, cabinet-level advice from his wife. Abigail had become not only a shrewd partner, but a top-notch savvy political consultant.

Consequently, his farewell address was well received. "I assure you it was a tender Scene at parting,"[23] John confirmed to Abigail. She wrote back a sweet sentiment to celebrate their personal moment: that Abigail had been corresponding with the person who was previously the vice president: "I see by the paper your address of leave to the senate. . . . I shall now take my leave of the Vice President, and address my next Letters to the President, whom neither Rank or station can more permanantly fix in the Heart of His / ever affectionate."[24]

On Monday, March 4, 1797, John Adams was inaugurated the second President of the United States of America. The specialness of the event may have been lost in the moment: it was the first peaceful transition of government in world history between two differing factions—the Federalists and the Democratic-Republicans.

The previous president, George Washington, attended the inauguration ceremony in the House of Representatives in Federal Hall before a joint session of Congress. Chief Justice Oliver Ellsworth administered the oath of office. Abigail missed John's inauguration as she was still in Quincy tending to John's sickly eighty-eight-year-old mother, hiring and firing labor hands, and supervising the farm work. There were no other Adams family members present at the inauguration ceremony. John wrote to Abigail of that slight disappointment, along with stating that he almost fainted during the ceremony: "It would have given me great Pleasure to have had some of my Family present, at my Inauguration which was the most affecting and overpowering Scene I ever acted in—I was very unwell had no sleep the night before, and really did not know but I should have fainted in Presence of all the World."[25]

Abigail was in the process of completing needed chores around the house, farm, and fields to get ready for spring in 1797 and her diplomatic absence. Aside from helping John's ailing mother, additional tasks were finalizing what was to be taken to Philadelphia and what was to stay in Quincy. But she was interrupted by an irksome occurrence. On Monday, February 13, Abigail wrote an aggravated letter to John about a real-life sarcastic example of "the so much boasted principle of Liberty and equality."[26] Abigail vividly told her story: One of her Black indentured stable servants named James had approached Abigail with a request. He said that a new "Evening School" had just opened not far away taught by "Master Heath." Abigail explained to John that the classes were to instruct a "Number of Apprentices Lads cyphering, at a shilling a week, finding their own wood and candles. James desired that he might go. I told him to go with my compliments to Master Heath and ask him if he would take him. he did & Master Heath returnd for answer that he would. accordingly James went after about a week."[27]

James was accepted, enrolled, and began attending night classes at the school. One evening there was a knock on the Adamses' door. It was a neighbor, James Faxon, who had seven school-age sons who all attended the same classes as James. Abigail explained to John: "Neighbour Faxon . . . requested to Speak to me. his errant was to inform me that if James went to School, it would break up the School for the other Lads refused to go."[28]

Abigail wasn't going to let the subject drop there. She asked Faxon if James had misbehaved. "O no, there was no complaint of that kind, but they did not chuse to go to School with a Black Boy," Faxon replied. Abigail countered with the fact that James went to the same church as Faxon boys and yet there had been no problem.

She cleverly turned the argument back on Faxon when she stated that there didn't seem to be a problem when James, who apparently played a musical instrument, supplied music at dances: "did these Lads ever object to James playing for them when at a Dance. how can they bear to have a Black in the Room with them then?"[29] Faxon's attack premise collapsed under Abigail's grilling. Soon Faxon was claiming it was others who wanted James out of the school: "O it is not I that Object, or my Boys, it is some others." Abigail quickly struck back, asking "who are they? why did not they come themselves?"

Abigail, in essence, the First Lady of the United States, reportedly then gave Faxon a firm lesson: "the Principle of Liberty and equality upon the only Ground upon which it ought to be supported, an equality of Rights the Boy is a Freeman as much as any of the young Men, and merely because his Face is Black, is he to be denied instruction. how is he to be qualified to procure a livelihood? is this the Christian Principle of doing to others, as we would have others do to us?"[30]

Faxon replied, "O Mam, You are quite right. I hope You wont take any offence."

Abigail reassured him, "None at all mr Faxon, only be so good as to send the Young Men to me. I think I can convince them that they are wrong. tell them, mr Faxon, that I hope we shall all go to Heaven together—upon which Faxon laugh'd, and thus ended the conversation I have not heard any more upon the Subject."

Abigail added a P.S. to John's letter. It was about the Adamses' other young black servant, Prince. "I have sent Prince Constantly to the Town School for some time, and have heard no objection."[31]

Twenty days after John Adams was inaugurated president, he already was in a predicament. It didn't help that "a violent cold and cough, fa-

tigues me,"[32] as he wrote to Abigail. "There are so many Things to do.
. . . I have every Thing else to hurry me: so that I must entreat you to
come on as soon as you can."[33] "I never wanted your Advice & assistance
more in my Life,"[34] he begged. He desperately needed Abigail's counsel
on many matters of high importance along with her calm organizational
and communication skills. The matters varied from "furnishing the
[President's] House" to advising him on political issues to figuring out
his expenses: "My Expences are so enormous, that my first Quarters
salary will not discharge much more than half of them. You must come
and see for yourself."[35]

The new US Constitution gave Congress the power to tax Americans. Raising much-needed federal revenue was the first matter on the 1797
agenda of Congress, since war with France seemed imminent. France,
of course, had once been friends to the United States. But twenty years
later, things had changed. The French navy had started seizing American
merchant vessels, and the United States had no navy to speak of to protect itself. The situation was already called the "Quasi-War" or "half
War,"[36] as John referred to it. Abigail agreed that a federal tax was
needed, so "we certainly ought to have Some resource of Revenue which
is not subject to the piratical plunder of Foreign Nations."[37] France was
also angry that the US passed the Jay Treaty, which France claimed favored Great Britain. France also refused to receive the new American
minister to their country. In return, the US stopped making debt payments to France and refused to pay a substantial bribe. War was on the
minds of most Americans.

However, America was in no shape to jump into a transatlantic war.
Outgoing President George Washington knew that fact, as did the new
President. But facing Adams from the first day of his administration
was the question of taxes and if and how to raise them to boost the military. Almost immediately, John was missing his most valuable counsel—Abigail.

Unfortunately, and without Abigail's counsel, John was talked into
endorsing a two million dollar "Direct Tax" by Congress, and it was the
first mistake of his presidency. Congress passed the Direct House Tax
of 1798. It was a disaster and sparked Fries's Rebellion, an armed revolt
by Pennsylvania Dutch farmers against the direct tax. An even worse
proposal by Congress was being debated. It would carry the historical
name of the Alien and Sedition Acts.

By April 1797, John was beyond desperation to get Abigail to Philadelphia, to "assist me with your Councils, and console me with your Conversation. . . [I] urge your immediate departure for Philadelphia. I must now repeat them with Zeal and Earnestness. I can do nothing without you."[38] John's April 11 letter pleading for Abigail's presence was preceded only by a few days of the death of John's mother, Susanna Boylston Adams. Six days later Abigail wrote to John: "To-morrow I have the last duties to pay to our venerable parent. I have taken upon me the care and charge of the funeral. . . . It is not for me to say when I will leave here; the will of heaven has detained me."[39] For nearly five years, Abigail had been caring for her ailing mother-in-law in Braintree/Quincy. Now a new chapter of her life opened. She was returning to Philadelphia—this time (as Abigail had foreseen in a dream), as First Lady and unofficial presidential advisor.

Shortly after the funeral, Abigail left on the arduous journey to Philadelphia. Abigail learned on the road that Mary "Polly" Smith, a twenty-one-year-old daughter of Abigail's late brother William Jr. had died from tuberculosis, or "consumption" as it was called. More agonizing news awaited Abigail when she stopped to visit Nabby and her family in East Chester, New York. Abigail learned that Nabby's husband, Colonel Smith, was missing and was barely one step ahead of the law for defaulting on his speculation debts. Abigail bitterly wrote to her sister Mary that the visit with Nabby "took from me all appetite to food, and depresst my Spirits. . . . the col gone a journey, I know not where I could not converse with her, I saw her Heart too full. such is the folly and Madness of speculation and extravagance."[40]

"These melancholy harbingers following, so closely each other, cast a Gloom over every object, and saddend the otherways Cheerfull Scenes of Nature, which were just waking into Life, and putting on new verdure after a long and severe winter,"[41] Abigail wrote in a letter to John Quincy. While Abigail was on the road, President Adams gave his first state of the union speech to Congress on May 16. Most of it was critical of French foreign policy, a slight the French didn't appreciate. The French ruling body planned their revenge during the summer break while John and Abigail were relaxing in Quincy.

Making one more stop on her way down to Philadelphia, Abigail checked in on her son Charles and his wife, Sarah "Sally" Smith Adams. The couple had a one-year-old daughter, Susanna Boylston Adams. Abigail informed her sister Mary that "Charles lives prettily but frugally. he has a Lovely Babe and a discreet woman I think for his wife, quite different from many of the Family."[42]

When First Lady Abigail arrived in Philadelphia on May 10 she was engulfed with visitors and well-wishers. Meeting and greeting everyone was becoming the chief event for her each day, aside from advising her husband on issues. She realized that to have any personal time to herself, she needed to publish and enforce times of the day in which she would receive visitors. "I keep up My old Habit of rising at an early hour. if I did not I should have little command of my Time at 5 I rise from that time till 8 I have a few leisure hours. at 8 I breakfast, after which untill Eleven I attend to my Family arrangements. at that hour I dress for the Day. from 12 untill two I receive company, sometimes untill 3. we dine at that hour. . . I begin to feel a little more at Home, and less anxiety about the ceremonious part of my Duty."[43]

Abigail had left Peacefield closed when she departed for Philadelphia since she couldn't find a trustworthy person to live in it while she and John were gone. Mary offered to occasionally go over or ride by the residence to check on it. "I have been to your House," Mary wrote, and "the mice have taken possession of your Store Room. there were several things wanted to be taken care of. the Loaf Sugar was in a sad plight the mice had got into the cask & fatten'd upon it. every loaf was cover'd with their dirt & those which were in a Bag were wet & smelt badly."[44] In her next paragraph, Mary offered to open the house and air it out. But in this mid-June letter Mary was hesitant to ask about Abigail's original plan for the summer: "I am affraid to ask you if we shall not see you this Summer. tis a long journey in hot weather I know but you had better take it than remain in that hot city."[45]

Abigail's plan to get out of Philadelphia to avoid the summer heat and diseases was delayed, she advised Mary. She and John still had to contend with the July Fourth festivities started by President Washington. The Chief Executive of each following administration was tasked with also paying for the huge happening out of their own pockets; a burden the Adamses could barely manage: "then comes the 4 July which is a still more tedious day, as we must then have not only all Congress, but all the Gentlemen of the city, the Govenour and officers and companies, all of whom the late President used to treat with cake punch and wine. what the House would not hold used to be placed at long tables in the Yard. as we are here, we cannot avoid the trouble nor the expence. I have been informd the day used to cost the late President 500 dollors. more than 200wt of cake used to be expended, and 2 quarter casks of wine besides Spirit. you will not wonder that I dread it, or think President Washington to blame for introducing the custom, if he could have avoided it."[46]

John had a few other duties and appointments to engage in as president before he and Abigail could leave Philadelphia for the remainder of the summer. The open post of minister plenipotentiary to Prussia was given to his son John Quincy Adams. John Quincy was more than qualified for the position. But the loud cries of nepotism were expected and delivered. "The appointments of Envoys extraordinary, like every other measure of Government will be censured by those who make a point of abusing every thing,"[47] Abigail wrote. As an ambassador John Quincy needed an experienced secretary, so he employed his youngest brother, Thomas Boylston Adams in the duty.

John and Abigail finally left Philadelphia for Peacefield on July 19. Abigail reasoned that the summer of 1797 spent in Quincy was meant for John "to be a month or twos relaxation in the rural occupations of his Farm, which are so necessary for his Health of Body and vigor of mind."[48] But more family news reached the Adamses' farm that summer. On July 26, John Quincy Adams married Louisa Catherine Johnson in London while he was waiting for congressional approval of his new position. The two had courted for a few years until John Quincy was assured that he could support a wife and future family. The newlyweds and Thomas then headed off for Hamburg and to John Quincy's new position.

Abigail had to wait for four years before she met Louisa. During that time preconceived ideas on the parts of both women began to take root. Abigail had learned that the Johnson family, and specifically Louisa's father Joshua Johnson, had been the American emissary in London. But as of late the Johnson family fortune had been lost, prompting them to move back to Maryland.

The next piece of family information was also not good. The money that son Charles had invested in speculative ventures had disappeared in a "bubble" funds collapse—including $4,000 which belonged to his brother John Quincy and represented nearly all his savings. John Quincy had expressed complete confidence with Charles's "safe security"[49] of his money: "As I place an entire confidence in your integrity and prudence, as well as in your fraternal affection, I presume you will have no occasion to make use of my name in the employment of the money."[50]

Abigail and John had always had the trusted agreement of each one having permission to open the other's mail. Of course, in all the years when John was away, it was necessary for Abigail to open John's mail to keep his correspondence active or to keep his legal business afloat—such as receiving payments to John on loans that were overdue. Occasionally when John was at home, he sometimes opened Abigail's mail; it seemed like when he did it was out of boredom or innocent curiosity. Of course, as a married woman in colonial times, Abigail had no legal right to prevent her husband from opening her mail. Usually, Abigail wouldn't be bothered with it, except for a few times when she wanted to keep a good-intentioned secret from John.

In 1797, Abigail had a new reason for her intercepting any of her delivered letters before they may have been picked up by John. She had decided to greatly expand Peacefield as a retirement gift to John for when his political career was over: it was to be "our Ark of safety" for when "we are four Years older if we should live to see the Day."[51] Abigail wanted it to be a surprise.

But in late 1797, John opened an innocent letter to Abigail. She had to "scold" John about his letter-opening practice, and she told Mary about it: "The President has agreed that he will not open any more Letters to me, and will be satisfied with such parts as I am willing to communicate. accordingly he has not opend any since I scolded So hard about it."[52]

The surprise was spoiled however in 1798. A neighbor to the Adamses, "Mr soper from Braintree"[53] traveling through Pennsylvania, had stopped in to say "hello" to the President and to remark about all the construction going on at Peacefield. John took the leaked news very well and even wished the surprise would have been kept secret.

A November 1797 letter from Abigail to Mary touched on a subject that had become controversial within the fragile union of states: that of females voting. In 1776 the New Jersey state constitution stated that "all inhabitants of this colony, of full age, who are worth £fifty . . . and have resided within the county . . . for twelve months" could cast a ballot. In 1790, important and historic steps were taken by that single state to ensure that a large group of Americans could freely cast ballots. The New Jersey legislature reworded the law to say, 'he or she,' clarifying that both men and women had voting rights. However only single women could vote because married women could not own property. Unfortunately in 1807, the New Jersey state legislature went backward and restricted suffrage (voting rights) to tax-paying, white male citizens.[54]

Erasing any doubt that Abigail would vote if she had the chance, she wrote, "if our state constitution had been equally liberal with that of New jersey and admitted the females to a Vote, I should certainly have exercised it."[55]

By the first week of October 1797, John decided that he needed to be closer to the center of the federal government. Although the summer yellow fever epidemic in Philadelphia hadn't yet abated after a couple frosts, John felt the epidemic would vanish while he and Abigail made the long journey back to the capital. John and Abigail packed up their belongings and left. But when they got to Nabby's house in East Chester, New York, word had reached the Adamses that the Philadelphia yellow fever epidemic still raged, and it was unsafe to go back into the city. Congress itself had temporarily moved to New York City to avoid the epidemic. While they were at Nabby's house, a letter reached Abigail from John Quincy explaining that his new bride, pregnant for only three months, had suffered a miscarriage—possibly due to the very primitive road conditions they had encountered traveling to Hamburg.

In the meantime, global events had not shut down for the summer. By early November 1797, as Abigail expressed, the country would be "happy indeed if we may be permitted to escape the calamities of War."[56] John returned to his administration in Philadelphia as did Congress. It was discovered in late summer that the French had maneuvered to place the United States and President John Adams purposely on the brink of war.

To friend Elizabeth Ellery Dana, Abigail warned, "My dear Madam the situation of our Country becomes daily more and more Dangerous, and I fear we shall find ourselves involved in a War wholy unprepaird for it, a War which we have not provoked."[57]

"Much of the Scum Rising"

1798–1800

C *atherine Nuth Johnson*, John Quincy Adams's mother-in-law, had expressed how fascinating it would be to be associated in a seat of power, as was Abigail's position. Abigail bluntly answered Mrs. Johnson's perception, "Indeed my dear Madam, the service of this Government is not a Bed of Roses—in any department of it."[1]

On the heels of the disastrous Direct House Tax of 1798 came the congressional passage of the controversial Alien and Sedition Acts. Unfortunately, it is the defining event in the presidency of John Adams. Rarely is it ever balanced with the fact that the Adams administration prevented the United States from being pulled into a world war—a war that it was ill-equipped to fight so soon after the country was founded.

Abigail was by now unofficially serving as what we today would call chief of staff [2] and policy advisor to the president. Fisher Ames, a popular orator and Federalist representative from Massachusetts, acknowledged: "The good Lady his wife . . . is as complete a politician as any Lady in the old French Court."[3]

However, with the good came the bad. Abigail had also been linked to history's blame for the "Alien Bill,"[4] as Abigail called it, and which she fully supported. It's rare that Abigail ever gave flawed advice to John, but that perspective is easy in hindsight. It's always uncomplicated to have the luxury of 250 years of history to judge a measure. From Abigail's point of view, when these events were happening, her conservative decisions are understandable.

The Alien and Sedition Acts were a bundling of four laws passed by the Federalist-controlled US Congress and President John Adams in June and July of 1798. It was felt that war with France would break out at any moment, and the acts sought to suppress freedom of the press and of speech during that time when French spies allegedly were secretly embedded in American society. The acts also restricted French persons, as well as French enemies, moles, influencers, and infiltrators, from freely traveling in the United States.

The older Abigail became, the more conservative she became on most matters. Her frustration and outward anger at false criticism had been formed during her time in London where she saw firsthand how unfairly the British press treated John. Sometimes the blatant lies printed by newspapers made her blood boil and she said so in her letters. She brought that animosity against the press back with her from Europe and into the offices of vice president and now president. Her feelings came to a head with passage of the Alien and Sedition Acts and the events that had brought on that legislation.

There were four separate new laws. The Alien Friends Act authorized President Adams to deport non-citizens during war or non-war and was passed June 25, 1798; the Naturalization Act raised the residency requirements for American citizenship from five to fourteen years and was passed June 18; the Alien Enemies Act permitted the arrest, imprisonment, and deportation of enemy male citizens during wartime and was passed July 6; and the fourth law, the Sedition Act, made it a crime for American citizens to "print, utter, or publish . . . any false, scandalous, and malicious writing"[5] about the government; and was passed July 14. During the Adams administration, ten newspaper printers and editors were convicted under the Sedition Act. One was James D. Callender, a notorious muckraker whose work would play a major role in the upcoming election of 1800.

Abigail firmly observed that the Alien and Sedition Acts were designed to protect against any perceived French plans to undermine the bedrock of the United States; as well as Americans' rights for peaceful commerce upon the sea, "for our very coasts are infested with French Privateers, who insult us in our own Waters."[6] There had always been a chance, Abigail cautioned John Quincy, that the four laws could have been debated to death and hacked up by Congress, "shaved and pared, to almost nothing."[7]

In a letter to her sister Mary Cranch, Abigail put full blame for the recent American Francophobe frenzy upon the Directory, the name of the current government of France. She added in parenthesis "(to call it a Republick, would be a subversion of terms)."[8] Abigail continued claiming she knew the malicious motives of the post-revolutionary French, "the base veiws and designs of France to Plunder us of all we hold dear & Valuable, our Religion our Liberty our Government and our Property."[9] Furthermore, she asserted that the French either demanded that President Adams apologize after his anti-French remarks in a recent address, or that France be paid an extra amount of hush money: "even the Presidents speech at which they have the insolence to pretend they are offended, may be expiated by money!"[10]

But it was the death threats mailed to John that most alarmed Abigail, "base and incendary Letters sent to the house addrest to him, that I really have been allarmd for his Personal safety tho I have never before exprest it."[11]

With the passing of the Alien and Sedition Acts, Abigail at least felt a degree of protection against newspaper writers who resembled to her, "an envenomed toad spit[ting] forth his poison."[12]

Initially John was widely acclaimed for signing the bills into law in June and July 1798. To show his personal gratitude, John decided to send each town that supported him a thank-you letter specific to that individual town. It turned out to be a huge task. Even asking Abigail to proofread, edit, or rewrite each letter required a degree of secrecy. No one in the government could know that a woman was taking part in crafting presidential material. Abigail confided to Mary, "I did get an alteration in it, but between ourselves . . . this is confidential."[13]

As the president's Fourth of July festivities grew closer, the incessant heat in Philadelphia made Abigail feel like she was "in an oven the bricks are so Hot." "The extreem heat of yesterday & the no less prospet of it this day, is beyond any thing I ever experienced in my Life. the Glasses were at 90 in the Shade yesterday. tomorrow will be the 4 July, when if possible I must see thousands. I know not how it will be possible to get through." She apologized to Mary for such a short letter, "tis so Hot I cannot think or write more."[14]

Abigail successfully endured the holiday's heat. It wasn't until late July that John and Abigail were able to leave Philadelphia for Quincy, delayed by the ever-present French crisis. On the rough road to Quincy, Abigail became extremely sick. The pair stopped at Nabby's house in East Chester, New York, where Abigail sent this note on to Mary: "we found clouds of dust for want of Rain, troops and calvacades did not lessen it, and the Heat was intolerably oppressive, so much so as to nearly kill all our Horses, and oppress me to such a degree as to oblige me to stop twice in a few hours, and intirely undress myself & lie down on the Bed, at night we could not get rest. small Rooms bad Beds & some company obliged me to stretch my wearied Limbs upon the floor upon a Bed not longer than one of my Bolsters. . . . I never sufferd so much in travelling before."[15] Abigail stayed ill and weak from an unknown cause throughout the late summer and fall of 1798. She wrote little during that time.

When John was due to leave Quincy for Philadelphia on November 12, it was obvious to him that he must once again travel alone and leave Abigail behind to recover. Without Abigail's steady demeanor and counsel, John felt that his political future was on dangerous ground. He confided as much to retired President George Washington that Abigail was "confined to the Bed of Sickness for two Months her Destiny is Still very precarious, and mine in consequence of it."[16] However John had to return to address Congress about a continued military mobilization if the Quasi War with France turned hotter. By 1798 the cost for Adams's military buildup was beyond budgetary limits, which included launching "Old Ironsides"—the USS *Constitution*. The country would have to take on debt to pay for the rest of the proposals.

This was accomplished by issuing federal certificates and securities, a tool that Abigail had long been familiar with and welcomed. She learned that to attract more investors, the new certificates paid out a 3, 6, or 8 percent interest rate. Also being offered were the attractive certificates which carried an interest payment delayed or "defer'd" until 1801. She notified John that "our stocks are high. there have not been any at Market untill lately, no defer'd stock to be had at all Six pr ct at seventeen. I have observed that it has been the same at Philadelphia."[17] Abigail had encouraged John to also buy some of the attractive securities through Abigail's agent and uncle Doctor Cotton Tufts. However, John still couldn't completely change his Puritan values of investing in tangible real estate instead of buying securities. Abigail told Tufts, "I have wanted the P——t to get you to draw for 2000 dollars which I think might be spaird, and to get you to vest it in stock but he says he believes he must Build a Barn & Stables with it."[18]

On October 23, 1798, Massachusetts Governor Increase Sumner had proclaimed November 29 as a day of Thanksgiving within the state. Abigail wrote a lonely letter to John: "This is our Thanksgiving day. when I look Back upon the year past, I perceive many, very many causes for thanksgiving, both of a publick and Private nature." Abigail had invited a few people to her house to celebrate, but most, including the Cranches, were too ill to come. "No Husband dignifies my Board, no Children add gladness to it, no Smiling Grandchildren Eyes to sparkle for the plumb pudding, or feast upon the mincd Pye. . . . I had but one resource, & that was to invite mr & mrs Porter to dine with me; and the two Families to unite in the Kitchin with Pheby the only surviving Parent I have, and thus we shared in the [']Bounties of providence.'"[19]

In the same letter Abigail praised a speech given by Maryland Governor John Henry on November 7. Henry had called for a strong offensive against France and continued cooperation between the states and Congress, "Govr Henry, tho I like his speech" and she added, "[I] belive he made it without the aid of Laudanum."[20] Even in Abigail's weakened state, she could still supervise the construction of a new carriage house and barn at Peacefield. As she brought John up to date, he in turn cautioned Abigail that the look of the buildings should not appear flashy. "Foppery" was the word John used. In his letter to Abigail he wrote, "My Fortune is small—Family large—and expensive—And shiftless Children and Grand Children enough to distract me."[21]

A family embarrassment occurred when the Adamses' son-in-law, Colonel William Stephens Smith (Nabby's husband), was promoted by President Adams to adjutant general and appointed to be third in command of a new army being created in case of a French attack. George Washington had been called out of retirement to be the commanding general, but in name only. The real command had gone to Major General Alexander Hamilton, due to Washington's insistence and despite John's reluctance. All high-level appointments had to be confirmed by Congress, and it was at that step that Colonel Smith was flagged as undesirable because of his prominent bankruptcy. Smith was offered a much smaller and insignificant job, that of surveyor and inspector of the port of New York. Smith had to take it out of necessity. Profoundly disappointed, John wrote to Abigail, "The General Officers nominated Smith for the command of a Regiment. . . . All the Actions of my Life and all the Conduct of my Children have not yet disgraced me so much as this Man. His Pay will not feed his Dogs."[22]

Before leaving Philadelphia in March 1799 for Peacefield's tranquility and Abigail's counsel, John had a surprise up his sleeve which baffled his fellow Federalists. It appeared as if war with France was only a matter of time, and very much wanted by the Federalists. John secretly ordered the American ambassador to the Netherlands, William Vans Murray, to travel to France with a peace offering. Abigail, in Quincy, heard of the peace offering outrage from the Federalists, who claimed it never would've happened if Abigail had been advising John in Philadelphia: "some of the Feds who did not like being taken so by surprize, said they wisht the old woman had been there; they did not believe it would have taken place; this was pretty sausy, but the old woman can tell them they are mistaken, for she considers the measure as a master stroke of policy." Abigail added the whimsical question to John, "Pray am I a good politician?"[23]

It was a warm mid-July of 1799 and John had been home in Quincy since March. Abigail was now recovered from her mysterious illness and well enough to send a family gift, which she often tried to do. Abigail had sent a book to her eight-year-old niece and namesake, Abigail Adams Shaw, the youngest daughter of Abigail's youngest sister, Elizabeth Smith Shaw Peabody of Atkinson, New Hampshire. However, Abigail hadn't looked over the book for content before buying it. Abigail apparently wasn't pleased with some of the messages in the book, but she decided to send it anyway tagged with a strong message. It is unknown what book it was, or what content was deemed offensive to Abigail. However, it again instigated intense words from Abigail about the relationships between men and women. Women, Abigail wrote, should never feel inferior to men: "I send my little Neice a Book I did not Read it untill I bought it. there is no harm in it, many usefull lessons—but some which I do not assent to or approve of—I will never consent to have our sex considered in an inferiour point of light. let each planet shine in their own orbit, God and natur designd it so—if man is Lord, woman is Lordess—that is what I contend for." Abigail then added a political edge to her feelings: "and if a woman does not hold the Reigns of Government, I see no reason for her not judging how they are conducted."[24]

John was preparing to leave for Congress in late September, but this time he was heading to Trenton, New Jersey, where Congress had fled because of the still-raging yellow fever epidemic in Philadelphia. Abigail joined John within a month. Just before John left, he and Abigail had received news that their alcoholic son Charles was bankrupt and had deserted his family. John traveled to East Chester, New York, to check on Nabby and her family, who were also reeling from her husband's sordid money problems. When John arrived, he discovered that Sally, Charles's wife, and their two young children had also taken up residency with Nabby. John sent Abigail an agonized letter: "Sally opened her Mind to me for the first time. I pitied her, I grieved, I mourned but could do no more. a Madman possessed of the Devil can alone express or represent.—I renounce him.—[My son] is a mere Rake, Buck, Blood & Beast."[25] John had painfully disowned one of his three sons. "Charlie" no longer existed to John.

After Abigail's similar stopover in East Chester, she reached Philadelphia in November at about the same time as John and Congress. The yellow fever epidemic was gone, at least until the next summer. Once arrived, First Lady Abigail began again receiving the formal visits expected by the public. The "Countess de Tilly," the fifteen-year-old daughter of Anne Bingham, was one such caller. Married to a reckless, bon vivant Frenchman, Abigail sarcastically noted that the countess "has all the appearence and Dress of a Real French woman, Rouged up to the Ears."[26]

In mid-December 1799, they received the shocking news that rolled through Philadelphia and the rest of the United States: George Washington had died on December 14. Abigail had known Washington very well through the eight years of John's vice presidency. His aura never diminished in her eyes. On December 22, Abigail wrote to Mary praises of "the account of the Death of Gen'll Washington . . . if we look through the whole tennor of his Life; History will not produce to us a Parrallel."[27]

The year 1800 would bring about one of the most contentious presidential elections in American history. The incumbent President Adams, not even popular within his own Federalist Party, was to face Vice President Thomas Jefferson, the nominee from the Democratic-Republican Party. Charles C. Pinckney of South Carolina was the Federalist nominating caucus's choice to balance their Adams–New England ticket with a person from the South. Jefferson, a Virginian, was balanced out with Aaron Burr of New York. Adams had virtually no say in who his running mate would be. The two opposing points between the parties were the Quasi War with France and the Alien and Sedition Acts. Since campaigning for the presidential office was also not allowed, John and Abigail would spend the summer of 1800 in Quincy silently observing the pre-election events through newspaper accounts. It was no illusion that electoral strings were being pulled behind the scenes in Philadelphia by Alexander Hamilton, the former Secretary of the Treasury. It was discovered that he had met with New England Federalists and urged them to switch the positions of John Adams's presidential spot with Pinckney, the Federalists' vice presidential candidate. Abigail called Hamilton the "little General,"[28] as it was obvious to her that he was using his appointment as army commander to travel around cementing the power of the Federalists Party. Hamilton could control Pinckney; he could not control Adams. Abigail realized that Hamilton was splitting the party, which would make it easier for Jefferson to claim victory.

Before Abigail took her summer break and left Philadelphia for Quincy, she reported to Mary her growing disillusionment with the whole electoral process: "One or two more Elections will be quite sufficient I believe to convince this people that no engine can be more fatally employd than frequent popular Elections, to corrupt and destroy the Morals of the people, the Electionering campaign I presume will bring all their forces into action."[29]

To counterweigh her anxiety, Abigail greatly anticipated her summer return to Quincy and her flowers and garden. She asked her sister Mary "for the Garden do not let my flowers be neglected."[30] "[T]he lively song of the Birds hail the welcome approach of the renovating Season; reminding Me of my Garden at Quincy & that like Eden of old it calls for culture, the pruning knife & the labourer."[31] In Philadelphia Abigail even missed a tree from Peacefield, "the weeping Willow, which is a favorite tree with Me, from the gracefullness of its slender branches, which float and wave to every breaze."[32]

The people of Philadelphia knew that regardless of who won the upcoming election, this was their final season of fashion and drawing rooms. The president and government would be moving to the new "Washington City." Therefore, Abigail's drawing room socials were very crowded in the spring of 1800. The First Lady officially announced "my last Drawing Room is notified for the 2d of May."[33] Although Abigail generally enjoyed the drawing rooms, she wasn't thrilled with a female fashion aspect that had recently crept into the events. It was a renewal of the classical "Empire style" of ancient Rome and Greece in art, literature, architecture, and fashion. The Empire style of dresses (raised waistlines to just below the bosom, short sleeves, low necklines, flowing skirts) was showing up at the drawing room events, and their appearance wasn't lost on Abigail, who considered them sensational and not in good taste. She noticed the hush in the room as a woman curtseyed wearing such a dress, "every Eye in the Room has been fixd upon her, and you might litterally see through her—but in this stile of Dress, She has danced nor regarded the splitting out of her scanty coat. upon the occasion, I askd a young Gentleman, if Miss ——— was at the dance last Evening. the replie, was yes most wickedly—to do justice to the other Ladies—I cannot accuse them of Such departures from female decorum, but they most of them wear their Cloaths too scant upon the body & too full upon the Bosom for my fancy; not content with the show which nature bestows; they borrow from art, and litterally look like Nursing Mothers."[34] Abigail summed it up to Mary as: "in short a drawing room frequently exhibits a specimin of Grecian Turkish French and English fashion at the same time, with ease Beauty and Elegance equal to any court."[35]

In one of the final events in Philadelphia, Thomas Adams asked his parents if he could host a tea party and dance in the President's House with some of his friends and their dates. John and Abigail said yes. Abigail described the evening and the Empire dress one of the girls was wearing:

> on thursday we had 28 young or rather unmarried Ladies and Gentlemen to dine with us. they were from Families with which our Young people have been most intimate, and who had shewn them many attentions & civilities. just before I rose from table, Thomas came round to me and whisperd me: have You any objection to my having a dance this Evening? none in the world, provided it comes thus accidential; the company soon came up to the Drawing Room to Tea, and in an hours time, the tables were removed, the lights light & the Room all in order. at 8 the dancing commenced, at 12, it finishd—more pleasure ease and enjoyment I have rarely witnessd. the President went down about an hour & then retired. I tarried it out, but was obliged to go to Bed at 8 oclock last night in concequence—Several of the company declared that they should always remember the Evening as one of the pleasentesst of their Lives— amongst the company was miss B——m, with manners perfectly affable, polite and agreable, with out affectation, or any haughtyness of Demeanour, but really fassinating; I could not but lament, that the uncoverd bosom should display, what ought to have been veild, or that the well turnd, and finely proportiond form, Should not have

been less conspicuous in the dance, from the thin drapery which coverd it. I wishd that more had been left to the imagination, and less to the Eye.[36]

Abigail possibly felt like a conservative "fuddy-duddy" when chaperoning the younger generation. John's reaction was to go to bed.

Never could Abigail imagine that the "fatally employd" election campaign would stoop so low and dirty as it did in 1800. A mud-slinging editor and pamphleteer in Virginia, James D. Callender, had a grudge against John Adams. The Adams administration had prosecuted and jailed Callender under the Sedition Act. However, Jefferson secretly hired Callender to dig up some election dirt on Adams. Callender's outrageous series of essays became a pamphlet, "The Prospect Before Us." Callender called President Adams "a blind, bald, crippled, toothless man who is a hideous hermaphroditic character with neither the force and fitness of a man, nor the gentleness and sensibility of a woman."[37]

In response to those claims, the Adams administration allegedly came back with the sensational claim: "Tom Jefferson, for the Presidency, who, to make the best of him, was nothing but a mean-spirited, low-lived fellow, the son of a half-breed Indian squaw, sired by a Virginia mulatto father, as was well known in the neighborhood where he was raised."[38]

Shortly after leaving Philadelphia for Peacefield, Abigail expressed to Mary in no uncertain terms how tired she was of the election process and all the corruption and lies that went with it: "I have heard of so Many lies and falshoods propagated to answer Electioneering purposes since I left Philadelphia, and for the last three weeks that I was there, that I am Disgusted with the world and the chief of its inhabitants do not appear worth the trouble and pains they cost to save them from Destruction—you see I am in an ill humour. when the rain subsides and the sun shines, it will dispell some of the gloom which hangs heavey at my heart."[39]

One week before the October 31 opening of the election dates, Alexander Hamilton published an essay-pamphlet, "Letter from Alexander Hamilton, Concerning the Public Conduct and Character of John Adams, Esq. President of the United States, [24 October 1800]."[40] Hamilton sent it in secrecy to some high-level Federalists in a bid to take party support from Adams. But Jefferson's Democratic-Republican Party acquired a copy of it and widely published it. In it, Hamilton had declared John Adams as totally unfit for the presidency. "Not denying to Mr. Adams patriotism and integrity, and even talents of a certain kind, I should be deficient in candor, were I to conceal the conviction, that he does not possess the talents adapted to the Administration of Government, and that there are great and intrinsic defects in his character, which unfit him for the office of Chief Magistrate."[41]

Hamilton's late season biased essay drove the final wedge between the fractured Federalist Party and tipped the election toward Jefferson. It also brought an end to Alexander Hamilton's standing as head of the Federalist Party and his political future. With a veiled criticism of Hamilton, Abigail summed up the politics of that early time: "the zeal pot of politicks is boiling over, and much of the Scum rising."[42] Abigail wasn't the only one name-calling. John referenced Hamilton's libelous pamphlet couched in a crude, but true, assessment: "a hundred lies besides published in a Pamphlet against me, by an insolent Coxcomb, who rarely dined in good Company where there was good wine, without getting silly, and vapouring about his Administration, like a young Girl about her brilliants and trinketts: Yet I loose all Patience, when I think of a bastard brat of a Scotch Pedler."[43]

In later years after Hamilton's early death, John would continue his sensational tirade against him: "What a pity it is that our Congress had not known this discovery, and that Alexander Hamiltons project of raising an Army of fifty thousand Men, ten thousand of them to be Cavalry and his projects of Sedition Laws and Alien Laws and of new Taxes to Support his army, all arose from a superabundance of secretions which he could not find Whores enough to draw off? and that the Same Vapours produced his Lyes and Slanders by which he totally destroyed his party forever and finally lost his Life in the field of honor."[44]

In the world of 1800, news still traveled at the speed of a horse or schooner. Had the pace been faster, history may have changed in favor of the incumbent President Adams. On September 30, Adams's peace envoy William Vans Murray and French dignitaries signed the Convention of 1800, also known as the Treaty of Mortefontaine. It ended the undeclared naval war between the United States and the French government now led by Napoleon Bonaparte. The treaty opened the relationship between the two nations that eventually led to the Louisiana Purchase. Adams would always list the Treaty of Mortefontaine as one of the public service pinnacles of his life, along with obtaining four financial loans for the United States from the Netherlands.

However, news of the Treaty of Mortefontaine wouldn't reach the United States until after the national election. By then John Adams had been defeated by Thomas Jefferson in his bid for a second term as president.

The results would all be revealed in time. But in October 1800, voters were casting their ballots. The Electoral College would then meet to determine the winner. It would be months before the election results would be known. In the meantime, the existing First Family, the Adamses, had to move out of the President's House in Philadelphia and into the new President's House in Washington, District of Columbia, for the final months of his term. The residence wouldn't be called "The White House" until 1812.[45] The District of Columbia would exist within "Washington City" or "Federal City." John left Quincy on October 11 and arrived at the house in "Washington City" in early November. Abigail was expected to arrive sometime later that month.

The decision had been made in 1790 to build an entirely new city out of Potomac swampland. The cornerstone of the President's House in Washington, DC, had been laid on October 13, 1792, by President Washington. In a letter to Abigail the day after John moved in, he wrote, "The Building is in a State to be habitable," though that was somewhat generous as the interior was far from finished.[46] John also signed off the letter to Abigail with now-famous words about the building—now etched into the State Dining Room fireplace mantle of the White House—"Before I end my Letter I pray Heaven to bestow the best of Blessings on this House and all that shall hereafter inhabit it. May none but honest and wise Men ever rule under this roof."[47]

To join John in Washington, Abigail left Quincy with her entourage of "ten Horses and nine persons"[48] on about October 19, 1800. However, she first had to say her good-byes to her sister Mary, who was at the time in very poor health, the same as Abigail herself. "It is a great Grief to me my dear sister that I can do so little for you in your trouble when I owe So Much to you. beside being much of an invalide myself."[49]

On her way, Abigail stopped in Manhattan to check on Charles's health. She expected to find Charles in bad health and knew in her heart that there would be nothing she could do to help her son. She found exactly that: "at N york I found my poor unhappy Son, for so I Must still call him, laid upon a Bed of sickness destitute of a home, the kindness of a friend afforded him an assylum. a distressing cough, an affection of the liver and a Dropsy will soon terminate a Life, which might have been Ma[de] valuable to himself and others. you will easily suppose that this Scene was too powerfull and distressing to me: Sally was with him but his Physician Says, he is past recovery—I shall carry a Melancholy report to the President, who passing through new york without Stoping knew not his situation."[50]

Abigail continued the journey until late in the afternoon of November 15 when, in the dense, dark, wild woods of Maryland, it became obvious to both the carriage driver and Abigail that they were lost.

Chapter Twenty-Five

"I Want to See the List of Judges"

1800–1804

Abigail arrived in the unfinished and malarial swamp town of "Washington City" on November 16, 1800—four weeks later than originally expected. The final leg of her journey had been harrowing. Her driver had become hopelessly lost in the dangerous woods past Baltimore. To make it worse, the sun had been setting. Nearly a week later, November 21, Abigail wrote Mary of the ordeal:

I arrived in this city on Sunday the 16th ult—having lost my way in the woods on saturday in going from Baltimore we took the road to Frederick and got nine miles out of our road. You find nothing but a Forest & woods on the Way, for 16 and 18 miles not a Village, here and there a thatchd cottage without a single pane of glass— inhabited by Black's—my intention was to have reachd Washington on saturday. . . . I sit out early intending to make my 36 Miles if possible: no travelling however but by day light; we took a direction as we supposed right, but in the first turn, went wrong—and were wandering more than two hours in the woods in different paths, holding down & breaking bows of trees which we could not pass—untill we met a solitary black fellow with a horse and cart. we inquired of him our way, and he kindly offerd to conduct us—which he did two miles, and then gave us such a clue as led us out to the post road and the Inn where We got some dinner.[1]

Back on the road again, they were stopped by Major Thomas Snowden, the owner of Patuxent Iron Works who had also been an officer serving under General Washington. Snowden begged Abigail and her procession to come to his house on the Old Post Road to rest up and safely spend the night. Abigail declined the generous offer because she "could not get courage to go to his House with ten Horses and nine persons."[2]

But shortly afterward she gave in when Major Snowden returned to plead once more; "we were stoped by the Major [Snowden] in full speed . . . in the kindest, and politest Manner he urged my return to his House, represented the danger of the road, and the impossibility of my being accomodated at any Inn I could reach: I plead My numbers, that was no objection he could accomodate double the number—there was no saying nay and I returned to a large Handsome Elegant House, where I was received with My Family, with what We Might term true English Hospitality Friendship."[3] Abigail added that the major was no follower of Jefferson: "I need not add that they are all true federal Characters."[4]

When Abigail and her entourage safely arrived in Washington, Abigail reserved the most vivid words to describe to Mary her first glimpse of "the President's House" and its grounds: "I arrived about one oclock at this place known by the name of the city, and the Name is all that You can call so—as I expected to find it a new country, with Houses Scatterd over a space of ten miles, and trees & stumps in plenty with, a castle of a House—so I found it—the Presidents House is in a beautifull situation in front of which is the potomac with a view of Alexandra—the country arround is romantic but a wild—a wilderness at present."[5]

"[N]ot one room or chamber is finished of the whole it is habitable by fires in every part, thirteen of which we are obliged to keep daily, or sleep in wet & damp places," Abigail remarked about the President's House. She famously noted, however, that "this House is built for ages to come."[6] Georgetown, however, didn't rate as highly for Abigail: "I have been to George Town and felt all that mrs Cranch described when she was a resident there. it is the very dirtyest Hole I ever saw for a place of any trade, or respectability of inhabitants. it is only one mile from me but a quagmire after every rain."[7] Abigail wrote a much more critical description of Washington, the town, to Nabby, but added, "You must keep all this to yourself, and, when asked how I like it, say that I write you the situation is beautiful, which is true."[8]

The fact that the President's House was being built by enslaved labor was in evidence every day Abigail looked out of a window. "The effects of Slavery are visible every where . . . the Slaves half fed, and destitute of cloathing, or fit for Rag faire, to labour, whilst the owner walks about Idle." Not much better were the accompanying "lower class of whites. . . they look like the refuse of human nature."[9]

Abigail had just gotten settled into the President's House when she learned the news that she probably expected: the death of her son Charles. "[H]is constitution was so Shaken, that his disease was rapid, and through the last period of his Life dreadfully painfull and distressing; he bore with patience & submission his Suffering's and heard the prayers for him with composure; his Mind at times was much deranged thro his sufferings, and through a total want of rest; he finally expired [wi]thout a groan on sunday week [November 30]. . . . I was Satisfied I had seen him for the last time when I left him. . . . [Y]et he did not look like an intemperate Man—he was bloted, but not red—." Alcoholism—specifically cirrhosis—was the likely cause of Charles's death.

On November 10, nearly three weeks before Charles died, Abigail had described Charles's imminent death as "an affection of the liver and a Dropsy"[10] (pleurisy). "[H]e was no Mans Enemy but his own—he was beloved, in spight of his errors, and all spoke with grief and sorrow for his habits," Abigail added.[11]

Polls for the election of 1800 closed on December 3, 1800. The results would be unknown for two months. But John Adams had already lost, by coming in third in the electoral votes with a total of sixty-five. Tied for first place with seventy-three votes each were Thomas Jefferson and Aaron Burr. On February 17, 1801, the voting process to break the tie moved to the House of Representatives as outlined by the US Constitution. During thirty-six rounds of balloting and negotiations, the latter mostly by Alexander Hamilton, the tie was broken. Thomas Jefferson would become president and Aaron Burr vice president.

To her uncle, Abigail bemoaned the Democratic-Republican win as "an unchecked spirit of calumny, lieing, and Slander; which has Spread through our country, to its infamy and disgrace, bearing down honour virtue and integrity like a besom of destruction."[12] She had definite bad feelings personally toward Jefferson, too, as she wrote to Mary that Jefferson "believes Religion only usefull as it may be made a political Engine, and that the outward forms are only as I once heard him express himself, Mere Mummery."[13] With news of the election results, the infant stock market also fell. Son Thomas anxiously asked his mother if he should sell all the equities he held. Abigail calmly replied, "tho Stocks have fallen, I would not advise to selling out; nay if I had money to spair, I would vest it in them. I think they will rise again. . . things will not suddenly Change."[14] Abigail, of course, was correct.

Abigail received a "pressing invitation of Mrs Washington"[15] dated December 21, 1800; George Washington had died almost exactly one year earlier on December 14, 1799. Martha was requesting Abigail make a last visit to Mount Vernon. Abigail responded that she would visit, even though she "had been ill a Week or ten days, confined to my Room,"[16] Abigail disclosed to Mary. Though traveling in bad winter weather was never welcomed, Abigail was still feeling the loss of Charles and "the sight of an old Friend, and the cordial reception I met With. . . . Served to sooth my Heart, wounded by a recent Grief, and penetrated with a sorrow which time may Soften, but cannot heal."[17]

Abigail found Mount Vernon curious and sad: "the House has an ancient appearance . . . the Rooms are small & low, as well as the Chambers." But she also noted that "the grounds" that used to look "highly ornamental" were now "going to decay." Martha Washington was still trying to deal with her husband's death and the profound changes it had brought to Mount Vernon. George Washington's will from July 9, 1799, first gave immediate freedom to Billy Lee, Washington's enslaved personal assistant, plus a lifetime pension. Billy had ridden alongside Washington for the full Revolutionary War. Washington then directed that upon Martha's death, 123 of the 317 enslaved persons at Mount Vernon were to be given their freedom. Those were the slaves that Washington himself owned. The remaining 153 enslaved people by law could not be freed by George or Martha Washington because they belonged to the Custis estate, in the aftermath of the death of Martha's first husband, Daniel Parke Custis, who had died without a will. Only Martha's death could bring about their freedom. Abigail observed, "Mrs Washington with all her fortune finds it difficult to support her family, which consists of three Hundred souls—one hundred and fifty of them, are now to be liberated."[18] The prospect of waiting to be freed upon Martha's death, she told Abigail, was very unsettling. Martha felt her life would be in danger to wait too long to free her enslaved people. So, she instead set January 1, 1801, as the announced date of freedom or "manumition." But even with that, she was still worried about what would happen to the suddenly freed slaves: "Men with Wives & Young children who have never Seen an acre, beyond the farm, are now about to quit it, and go adrift into the world without house Home or Friend. Mrs Washington is distrest for them."[19]

Abigail noted, "in the state in which they were left by the General, to be free at her death, she did not feel as tho her Life was safe in their Hands, many of whom would be told that it was there interest to get rid of her—She therefore was advised to sit them all free at the close of the year."[20] Washington's will also stipulated money to support elderly freed slaves or those who were unable to support themselves. Martha herself died in May 1802. In Abigail's letter to sister Mary, she summarized her feelings about slavery after visiting the "decay" of Mount Vernon: "if any person wishes to see the banefull effects of slavery, as it creates a torpor and an indolence and a spirit of domination—let them come and take a view of the cultivation of this part of the United states."[21]

Along with the visit with Martha Washington in December, Abigail corresponded with her friends and family about the Adamses' plans. "My spirits you See are low—I am not very well,"[22] she disclosed to Mary. "[T]he concequence to us personally, is that We retire from public Life: for myself and family I have few regreets; at My age and with my bodily infirmities I shall be happier at Quincy."[23]

Teasing post-election nicknames for John were being bantered around in the executive hallways, such as "Farmer Adams."[24] Aside from Abigail worrying about how John would take to retirement, she also was sad that her own compassionate activities of helping her "fellow creatures" would now be lessened: "I can truly and from my heart say, that the most mortifying circumstance attendant upon My retirement from public Life is, that, my power of doing good to my fellow creatures is curtaild and diminished."[25]

Abigail's twenty-three-year-old nephew, William "Billy" Smith Shaw,[26] son of her sister Elizabeth, was working as John's private secretary in Washington. When the 1800 election results were first announced, Billy sent a note out to his traveling Aunt Abigail confirming, "Soon after you left us the election was decided in favor of Mr. Jefferson for President."[27]

John and Abigail had only spent three months as the first occupants in the new President's House, but by then Abigail had enough of politics, at least outwardly. She would, however, always take an interest in politics for the rest of her days.

Though it was dangerous winter traveling, Abigail left Washington for Quincy during the last weeks of her husband's term and before roads got worse. Her nieces had warned her about traveling without a male escort: "Aunt how could you consent to come this horrid road through this shocking wilderness without some Gentleman with you."[28] Aunt Abigail replied with her typically honest truth: "I was too independant to want a Gentleman always at my apronstring—tho be sure it would be very agreable to have one in the way We traveld—yet I had been accustomed to get through many a trying scene, and combat many difficulties alone I was therefore not very timid."[29]

With their dual retirement from public life, the letters that Abigail and John exchanged over the decades were also coming to an end. However, a remarkable and often overlooked phrase can be found in a final letter illustrating Abigail's continued political influence that she exercised with John. John had indicated to Abigail, who was on the road back home, that in his final days as president he was appointing Federalist circuit court judges—a privilege the US Constitution allowed the president. As always, he asked for her opinion of the prospective candidates. The final sentence written by Abigail, in her final letter to John, demonstrates the depth of influence Abigail held, even up to the final days. Abigail wrote to John, "I want to see the list of judges."[30]

Those often called "midnight appointments"[31] greatly angered incoming President Thomas Jefferson and his Democratic-Republican Party members. Often in the early workings of the new republic, which had no model or precedent to copy from, habits and personal likings of the individual executive were sometimes codified into actions that are still practiced today. George Washington was aware that nearly everything he said and did could become precedent. One example was improvising "So help me, God" at the conclusion of his oath. Those words weren't in the original.

On March 4, 1801, Thomas Jefferson was to take the same oath—which Abigail thought hypocritical. Although Jefferson was largely considered a Christian Deist, Abigail thought of Jefferson's faith in less glowing terms: he was a Bible-defacing atheist and "Infidel." On Abigail's journey back to Quincy, she expressed to John her feelings about the new president's support of separation of church and state: "I have heard Some of the Democratic rejoicing Such as Ringing Bells & fireing cannon; what an inconsistancy Said a Lady to me to day, the Bells of Christ Church ringing peals of rejoicing for an Infidel President!"[32]

In later years another tradition, but not a law, dictated the outgoing president was to be present during the inauguration of his (or her) elected successor. It symbolized the democratic continuity and strength of the republic through a nonviolent change of power. But in John Adams's time that tradition of requiring the former president's attendance didn't exist. Adams had his carriage loaded and he and William Shaw left the President's House at 4:00 a.m. on Jefferson's inauguration day. John may have even felt that he wasn't welcome had he shown up unexpectedly at the inauguration, since he'd received no invitation. Perhaps it was also a bit of jealousy on John's part as well. He had never written his reason for the early departure, so we'll never know. John seemed outwardly content with a return to his agrarian lifestyle where he would wear the jocular titles of "Monarch of Stony field, Count of Gull Island, Earl of Mount Arrarat, Marquis of Candlewood Hill, and Baron of Rocky Run."[33]

The frosty feeling among Abigail, John, and Thomas Jefferson would go on for another three years with neither person writing to the other. Abigail would finally break the ice with her compassionate 1804 letter to Jefferson upon the death of his daughter Polly. But for John, the silence with Jefferson would last until 1812.

A last-minute decree made by President Adams was to recall his eldest son, John Quincy, from Berlin. The reasoning was that removing John Quincy Adams from his post would save face for both Adamses since it could be one of the first vindictive actions taken by President Jefferson. Abigail was delighted since an innermost desire of hers was now to have her two remaining sons, John Quincy and Thomas, near her in Quincy. She would have her wish. Much of her time in the years to follow would be spent with her children and grandchildren, and since she now lived with John and they didn't write to each other anymore, most of her letters were to her sisters and her children.

Meanwhile on April 12, 1801, John Quincy and his wife Louisa celebrated the successful birth of son George Washington Adams in Berlin. Louisa had lived through two miscarriages (ultimately, she would have three), so celebrating a baby's birth was joyful. However, the birthing name caused a quiet uproar in Peacefield when it came to light. It was a common rule of respect and honor to name baby boys after parental fathers or grandfathers. The fact that the new baby's name was "George Washington Adams" was curious. Abigail tried to work out the answer to that question in a July 1801 letter to son Thomas: "He has calld his Son George Washington. This I think was ill judged. I feel that it was wrong; Children do not know how much their parents are gratified by the continuation of their Name in their Grandchildren. I was not myself Sensible of it, and neither of my own Children bear the names of their Grandparents by the Maternal Side, Yet I now recollect, when you was named, that your Grandfather appeard hurt by it. I am sure your Brother had not any intention of wounding the feelings of his Father, but I see he has done it—Had he calld him Joshua, he would not have taken it amiss."[34]

John Quincy, Louisa, and their baby arrived in Philadelphia on September 4, 1801. They rested at the Philadelphia house of Thomas Adams. Then the newly arrived Adamses split up for visiting efficiency: John Quincy left for Quincy, Massachusetts, to reacquaint himself with his parents and to purchase a law office/home in Boston. Louisa and her infant, George, left for Washington to see her parents. Louisa got to Peacefield in November 1801, and the uncomfortable first impressions of both parties were evident. Abigail had heard that Louisa was generally always sick. That was confirmed by Abigail's writing soon after Louisa's arrival: "Mrs Adams has had a very allarming cough and pain in her Breast which confined her almost the whole time she was here, and it has not left her yet, tho she has been both Bled and Blisterd; her frame is so Slender and her constitution so delicate that I have many fears that she will be of short duration."[35]

Louisa assumed that she'd be made to feel inadequate and spurned when meeting John and Abigail—American royalty. More so, she disdained the rural atmosphere of Peacefield. Louisa had been born in London and had lived and been schooled in France and England. She was learned and always carried herself as a privileged woman. Many years later Louisa sarcastically recalled her surprise in meeting the Adams family and all of Abigail's pets for the first time, "Quincy! What shall I say of my impressions of Quincy! Had I steped into Noah's Ark I do not think I could have been more utterly astonished. . . . It was lucky for me that I was so much depressed, or so ill, or I should certainly have given mortal offence." Even "snuffling through the nose"[36] during church services by parishioners was foreign to her.

Adding to Louisa's "Noah's Ark" remark, Abigail, an animal lover, had just been gifted with a Newfoundland puppy she named Juno. At the bottom of a letter to Thomas's wife, Ann Harrod, who went by "Nancy," Abigail added, "P S Miss Juno wags her kind remembrance to you."[37]

At the start of 1802, Abigail sent another letter to Thomas, but she discreetly enclosed some money this time. Before she mentioned the money, she decried the deep divisions developing in the country during the Jeffersonian reign that she labeled "Southern despotism" and warned that "faction and party Rage will soon involve us in a civil war."[38] While pretending the reason for her letter was purely political, she knew that Thomas's legal work in Philadelphia wasn't prospering. Abigail may have still been mourning the death of Charles, but she retained the goal of having John Quincy and Thomas near her. She was very compassionate in her approach to Thomas to offer help, on one condition. He could not openly acknowledge the receipt of the money (which she called "my pin money") in any reply letter to her.[39] "I inclose it to you, requesting you to accept it as a small token of the Love and affection I bear you, wishing at the same time, that it was ten times the value. I have but one injunction to make you. It is that you make no mention of it; further than to say you received my Letter safe of the 28th of Feb'ry."[40]

In 1801, John Quincy had bought a house on Hanover Street in Boston to begin his law practice. In early 1802 he was elected to the Massachusetts Senate and in November was narrowly defeated in a close race for the US House of Representatives. In February 1803, he was successfully elected to the US Senate seat from Massachusetts. Abigail and John were happy with their son's success and their retirement was one of contentment. However, financial disaster was imminent for Abigail and John.

Norton Quincy, Abigail's mother's brother, was widowed, childless, and reportedly one of Abigail's favorite uncles. When Norton died in 1801, his large estate of the Quincy family's Mount Wollaston had to be distributed among heirs who were related to the Quincy family, namely Cotton Tufts Jr., Abigail, and her sisters. John, as always, had expressed a determination to own land rather than paper securities. He wanted to own the whole Mount Wollaston estate. Abigail enthusiastically agreed with him about owning a childhood property where she had such good memories. Through Abigail's uncle-trustee Cotton Tufts Sr., the Adamses set about buying the other claimants out.[41] Abigail's sisters, Mary and Elizabeth, were each given a lump sum of $2,251 in exchange for their claims on the estate. Married women, such as Mary and Elizabeth, could not legally hold cash. To get around that detail, Abigail informed their husbands, Richard Cranch and Reverend Steven Peabody, that her sisters' money was being deposited into a trust in the name of the sisters' eldest sons. Initially Cotton Tufts, Jr., was hesitant to sell his share, but eventually relented.

John and Abigail needed $13,000 to complete the transaction of buying Mount Wollaston and other parcels. John knew he had at least that amount in securities in an Amsterdam bank since the days when John was an ambassador in the Netherlands.

To route the funds discreetly, John asked John Quincy to handle the business deal. His son knew that if the funds first were channeled through a British bank and its pound currency, that the existing exchange rate would favor the American dollar. Or as Abigail understood it, "the exchange was more in favour of England than Holand."[42]

John Quincy was familiar with the British merchant investment firm of Bird, Savage & Bird. The bank was even designated a reliable banking/fiscal agent in Great Britain for the United States government. In late 1802, John Quincy deposited his parents' Dutch guilders in Bird, Savage & Bird and never gave it a second thought—until early 1803, when Bird, Savage & Bird declared total bankruptcy.

John and Abigail were stunned at the news that their money was gone. They were still in debt to pay off $7,000 already owed on the Mount Wollaston purchase. Abigail spelled out the truth for her unsuspecting son Thomas: "the House which has lately faild, Bird Savage & Bird; a Catastrophe so unexpected to us, and at a time when we had become responsible for so large a sum; has indeed distrest us, at no other–time of our lives could we have been equally affected by it."[43] She added, "I do not dread want, but I dread debt."[44]

The legal unwinding of the Bird, Savage & Bird claims dragged on and on. John Quincy updated his mother with the best news he could send: "I have nothing satisfactory to tell you of the demands against Bird, Savage and Bird—I have had the debt proved under the Bankruptcy of Robert Bird at New-York, and by a letter I received last Evening from Bird and Savage in London, I find Mr. Williams had received the papers I sent him to prove the debt there."[45] It was still unknown if any money or assets were left by Bird, Savage & Bird. If there was, the question would be whether anything was left to reimburse their clients.

John Quincy Adams did the honorable thing. He sold his recently purchased townhouse in Boston and, using his savings, he bought from his parents the two old Adams salt box homes[46] along with their farmland property—and he deliberately overpaid. John Quincy expressed, "The error of judgment was mine, and therefore I shall not refuse to share in the suffering."[47]

With Abigail and John's domestic security now settled, Abigail reported to their eldest son about his father's most recent winter project.

As unusual as it may have seen, "Your Father has read two Romances this winter. . . . I think he enjoyed them as highly as a Girl in her teens."[48]

Otherwise during the daytime hours of spring through late summers, a retired John (like Abigail) wasn't so retired. He rose early at dawn and after a hardy breakfast, engaged in the manual labor it took to keep their property functioning. His famous "Heaps of Compost"[49] were sometimes substituted by John as appropriate substitutions for politics. In that vein, John had written that he had exchanged "honors & virtues, for manure."[50]

In May 1804, Abigail read in the newspaper of the tragic death[51] of President Thomas Jefferson's daughter Mary Jefferson Eppes. In the happier days of 1787 Abigail knew Thomas Jefferson's daughter as "Polly," and she recalled the closeness that the two had shared when Abigail joyfully looked after the scared, motherless, eight-year-old in London. As someone who had also grieved the loss of life of younger children (Susanna, Elizabeth, and Charles), Abigail wrote to Jefferson despite their political quarrel. It wasn't a long letter, but mainly words of shared grief. It was her hope that her remarks could help Jefferson cope with the unimaginable loss.

> Had you been no other than the private inhabitant of Monticelo, I should e'er this time, have addrest you with that Sympathy which a recent event has awakened in my Bosom, but reasons of various kinds withheld my pen, untill the powerfull feelings of my Heart, burst through the restraints, and call'd upon me to shed the tear of sorrow over the departed remains of your beloved and deserving daughter, an Event which I most Sincerely mourn. The attachment which I formed for her, when you committed her to my care upon her arrival in a foreign land, under circumstances peculiarly interesting, has remained with me to this hour. . . . I have tasted the bitter cup. . . . [and] you may derive comfort and consolation in this day of your sorrow and affliction, from that only Source calculated to heal the wounded heart, a firm Belief in the Being.[52]

President Jefferson replied to Abigail from Washington, DC, about three weeks later. He wrote that the first half of her letter had "awakened in me sensibilities natural to the occasion, & recalled your kindnesses to her which I shall ever remember with gratitude & friendship." He wrote that Polly had asked "whether I had heard lately of you, and how you did." Jefferson shared that he had "regret that circumstances should have arisen which have seemed to draw a line of separation between us."[53] But he just couldn't resist reopening an old election wound that he still carried: "I can say with truth that one act of mr Adams's life, and one only, ever gave me a moment's personal displeasure. I did consider his last appointments to office as personally unkind. they were from among my most ardent political enemies."[54] Jefferson had raised the specter of outgoing President Adams's "midnight appointments" of 1801. Jefferson was still angry enough to use a sympathy card reply to carry out a new attack upon John.

By 1804, Abigail was an extremely astute and toughened political player. She wouldn't let attacks upon her husband go unchallenged. The third letter[55] in the series of eight letters between Abigail and Jefferson was Abigail's reply letter to Jefferson on July 1. She informed Jefferson of the precedent of the "midnight appointments" and insisted that they came from no grudge against him. Abigail then alluded to James Callender, whom she called a "wretch."

Callender had been in prison, charged under the Alien and Sedition Acts, but John released him on his last day as president. Jefferson then pardoned Callender and paid him two installments of fifty dollars, secretly via Jefferson's secretary Meriwether Lewis,[56] to dig up election dirt on Adams. After Jefferson won the presidency, Callender demanded a government job as postal inspector in Richmond, Virginia, which Jefferson denied him. Feeling betrayed, in retaliation Callender dug up dirt about Jefferson alleging that at Monticello he kept African American concubines. Callender also claimed that Jefferson had fathered children by Sally Hemings, an enslaved girl at Monticello.

Abigail vigorously responded about "midnight appointments" and Callender: "our correspondence would have terminated here: but you have been pleased to enter upon some Subjects which call for a reply. . . . The constitution empowers the president to fill . . . offices as they become vacant. it was in the exercise of this power that appointments were made. . . . This was done by president Washington equally, in the last days of his administration."[57]

The fourth, fifth, sixth, and seventh letters in the exchanges between Thomas Jefferson and Abigail Adams became progressively heated. Abigail kept up her replies and counter statements to Jefferson as if she were a skilled lawyer, deflecting any attack by Jefferson, a leading barrister himself.

In the eighth and final letter, Abigail clearly saw where their subject was going and said goodbye to her old friend forever. She had "once entertained for you a Respect and esteem, founded upon the Character of an affectionate parent, a kind Master, a candid and benevolent Friend. . . . [I]t was not untill circumstances concured to place you in the light of a rewarder, and encourager of a Libeler whom you could not but detest and despise, that I withdrew the esteem I had long entertaind for you. . . . I will not any further intrude upon your time."[58]

Over one month later, Abigail told John of the intense communication she'd had with Jefferson. She showed him Jefferson's letters and her letter drafts to him. Curiously at the bottom of Abigail's final eighth draft-copy to Jefferson, John, perhaps ever the lawyer, endorsed the following on the sheet, "The whole of this Correspondence was begun and conducted without my Knowledge or Suspicion. Last Evening and this Morning at the desire of Mrs Adams I read the whole. I have no remarks to make upon it at this time and in this place. J. Adams."[59]

And yet it wouldn't be the last correspondence between the three old acquaintances.

Part V

Legacy

"A Happy Domestic Circle"

1805–1811

A *bigail was most happy* when Peacefield was filled with people. It was especially so in her retirement years, with daughters-in-law and their children, relatives, guests, and servants drifting in and out with everyone talking and laughing. It was "a happy Domestic Circle,"[1] as Abigail remarked. "My own Family when collected together consists of 21 persons,"[2] Abigail also boasted. She treasured the rare times when nearly all of her offspring were together with her at Peacefield: "I have scarcly ever been able to collect my Family together tho so small a Number at these Annual festivals—they have been scatterd over the Globe—I had the largest collection of them together the last Sunday you dinned with us—all my Children, and all but one of my Grandchildren."[3] Son Thomas Boylston Adams had just married a young woman from Haverhill, Massachusetts, Ann Harrod, on May 16, 1805. The couple presented a granddaughter named Abigail Smith Adams to her namesake grandmother on July 29, 1806.

A memoir published in the early 1800s by Doctor Benjamin Rush was his attempt to document some accurate historical memories for posterity. He felt the need to identify the key patriots who brought America its independence before the misinformation that was being circulated took hold. He paid homage to John Adams as a chief architect of the nation. Right along with John, he identified "Mrs. Adams" as a compatriot of independence: "The pleasure of those evenings was much enhanced by the society of Mrs. Adams, who in point of talents, knowledge, virtue, and female accomplishments, was in every respect fitted to be the friend and companion of her husband in all his different and successive stations, of private citizen, member of Congress, foreign Minister, Vice President and President of the United States."[4]

Dr. Rush wasn't the only member of the Revolutionary War veterans who were still alive and eager to write the history of the historic epic.

The year 1805 marked the publication date of a massive three-volume set of books written by Abigail's old friend and mentor Mercy Otis Warren, *History of the Rise, Progress, and Termination of the American Revolution.* It was one of the first history books about the American Revolution.[5] The falling out that the Warrens had with the Adamses hadn't healed yet. As president, John refused to give some of the Warren boys lucrative but meaningless patronage posts in his administration. Accordingly, the Warrens supported Thomas Jefferson in the national election. President Jefferson liked how he was portrayed in Mercy's history book, so he ordered book subscriptions for his entire cabinet and himself. Jefferson wrote to Mercy "with great satisfaction that mrs Warren's attention has been so long turned to the events which have been passing. the last thirty years will furnish a more instructive lesson to mankind than any equal period known in history."[6]

Of course, when John read the three books, their inaccuracies and favoritism made him livid.[7] He probably had each volume page heavily edited in the margins with remarks, arguments, and corrections, as was his style. For a year and a half after publication Mercy did not hear from Abigail or John with any book reviews of Mercy's biased, unflattering trilogy.

However, by summer 1807 John was ready to have a robust written dialog with Abigail's former friend about her books. "Dear Madam, I have read much if not all your history of the *Rise Progress and termination of the American Revolution.* . . . there are several Mistakes. I propose that you may have an opportunity, to correct them for any future Edition of the Work."[8] Adams cited many pages and text that were in error; he specifically listed their volume, page, and line numbers.

John noted words taken out of context, offering one sample among many others. He had once been joking with the Warrens, and "I said jocularly, laughing, in that Style of familiarity which had been long habitual between Us 'For my Part I want King Lords and Commons.'"[9] That sentiment and many more erroneous utterances supposedly said by John Adams found their way into the book as fact. Throughout the remainder of 1807 John and Mercy sent sixteen heated letters back and forth—mostly from John flooding Mercy with incredibly long and detailed claims and proof of John's defense points. "Now Madam, I demand of you to shew me when are where and how I have relinquished the Republican System, and what Principle of the American Revolution I have forgotten."[10] Mercy answered John's "frivolous criticisms"[11] with claims of her own.

Abigail decided to stay out of the rift. Though her friendship with Mercy had run its course, the battle of words between John and Mercy was painful to her. The letters had stooped to such low language as threats of blackmail by Mercy and claiming John was mentally instable. In her last letter to John, Mercy told him that she would never condone any edits or corrections to her work "to satiate your thirst for revenge for imaginary crimes."[12] She titled his claims against her as an "insolent composition" and wrote threateningly, "the lines with which you concluded your late correspondence cap the climax of rancor, indecency, and vulgarism."[13]

Even more shockingly, Mercy alleged that from the very first meeting with John, she considered him mentally unstable, "This truth I have witnessed from my first acquaintance with you;—your nerves have not always been wound up by the same key."[14] Finally, she disclosed to John that she'd kept all of his letters and hinted of blackmail to him: "Shall I refresh your memory with a small part of this curious conversation?"[15] such as to which fellow Congressmen that John had labeled as, "such Summer-flies,—such Blood-suckers!"[16] Mercy warned that she had many examples of John's rantings that the general public would find interesting.

When John ceased to have any contact with her, Mercy composed a letter to Abigail, "Deeply wounded" as she was. She'd found, "not one solitary line of retraction . . . in reply to Mr Adams's unkind & cruel Letters to his aged friend." Mercy ended her entreating letter to Abigail, "With every desire to meet and reciprocate with you, former friendship. . . . Our correspondence has been long suspended, but at no moment has affection been obliterated from my heart. . . . May we stand prepared to renew our amities where all is harmony, and truth, and love."[17]

The close Adams-Warren relationship was essentially over. It would be two more years, in 1809, when Abigail would send Mercy a melancholy letter about the sad death of their friendship over errors that Mercy could have fixed: "If in a History to be transmitted to posterity you had not misrepresented and mis-construed, not merely facts, but principles, views, and designs, all together foreign to the Character you have delineated, and whom from a long and intimate acquaintance and a frequent correspondence with him, I should have supposed it, impossible you could have thus mistaken. But I have still thought more unkind, is, that when those Errors were pointed out, and means furnished you for rectifying them, not a Solitary line ever acknowledged the receipt of a Letter or any disposition to retract. It was this which dried up the fountain of my ink."[18]

In 1808, when Mercy's husband, "Genll. Warren," died, Abigail wrote to Nabby, "I felt as tho former Friendship demanded from me a Sympathizing Letter, and requested that the bitterness of party Spirit had severd us, but after the injustice she had done your Fathers Character in her History, and the opportunity he had given her of making some acknowledgment for it, which she wholy omitted to do. I thought a Letter of the kind would appear insincere, and altho I feel for her bereavement, and know how keenly she must feel it, I have declined writing to her."[19]

Abigail and Mercy still sent occasional letters to each other until Mercy's death in May 1814. Mercy's unflattering portrayal of John Adams as a failed president seems to have stuck with Americans for the better part of two centuries. Not until recently did historians such as David McCullough, Page Smith, and John Ferling strip away the false veneer to reveal the real John Adams. With those tributes, the valuable support that Abigail gave to John started to be more widely acknowledged. An associated truth that was obvious to Abigail: "no man ever prospered in the world, without the consent, and cooperation of his wife."[20]

Nabby's absent husband, Colonel William Stephens Smith, was Surveyor of Customs for the Port of New York, a position given to him by John Adams, thanks to the federal civil service system. But Smith had started to fancy himself a revolutionary and romantic freedom fighter, even if it was an imaginary endeavor. The "liberator" title was intoxicating to Colonel Smith. Then one day, Smith met Generalissimo Sebastián Francisco de Miranda y Rodríguez de Espinoza, who went by the shorter name of Generalissimo Francisco de Miranda. He was a contemporary revolutionary military leader from Venezuela. In 1779, Spain had entered the American Revolution in a bid to win back South American territories lost to the British. Miranda, commissioned as a Spanish officer, took part in battling the British in Florida and Louisiana, as well as during the Siege of Pensacola.

In late 1805, Miranda was in New York City building up financial support to fund an attack on Caracas to liberate the Venezuelan Province from Spanish rule. Colonel Smith and Generalissimo Miranda met and hit it off. Smith started raising supplies, cash, guns, and men for Miranda's cause. One such enlistee was Nabby and Colonel Smith's own nineteen-year-old son—William Steuben Smith, who had just dropped out of Columbia College to somehow fight in the Spanish war for liberty. Abigail had read about Miranda in the newspaper and didn't trust him. "Miranda is. . . . capable of troubling the waters, and fishing in them too," she wrote.[21] In other words, Miranda was a pirate, masquerading as a liberator, and it seemed that her grandson had just signed on to a Caribbean pirate ship.

Miranda had promoted Colonel Smith to shore-bound supply officer, so he had to stay behind while William Steuben Smith sailed from New York City in February 1806. Miranda's ships gathered military volunteers in Haiti, then sailed about the Caribbean en route to Venezuela. Spanish warships had been alerted and were waiting for Miranda in an ambush. They captured some of Miranda's schooners and sailors. However, while Miranda and his flagship escaped, William Steuben Smith was captured.

Word reached the Adams family in Massachusetts that grandson William Steuben had been taken prisoner and following a trial he would be executed as a pirate. John Adams was so disgusted with Colonel Smith and his lack of ambition and intelligence that he defiantly expressed that he didn't care what happened to Colonel Smith or his son: "News came that my Grandson was in Prison at Caraccas with many of his Companions, waiting for Tryal and Execution. Yrujo [the Spanish ambassador to the US], who had known me in Europe and America came forward with an Offer to interpose for a Pardon for my Grand Son. I took no notice of it. No! my blood should flow upon a spanish scaffold, before I would meanly ask or accept a distinction in favour of my Grandson. No! He should share the Fate of his Colleagues Comrades and Fellow Prisoners."[22]

John Quincy appealed to administration officials for the boy to be pardoned and released. Then it was learned that William Steuben Smith had escaped from the Spanish jail and was safe on the island of Trinidad awaiting rescue. However, his father, Colonel Smith, had been arrested in New York for violating the Neutrality Act of 1794. Colonel Smith was charged with attempting to overthrow a government; and since authorities couldn't find Miranda to place him under arrest, Smith, his assistant, would do. In his defense, Colonel Smith claimed that the expedition was approved by President Jefferson and Secretary of State Monroe, who both refused to testify.

Colonel Smith was tried and acquitted in a New York state trial but fired from his customs job. He decided to move his family into the dense wilderness of Lebanon, New York, west of Albany, and he started to build a large farmhouse there.

Abigail was devastated when she heard Colonel Smith's plans. She imagined never seeing her beloved daughter Nabby and their four children ever again. The colonel arrived at a compromise with his mother-in-law, who had said "I cannot think of her going into the Wilderness at this season of the year."[23] He agreed with Abigail that while he was building his house, he would allow Nabby and two of their children to live at Peacefield until he would send for them. To Abigail's distress in January 1808, Colonel Smith kept his word and drove his sleigh to Quincy to collect Nabby and their children.

On August 18, 1807, the third son of John Quincy and Louisa Catherine was born and named Charles Francis Adams.[24]

Abigail generally liked the political independence her son and now Federalist US Senator John Quincy Adams displayed. However, in 1807 President Jefferson, a Republican, felt that the best way to keep the United States from going to war with Britain or France was to cut trade ties with both countries, thereby demonstrating no favoritism. The thought of an embargo was horrifying to the Federalists and to Abigail. It would create commercial chaos in the country, but John Quincy saw the logic in the decision and voted for it. He was immediately attacked by his fellow Federalists and was convinced by them that his political life, at least as a Federalist, was finished. Abigail, a devout Federalist, told John Quincy that she supported his decision, "Altho you must expect that it will raise a Hornets nest arround you, the Consciousness of having uprightly discharged your duty to your country, will serve to shield you from their Stings."[25] In her life, Abigail had seen plenty of political attacks on herself and John. Now the attacks were on her eldest son.

John Quincy wrote to his mother, "I could wish to please my Country—I could wish to please my Parents—But my duty, I must do—It is a Law far above that of my mere wishes."[26] It was only a few months after, in spring 1808 when John Quincy did the unthinkable: he changed political parties from Federalist to Democratic-Republican.[27] As his mother had predicted, the stinging hornets came out in force against John Quincy.

But fate could work the other way as well. On June 27, 1809, Republican President James Madison nominated John Quincy Adams to the post of American ambassador to Russia. In August John Quincy left for his post with his wife, Louisa Catherine, and their toddler Charles Francis. Their two older boys, George and John, were enrolled in the Atkinson, New Hampshire, school owned by his Aunt Elizabeth and Reverend Stephen Peabody. Acting as secretary and traveling to St. Petersburg with John Quincy and family would also be twenty-two-year-old William Steuben Smith. Smith had returned after his short pirating adventure and was ready for another challenge, this time in the "severe shocks of a Russian Winter."[28]

"Thursday the 30th of November was our thanksgiving day" wrote sixty-five-year-old Abigail in 1809 to her fourteen-year-old granddaughter, who, "although not present, [was] remembered, and asked for."[29] She was Caroline Amelia Smith, the fourth and youngest child of Nabby and Colonel Smith. Abigail "rejoiced over. . . plumb pudding and minced pies" and for having lived long enough to appreciate "the lives and health of every branch be prolonged, until like a shock of corn fully ripe we may be gathered to our Fathers."[30]

Abigail sent her apologies to Caroline for her "very pretty letter"[31] having gone unanswered for so long. Abigail's health, which had often been poor, was seemingly in decline. However, her grandmotherly fingers and eyes, she wrote, "have prevented my writing. . . my hearing is not at all impaired, but memory, and recollection are not what they once were, my heart is still warm."[32]

Abigail wrote that she was especially proud of Caroline's intelligence and self-reliant personality. She gave her granddaughter some advice: "the more we are qualified to help ourselves, the less dependent we are upon others."[33] Abigail was not just voicing womanly self-reliance, she practiced what she preached. Even if the work around the farm was very tiring, she explained to her sister Betsy, "I am really So Self-Sufficient as to believe that I can do it better than any of my Family—So I am punished for my Self conceit & vanity."[34]

John Quincy and his family arrived in St. Petersburg, Russia, in October 1809 after a two-and-a-half-month sea "Voyage of 6000 miles."[35] Louisa Catherine wrote a few letters to Abigail before the Neva River froze. She painted a bleak picture, "It is customary here to go to bed at 4 o-clock in the morng. and to rise at 11 dine at 5 take Tea at 10 and sup at one. The rest of time you are expected to pass in your Carriage paying a perpetual round of visits which are never finished."[36] Louisa continued with an unflattering description of the Russian women. "The Women in this Country are in general very large, with very fine complexions, and when quite young . . . are very, handsome. but they fade remarkably early. they are cold and haughtily-repulsive in their manners."[37]

For unknown reasons, about ten months after John Quincy's arrival in Russia, Abigail petitioned President James Madison on August 1, 1810, to recall her son from Russia. John Quincy had no knowledge that his mother had made such a request. Abigail started her letter to Madison, "Sir I take the Liberty of addressing you in behalf of my son, now at st petersburgh, and to ask of you, permission for his return to his native Country."[38] She then stated that his salary was too small for his expenses at the post and that he had written to Abigail of his "embarrassment" with the "extravagance" expected to carry out his "public duty."[39]

John Quincy addressed his mother's concern for his safety and security and that of his family which led her to write to the president. "Let me turn to your letter—The President had informed me of that which you had written to him, and of which you have now sent me a copy. to stay though it should be at my own cost and in my capacity as a private individual—I wrote so to the President. . . . I know that your letter to the President was written from the tenderest and most affectionate concern for myself and my family—And I see that our letters to you on our first arrival here, fully justified all your alarm."[40]

John Quincy assured his mother that all was well, which was true. John Quincy had gained the trust of Czar Alexander I and the relationship was a good one as they both kept eyes westward for the threats of Napoleon. To counter the perception of Russia being the frozen wasteland that Louisa had painted, John Quincy ended his letter with a familiar scene that his mother might recognize even at Quincy: "We have been suffering nearly a week from the excessive heat of the weather—The Sun is eighteen hours and a half of the twenty-four above the horizon, and the night is scarcely cooler than the day."[41]

More sadness was in store for sixty-seven-year-old Abigail as the calendar turned over to 1811. She had learned in March 1810 that Nabby, living in the wilderness of upstate New York, had felt a swelling in her right breast. Thinking that it was just a harmless nodule, Nabby tried to ignore it and continue with her life, which at that time included caretaking for her husband who had contracted a long-term illness. However, he kept urging Nabby to leave him and travel to Boston to consult physicians there for her own problem. Abigail, of course, was filled with "anxiety" with the news: "My anxiety is great also for my dear and only daughter I have not mentiond it before, I know that It would distress william—She is apprehensive of a cancer in her Breast. I have besought her to come on to Boston and take advise, and I have consulted dr Welch, and Holbrook. they have advised as well as they could without Seeing her, but wish her to come he[re] I cannot yet prevail upon her. She thinks that She cannot leave home [without] the Col. and that he cannot come, but the real Truth is, I believe, She thinks the Physicians would urge the knife, which she says, the very thoughts of would be Death to her."[42]

By June 1811 Nabby's pain was so great that she decided to travel the three hundred miles to Quincy to see a doctor. The first diagnosis of Nabby's condition was of an "obstructed gland"[43] and to just take "cicuta"[44] (water hemlock pills). But by midsummer other doctors called in for consultations were starting to agree that Nabby's condition was breast cancer, and a radical mastectomy was the only reliable treatment. In the meantime, Nabby had acquired and read a scientific paper on cancer that had been published by the eminent physician friend of her father and signer of the Declaration of Independence, Benjamin Rush. His article was about nonsurgical approaches to curing cancers, so it piqued Nabby's hopes. On September 12, 1811, Nabby wrote a letter to Doctor Rush:

you will I hope pardon the Liberty I have taken to address myself to you . . . since I have been on a visit to my Parents, I have met with a volume of your Medical inquiries, in which are contain some observations upon the use of Arsenic in the cure of Cancers and schirrous complaints.

about May 1810 I first perceived a hardness in my right Breast just above the nipple which occasioned me an uneasy sensation, like a burning sometimes an itching & at time a deep darting pain through the Breast, but without any discolouration at all. it has continued to Contract and the Breast has become much smaller than it was. the tumor appears now about the size of a Cap and does not appear to adhere but to be loose. . . . Still I am uneasy upon the Subject—for I think I observe it becoming harder and a little redness at times on the skin Dr Warren who has seen it told me that in its present state he would not advise me to do anything for it.[45]

Doctor Rush preferred to answer Nabby's letter by writing to her father, instead of Nabby, for two reasons. One was that it was just more decent to be writing a letter to her father instead of directly to her about such a delicate subject. Two, was that it would allow John and Abigail to have a joint conversation with Nabby about the success rate of non-surgical holistic breast cancer treatments. Nabby, Doctor Rush feared, might have false hopes.

Doctor Rush wrote to John and Abigail: "I shall begin my letter by replying to your daughters. I prefer giving my Opinion & Advice in her Case in this way. You and Mrs Adams may communicate it gradually and in such a manner as will be least apt to distress and alarm her. After the experience of more than 50 years in cases similar to hers, I must protest agst: all local applications, and internal medicines for her relief. They now and then cure, but in 19 Cases Out of 20 in tumors in the breast, they do harm, or suspend the disease Until it passes beyond that time in which the only radical remedy is ineffectual. This remedy is the knife. . . . I repeat again—let there be no delay in flying to the knife."[46]

John was so distraught at the advice given by Doctor Rush that he couldn't be with Abigail when she told Nabby the news. And while in the months past, Abigail had also taken steps to keep Colonel Smith from being with Nabby, she now sent for him to come at once and be by Nabby during the operation. However, Nabby had scheduled her surgery for October 8, an impossible date for her husband's attendance.

Early that autumn morning, four surgeons rode out from Boston to the Adams house in Quincy. The lead surgeon for Nabby's mastectomy was Doctor John Warren, the brother to the famous patriot martyr Doctor Joseph Warren who was killed at Bunker Hill. Accompanying his father was young Doctor John Collins Warren, and two other assistant doctors—"Dr Welch & Hoolbrook." Nabby's only anesthetic was a swig of laudanum (opium) before the operation. Nabby was in the upstairs bedroom next to her parents' bedroom when Doctor Warren skillfully performed the breast and tissue removal within twenty-five minutes. The dressing of the wound took nearly twice as long, John wrote to Doctor Rush. All parties present there felt good that the whole of the cancer mass had been removed. John wrote, "The Surgeons all agree that in no Instance did they ever witness a Patient of more Intrepidity than she exhibited through the whole Transaction. They all affirm that the morbid substance is totally eradicated and nothing left but Flesh perfectly sound. They all Agree that the Probability of compleatt and ultimate success is as great as in any Instance that has fallen under their Experience."[47]

Nearly a month later Abigail wrote to John Quincy to tell him of the ordeal; she had kept the news from him until then:

> This was an opperation upon your Sister, who came here with Caroline in july to consult the Physicians upon a tumour in her Breast, and which was pronounced a cancer—after taking the opinion of Drs Warren Welch & Hoolbrook, she wrote her case to dr Rush— who gave a decisive opinion, that there was no chance for her Life, but by an immediate opperation, to this with the persuasion of her Friends She finally consented and five weeks since was performed by dr. Warren and his son attended by Dr Welch and Hoolbrook— She supported herself through it with calmenss & fortitude, & bears with much patience, all the concequences of weakness and confinement, and loss of the use of the Arm, as any Heroine—She is doing well, and recovering as fast as could be expected after an opperation in which the whole Breast was taken off—the wound is intirely healed, and every affected part was removed, So that we have every prospect of her perfect recovery to Health and Usefullness again. but She remains with us this winter not being able to ride, only a short distance at a time.[48]

During that fall and winter of 1811 Abigail seemed to be the only healthy person among her friends and family. Nabby was battling cancer, and Abigail's sister Mary and her husband Richard, Sally (Charles's widow), son Thomas, and husband John were all afflicted with serious ailments which Abigail was attempting to nurse.

Richard Cranch died of a stroke on October 16, about a week after Nabby's operation: "[H]e was Seized with a lethargy which deprived him of his Speech."[49] Mary Cranch "Sickened the beginning of June, with a plurisy fever, and from that, fell into a consumption" (tuberculosis),[50] from which she died on October 17, the day after her husband. Sally Adams, the widow of Charles, started spitting up blood and was confined to bed rest at Peacefield for nearly four months while doctors treated her. John and Abigail's son Thomas had a horse fall on him, nearly crushing him.

John had been excited to see "The great comet of 1811," a popular attraction in the dark night sky that autumn. But an accident in that darkness laid John up for months: "Two Month's since going out in the dark in my Garden to look for the Comet, I Stumbled over a Knot in a Stake and tore my Leg near the Shin in Such a manner that the Surgeon with his Baths Cataplasms, Plaisters and Bandages has been daily hovering about it and poor I, deprived of my horse and my Walks have been bolstered up with my Leg horrizontal on a Sopha."[51]

As 1811 drifted into the new year of 1812, Abigail reflected to John Quincy, still in Russia, on her trials of the year past, "I have past through Scenes, my dear Son in this last year; most Solemn."

"My Fire Is Out, My Wit Decayed"

1812–1815

D*octor Benjamin Rush* was an ardent American patriot who played many important roles during America's rebellion for independence. As a physician, some of his techniques and practices were worthy of praise, such as advocating more humane treatment of the mentally ill. However, Rush was mistaken in other ways and still believed in pseudo-scientific theories such as bloodletting, purges, and the mystical power of dream prophecies.

In 1805 Rush and John Adams had begun writing to each other—two old revolutionary friends. John had become aware of Rush's amazingly predictive dreams as the doctor described them to him. John wrote, "Your Dreams and Fables have more Genius in them than all my Life."[1] However on October 17, 1809, Rush wrote to John about the contents of a very stirring dream he had just experienced. In his dream he was asking his son about a book he was reading: "What book is that in your hands said I to my son Richard a few nights ago in a dream?"[2]

Rush then dreamed of opening the cover and reading inside the book, "1809. Among the most extraordinary events of this year was the renewal of the friendship & intercourse between Mr John Adams and Mr Jefferson, the two expresidents of the United States."[3] Rush's dream description letter to John written in 1809 seemed to prophesy the events between John Adams and Thomas Jefferson from 1812 on to 1826: "A difference of opinion upon the Objects and issue of the French Revolution seperated them during the years in which that great event interested and divided the American people. . . . Mr. Adams addressed a short letter to his Old friend Mr. Jefferson in which he congratulated him upon his escape to the shades of retirement and domestic happiness. . . . Mr Jefferson replied to this letter, and reciprocated expressions of regard and esteem. These letters were followed by a correspondence of several years. . . . These gentlemen sunk into the grave nearly at the same time, full of years, and rich in the gratitude and praises of their country."[4]

Prophetic or not, Doctor Rush coerced both John Adams and Thomas Jefferson into writing to each other for nearly a decade and one-half, for the sake of history. John Adams sent Jefferson a short holiday greeting note on January 1, 1812. It was followed by Jefferson on January 21, 1812. "You and I, ought not to die, before We have explained ourselves to each other," wrote Adams to Jefferson.[5]

The two continued to write each other for fourteen years, until both were near death on July 4, 1826, the fiftieth anniversary of the Declaration of Independence—as Rush's dream had mostly foretold. Abigail was happy that the two national celebrities had started their communication again. She noticed that the renewal of the letter writing between the two elderly ex-presidents seemed to have given John more energy and happiness. She, however, thought that she would never have an occasion to ever write anything to Jefferson. Abigail was still smarting from her last communication with him in 1804. In the end, she was in error. Abigail would write to him after experiencing a tragic, life-shattering event still to come.

Since 1809 the United States and Great Britain had been at odds, embroiled in a dispute. France, under Emperor Napoleon Bonaparte, was an enemy of Britain, leaving America caught between the two warring countries. The British Navy had been preventing neutral American ships at sea from conducting trade with France. The British were boarding American ships while docked in neutral harbors, searching for contraband destined for or from French ports. Occasionally they would also impress or kidnap American sailors to work on British vessels. President James Madison demanded that Britain end such practices, but Britain refused. The British claimed that Americans were under the impression that Britain was supporting Indian attacks against the American settlers on Indian land in the West.

When false and treasonous claims against the American government were printed in a newspaper, Abigail reacted as she had during the Alien and Sedition Acts. She called for the printer to be arrested and jailed: "a federal grand jury thought it necessary to present one Printer. Bill were found against him. he pleaded guilty, and a federal judge condemnd him to [a] fine and six Months imprisonment. I confide in the good sense and intelligence of our people to support the National Government, in a particular manner at this juncture, when union is necessary for our existance—and those who prefer the government of great Britain should have liberty to retire to it, with this proviso, that they never return to us again—their banishment should be for Life."[6]

President James Madison and the United States Congress declared war on Great Britain on June 18, 1812. John and Abigail supported the war and Madison, but many New Englanders did not. Abigail noted, "We are indeed a happy Land, but a grumbling Nation."[7] Some New England factions even called for those northernmost states to secede from the union: "You will hear much of the NE. opposition to the war,"[8] warned Abigail to John Quincy, still the ambassador to Russia.

Many people in northern states like Massachusetts and Connecticut believed that the war was unneeded and that the real enemy to the American union was Napoleon. New Englanders also felt they were shouldering an unfair portion of the war through commercial disruptions affecting the region's economy. Additionally, as would be the case during the Civil War and the Vietnam War, families throughout the United States were split in different allegiances. Even Abigail and her sister Elizabeth were divided on the subject. Elizabeth's pastor husband Reverend Stephen Peabody was against the war and Elizabeth supported her husband. Abigail wrote Elizabeth, "I could not agree with you in your politic's you seem to have imbibed an undue prejudice against the chief Majistrate [Madison]. . . . You may [be] assured that mr Madison is an honest upright Man, who would no sooner sacrifice the interest or independence of the Nation than any of his predecessors. no more than Washington or His immediate successor."[9]

Elizabeth wrote Abigail that even members of her Shaw-Peabody family did not all agree: "I do not mean to mention any more than you, a word of Politicks. . . . Our own House, is nearly equally divided—Mr Peabodys Son, & Son in Law are quite opposite—but we agree not to love each other less—& agreed, with myself to love every thing that contributes to the good, & honour of our Country."[10]

Abigail was starting to feel her age. She wrote to daughter Nabby, "When I sit down to write, I feel as though I could not pen a paragraph worth penning. My fire is out, my wit decayed, my fancy sunk."[11] Abigail also humorously equated her old age behavior to that of her dog, Juno: "you will be glad to learn that Juno yet lives, although like her mistress she is gray with age. She appears to enjoy life and to be grateful for the attention paid her. She wags her tail and announces a visiter whenever one appears."[12]

Abigail's light-hearted moments stood in stark contrast to the seemingly never-ending bad events now in her later life. In 1812 there would be yet more deaths for Abigail to mourn. The infant daughter of Thomas and Ann Adams died on March 4. In Russia, Louisa Catherine, the one-year-old daughter of John Quincy and Louisa, died on September 15.

Phoebe, Abigail's lifelong family friend, died during the fall of 1812. Phoebe's trust that had been set up for her by Abigail's minister father had long ago run out of funds, but the town of Quincy had voted approval for a small caretaker's salary. However, the reliability of the transient caretakers to help Phoebe was the big issue. According to Abigail, "our great difficulty is to get a person, Sober, and prudent to attend her."[13] Abigail wrote her sister Elizabeth, "it requires two of a night to look after her, as she has frequent need to be got out of Bed. She has lived to an Age when she has out lived not only her own personal comforts, but the means our dear parent left to support her. . . . when I go, she held me by the hand, and cannot bear that I should leave her, and when shall I see you again, is her daily inquiry?"[14] Abigail gave this prayer when she heard Phoebe was mortally ill, "I love and respect and venerate her and would not See her want, while I had Bread to divide with her."[15]

Recently Abigail had also grown dissatisfied with her grandsons' learning at Atkinson Academy, mainly owing to eleven-year-old George Washington Adams's slovenly handwriting. Well-formed cursive writing was a very important skill among the upper class. George's handwriting would have to dramatically improve or he stood the chance of being looked down upon his whole life, regardless of his pedigree. Abigail moved George and his brother, John Adams 2nd, to Hingham Academy and wrote to Elizabeth that the reason for her move was

George's handwriting. Elizabeth defended their academy teacher and claimed that she had helped George. She also had warned the boys, "they well know if they did not improve, it was their own Fault—I did all I could to encourage George to write well—I have ruled his paper—I have guided his hand times, & times." Within a month's time at Hingham Academy, George's handwriting was better, judging by a letter he sent his grandmother. Abigail praised George in a reply: "I was much pleased with the improvement in your hand writing. I have had to regret all my Life time the want of that accomplishment. when I was young, I was brought up in a Town where it was at that time, customary for Girls to attend Schools for writing, and female Education was much less attended to than at the present day; indeed it was almost wholy neglected."[16]

More losses of Abigail's friends and family occurred as 1813 came into view. Abigail knew these sorrowful occurrences would continue until one day she would be counted among the dearly departed. It was the way of the world and of God, she submitted. Abigail, not usually a gloomy person, was now being visited by feelings of darkness. In a pensive mood, Abigail wrote to Mercy Otis Warren, now aged eighty, in December 1812: "the longer I live, the more wrapt in clouds & darkness does the future appear to me."[17] And to Mercy, Abigail forwarded, "to you my Dear Friend a token of Love and friendship——a lock of my own Hair as [that of the] 'ancient Friends' [they were]. the lock of hair you gave to me I have placed in an hankerchif pin set with pearl in the Same manner with the Ring and shall hold it precious."[18]

April 19, 1813, brought the news of the death of Doctor Benjamin Rush of typhus in Philadelphia. The doctor who had encouraged Jefferson and Adams to write to each other had passed away leaving his unique mark upon American history. He was also the doctor who had stressed that the "remedy is the knife"[19] for Nabby to save her life in 1811.

Throughout 1813, Nabby had suffered with her self-diagnosed bouts of inherited rheumatism. Nabby had been cancer free for over a year. Instinctively, however, she felt that the cancer had returned. By summer Nabby was very ill and yet another tumor could be felt in her remaining left breast. In past years, Abigail would have wasted no time in traveling to Nabby no matter where she was living, or ask Nabby to travel to Quincy. But in 1813 both parties were unable to travel to the other. Faced with that situation, Nabby, her children John and Caroline, and Colonel Smith's sister Nancy traveled the three hundred miles in a very bumpy carriage to reach Quincy and the sanctuary of Peacefield. She arrived on July 26 and had to be carried into the house. Colonel Smith, who was in the US House of Representatives, arrived from Washington to be by Nabby's side. Even the administration of laudanum[20]—then the only effective pain medication available—was barely helping Nabby. Abigail wrote of Nabby's situation to Mercy: "So helpless in her Limbs as not to be able to walk across the Room, obliged to be carried in a chair from the Chamber to the Carriage. . . . Schirrous Cancer Seated in the Breast and extending itself over the Stomack contracting the mussels both of that, and the Bowels so as frequently to create Spasms over the whole Surface, like being as She expresses it cased up in Armour."[21]

Nabby died at the age of forty-nine on August 15, 1813. Abigail was shattered at the premature death of her lovely and devoted daughter. To lose a precious daughter, sister Elizabeth dramatically wrote, "It makes Nature bleed at every pore."[22] Helping her grandmother Abigail through the following days of grief was Nabby's nineteen-year-old daughter Caroline. Her help and words spoken to Abigail, plus the fact that she bore a resemblance to her mother, were supportive to Abigail in the dark days following Nabby's death.

Near the bottom of a letter to Thomas Jefferson, John Adams stopped writing and explained "Quincy August 16. 1813. I can proceed no farther, with this Letter, as I intended. Your Friend, my only Daughter, expired, Yesterday morning in the Arms of her Husband her Son, her Daughter, her Father and Mother, her Husbands two Sisters and two of her Nieces, in the 49th. Year of her Age, 46 of which She was the healthiest and firmest of Us all: Since which, She has been a monument to Suffering and to Patience."[23]

A distraught Abigail wrote Julia Stockton Rush, the widow of Benjamin Rush, of Nabby's struggle to live:

my dear Friend Since I wrote you last I have been calld to drink deep of the bitter cup of affliction—my Dear and only daughter Mrs Smith died here the last Month. you will recollect that the advice given her by our dear Friend determined her to Submit to an opperation for a cancer—it Succeed So as to remove all our fears—but early in the last year, the other Breast became hard—and callous. She Sufferd Severe pain in her Back and Limbs. the poison diffused itself through her whole frame deprived her of the use of her Limbs—and renderd her a mere criple—weak suffering and debilitated—She determined upon comeing to her Native house, to See her parents once more, was her most earnest desire. with uncommon resolution She undertook the journey attended by her Sister Nancy Smith & her son and daughter they reachd here in july. every aid advice and assistance was calld in by us, but the decree was gone forth. continual spasms in her stomack & Bowels could only be releived by opium, and three weeks after She arrived She expired to the inexpressible grief of her Parents Husband & children—a pattern of patience Resignation & Submission, her Death was but a transcrip of her Life—for many and various were the Changes through which She had past.[24]

On August 22, one week after Nabby's death, Thomas Jefferson wrote to Abigail. John had suggested prior to Nabby's death that a letter to Abigail would be well received. Jefferson began the letter, "A kind note at the foot of mr Adams's letter of July 15. reminds me of the duty of saluting you with friendship and respect,"[25] Jefferson wrote, not knowing of Nabby's death.

Abigail, who had resolved never to write to Jefferson again after their last feud in 1804, was touched by Jefferson's kind but unknowing letter. She replied to him,

your kind and Friendly Letter found me in great affliction for the loss of my dear, and only daughter, mrs Smith. She had been with me only three weeks having undertaken a journey from the state of Nyork, desirious once more to see her parents, and to close her days under the paternal roof. she was accompanied by her son and daughter. who made every exertion to get her here, and gratify what seemd the only remaining wish she had, so helpless and feeble a state as she was in. it is wonderfull how they accomplished it. two years since she had an opperation performed for a Cancer in her Breast. this she supported, with wonderfull fortitude, and we flatterd ourselves that the cure was effectual, but it proved otherways. it soon communicated itself through the whole mass of the Blood, and after severe sufferings, terminated her existance. you sir. who have been called to seperations of a similar kind, can sympathize with your Bereaved Freind.[26]

Abigail's "Scene of distress, grief and Sorrow"[27] of the past couple years was not over. The fourth child and the only daughter of John Quincy and wife Louisa Adams had been born in St. Petersburg on August 12,

1811. John Quincy described to Abigail his baby daughter being inoculated for smallpox, and although she was currently sick with an unknown ailment, she was otherwise healthy: "our daughter Louisa having just past through the vaccine inoculation—As the fashion of the Ladies is in full dress, to bare entirely their arms, she was inoculated on the shoulder, so that the scar might not be visible—But the Doctor inoculated her in two places, both of which took the infection; and the inflammation of her arm was greater than it had been with either of our other children—Just at the time when it was at the highest, she took another disease which passes here for a species of the mumps, but which I believe was only a severe Cold, and sore throat—Between the two complaints however a third worse than either was bred, which was a high fever; and her mother was at the same time quite unwell, threatened with a sore breast—They are now both much better and I trust in a day or two more will be quite well—With this exception the Child has been the strongest and healthiest we ever had."[28]

But soon after John Quincy had written his mother, at just thirteen months old their baby daughter Louisa Catherine had died.

> my dear wife and me tidings of affliction by the death and sorrows of those whom we loved—The turn has now come to me to ask your sympathy for our own peculiar distress—We have lost our dear and only daughter. . . . as lovely and promising a child, as ever was taken from the hopes of the fondest parent—She had been untill a full year old in general healthier than any of our other children were at the same period of their lives—She had already six teeth—But she sickened on breeding five or six at once, and very soon after being weaned—So soon indeed that on the appearance of her illness she was by the advice of the physicians taken back to the Breast—The illness began by a violent Dysentery, which was succeeded by a nervous fever, and terminated with Convulsions—She died at half past One O'Clock on Tuesday Morning the 15th. of this Month—to the inexpressible anguish of both her Parents.[29]

With so much death happening all around them, Abigail persuaded John, who like Abigail had just recovered from a undiagnosed illness, to take a February sleigh ride down to Weymouth, Abigail's birthplace. They wanted to make a social call to Doctor Cotton Tufts. They were both amazed and encouraged when they beheld his energy and mental acuteness: "your Father and I have So far recoverd from our late sickness, as to ride the last week to weymouth, to visit our old Friend Dr Tufts, who in his 82d year, still enjoys So much vigor, as to mount his Horse, and ride Several miles in a Day. his mental faculties are Still active, and correct, altho the outward frame decays."[30]

Dutch minister François Adriaan van der Kemp had been a radical supporter of the American cause while residing in the Netherlands during the Revolutionary War. There and in "Holland, Utrecht and . . . near New-york," he would meet with both John and Abigail, and they always enjoyed each other's company. After van der Kemp immigrated to New York he continued to see his friends "mr and mrs Adams" as often as he could while doing governmental business in New York or Philadelphia. In late 1813, however, van der Kamp wrote to Abigail of a disturbing dream he'd had of meeting her in a large crowd of people and not recognizing her. "I wildly looked for mrs Adams, when mr Eliot addressed an elderly Lady. She threw a glance on me, while I remained motionless: Her mien, her countenance; her piercing eye, her dignified port could not awake me. She advanced, and my dream continued. . . . I did not consider, what ravages time and affliction could effect; I was thunder Struck."[31]

Abigail was not offended at all with van der Kemp's innocent slight. She simply wrote him back and with a faint sense of humor said, "Be assurd my dear Sir that I took no exception to your expression of Surprize at the vast change time had wrought upon the face of your Friend, my faithfull Mirrur had told me the Same serrious truth long before."[32]

That dark-humored letter that Abigail wrote van der Kemp in February 1814 was followed up with the death of Abigail's long-time friend and mentor, Mercy Otis Warren in October 1814 at eighty-six. No cause of death was ever registered, but most likely it was age related. Abigail had commiserated with Mercy that many of the revolutionary generation were now gone, and with them, much of the danger that their generation faced: "The old Actors are gone off the Stage. few remain who remember the perils and dangers to which we were then exposed."[33]

Also in 1814 Abigail wrote a philosophical thought about retirement and how unfair it was to be free from work turmoil and to still be "active," just when the sun sets prematurely. "I am Sometimes tempted to complain that at a period of Life, when we must retire from the active Scenes of it, we Should be deprived by loss of Sight, from the mental food, which we most need for Support, when the world is receeding from us. but as it is the order of nature, and there is as morning and a noon, there must be an Evening, when the Lengthening Shadows admonish us of approaching Night—and reconcile us to our Destiny."[34]

On the other hand, the year also marked a celebratory event and one which made Abigail extremely proud. On Christmas Eve 1814, a peace treaty was signed in Ghent, Belgium, ending the War of 1812 between the United States of America and the United Kingdom of Great Britain. John Quincy Adams had been the lead negotiator on the terms of the treaty. Abigail wrote to her illustrious son, "I rejoice as a Lover of peace, harmony and humanity, that a termination is put to the War, and I rejoice that it has terminated so gloriously for our Country."[35] In one of Abigail's last astute political reflections upon a worldwide event, she stated, "Britain for once, acted wisely in concluding a peace with America. the war has given us many usefull lessons—it has taught us to feel our own strength, and to use it,—it has convinced us, that we can, and we will share the waves—that we can combat, and conquer both by land and sea."[36]

With her brother William and sister Mary now gone, Abigail occasionally wondered who in her immediate family of siblings would be next to die. Abigail had every reason to believe that Elizabeth, her younger sister by six years, would be the final Smith to pass on. Abigail was visiting Elizabeth the night of April 10, 1815, when, much to Abigail's surprise, Elizabeth had "Taken God's leave to die."[37] Abigail described Elizabeth's last hours: "She went to Bed on Saturday night well except a Slight Soar throat, which she complaind of, having read two sermons in the evening's about 12 oclock she awoke, complaind that She was chill'd and oppresst upon her lungs. Mr Peabody rose, call'd up a Maid Servant. Abbe also got up, sent for the doctor, Who soon came, but found the spirit had taken Wing, Without the knowledge or least suspicion of her attendents. . . . So tranquil was her exit; so few her sufferings, a translation from this earthly abode, to the mansions of glorified Spirits. . . . To me, She was most dear, and now I am left alone; the Sole Surviving branch from the parent Stock."[38]

Abigail received word of the death of her beloved uncle and mentor, Doctor Cotton Tufts, on December 8, 1815. When Abigail and John had last visited Tufts in February 1814, not quite two years before, they'd found him in great health despite his advanced age. But on their latest visit of December 7, 1815, the day before Cotton died, Abigail described to John Quincy: "I Said to your Father, He is going. altho I did not consider the event So near at hand, he Survived only one day— he fell asleep—for his death was not preeceeded by any Sickness or allarming Symptoms."[39]

Upon leaving her uncle's bedside that final day, Abigail described him lovingly squeezing her hand, "when I took leave of him, he gave me a pressure of the hand, and an earnest expression in his countanance which Sunk deep to my heart."[40]

The deaths of Abigail's many relatives and friends were wearing her down. She now frequently had depressed days, when "melancholy thoughts will frequently get the better of me."[41] She confided in a letter to Louisa, John Quincy's wife, "the Death of many near and dear Friends, and relatives, have broken me down, and give me little reason, to boast myself of tomorrow, as I know not, what a day may bring forth, So that when they go from me it is with the painfull Idea; that I shall see their faces no more, may we all finally meet in a better world."[42]

Abigail had experienced another reminder that her body was starting to wear out. In February 1814, sixty-nine-year-old Abigail and John had spent many a happy retirement day each reading books or reading to each other. However, Abigail noticed an alarming trait developing inside of her: she was having a difficult time remembering what she had just read. She wrote that her "memory" was "like a Sieve. I feel more anxious for information and read with more solicitude to retain what I read than ever. yet the impression is like a press coppy; faint, difficult to retrace, and often escapes me. your Father retains what he reads much better, but Since his Sickness, his Eyes Suffer, with the general debility of his Body, and mine Share in the Same calamity."[43]

Abigail felt it was time to make out her will—without consulting John or even informing him that she was doing so. Married women, of course, were prohibited by the law of coverture from exercising the "will option" because they could own no personal property, therefore they needed no will. Everything of the wife belonged to the husband.

However, contrary to the law of coverture, Abigail owned considerable assets in her name that she had built up over decades. Now she was going to draw up her own will and leave what she wanted to whom she desired—nearly all to women. Abigail's actions were illegal under the law, leaving John in one of the most difficult legal positions of his life.

Chapter Twenty-Eight

"Her Letters Yet Remain"

1816–1818

The *frozen soil of March 1816* was late in thawing that year. Even the eventual spring buds were still lost on Abigail, who was in a persistently melancholy mood. She wrote to Louisa Catherine, "my strength failed me, and I have been ever since, in so low, and debilitated a state of Health, as to despair of ever recovering strength again, but for the last ten days, I have gained some, and my physician, encourages me, that I shall be benefitted by the returning Spring. I have not had any disease, such as fever, cough, or pain, except in my Head occasionally. It seems to me to be an universal debility, and dissolution of my constitution."[1]

Abigail was nearly sure that she would not be seeing John Quincy and his family ever again. She ended her letter to Louisa Catherine with these words: "Let me my dear daughter hear from you as often as possible. Letters from abroad refresh my drooping Spirits, and Light up the Lamp of Life afresh."[2]

And yet as with the spring of 1816, Abigail saw in the later flowering a new optimism. Her winter despair was cast off. There was a rising spirit in the country of cheerfulness, perhaps from the recent victory of the United States over Great Britain. There was also a good feeling that in the upcoming national election the protégé of James Madison—James Monroe—would be elected president. John and Abigail had supported Madison, although they were highly criticized in New England. They intended to give the same level of support to Monroe, the last president who had served in the Revolutionary War (he had been severely wounded in the crossing of the Delaware). Thomas Jefferson never fought in any armed conflict. That difference was a distinction of merit which Abigail and John both honored about Monroe.

John, in contrast, was one of the last surviving Founding Fathers of the United States and of the Revolutionary War as well. His guidance in the fragile years following independence allowed time for the fledgling nation to get on its feet. Now new generations of Americans wanted to meet the living legend. Summer had brought an unexpected surge in party invitations and visitors to Peacefield to behold the Adamses. As Abigail wrote John Quincy, "your Father, and I have Lived to an Age, to be sought for as Curiosity's—accordingly we have more strangers to visit us, and more company, than for years past."[3] The commotion took the Adamses by surprise: "Bless my heart,! how many feet have your Mother and your Father in the Grave,? and yet how frolicksome We are?"[4] is how John described he and Abigail to John Quincy in the summer of 1816. "Frolicksome" was never a word used to describe Abigail and John. But they were enjoying every minute of it.

Change was occurring all around the Adamses, even in their religious beliefs. Since her birth into a devout household, religion had always occupied a solemn place with Abigail. However, in the early 1800s some outspoken and reformed ministers had been challenging several of the fundamentals of Calvinism, of which Congregationalism was a part. Abigail adamantly wrote to her son John Quincy, "I profess myself a unitarian."[5] John Quincy had expressed a differing theology than his mother,[6] but they were both wise enough not to let the difference drive a wedge between them. One of the differences discussed was the Calvinistic concept of "trinitarianism," the idea that God is three different beings. Abigail expressed her immovable disbelief, writing, "There is not any reasoning which can convince me, contrary to my Senses, that Three, is one, and one three."[7]

In spring 1816 Abigail described to Louisa Catherine in playful terms the progress that her grandson George Washington Adams was making in his penmanship, "I am rejoiced to find George so fond of writing,

and really do think, that he improves in his hand writing altho his su-
perscriptions look a little as if the Spiders had dipt their Legs in the
Ink; and crawld over the paper."[8]

In the national election of 1816, James Monroe was on the ballot
against New York Senator Rufus King. Monroe had been Secretary of
State and Secretary of War for Madison, and he seemed a likely successor.
The election results were a near sweep, with Monroe taking all of the
electoral votes except for those of three states: Massachusetts, Delaware,
and Connecticut. President Monroe then appointed John Quincy Adams
as his administration's Secretary of State on March 5, 1817. Monroe's
selection meant that John Quincy and his family could leave Russia and
return to the United States, which they did on August 6, 1817. John
Quincy knew that his mother was quite ill, so the family first headed
to Peacefield in Quincy.

At the first sign of a "carriage & four comeing down the Hill," Abigail
wrote, "I ran to the door, it arrived in a few moments, the first who
sprang out was John [Adams II], who with his former ardour was round
my neck in a moment." Grandson John was then followed by his brothers George and Charles. Finally, out came John Quincy and Louisa, "Father and Mother, well both out, and mutually rejoicing with us."
Abigail noted that her husband John was slowly moving to greet each
family member, "tho his retired Life has injured his Health for want of
exercise."[9]

During this time, John was also plagued with trembling hands. "Bad
as my Eyes are, they are better than my hands. . . . But my hand trembles
So that I can hardly / hold it to write."[10] It's unknown if John had trembling hands from an inherited palsy or from Parkinson's disease, which
was given the name by Doctor James Parkinson in the same year of
1817. Since 1811, when John originally noticed the shaking, he called
the affliction "Quiveration." He wrote to Benjamin Rush, "So much for
the bright Side. On the other I have a 'Quiveration.' What in the Name
of the Medical Dictionary, you will Say, is a 'Quiveration?' A wild Irish
Boy, who lives with my son T.B., let a Horse run away with a chaise.
One of the Family ran out and cryed out Nat! why did you not Scream
out and call for help. Sir! Sir! said Nat, I was Seized with such a Quiveration that I could not Speak. Nat's Quiveration is the best Word I
know to express my Palsy."[11]

Amidst so much sorrow and tragedy, one couple brought Abigail and
John much happiness. Caroline Amelia Smith, Nabby's daughter, had
married John Peter De Windt in 1814, and their subsequent lives

seemed blessed. The De Windts would go on to produce twelve children (Abigail's great-grandchildren). In the Indian summer of 1816 John and Caroline came to visit at Peacefield. Aside from the happy family get-together, the incredible news was how quickly the De Windts had traveled. Not long before, a trip from New York to Boston had taken a week. The De Windts made it in forty-eight hours, on a new steamboat.

President James Monroe was making a goodwill tour of New England in the summer of 1817 to celebrate his election victory and to mend any fences with the northern constituency who might have opposed him. On July 7 to thank Abigail and John for their support, Monroe stopped at their home in Quincy. The Adamses, President Monroe, and about forty guests celebrated that evening. It was a scene that in the past would have seemed impossible, the sight of two political party icons, Adams and Monroe, dining together in harmony. By mid-1817 party spirit and bad feelings had mostly dissipated; now the atmosphere was filled with peace and prosperity. Even Abigail had felt her animosity toward the Federalist Party, in fact all party politics, start to wane: "I am determined to be very well pleased with the World, and wish well to all its inhabitants . . . this is a very good world and I always thought the laughing phylosopher a much wiser man, than the Sniveling one."[12]

The summer months of 1817 were beautiful and gentle for Abigail. Accordingly, "several of those who came to call at about this time would remember Abigail outside seated on a couch sorting a basket of laundry or shelling beans as she talked." Visiting Salem clergyman William Bently wrote, "I found a freedom in conversation [with her]. . . . She was possessed of the history of our country and the great occurrences in it. . . . She had a distinct view of our public men and measures and had her own opinions."[13]

In August 1817, John went to the Boston studio of the renowned painter Gilbert Stuart to pick up a portrait of himself to hang at Peacefield. Stuart had painted John while he was president. Abigail had also been painted at the same time. When Abigail saw the paintings, she thought that John's rendering still looked like him, even over the course of decades. However, Abigail was aghast at her own image: "he has promised to finish that which twenty years ago he took for me, but now, no more like me."[14] She added, "I am much fallen away, and am but the Specter of what I once was."[15]

November 27, 1817, was Abigail's near-perfect kind of holiday. It was Thanksgiving Day, and she was surrounded by her family, and her many grandchildren. She wrote of the day to Louisa Catherine Johnson Adams,

John Quincy's wife. John Quincy could not break away from his Washington workload, but he and Louisa had ensured that their three children attended Grandmother's house: "we had a pleasent Thanksgiving Day . . . George John and Charles made three of the Nine Grandchildren present—we wished for their Parents to have compleated the festival—with nine Boys, and Girls we made a full chorus."[16]

As early as 1815, Abigail had seemed to be starstruck with the dashing and brave General Andrew Jackson and his War of 1812 victory at New Orleans.[17] To her son John Quincy, still in Russia at that time, she sent a newspaper clipping about his thrilling exploits: "I inclose to you a Character of Gen'll Jackson which I cut from a news paper, as he is the Hero of the day, and must excite great curiosity as the defender of New orleans, as the conqueror of British Allies; the Savages of the Wilderness, and the pirates of Barataria and last of all the veteran Troops of Lord Wellington, confident of their skill and strength, despiseing their Enemy, flushd with former victories. they became victims to their audacity, and fell by thousands before the consumeing fire of our cannon."[18]

On the freezing morning of February 27, 1818, Abigail wrote to her daughter-in-law Louisa Catherine on a variety of subjects, which was always her style. John Quincy had been ill, and Abigail, always the medical consultant, suggested an alternative remedy to her usually prescribed practice of bleeding. Her updated recommendation was "excercise is better than bleeding if he can take it."[19] Then she gave a heartwarming report on her songbird and dog: "the Bird and dog are both in fine health and spirits. . . . the Bird is under no controul, and sings so loud, especially if we are reading as to be quite a Nuisance—he is a true worshiper of the riseing sun."[20]

Abigail had included a small request in an earlier letter which reflected her lifelong love of furry and feathered creatures. It was a request to her son to please write a tribute to her favorite and faithful companion—Juno, her Newfoundland dog of which she was very fond. "I have a request to make to you. it is to immortalize my Juno. You know many of her virtues, her affectionate attachment, her good humour, her watchfullness, and her sportive graces together with her personal Beauties. . . . Homer has immortalized the dog of Ulyssus . . . and why not my favorite Juno?"[21]

In 1818, the glitter from Andrew Jackson's fabled armor still had not worn off for Abigail. Writing to Louisa Catherine, after a quick local weather report, Abigail again praised Jackson while reading the biography of him: "We are burnt up here, with the Severest drought that I ever knew at this Season. I have just been reading the Life of Genll Jackson—and I admire the Man; as his character is represented—I esteem him, much more highly than I did before, I read it. He appears to have been raised up for the Command he had, and for the defence he made He is as Brave as Buonaparte [Bonaparte], without his embridled Ambition—I wonder if my Son has read it?—tho Jackson has lately given him Specimins of his Character—which have some what embarrassed the President, I fancy."[22]

Abigail lived long enough to see her son, John Quincy, be appointed Secretary of State under President Monroe. But she would not see John Quincy become the chief designer of the Monroe Doctrine and its policy of Manifest Destiny. She also would never see him be elected to one term as President of the United States, ironically running twice against the man Abigail admired very much at the end of her life, General Andrew Jackson. Those elections of 1824 and 1828 were vicious and filled with dirty tricks, accusations, secret backroom agreements, and name calling by both sides.

John Quincy and Louisa Catherine were relieved when the US government went on summer vacation during the hot summer of 1818. The young Adamses took advantage of the break to travel to Quincy to visit Abigail. John Quincy and Louisa had barely returned to the capital in October when word reached them that Abigail had taken ill with typhoid fever.

Typhoid fever was a dangerous disease that was widely misunderstood at the time. It was caught by eating or drinking substances containing the infectious *Salmonella typhi* bacteria, which is related to the salmonella that causes food poisoning. Once inside a person's body, the bacteria can travel through the bloodstream and infect the organs. The only known, and highly ineffective treatment of the time, was offering the afflicted person quinine mixed with brandy, Madeira, or turpentine. When the bacteria got inside of organs, as it often did in Abigail's time, it was nearly always fatal.

The symptoms, some of which Abigail developed, were a very high fever, a general weakness, headache, and stomach pain. Abigail's doctor, Amos Holbrook, also prescribed complete silence from her. Although not widely medically recognized, refraining from speaking was sometimes prescribed by a doctor to conserve the strength of the patient. The body could then, in theory, have enough vigor to fight off the high fever. Abigail's doctor was in that minority of medical science physicians. John, now feeling helpless, wrote to Jefferson about Abigail's illness,

"The dear Partner of my Life for fifty four Years as a Wife and for many Years more as a Lover now lyes, in extremis, forbidden to Speak or be Spoken to."[23]

Abigail's silence may have been from other causes. It was possible that she had also suffered a stroke. Or she may have suffered from a less frequent effect of typhoid, that of lapsing into a "typhoid state," which renders the victim motionless.

On October 21, Doctor Benjamin Waterhouse[24] wrote to John Quincy Adams to tell him to brace himself for the likelihood of bad news soon about his mother. He reminded John Quincy that his mother had survived equally dangerous diseases in her lifetime, but now at the age of seventy-four, she was not as strong as she had been.

Family friend Harriet Welsh reported to Caroline Amelia Smith De Windt, Nabby's daughter: "She was very weak but we had hopes which did waver much till Dr Holbrook came on Thursday [Oct. 22] he then declared that 24 hours were very important—that if the Bark [quinine] did not produce some addition to her strength she must fail very shortly after."[25] Taking turns of sitting by Abigail's bedside were Lucy Greenleaf, Harriet Welsh, Louisa Adams, and Rebecca Dexter. "[W]e have the best of assistance night & day—& more than we want is offered hourly—Mrs. Greenleaf Mrs. Adams Louisa myself & Mrs. Dexter are only admitted by turns day & night."[26]

On October 26, 1818, Abigail's condition seemed stable: "Mrs. Adams remains very much the same not worse than the two days past—we have still hopes."[27] Even Abigail's sense of humor was still recognizable during those times "blisters were applied & she [Abigail] called them a present from Dr. Welsh."[28]

Abigail died at about one in the afternoon on Wednesday, October 28, 1818, twenty-eight days before her seventy-fourth birthday. Her son Thomas wrote that his mother was "seeming consciousness, until her latest breath."[29] John was in shock about Abigail's passing. He was ten years older than Abigail, and had every assumption that he would die before Abigail. Her physical strength had always persevered through a lifetime of illnesses, and she had always recovered. But not this time.

Abigail's funeral and burial was set for Saturday, November 1. John was inconsolable with grief but said a few times that he was so grateful that Abigail's pain was gone.

Again, John wrote to Jefferson. "The public papers, my dear friend, announce the fatal event of which your letter of Oct. 20. had given me ominous foreboding. tried myself, in the school of affliction, by the loss of every form of connection which can rive the human heart."[30]

The year 1818 brought record heat in New England. It was unseasonably hot on November 1, when John accompanied Abigail's coffin to the Braintree meeting house for her funeral, then burial.

Thomas Boylston Adams described how their father handled the day for his brother John Quincy:

> He insisted on walking to the Meeting house in the procession, and supported himself very well for the greatest part of the way, but perceiving that he faultered a little, I took his arm and he was able to reach the house. It was only a momentary dizziness, occasioned by the heat of the weather and too thick clothing. He went through with all the rest with great composure and serenity, and has attended meeting all day. The Assembly of our relatives and friends was numerous at the interment. Mr: Whitney Officiated alone, and in a manner perfectly acceptable to my Father and all the Family. His discourse delivered this Afternoon was soothing to our sorrows as a just, though, from necessity, a short, delineation of the life & character of our Saint like Mother.[31]

Abigail initially was buried in Hancock Cemetery, across from the United First Parish Church in Quincy.[32] John had expressed his displeasure of being buried in the same open-air cemetery when his time came. Both he and Abigail are now entombed in the basement of the church across from the cemetery, along with John Quincy Adams and his wife Louisa Catherine Johnson Adams.

During the week following Abigail's death, the expected tributes began flowing in. A short note that Louisa Catherine sent Harriet Walsh captured the grief of the two women who knew Abigail so well in those later years: "The soul which actuated every thing is fled and left nothing but sadness and mourning to supply her place."[33]

John had not known Abigail had written a will dated January 18, 1816, two years earlier, until it was found mixed in with her personal possessions after her death. John now faced a dilemma: he could either throw it away according to the law dictating non-legal documents, such as a will written by a married woman. Or he could take it upon himself to ensure that Abigail's written wishes were honored and carried out. It likely didn't take long for John to reject the first option. Instead, he took pains to ensure that Abigail's last wishes were respected to the letter. With the assistance of their son Thomas, whom Abigail had entrusted in her will to be executor, John ensured that every aspect of Abigail's will was carried out. Since John was a longtime sworn officer of the court, recognizing the validity of the will and assisting with its disposition made the will somewhat legal in the eyes of the law. In fact, no legal challenge was ever raised about the document.

But Abigail's will violated the law in three areas. First, as a married woman she illegally made out a will by herself for herself, with no witnesses. Second, she decided her executor(s) would divide up her unlawful estate which she had acquired over the decades. Third, except for some items bequeathed to her two surviving sons, her will's recipients were females, most of whom could not legally accept the items. Abigail named twenty-one female recipients in her will: nieces, granddaughters, daughters-in-law, widows, and friends.

In her will, she left Thomas and John Quincy deeds or partial deeds to nearby farms and other items: "I also give one share in Weymouth bridge to my Son John Q Adams and one to my son Thomas B Adams. . . . It is my request to my dear Husband, that the old Silver Tankard given me by my Father as a piece of family plate, may be given to our Son Thomas B Adams. The Quincy Tankard, I hope, will go with its name to our Son JQ Adams. . . . to my Son John Quincy Adams a ring with my Unckle Quincy's hair and name."[34] Abigail then bequeathed the rest of her money, deeds, stocks, and personal items to the living women whom she knew and had played personal parts in her later life:

"my Grand daughter Caroline Amelia DeWint" [Nabby's daughter]
"my Neice Louisa Catharine Smith" [William's daughter]
"my Grand daughter, Susanna B Adams" [Charles' daughter]
"Abigail Louisa Smith Johnson" [Charles Francis Adams' daughter, "Abbe"]
"my grand daughter[s] Abigail Smith Adams and Elizabeth Coombs Adams" [Thomas' daughters]
"Catharine Louisa Adams" [John Quincy's wife]
"Sarah Adams, Widow of my Son Charles"
"Ann Adams wife of my son Thomas B Adams"
"my Sister in Law Catharine Louisa Smith"
"my Neice Mary Turner, Widow of Elisha Turner"
"Lucy Greenleaf wife of John Greenleaf"

"Charlotte Bailey [stepdaughter of Abigail's cousin Abigail (Kent) Welsh] and to Harriet Welsh" [Harriet was a long-time family friend who helped John with his writing and filing.]

"Abigail Smith Shaw" [daughter of Abigail's sister Elizabeth] "The name of Abigail Smith Shaw, is intended for Abigail Adams Shaw, now Mrs: Felt." [Notation by Thomas Adams]

"Elizabeth Foster my Neice, wife of James H Foster" [Mr. Foster was Abigail's "Boston Trustee"]

"Rebecca Dexter wife of Richard Dexter"

"Esther Briesler" [Esther was a long-time housekeeper for the Adamses]

"my Neice Louisa C. Smith, one share in Haverhill Bridge"

"Susanna B Adams, one share in Haverhill Bridge"

Abigail added these three statements to the bottom of her will:

"To any of the girls who may live with me at my decease, I give each a Calico-gown to be chosen out of mine which I leave and ten dollars in money."

"My will is that all my clothing—body linen &ca not already named shall be equally divided between my five Grand daughters and Louisa C Smith, Caroline Amelia DeWint, Susanna B Adams, Abigail Louisa Smith Johnson, Abigail Smith Adams, & Elizabeth Coombs Adams, and the same, if any Surplus of money remain."

"Louisa Catherine Smith will deliver the clothing agreeable to my request."[35]

Finally, Abigail sought to quell any jealousies or claims by her survivors against Louisa Catherine Smith, the daughter of Abigail's brother William. Louisa had been Abigail's nurse during her retirement years and more so had been a constant companion for over forty years. Abigail's final instructions read: "I hope that no unkind or hard thoughts will be entertained that I have given to Louisa more than the rest. Her case is peculiar, having no relative upon her Mother's side but a Sister. I commend her to the kindness of my children."[36]

Abigail had noticed that over the course of her life, her mood and her feelings of happiness and well-being were driven by a bright sun in the sky. She would allude to such phrases as: "I am glad to See the Sun Beams"[37]—"the genial influence of the Sun is so necessary, both, to my health and Spirits."[38]

It is fitting then that in the final words of Abigail's obituary notice of October 28, her own affinity for the sun was, for that day, symbolizing not a gloomy death but a radiant sunset. Of Abigail it was said, "The leading patriots of that period well knew her intellectual worth. With many of the most distinguished, she long continued in the habits of correspondence. Her letters yet remain, and are monuments of refined taste and pure sentiment. . . . Clear and shedding blessings to the last, her sun sunk below the horizon, beaming with the same mild strength and pure radiance, which distinguished its meridian."[39]

Abigail's "letters yet remain"[40] with us, even though she asked for their destruction at the time of writing nearly each one. They tell us the story of remarkable people and the Founding of a nation, all chronicled and acted upon by a remarkable woman and Founder in her own right.

Her incurable optimism, in her own words, can still guide us today: "It is true, we have not always power over our own lot, to carve it out as we please, but the mind has power over itself; and happiness has its Seat in the mind."[41]

Notes

PROLOGUE: THE WORLD OF ABIGAIL ADAMS

1. "From Abigail Smith Adams to Elizabeth Smith Shaw Peabody, 5 June 1809," Founders Online, National Archives.

2. Charles Francis Adams's 1840 book *Familiar Letters of John Adams and His Wife Abigail Adams during the Revolution with a Memoir of Mrs. Adams* (Boston: C. C. Little and J. Brown, 1840) was born out of a highly popular lecture he gave of his grandmother's letters in 1838 at the Masonic Grand Lodge in downtown Boston on behalf of the Massachusetts Historical Society.

3. "Abigail Adams to John Adams, 5 May 1789," Founders Online, National Archives.

4. "Abigail Adams to Royall Tyler, 14 June 1783," Founders Online, National Archives.

5. Edith Belle Gelles, *Abigail Adams: A Writing Life* (New York: Routledge, 2002), 26.

6. Edith Belle Gelles, "Abigail Adams to John Adams, 23 September 1776," Founders Online, National Archives.

7. "Abigail Adams to Abigail Adams 2d, 11 February 1779," Founders Online, National Archives.

8. *A Dictionary of the English Language* by Samuel Johnson had been printed in England in 1755, but copies were hard to come by in the American colonies.

9. "Abigail Adams to Mary Smith Cranch, 5 May 1800," Founders Online, National Archives.

10. Until even after American independence.

11. "Abigail Adams to John Adams, with a List of Articles wanted from Holland, 17 June 1782," Founders Online, National Archives.

12. This was a common colonial phrase used by women to explain new duties thrust upon them when the husband went off to war.

13. "Abigail Adams to John Adams, 5 August 1777," Founders Online, National Archives.

14. "Abigail Adams to John Adams, 30 June 1778," Founders Online, National Archives.

15. "From Abigail Smith Adams to Louisa Catherine Johnson Adams, 21 August 1818," Founders Online, National Archives.

16. "John Adams to Abigail Adams, 25 August 1776," Founders Online, National Archives.

17. Elizabeth Cobbs, *Fearless Women: Feminist Patriots from Abigail Adams to Beyoncé* (Cambridge, MA: Belknap Press of Harvard University Press, 2023), 52.

18. "From Abigail Smith Adams to Louisa Catherine Johnson Adams, 20 March 1816," Founders Online, National Archives.

19. "Abigail Adams to Catherine Nuth Johnson, 19 January 1800," Founders Online, National Archives.

20. "From Abigail Smith Adams to Louisa Catherine Johnson Adams, 21 January 1811," Founders Online, National Archives.

21. "Abigail Adams to John Quincy Adams, 17 January 1787," Founders Online, National Archives.

22. "Abigail Adams to John Quincy Adams, 17 January 1787," Founders Online, National Archives.

23. "Abigail Adams to John Adams, 13 July 1776," Founders Online, National Archives.

24. Edith Belle Gelles, *Abigail Adams: A Writing Life* (New York, Routledge, 2002), 3.

CHAPTER ONE: "MY OWN GIDDY DISPOSITION"

1. "From Abigail Smith Adams to John Quincy Adams, 30 December 1804," Founders Online, National Archives.

2. Weymouth, Massachusetts, celebrated its four hundredth anniversary in 2022.

3. The Adams Papers editors listed in the final possessions of Rev. Smith over "430 volumes, of which 85 were in French." "Will of Reverend William Smith, 12 September 1783," Founders Online, National Archives. The additional inspiration for AA's advanced learning, especially in French, came from Richard Cranch—her sister Mary Smith's boyfriend, then fiancé. He reportedly recognized the literary spark in young AA and tutored her.

4. This two-story, seven-room saltbox structure which dates from 1685 would become known as "Abigail Adams's Birthplace." It is still a popular tourist attraction in North Weymouth, having opened to the public in the 1950s. In 1838, it was moved from its original location near the corner of North and East Streets a mile away to Bridge Street. But in 1947 it was sawed in two and moved back to 180 Norton Street.

5. "Decr. 25th. 1765. Christmas," Founders Online, National Archives.

6. "Abigail Smith to Cotton Tufts, 9 April 1764," Founders Online, National Archives. A "bugbear" was a form of the boogeyman during colonial times.

7. All the dates are in "Old Style" or "O.S.," since they occurred before 1752. Simply put: in the 1500s astronomy experts estimated that there was a big error counting the Julian calendar days in a year. Everything was off by eleven days due to leap years. So, Pope Gregory XIII decreed the new and corrected Gregorian calendar should be used. But countries like Great Britain weren't going to be told what to do by a pope. It wasn't until 1752 when the British and other countries joined the New Style (N.S.) calendar club. To convert from an O.S. date to a N.S. date, add eleven days to the O.S. date.

8. Regardless, the diary of Rev. William Smith at the Massachusetts Historical Society records that Smith baptized "my Negro man Thomas" on March 22, 1741.

9. Annika Hom (February 6, 2019). "The Untold Stories of Slaves Who Lived in Abigail Adams's Birthplace," BostonGlobe.com.

10. "Elizabeth Smith to John Adams, 14 October 1774," Founders Online, National Archives.

11. Larissa R. Schumann, "Epidemics in Colonial North America, 1519–1787: A Genealogical Perspective," in "Disease & Death in Early America," *Tully (NY) Area Historical Society News & Databases*, https://www.tullyhistoricalsociety.org/tahs/medical.php#epidemics.

12. "Abigail Adams to Mary Smith Cranch, 12 October 1786," Founders Online, National Archives.

13. "From Abigail Smith Adams to Elizabeth Smith Shaw Peabody, 26 February 1811," Founders Online, National Archives.

14. "From Abigail Smith Adams to Elizabeth Smith Shaw Peabody, 26 February 1811," Founders Online, National Archives.

15. According to the Adams Papers editors, this diary entry records possibly the first visit to the Smith parsonage by John Adams and meeting the Smith girls.

16. "The Diary of John Adams [Summer 1759]," Founders Online, National Archives.

17. "The Diary of John Adams [Summer 1759]," Founders Online, National Archives.

18. Parson Smith's original house had seven rooms in total: five rooms downstairs and two rooms upstairs. The five rooms downstairs counterclockwise were the parlor, back door/mud room, kitchen, Parson William Smith, Sr. and wife's bedroom, library/study. Climbing the narrow stairs, you will find two upstairs bedrooms. To the left was William Smith, Jr.'s bedroom. To

the right was the larger bedroom of the three girls: Mary, Abigail, and Elizabeth. An indication of occupied bedrooms came from Abigail, writing a letter to John late at night. She signed off the letter writing, "My Mamma has just been *up* and asks to whom I am writing." This information is from the generous tour given to the author in May 2023 by Cathy Torrey, the president of the Abigail Adams Historical Society. "Abigail Smith to John Adams, 12 April 1764," Founders Online, National Archives.

CHAPTER TWO: "AS SPECKLED AS YOU DESIRE TO BE"

1. Most likely diphtheria, scarlet fever, or a form of strep throat.
2. Now called the John Quincy Adams Birthplace, it is located at 141 Franklin Street in Quincy, Massachusetts, near the older John Adams Birthplace home. The two houses still remain in their original locations, approximately 75–100 feet from each other. Including the nearby "Peacefield Old House," the three Adams homes in Quincy, Massachusetts, are called Adams National Historical Park and are managed by the National Park Service (NPS) and open to public tours via reserved tickets.
3. "Freeholder" generally meant someone who held undisputed property "free" and clear of title.
4. "Abigail Smith to John Adams, 30 April 1764," Founders Online, National Archives.
5. "Abigail Adams to Thomas Brand Hollis, 6 September 1790," Founders Online, National Archives; Woody Holton, *Abigail Adams* (New York: Free Press, 2009), 13.
6. In possibly the first (expressly undated) love letter that John sent Abigail, he called her "Miss Jemima," presumably named after one of the daughters of the biblical person Job. That nickname appears to have been used just once. "John Adams to Abigail Smith, 1762–1763," Founders Online, National Archives.
7. "John Adams to Abigail Smith, 4 October 1762," Founders Online, National Archives.
8. "John Adams to Abigail Smith, 4 October 1762," Founders Online, National Archives.
9. "John Adams to Abigail Smith, 20 April 1763," Founders Online, National Archives.
10. Dr. John Gregory of Edinburgh. "*A Father's Legacy to His Daughter*," London, Wood & Innes Printers, 1808, Poppin's Court, Fleet Street. Originally published in 1761.
11. "Abigail Smith to John Adams, 11 August 1763," Founders Online, National Archives.
12. "Abigail Smith to John Adams, 12 September 1763," Founders Online, National Archives.
13. "Abigail Smith to John Adams, 12 September 1763," Founders Online, National Archives.
14. JA had a crush on and was on the verge of proposing marriage to Hannah in 1762 before she married Joshua Green.
15. The text of Hannah's reply letter has been added by the Adams Papers to the bottom editorial section page of "Abigail Smith to John Adams, 12 September 1763," Founders Online, National Archives.
16. In earlier years, John had been a teacher in the Worcester area.
17. "Abigail Smith to John Adams, 12 September 1763," Founders Online, National Archives.
18. "John Adams to Abigail Smith, 13 April 1764," Founders Online, National Archives.
19. "Abigail Smith to John Adams, 19 April 1764," Founders Online, National Archives.
20. "Abigail Smith to John Adams, 15 April 1764," Founders Online, National Archives.
21. "Abigail Smith to John Adams, 30 April 1764," Founders Online, National Archives.
22. "John Adams to Abigail Smith, 26 April 1764," Founders Online, National Archives.
23. [A Letter to Richard Cranch about Orlinda, a Letter on Employing One's Mind, and Reflections on Procrastination, Genius, Moving the Passions, Cicero as Orator, Milton's Style, &c., October–December 1758.]
24. "John Adams to Abigail Smith, 30 September 1764," Founders Online, National Archives.
25. "John Adams to Abigail Smith, 30 September 1764," Founders Online, National Archives.
26. "*City of Washington*" was how Abigail referred to the new national capital addressing an envelope to John on February 21, 1801.
27. "Abigail Smith to John Adams, 4 October 1764," Founders Online, National Archives.
28. "Abigail Smith to John Adams, 13 October 1764," Founders Online, National Archives.
29. Diane Jacobs, *Dear Abigail: The Intimate Lives and Revolutionary Ideas of Abigail Adams and*

Her Two Remarkable Sisters (New York: Ballantine Books, 2014), 22.

30. Vital Records of Weymouth Massachusetts to the Year 1850; Volume II—Marriages and Deaths; Published by the New England Historic Genealogical Society at the Charge of the Eddy Town-Record Fund Boston, Mass., p. 11.

31. So called because it resembled a lidded box of its time where salt was kept.

32. The exact number of acreages differed with various records.

33. The John Adams birthplace was built in 1681. The John Quincy Adams birthplace was built in 1663.

CHAPTER THREE: "COME PAPPA COME HOME"

1. J. A. Leo LeMay, ed., *Robert Bolling Woos Anne Miller: Love and Courtship in Colonial Virginia, 1760* (Charlottesville: University of Virginia Press, 1990).

2. "Abigail Adams to John Adams, 10 July 1777," Founders Online, National Archives.

3. "From John Adams to Benjamin Rush, 4 January 1813," Founders Online, National Archives.

4. The baby, Abigail the second, was baptized by Rev. Smith on the very same Sabbath day of her birth.

5. The Adams Papers editors wrote: "Poultices of boiled chamomile flowers and of heated white bread and milk were used to treat sore and broken breasts" (Henry Wilkins, *The Family Adviser; or, A Plain and Modern Practice of Physic*, 3d ed., Philadelphia, 1801, p. 22, Shaw-Shoemaker, No. 1658; Eliza Smith, *The Compleat Housewife; or, Accomplish'd Gentlewoman's Companion*, 5th ed., Williamsburg, Va., 1742, p. 204, Evans, No. 5061); "Abigail Adams to Mary Smith Cranch, 21 April 1790," Founders Online, National Archives.

6. "1765. December. 23d. Monday," Founders Online, National Archives.

7. The Navigation Acts, the Wool Act, Naval Stores Act, the Hat Act, the Molasses Act, and the Iron Acts are some examples.

8. "[The Stamp Act, 1765]," Founders Online, National Archives.

9. JA's name is on a list of three hundred members of the Sons of Liberty at the Massachusetts Historical Society.

10. "1766. Jany. 2d. Thursday.," Founders Online, National Archives.

11. "Braintree Decr. 18th. 1765. Wednesday.," Founders Online, National Archives.

12. "Braintree Decr. 18th. 1765. Wednesday.," Founders Online, National Archives.

13. Unfortunately Parliament replaced it with the Declaratory Act which stated that at any time Parliament could pass any act they wanted to and colonists couldn't do anything about it. It sewed the future seeds for revolution.

14. "Abigail Adams to Mary Smith Cranch, 15 July 1766," Founders Online, National Archives.

15. "Abigail Adams to Mary Smith Cranch, 15 July 1766," Founders Online, National Archives.

16. "Abigail Adams to Mary Smith Cranch, 15 July 1766," Founders Online, National Archives.

17. "Tuesday Aug. [5 or 12] 1766.," Founders Online, National Archives.

18. "Wednesday Aug. [6 or 13] 1766.," Founders Online, National Archives.

19. "Thursday Aug. [7 or 14] 1766.," Founders Online, National Archives.

20. "Abigail Adams to Mary Smith Cranch, 6 October 1766," Founders Online, National Archives. It was sometimes a custom then to take a knife and cut out a wedge of a silver coin or some other semi-precious metal; then continue to pass off the coin as full specie. If one had bad luck, the lesser-valued penny ("a bad penny") would return to the unfortunate owner. "What goes around, comes around."

21. "Abigail Adams to Mary Smith Cranch, 13 October 1766," Founders Online, National Archives.

22. John Adams Diary "[January 1768]," Founders Online, National Archives.

23. Obviously Mary Smith Cranch did not destroy the letter.

24. "[First Residence in Boston, 1768] ," Founders Online, National Archives.

25. "Abigail Adams to Mary Smith Cranch, 6 October 1766," Founders Online, National Archives.

26. "Abigail Adams to John Adams, 13 September 1767," Founders Online, National Archives.

27. "Monday August 14.," Founders Online, National Archives.

28. "Monday August 14.," Founders Online, National Archives.

29. Suggestion from the Adams Papers editors.

30. The Adamses had four paid servants by this time, so it was presumed that two would move to Boston with them, while two would stay behind at the Braintree house.

31. "[First Residence in Boston, 1768]," Founders Online, National Archives.

32. Brattle Street was demolished in the early 1960s to make way for the Boston Government Center's City Hall Plaza.

33. "[1768–1770]," Founders Online, National Archives.

34. Some old references call the street "Cole Lane." So does Adams himself: "removed to Cole Lane, to Mr. Fayerweathers House."

35. "[November 1772]," Founders Online, National Archives.

36. "John Adams to Abigail Adams, 29 June 1769," Founders Online, National Archives.

CHAPTER FOUR: "I SHOULD CERTAINLY HAVE BEEN A ROVER"

1. David McCullough, *John Adams* (New York: Simon & Schuster, 2001), 65.

2. Charles Adams, the Adamses' second son, died of alcoholism in 1800.

3. "From Elizabeth Smith Shaw Peabody to Thomas Boylston Adams, 14 March 1812," Founders Online, National Archives.

4. "[1770]," Founders Online, National Archives.

5. "[1770]," Founders Online, National Archives.

6. "1773. March 5th. Fryday.," Founders Online, National Archives.

7. J. L. Bell, "Naming a Massacre," *Boston 1775,* March 8, 2016, https://boston1775.blogspot.com/2016/03/naming-massacre.html.

8. The British troops, garrisoned inside Boston since their arrival in 1768, knew that they were despised by the locals, and frequent shoving incidents and scuffles between the two groups had occurred. On that evening in March, after a few more brawls at Grey's ropewalk and then at the Customs House on King Street, an angry mob gathered in front of a redcoat sentry at the Customs House. They began hurling taunts, rocks, and snowballs at the helpless sentry until Captain Thomas Preston, the officer of the watch, arrived with reinforcements. The situation deteriorated until shots were fired by the British. Three civilians were killed outright, two others would later also die, and eight citizens were wounded. "The next Morning I think it was, sitting in my Office, near the Steps of the Town house Stairs, Mr. Forrest came in," John continued in his diary. "With tears streaming from his Eyes . . . [he] said I am come with a very solemn Message from a very unfortunate Man, Captain Preston in Prison. He wishes for Council, and can get none." Adams immediately answered Mr. Forrest with conviction: "I had no hesitation in answering that Council ought to be the very last thing that an accused Person should want in a free Country."

9. "[1770]," Founders Online, National Archives.

10. "1773. March 5th. Fryday," Founders Online, National Archives.

11. "[1770]," Founders Online, National Archives. Trial preparations went on for months and months. However, John still had to earn a living as a circuit riding lawyer, so by a stroke of luck John's Boston-based friend Josiah Quincy, Jr. had agreed to assist with the evidence-and witness-gathering process. By fall 1770, the fervor of citizens' outrage had cooled a bit and the trials of the British soldiers had been set for October and November. Adams had been successful in having the trial of Captain Thomas Prescott separated from that of the six enlisted soldiers.

12. "Adams' Argument for the Defense: 3–4 December 1770," Founders Online, National Archives.

13. "[Braintree and Boston, 1771–1773]," Founders Online, National Archives.

14. "[Braintree and Boston, 1771–1773]," Founders Online, National Archives. Captain Preston's trial lasted for six days, with John's defense casting reasonable doubt on the claim that Preston had given the order to open fire on the angry crowd. Preston was acquitted. In the longer second trial, John gave a riveting defense of the six soldiers, but deftly placing the ultimate guilt upon the British order allowing the quartering of military troops inside of an already

enraged city. Out of that powder keg, Adams reasoned to the jury, emerged infuriated residents colliding head-long into armed and frightened combatants: "soldiers quartered in a populous town . . . are wretched conservators of the peace!" Adams called for acquittal of all six soldiers from the original charges of murder. Adams established that, based upon the facts, the soldiers had been acting in their own self-defense; that they had been attacked by a mob screaming, "Kill them! Kill them! Knock them over! . . . heaving snow-balls, oyster shells, clubs, white birch sticks three inches and an half diameter." To which Adams added the logical reaction of a pummeled British soldier, "Do you expect he should behave like a Stoick Philosopher lost in Apathy?" After the jury returned from a deliberation of over two hours, four of the six soldiers had been found innocent. The two remaining soldiers—Matthew Kilroy and Hugh Montgomery—who had fired their muskets, were found guilty of the lesser charge of "manslaughter, which is killing a man on a sudden provocation."

15. "1771. April 16. Tuesday Evening.," Founders Online, National Archives.

16. "Abigail and John Adams to Isaac Smith Jr., 4 January 1770," Founders Online, National Archives.

17. Isaac Smith, Jr. wrote separate letters to John and Abigail on the same day, February 21, 1771.

18. "Isaac Smith, Jr. to Abigail Adams, 21 February 1771," Founders Online, National Archives.

19. "Isaac Smith, Jr. to Abigail Adams, 21 February 1771," Founders Online, National Archives.

20. "Abigail Adams to Isaac Smith Jr., 20 April 1771," Founders Online, National Archives.

21. "Abigail Adams to Isaac Smith Jr., 20 April 1771," Founders Online, National Archives.

22. "Abigail Adams to Isaac Smith Jr., 20 April 1771," Founders Online, National Archives.

23. Catharine Sawbridge Macaulay (1731–1791) was an acclaimed conservative author of English sixteenth-century history. Her eight-volume series *The History of England from the Accession of James I to the Revolution* was widely read and she was noted as the world's only female historian. A widow, her 1778 scandalous marriage to William Graham (twenty-six years younger than herself) hurt her reputation. Following the American Revolution, she traveled to the United States where she met fellow female confidante Mercy Otis Warren. She also met Revolutionary figures Henry Knox and Richard Henry Lee. She was invited to stay at Mount Vernon as the guest of George and Martha Washington.

24. "Isaac Smith Jr. to John Adams, 21 February 1771," Founders Online, National Archives.

25. "Abigail Adams to Isaac Smith Jr., 20 April 1771," Founders Online, National Archives.

26. "[Braintree and Boston, 1771–1773]," Founders Online, National Archives.

27. John Adams's "Office Book for 1770–1774" shows that he handled sixty-six cases in the July term of the Suffolk Inferior Court, and his docket of actions in the August term of the Suffolk Superior Court, which ran into September, lists no fewer than seventy-eight continued and new cases in which he was concerned. Adams Papers, Microfilm Reel No. 183, Massachusetts Historical Society.

28. "1772. Septr. 22.," Founders Online, National Archives.

29. "1772. Septr. 22.," Founders Online, National Archives.

30. Suffolk County Deeds, Liber 122, folio 7.

31. "[Braintree and Boston, 1771–1773]," Founders Online, National Archives.

32. "John Adams to Abigail Adams, 17 September 1771," Founders Online, National Archives.

33. "[Notes for an Oration at Braintree, Spring 1772]," Founders Online, National Archives.

34. Library of Congress Digital Collections Documents from the Continental Congress and the Constitutional Convention, 1774 to 1789 Articles and Essays Timeline 1766 to 1767.

35. "John Adams to Abigail Adams, 29 June 1774," Founders Online, National Archives.

36. "Abigail Adams to Mercy Otis Warren, 16 July 1773," Founders Online, National Archives.

37. "Abigail Adams to Mercy Otis Warren, 16 July 1773," Founders Online, National Archives.

38. "From John Adams to Hezekiah Niles, 13 February 1818," Founders Online, National Archives.

39. No relationship to Dr. Joseph Warren, a revolutionary leader in Boston who would die at Bunker Hill.

40. "Abigail Adams to Mercy Otis Warren, 16 July 1773," Founders Online, National Archives.

41. "Abigail Adams to Mercy Otis Warren, 16 July 1773," Founders Online, National Archives.

CHAPTER FIVE: "THE TEA THAT BAINFULL WEED IS ARRIVED"

1. "Mercy Otis Warren to Abigail Adams, 19 January 1774," Founders Online, National Archives.

2. "Abigail Adams to Mercy Otis Warren, 5 December 1773," Founders Online, National Archives.

3. "Abigail Adams to Mercy Otis Warren, 5 December 1773," Founders Online, National Archives.

4. "Abigail Adams to Mercy Otis Warren, 5 December 1773," Founders Online, National Archives.

5. "Abigail Adams to Mercy Otis Warren, 5 December 1773," Founders Online, National Archives.

6. "Abigail Adams to Mercy Otis Warren, 5 December 1773," Founders Online, National Archives.

7. "Abigail Adams to Mercy Otis Warren, 5 December 1773," Founders Online, National Archives.

8. "1773. Decr. 17th.," Founders Online, National Archives.

9. "1773. Decr. 17th.," Founders Online, National Archives.

10. "Abigail Adams to John Adams, 30 December 1773," Founders Online, National Archives.

11. "Abigail Adams to John Adams, 30 December 1773," Founders Online, National Archives.

12. Pastor Smith had added on to their parsonage house to accommodate paying customers. The addition however burned to the ground later.

13. "Abigail Adams to Mary Smith Cranch, 1774," Founders Online, National Archives.

14. "Abigail Adams to Mary Smith Cranch, 1774," Founders Online, National Archives.

15. "John Adams to Abigail Adams, 12 May 1774," Founders Online, National Archives.

16. The illegal Massachusetts Provincial Congress met in Salem instead of in Boston and on June 17 elected their congressional delegates—one of whom was John Adams.

17. "[In Congress, September–October 1774]," Founders Online, National Archives.

18. "John Adams to Abigail Adams, 12 May 1774," Founders Online, National Archives.

19. "John Adams to Abigail Adams, 23 June 1774," Founders Online, National Archives.

20. "John Adams to Abigail Adams, 30 June 1774," Founders Online, National Archives.

21. "John Adams to Abigail Adams, 30 June 1774," Founders Online, National Archives.

22. "[In Congress, September–October 1774]," Founders Online, National Archives.

23. "John Adams to Abigail Adams, 30 June 1774," Founders Online, National Archives.

24. "1774. June 25th. Saturday.," Founders Online, National Archives.

25. "John Adams to Richard Cranch, 18 September 1774," Founders Online, National Archives. This particular letter was addressed "To Mr. Richard Cranch Boston favoured by Mr. Revere"; endorsed: "John Adams Phila. Sept. 18. 1774." Adams Papers editors.

26. The diary of Robert Treat Paine, MHS ["(August 1774)," Founders Online, National Archives; footnote 2].

27. "Abigail Adams to John Adams, 15 August 1774," Founders Online, National Archives.

28. "Abigail Adams to John Adams, 19 August 1774," Founders Online, National Archives.

29. "Abigail Adams to John Adams, 19 August 1774," Founders Online, National Archives.

CHAPTER SIX: "IF THE SWORD BE DRAWN"

1. John Adams always preferred to travel by horseback. There is no evidence that Abigail ever traveled that way; instead, she always went by a horse-driven carriage.

2. "1774 Aug. 16. Tuesday.," Founders Online, National Archives.

3. In fact, one of John's letters from Congress to Abigail was intercepted by the British, was published, and resulted in some embarrassment for John.

4. "John Adams to Abigail Adams, 8 September 1774," Founders Online, National Archives. In 1774, John Thaxter, Jr. (Abigail's maternal first cousin) and Nathan Rice were law clerks living above John's law office inside the Braintree house. Other clerks were William Tudor, John Trumbull, Edward Hill, and Jonathan Williams.

5. "John Adams to Abigail Adams, 8 September 1774," Founders Online, National Archives.

6. "John Adams to Abigail Adams, 8 September 1774," Founders Online, National Archives.

7. "Abigail Adams to John Adams, 14 September 1774," Founders Online, National Archives.

8. John's law clerk Thaxter was also a part-time live-in tutor to John Quincy.

9. "Abigail Adams to John Adams, 14 September 1774," Founders Online, National Archives; addition to the letter dated September 16.

10. The Powder Alarm was a false alarm to New Englanders claiming the British had captured their magazine of gunpowder in Cambridge, Massachusetts, on September 1, 1774. It occurred seven months prior to the actual alarm—the seizing of gunpowder in Concord, Massachusetts.

11. "Abigail Adams to John Adams, 14 September 1774," Founders Online, National Archives; addition to the letter dated September 16.

12. "Abigail Adams to John Adams, 22 September 1774," Founders Online, National Archives.

13. "Abigail Adams to John Adams, 22 September 1774," Founders Online, National Archives.

14. "Abigail Adams to John Adams, 22 September 1774," Founders Online, National Archives.

15. "Abigail Adams to Catharine Sawbridge Macaulay, 1774," Founders Online, National Archives.

16. "Liberty or death" was a popular phrase of the time. But Abigail used it here a full six months before Patrick Henry supposedly said it at the Second Virginia Convention on March 23, 1775.

17. "Abigail Adams to Catharine Sawbridge Macaulay, 1774," Founders Online, National Archives.

18. "Abigail Adams to Catharine Sawbridge Macaulay, 1774," Founders Online, National Archives.

19. Jonathan Williams and Edward Hill.

20. "John Adams to Abigail Adams, 29 September 1774," Founders Online, National Archives.

21. "John Adams to Abigail Adams, 7 October 1774," Founders Online, National Archives.

22. "Abigail Adams to John Adams, 16 October 1774," Founders Online, National Archives.

23. "1774. Monday. Octr. 24," Founders Online, National Archives.

24. "John Adams to Abigail Adams, 9 October 1774," Founders Online, National Archives.

25. "John Adams to Abigail Adams, 9 October 1774," Founders Online, National Archives; Cover addressed: "For Mrs. Abigail Adams Braintree favd. by Mr. Revere"; endorsed: "C 1 No 10."

26. "John Adams to Abigail Adams, 7 October 1774," Founders Online, National Archives; addressed: "To Mrs. Abigail Adams Braintree"; endorsed: "C 1 No 9."

27. "John Adams to Abigail Adams, 7 October 1774," Founders Online, National Archives; addressed: "To Mrs. Abigail Adams Braintree"; endorsed: "C 1 No 9."

28. Congress wouldn't be known as the "First Continental Congress" until the convening of the Second Continental Congress in 1775, after the bloodshed at Lexington and Concord.

29. One of which Abigail always felt was the "sin of slavery."

30. "Abigail Adams to John Adams, 16 October 1774," Founders Online, National Archives.

31. "Abigail Adams to John Adams, 16 October 1774," Founders Online, National Archives.

32. "The King's speech to both houses of Parliament on the 30th of November 1774. Together with their addresses to His Majesty," Library of Congress; https://tile.loc.gov/storage-services/service/rbc/rbpe03/rbpe037/03704100/03704100.pdf.

33. "Abigail Adams to Mercy Otis Warren, 3 February 1775," Founders Online,

34. "John Adams to Abigail Adams, 28 August 1774," Founders Online, National Archives.

35. "Abigail Adams to John Adams, 14 September 1774," Founders Online, National Archives.

36. "Abigail Adams to John Thaxter, 15 February 1778," Founders Online, National Archives.

37. "John Adams to Abigail Adams, 26 September 1775," Founders Online, National Archives.

CHAPTER SEVEN: "I WANT SOME SENTIMENTAL EFFUSIONS OF THE HEART"

1. "Abigail Adams to Mercy Otis Warren, 24 July 1775," Founders Online, National Archives.
2. "From John Adams to Joseph Palmer, 2 May 1775," Founders Online, National Archives.
3. "Mercy Otis Warren to Abigail Adams, 28 January 1775," Founders Online, National Archives.
4. "Abigail Adams to Mercy Otis Warren, 3 February 1775," Founders Online, National Archives.
5. "Mercy Otis Warren to Abigail Adams, 25 February 1775," Founders Online, National Archives. Package delivery during those turbulent early days was sketchy and unreliable, but the two requests were apparently fulfilled.
6. "Mercy Otis Warren to Abigail Adams, 28 January 1775," Founders Online, National Archives.
7. "Mercy Otis Warren to Abigail Adams, 28 January 1775," Founders Online, National Archives.
8. In his 2009 book *Abigail Adams*, Woody Holton claims that Abigail's favorite cousin, Isaac Smith, Jr., was the "Loyalist tutor" on "Cambridge common" who gave British officers good directions on how to get to Concord. Holton provides no documentary sourcing for that fact (p. 76).
9. "[Novanglus Papers, 1774–1775]," Founders Online, National Archives.
10. "[Novanglus Papers, 1774–1775]," Founders Online, National Archives.
11. "John Adams to Abigail Adams, 2 May 1775," Founders Online, National Archives; addressed: "To Mrs. Abigail Adams Braintree"; endorsed: "C No 2."
12. "Abigail Adams to John Adams, 5 July 1775," Founders Online, National Archives.
13. "John Adams to Abigail Adams, 2 May 1775," Founders Online, National Archives.
14. "Abigail Adams to John Adams, 24 May 1775," Founders Online, National Archives.
15. "Abigail Adams to John Adams, 24 May 1775," Founders Online, National Archives.
16. "Abigail Adams to John Adams, 24 May 1775," Founders Online, National Archives.
17. "John Adams to Abigail Adams, 6 June 1775," Founders Online, National Archives.
18. "Abigail Adams to John Adams, 4 May 1775," Founders Online, National Archives.
19. "John Adams to Abigail Adams, 29 May 1775," Founders Online, National Archives; (Adams Papers) - addressed: "To Mrs. Abigail Adams Braintree"; endorsed: "C No 5" (corrected from "No 6").
20 "John Adams to Abigail Adams, 29 May 1775," Founders Online, National Archives.
21. "John Adams to Abigail Adams, 11 June 1775," Founders Online, National Archives.
22. "John Adams to Abigail Adams, 2 June 1775," Founders Online, National Archives.
23. "A Summary View of the Rights of British America," Thomas Jefferson, 1775; the Avalon Project https://avalon.law.yale.edu/18th_century/jeffsumm.asp.
24. "John Adams to Abigail Adams, 10 June 1775," Founders Online, National Archives. "To Mrs. Abigail Adams Braintree"; endorsed: "C No 8."
25. Dr. Benjamin Church, a Boston Whig and one of the Sons of Liberty, was in Philadelphia consulting with Congress when in July 1775 he was named the first "Chief Physician" of the new Continental Army. Later it was discovered he had been a spy for General Thomas Gage, the British commander.
26. "John Adams to Abigail Adams, 10 June 1775," Founders Online, National Archives, addressed: "To Mrs. Abigail Adams Braintree"; endorsed: "C No 9."
27. "Abigail Adams to John Adams, 16 June 1775," Founders Online, National Archives.
28. "Abigail Adams to John Adams, 25 June 1775," Founders Online, National Archives.
29. "[In Congress, June and July 1775]," Founders Online, National Archives.
30. "John Adams to Abigail Adams, 11/17 June 1775," Founders Online, National Archives.
31. Penn's Hill is in Quincy, at the corner of Franklin Street and Viden Road. At the rock outcroppings at the top is a cylindrical rock monument called the "Abigail Adams Cairn." It marks the spot where Abigail and John Quincy watched the shelling of Charlestown and Bunker Hill, a moment John Quincy remembered for the rest of his life.

32. "Abigail Adams to John Adams, 25 June 1775," Founders Online, National Archives.
33. Brother Elihu Adams's farm was in what is now Randolph, Massachusetts.
34. "Abigail Adams to John Adams, 18 June 1775," Founders Online, National Archives.
35. "[In Congress, June and July 1775]," Founders Online, National Archives.
36. "Abigail Adams to John Adams, 12 July 1775," Founders Online, National Archives.
37. "Abigail Adams to John Adams, 5 July 1775," Founders Online, National Archives.
38. "Abigail Adams to John Adams, 5 July 1775," Founders Online, National Archives.
39. "Abigail Adams to John Adams, 5 July 1775," Founders Online, National Archives.
40. "Abigail Adams to John Adams, 12 July 1775," Founders Online, National Archives.
41. "Abigail Adams to John Adams, 12 July 1775," Founders Online, National Archives.
42. "Abigail Adams to John Adams, 12 July 1775," Founders Online, National Archives.
43. "Abigail Adams to John Adams, 12 July 1775," Founders Online, National Archives.
44. "Abigail Adams to John Adams, 12 July 1775," Founders Online, National Archives.
45. "John Adams to Abigail Adams, 28 July 1775," Founders Online, National Archives; addressed: "To Mrs. Abigail Adams Braintree favoured by Mr. Lux"; endorsed: "C No 17." Enclosed "Warning" from JA to his tenant Hayden not found.
46. "Abigail Adams to John Adams, 21 October 1775," Founders Online, National Archives.
47. "Abigail Adams to John Adams, 16 July 1775," Founders Online, National Archives.
48. "Abigail Adams to John Thaxter, 9 April 1778," Founders Online, National Archives.
49. "Abigail Adams to John Adams, 15 July 1775," Founders Online, National Archives.
50. Even though British-born Charles Lee was considered to be the most capable officer by Congress, the commander-in-chief title went to George Washington, followed by Gen. Artemas Ward. Lee would eventually be court-marshaled out of the Army for his disastrous (some say traitorous) leadership during the Battle of Monmouth, New Jersey, on June 28, 1778.
51. "Abigail Adams to John Adams, 16 July 1775," Founders Online, National Archives.
52. "Abigail Adams to John Adams, 16 July 1775," Founders Online, National Archives.
53. "Abigail Adams to John Adams, 16 July 1775," Founders Online, National Archives.
54. "Abigail Adams to John Adams, 16 July 1775," Founders Online, National Archives.
55. "Abigail Adams to John Adams, 5 July 1775," Founders Online, National Archives.
56. "Abigail Adams to John Adams, 5 July 1775," Founders Online, National Archives.
57. "Abigail Adams to John Adams, 16 July 1775," Founders Online, National Archives.
58. "Abigail Adams to John Adams, 16 July 1775," Founders Online, National Archives.
59. "Abigail Adams to John Adams, 31 July 1775," Founders Online, National Archives.
60. "Abigail Adams to John Adams, 25 July 1775," Founders Online, National Archives.
61. In 1775 William Barrell was a trusted agent based in Philadelphia for the Boston mercantile firm of Amory & Taylor.
62. "John Adams to Abigail Adams, 30 July 1775," Founders Online, National Archives; addressed: "To Mrs. Abigail Adams Braintree favoured by Mr. Barrell"; endorsed: "C No 18."

CHAPTER EIGHT: "THE SIN OF SLAVERY"

1. "[August 1775]," Founders Online, National Archives.
2. "Abigail Adams to Mercy Otis Warren, 27 August 1775," Founders Online, National Archives.
3. *Adams Papers* record "that Susy recovered and returned," "Abigail Adams to John Adams, 8 September 1775," Founders Online, National Archives; source note 3.
4. Patty was the second servant girl of the Adamses and she died from dysentery in October. "Abigail Adams to John Adams, 8 September 1775," Founders Online, National Archives; source note 3.
5. "Abigail Adams to John Adams, 8 September 1775," Founders Online, National Archives.
6. "Abigail Adams to John Adams, 8 September 1775," Founders Online, National Archives. JA also frequently shared her letters describing military intelligence with other congressional delegates; of course, JA did not destroy this letter as AA had requested.
7. It appears that in 1775 Abigail was very early in her use of the term "corn fed." The *Adams*

Papers editors noted, "The earliest use of this adjective recorded in DAE is by Joel Barlow in his *Hasty Pudding*, published 1793: 'Brown, corn-fed nymphs and strong, hard-handed beaux.' The more recent *Dictionary of Americanisms* records 'corn-fed pork' in 1787."

8. "Abigail Adams to John Adams, 17 September 1775," Founders Online, National Archives.
9. "Abigail Adams to John Adams, 17 September 1775," Founders Online, National Archives.
10. "John Adams to Abigail Adams, 26 September 1775," Founders Online, National Archives.
11. "Abigail Adams to John Adams, 25 September 1775," Founders Online, National Archives.
12. "Abigail Adams to John Adams, 25 September 1775," Founders Online, National Archives.
13. "Abigail Adams to John Adams, 29 September 1775," Founders Online, National Archives.
14. "Abigail Adams to John Adams, 29 September 1775," Founders Online, National Archives.
15. "Abigail Adams to John Adams, 1 October 1775," Founders Online, National Archives.
16. "Abigail Adams to John Adams, 22 October 1775," Founders Online, National Archives.
17. "Abigail Adams to John Adams, 9 October 1775," Founders Online, National Archives.
18. "Abigail Adams to John Adams, 22 October 1775," Founders Online, National Archives.
19. "Abigail Adams to John Adams, 12 November 1775," Founders Online, National Archives.
20. "Abigail Adams to John Adams, 9 October 1775," Founders Online, National Archives.
21. "John Adams to Abigail Adams, 13 October 1775," Founders Online, National Archives.
22. "John Adams to Mary Palmer, 5 July 1776," Founders Online, National Archives.
23. "Abigail Adams to John Adams, 25 October 1775," Founders Online, National Archives.
24. "Sister Betsy too is very unwell"; "I have been to day with my Sister Cranch who is very ill." "Abigail Adams to John Adams, 25 October 1775," Founders Online, National Archives.
25. https://allthingsliberty.com/2013/12/benjamin-franklin-americas-first-whistleblower/.
26. "John Adams to Abigail Adams, 12 November 1775," Founders Online, National Archives.
27. "Abigail Adams to John Adams, 5 November 1775," Founders Online, National Archives.
28. "Abigail Adams to John Adams, 12 November 1775," Founders Online, National Archives.
29. "Abigail Adams to John Adams, 25 October 1775," Founders Online, National Archives.
30. "Abigail Adams to John Adams, 31 March 1776," Founders Online, National Archives.
31. "Abigail Adams to John Adams, 12 November 1775," Founders Online, National Archives.
32. "John Adams to Abigail Adams, 26 September 1775," Founders Online, National Archives. The name of the English gentleman has never been disclosed.
33. "Abigail Adams to John Adams, 25 October 1775," Founders Online, National Archives.
34. "Abigail Adams to John Adams, 16 July 1775," Founders Online, National Archives. It's not known if Washington and Lee's mid-July 1775 visit to Abigail's Braintree house also came with Lee's ever-present pack of barking dogs who accompanied him everywhere.
35. "From John Adams to James Warren, 24 July 1775," Founders Online, National Archives.
36. Hichborn sent letters to JA for the next decade apologizing for the incident.
37. "From John Adams to James Warren, 24 July 1775," Founders Online, National Archives; initial source note.
38. "To John Adams from Charles Lee, 5 October 1775," Founders Online, National Archives.
39. The *Adams Papers* editors write, "AA's spelling 'Sparder' for Spada is a revealing example of New England phonetic or orthographic overcompensation or both." "Abigail Adams to John Adams, 10 December 1775," Founders Online, National Archives, note 5.
40. "Abigail Adams to John Adams, 27 November 1775," Founders Online, National Archives.
41. "Abigail Adams to John Adams, 27 November 1775," Founders Online, National Archives.
42. "Caughnawaga."
43. With new congressional delegate Elbridge Gerry and JA's aide Joseph Bass.
44. "John Adams to Abigail Adams, 24 January 1776," Founders Online, National Archives. Sent from Watertown, MA.
45. Saltpeter could be made by combining ashes, dirt, and urine to create potassium nitrate for use in gunpowder. The mixture can be explosive when combined with sulfur and charcoal.
46. "Abigail Adams to John Adams, 31 March–5 April 1776," Founders Online, National Archives.
47. "John Adams to Abigail Adams, 18 February 1776," Founders Online, National Archives.
48. "John Adams to Abigail Adams, 18 February 1776," Founders Online, National Archives.

Notes to Pages 80–89

CHAPTER NINE: "REMEMBER THE LADIES"

1. "To John Adams from Benjamin Kent, 24 April 1776," Founders Online, National Archives.
2. Initially people in America, England, and Europe thought John Adams had written it. But he, the trained British legal scholar, acknowledged that he couldn't write something so simple.
3. "From John Adams to William Tudor, 12 April 1776," Founders Online, National Archives.
4. "John Adams to Abigail Adams, 19 March 1776," Founders Online, National Archives.
5. "From John Adams to Thomas Jefferson, 22 June 1819," Founders Online, National Archives.
6. "Abigail Adams to John Adams, 2 March 1776," Founders Online, National Archives.
7. "Abigail Adams to John Adams, 21 February 1776," Founders Online, National Archives.
8. "Abigail Adams to John Adams, 2 March 1776," Founders Online, National Archives.
9. "John Adams to Abigail Adams, 28 April 1776," Founders Online, National Archives.
10. "John Adams to Abigail Adams, 27 May 1776," Founders Online, National Archives.
11. "Abigail Adams to John Adams, 9 May 1776," Founders Online, National Archives.
12. "John Adams to Abigail Adams, 27 May 1776," Founders Online, National Archives.
13. "Abigail Adams to John Adams, 2 March 1776," Founders Online, National Archives.
14. "Abigail Adams to John Adams, 2 [3] March 1776," Founders Online, National Archives.
15. "Abigail Adams to John Adams, 2 March 1776," Founders Online, National Archives.
16. "Abigail Adams to John Adams, 2 March 1776," Founders Online, National Archives.
17. "Abigail Adams to John Adams, 16 March 1776," Founders Online, National Archives.
18. General Howe could not negotiate directly with General Washington since Washington's army and rank were considered invalid. Washington was seen as the leader of an illegal rebellion and his rank had no military significance.
19. "Abigail Adams to John Adams, 16–17 March 1776," Founders Online, National Archives.
20. "Abigail Adams to John Adams, 16–17 March 1776," Founders Online, National Archives.
21. "Abigail Adams to John Adams, March 1776," Founders Online, National Archives.
22. "Abigail Adams to John Adams, 7 April 1776," Founders Online, National Archives.
23. "Abigail Adams to John Adams, 31 March 1776," Founders Online, National Archives.
24. "Abigail Adams to John Adams, 31 March 1776," Founders Online, National Archives.
25. "Saucy" meant flippant or jokingly. JA used that word to describe AA's women's rights request.
26. See discussion in the Introduction of this book.
27. "Abigail Adams to Mercy Otis Warren, 27 April 1776," Founders Online, National Archives.
28. "Abigail Adams to Mercy Otis Warren, 27 April 1776," Founders Online, National Archives.
29. This is a paraphrase of Daniel Defoe: "*Nature has left this tincture in the blood, That all men would be tyrants if they could.*" *Oxford Essential Quotations*, edited by Susan Ratcliffe (Oxford University Press, 2016), *The History of the Kentish Petition (1712–13)* addenda, l. 11.
30. The meaning of the word "Friend" used in this context was much different than what is implied today. John and Abigail, two married, loving people, often began their letters: "Dearest Friend." Back then the word could imply a deep, loving relationship.
31. "Abigail Adams to John Adams, 31 March 1776," Founders Online, National Archives.
32. "John Adams to Abigail Adams, 14 April 1776," Founders Online, National Archives.
33. "John Adams to Abigail Adams, 14 April 1776," Founders Online, National Archives.
34. "John Adams to Abigail Adams, 14 April 1776," Founders Online, National Archives.
35. "Abigail Adams to Mercy Otis Warren, 27 April 1776," Founders Online, National Archives.
36. "Abigail Adams to John Adams, 7 May 1776," Founders Online, National Archives.
37. "Abigail Adams to Mary Smith Cranch, 15 November 1797," Founders Online, National Archives.
38. Judith Apter Klinghoffer and Lois Elkis, "'The Petticoat Electors': Women's Suffrage in New Jersey, 1776–1807," *Journal of the Early Republic*, 12 (Summer 1992): 159–160, 162.
39. "Abigail Adams to John Adams, 14 April 1776," Founders Online, National Archives.

40. Variolation was the old process of inoculation where small amounts of live smallpox virus pus were collected and introduced into an open wound of an otherwise healthy person. For simplicity, this book uses the term "inoculation" versus the more correct "variolation."

41. It is unknown how many people went with Abigail.

42. Abigail may have been inoculated along with the children, but she didn't expressly state that.

43. "Abigail Adams to John Adams, 13 July 1776," Founders Online, National Archives. Unlike as shown in the HBO/Playtone miniseries *John Adams*, the inoculations had to be done within the city limits of Boston, although Abigail noted, "In many Towns, already arround Boston the Selectmen have granted Liberty for innoculation." The Adamses and all the relatives/friends listed went into Boston from Braintree for the procedure and quarantine. They stayed by invitation in the home of Uncle Isaac Smith, Sr., on Court Street, sometimes listed as Queen Street.

44. "Abigail Adams to John Adams, 13–14 July 1776," Founders Online, National Archives.

CHAPTER TEN: "I AM NOT APT TO BE INTIMIDATED YOU KNOW"

1. "John Adams to Abigail Adams, 3 July 1776," Founders Online, National Archives.

2. Some historians and scholars have debated this grandiose statement by JA. Did he mean from the Atlantic Ocean to the Pacific Ocean? Or just from New England to Georgia? "John Adams to Abigail Adams, 3 July 1776," Founders Online, National Archives.

3. "John Adams to Abigail Adams, 3 July 1776," Founders Online, National Archives.

4. JA wrote no letter to AA on July 4, but wrote two letters to her on July 3. This may have been what AA was describing with her mention of "two Letters."

5. "Abigail Adams to John Adams, 13 July 1776," Founders Online, National Archives.

6. Technically on this day, AA had already been exposed to smallpox through inoculation for six days, but was showing no signs of it. Since thousands of people had flooded into Boston for the express purpose of inoculation, many others in the congregation on King Street may have been similar carriers of the disease as AA possibly was. This may have been an example of what we call in the twenty-first century a "superspreader" event. "Abigail Adams to John Adams, 21 July 1776," Founders Online, National Archives.

7. The Adams Papers editors explain: "After Daniel Sutton (1735–1819), an irregular but highly successful practitioner of Ingatestone, Essex, and later of London. His method required only a small puncture, rather than a gash, to infect the subject and made use of less virulent matter." "Abigail Adams to John Adams, 21 July 1776," Founders Online, National Archives.

8. "John Adams to Abigail Adams, 20 August 1776," Founders Online, National Archives.

9. People wandered outside even though many inoculation hospitals, some inside large houses, were set up to house waiting patients.

10. "Abigail Adams to John Adams, 13 July 1776," Founders Online, National Archives.

11. "Abigail Adams to John Adams, 21 July 1776," Founders Online, National Archives.

12. "Abigail Adams to John Adams, 21–22 July 1776," Founders Online, National Archives.

13. "Abigail Adams to John Adams, 29 July 1776," Founders Online, National Archives.

14. "Abigail Adams to John Adams, 12 August 1776," Founders Online, National Archives.

15. "Abigail Adams to John Adams, 30 July 1776," Founders Online, National Archives.

16. "Abigail Adams to John Adams, 12 August 1776," Founders Online, National Archives.

17. "Abigail Adams to John Adams, 17 August 1776," Founders Online, National Archives.

18. "Abigail Adams to John Adams, 19 August 1776," Founders Online, National Archives.

19. "John Adams to Abigail Adams, 27 August 1776," Founders Online, National Archives.

20. "John Adams to Abigail Adams, 28 August 1776," Founders Online, National Archives.

21. This was the first time John had used the term "delicate" to describe his son Charles. It would continue to be used to describe Charles until his manhood by John, Abigail, JQA, and other friends of the family.

22. "John Adams to Abigail Adams, 30 August 1776," Founders Online, National Archives.

23. John Quincy Adams, after just one inoculation, had developed only a mild case of small-pox.

24. "John Adams to Abigail Adams, 30 August 1776," Founders Online, National Archives.

25. "John Adams to Abigail Adams, 3–4 August 1776," Founders Online, National Archives.

26. "Abigail Adams to John Adams, 14 August 1776," Founders Online, National Archives.

27. "Abigail Adams to John Adams, 31 August–2 September 1776," Founders Online, National Archives.

28. "Abigail Adams to John Adams, 29 August 1776," Founders Online, National Archives.

29. "Abigail Adams to John Adams, 29 August 1776," Founders Online, National Archives. JA answered AA's notice with this letter postscript: "Sunday Septr. 8. Yesterdays Post brought me yours of Aug. 29. The Report you mention 'that I was poisoned upon my Return at New York' I suppose will be thought to be a Prophecy, delivered by the Oracle in mystic Language, and meant that I should be politically or morally poisoned by Lord Howe. But the Prophecy shall be false."

30. "John Adams to Abigail Adams, 5 September 1776," Founders Online, National Archives.

31. In the colonial era a "bugbear" was a mythical creature like a boogeyman, hobgoblin, or monster. Parents would invoke it at bedtime to keep unruly children in bed.

32. "Abigail Adams to John Adams, 20 September 1776," Founders Online, National Archives.

33. [Diary of John Adams] "Travels, and Negotiations," Founders Online, National Archives.

34. Only one high-ranking member of Congress was captured and sent to the Tower of London during the war. Henry Laurens, the fifth president of the Continental Congress, was taken pris-oner by the British near the end of the war in 1780 and sent to the Tower of London. Although in December 1781 he was part of a prisoner exchange for General Lord Cornwallis, Laurens' health was never the same after his release.

35. First and foremost, one of the major figures of the King's description of *dangerous and ill-de-signing Men* would be John Adams. https://www.masshist.org/database/viewer.php?item_id= 818&pid=2

36. By the King, a *Proclamation, For suppressing Rebellion and Sedition* (Boston: John Howe, 1775), https://www.masshist.org/database/818

37. Carter Braxton to Landon Carter, April 14, 1776, *Letters of Delegates to Congress: Volume 3, January 1, 1776–May 15, 1776*, edited by Paul H. Smith et al. (Washington, DC: Library of Congress, 1978), 523.

CHAPTER ELEVEN: "A SACRIFICE TO MY COUNTRY"

1. Outgoing citizens leaving Boston had to undergo a "smoking" (fumigation) at the border. Smoking, like JA experienced ten years earlier, was thought to purify the subject from small-pox.

2. "Abigail Adams to John Adams, 7 September 1776," Founders Online, National Archives.

3. "Abigail Adams to John Adams, 20 September 1776," Founders Online, National Archives.

4. A "lighter" was an oar-powered, flat-bottomed barge which "lightened" the load that a ship bore as it was anchored offshore. It transferred people and goods back and forth. It's unknown when or under what circumstances JA acquired his "Lighter," but according to AA who in-spected it, it was near rotten from lack of upkeep.

5. "Abigail Adams to John Adams, 20 September 1776," Founders Online, National Archives.

6. "Abigail Adams to John Adams, 21 September 1776," Founders Online, National Archives.

7. "Abigail Adams to John Adams, 21 September 1776," Founders Online, National Archives.

8. "John Adams to Abigail Adams, 8 October 1776," Founders Online, National Archives.

9. "Abigail Adams to John Adams, 20 September 1776," Founders Online, National Archives.

10. "John Adams to Abigail Adams, 11 July 1776," Founders Online, National Archives.

11. "Abigail Adams to John Adams, 7 September 1776," Founders Online, National Archives.

12. "Abigail Adams to John Adams, 29 September 1776," Founders Online, National Archives.

13. "John Adams to Abigail Adams, 21 September 1776," Founders Online, National Archives; note 2.

14. "John Adams to Abigail Adams, 21 September 1776," Founders Online, National Archives; note 2, Letter to Warren is in JA's letterbook.

15. "Abigail Adams to Mercy Otis Warren, January 1777," Founders Online, National Archives.

16. "Abigail Adams to John Adams, 8 March 1777," Founders Online, National Archives.

17. "Abigail Adams to Mercy Otis Warren, January 1777," Founders Online, National Archives.

18. The secret password of the Trenton operation.

19. On December 9, 1776, the Continental Congress voted to move to Baltimore, Maryland, if Philadelphia became in danger of a British attack. By December 12, steps were being taken to pack up and transfer records and the treasury to Baltimore. On December 20, Congress convened in Baltimore. By February 26, no longer fearing a British attack, Congress voted to return to Philadelphia where it reconvened on March 13, 1777.

20. Records show that Lovell and John left for Baltimore from John's Braintree house. This was likely when Abigail first met Lovell in person.

21. "John Adams to Abigail Adams, 2 February 1777," Founders Online, National Archives.

22. The term "old maid" was a British expression replacing "spinster" in the early eighteenth century.

23. "Abigail Adams to John Adams, 8 March–9 March 1777," Founders Online, National Archives.

24. "Abigail Adams to John Adams, 8 March–9 March 1777," Founders Online, National Archives.

25. "Abigail Adams to John Adams, 26 March 1777," Founders Online, National Archives.

26. "Abigail Adams to John Adams, 8 March–10 March 1777," Founders Online, National Archives.

27. Abigail's sixth pregnancy in 1777 counts Susanna (Grace "Suky" Susanna Adams), who died at sixteen months old.

28. "Abigail Adams to John Adams, 17 April 1777," Founders Online, National Archives.

29. "Abigail Adams to John Adams, 8 March 1777," Founders Online, National Archives.

30. "Abigail Adams to John Adams, 1 June 1777," Founders Online, National Archives.

31. "Abigail Adams to John Adams, 15 June 1777," Founders Online, National Archives.

32. "Abigail Adams to John Adams, 8 June 1777," Founders Online, National Archives.

33. "Abigail Adams to John Adams, 8 June 1777," Founders Online, National Archives.

34. "Abigail Adams to John Adams, 9 July 1777," Founders Online, National Archives.

35. "Abigail Adams to John Adams, 10 July 1777," Founders Online, National Archives.

36. "Abigail Adams to John Adams, 10 July 1777," Founders Online, National Archives.

37. "Abigail Adams to John Adams, 10 July–11 July 1777," Founders Online, National Archives.

38. "Childbirth in colonial America was a difficult and sometimes dangerous experience for women. During the 17th and 18th centuries, between one percent and one and a half percent of all births ended in the mother's death because of exhaustion, dehydration, infection, hemorrhage, or convulsions. Since the typical mother gave birth to between five and eight children, her lifetime chances of dying in childbirth ran as high as one in eight. This meant that if a woman had eight female friends, it was likely that one might die in childbirth." "Childbirth in Early America," University of Houston, Digital History TOPIC ID 70. https://www.digital-history.uh.edu/topic_display.cfm?tcid=70.

39. A colonial-era word for depression.

40. "Abigail Adams to John Adams, 16 July 1777," Founders Online, National Archives.

41. "Abigail Adams to John Adams, 16 July 1777," Founders Online, National Archives.

42. "John Adams to Abigail Adams, 28 July 1777," Founders Online, National Archives.

43. Some counterfeit bills were produced so well that the superior quality alone was a tipoff of being bogus.

44. "Abigail Adams to John Adams, 1 June 1777," Founders Online, National Archives.

45. "Abigail Adams to John Adams, 15 June 1777," Founders Online, National Archives.

46. This stingy merchant was determined to be Thomas Boylston, a first cousin to JA's mother. The women also put the coffee up for sale at a reasonable cost and then gave the money to Boylston. On July 25, 1777, John Scollay, a Boston selectman, wrote of the Boston Coffee Riot that

the women "told him [Boylston] that they kept Little shops to sell Necessarys for Poor People." But Scollay agreed that Boylston "was very roughly handled." "Abigail Adams to John Adams, 30 July 1777," Founders Online, National Archives, note 2.

47. "Abigail Adams to John Adams, 30 July–31 July 1777," Founders Online, National Archives.

48. "Abigail Adams to John Adams, 1 June 1777," Founders Online, National Archives.

49. "Abigail Adams to John Adams, 1 June 1777," Founders Online, National Archives.

50. "Abigail Adams to John Adams, 1 June 1777," Founders Online, National Archives.

51. "Abigail Adams to John Adams, 1 June 1777," Founders Online, National Archives.

52. Abigail meant thirteen years of marriage.

CHAPTER TWELVE: "A VERY DANGEROUS MAN"

1. In 1775 the Continental Congress initiated free congressional franking for official business. This meant that a congressman could sign his name in the corner of a folded letter, which substituted for an envelope, and the postal fee would be suspended.

2. In fact, AA mentions having met Lovell twice, but the date of the second meeting is unknown: "I do not recollect that I ever had that opportunity with my correspondent, twice only in my life do I remember to have seen him," "Abigail Adams to James Lovell, 20 September 1781," Founders Online, National Archives.

3. "Abigail Adams to John Adams, 17 September 1777," Founders Online, National Archives.

4. It is possible that John had told Lovell this fact on their way to Congress.

5. "James Lovell to Abigail Adams, 29 August 1777," Founders Online, National Archives.

6. September 17 was the same day AA sent her letter to John telling him about Lovell's surprise letter.

7. "Abigail Adams to James Lovell, 17 September 1777," Founders Online, National Archives.

8. Jean C. O'Connor, "James Lovell: Schoolteacher, Prisoner, Patriot," *Journal of the American Revolution*, January 5, 2021. https://allthingsliberty.com/2021/01/james-lovell-schoolteacher-prisoner-patriot/.

9. Jean C. O'Connor, "James Lovell: Schoolteacher, Prisoner, Patriot," *Journal of the American Revolution*, January 5, 2021. https://allthingsliberty.com/2021/01/james-lovell-schoolteacher-prisoner-patriot/.

10. Jean C. O'Connor, "James Lovell: Schoolteacher, Prisoner, Patriot," *Journal of the American Revolution*, January 5, 2021. https://allthingsliberty.com/2021/01/james-lovell-schoolteacher-prisoner-patriot/.

11. Some of AA's letters may be in private ownership and therefore can't be counted.

12. Surprisingly, Congress did not hear of Burgoyne's surrender until October 31. The lackadaisical courier, Lieutenant Colonel James Wilkinson, took 12 days to ride from New York to York, Pennsylvania. "Dawdling sociably on the way," Wilkinson would soon reach new levels of detestability in the years to come. Samuel Adams cleverly said that as a reward for bringing Congress the surrender news, Congress should present Wilkinson with a new set of spurs. "John Adams to Abigail Adams, 24 October 1777," Founders Online, National Archives, note 2.

13. "Abigail Adams to John Adams, 20 October–22 October 1777," Founders Online, National Archives.

14. "Abigail Adams to John Adams, 20 October–22 October 1777," Founders Online, National Archives.

15. A bill of exchange was a promissory note between international parties to annually ensure that a fixed amount of money was paid to the investing parties.

16. [The Diary of John Adams] "Travels, and Negotiations," Founders Online, National Archives.

17. [The Diary of John Adams] "Travels, and Negotiations," Founders Online, National Archives.

18. [The Diary of John Adams] "Travels, and Negotiations," Founders Online, National Archives.

19. "Abigail Adams to John Thaxter, 15 February 1778," Founders Online, National Archives.

20. "Abigail Adams to Hannah Quincy Lincoln Storer, 1 March 1778," Founders Online, National Archives.

21. "Abigail Adams to John Thaxter, 15 February 1778," Founders Online, National Archives.

22. "Abigail Adams to James Lovell, 15 December 1777," Founders Online, National Archives.

23. "Abigail Adams to James Lovell, 15 December 1777," Founders Online, National Archives.

24. "Abigail Adams to James Lovell, 1 March 1778," Founders Online, National Archives.

25. "James Lovell to Abigail Adams, 1 April 1778," Founders Online, National Archives.

26. "James Lovell to Abigail Adams, 1 April 1778," Founders Online, National Archives.

27. "Abigail Adams to James Lovell, 4 January 1779," Founders Online, National Archives. Lovell indeed sent copies of congressional Journals to Abigail.

28. "Abigail Adams to James Lovell, 4 January 1779," Founders Online, National Archives.

29. "Abigail Adams to John Adams, 10 September 1777," Founders Online, National Archives.

30. "James Lovell to Abigail Adams, 21 March 1780," Founders Online, National Archives.

31. "Abigail Adams to James Lovell, 12 June 1778," Founders Online, National Archives.

32. "Abigail Adams to James Lovell, 24 June 1778," Founders Online, National Archives.

33. "James Lovell to Abigail Adams, 1 September 1778," Founders Online, National Archives.

34. "James Lovell to Abigail Adams, 19 January 1779," Founders Online, National Archives.

35. "James Lovell to Abigail Adams, 9 March 1779," Founders Online, National Archives.

36. "James Lovell to Abigail Adams, 16 July 1779," Founders Online, National Archives.

37. "James Lovell to Abigail Adams, 19 July 1779," Founders Online, National Archives.

38. "James Lovell to Abigail Adams, 13 January 1780," Founders Online, National Archives.

39. "James Lovell to Abigail Adams, 13 January 1780," Founders Online, National Archives.

40. "Abigail Adams to James Lovell, 23 June 1781," Founders Online, National Archives.

41. "James Lovell to Abigail Adams, 16 June 1781," Founders Online, National Archives.

42. "Abigail Adams to James Lovell, 20 September 1781," Founders Online, National Archives. Abigail was partially quoting from Psalm 137 here, telling Lovell that she only remembered seeing him twice in her life. There may have been another time, but at that moment John was leaving for Congress again, and Abigail was very sad and might not have noticed another's face. Weeping willow trees frequently symbolized loss, and harps being hung up meant the end of music and happiness.

43. Abigail called *herself* a "physiognomist" and John agreed with her. It is someone who supposedly can gain insights into another person's character by studying their physical features, especially the eyes. "Abigail Adams to James Lovell, 20 September 1781," Founders Online, National Archives.

44. "Abigail Adams to James Lovell, 20 September 1781," Founders Online, National Archives.

45. "Abigail Adams to James Lovell, 8 January 1782," Founders Online, National Archives, note 4.

46. "Abigail Adams to James Lovell, 22 April 1789," Founders Online, National Archives.

47. "Abigail Adams to James Lovell, 22 April 1789," Founders Online, National Archives.

48. "Abigail Adams to John Thaxter, 15 February 1778," Founders Online, National Archives.

49. The Adams entourage that traveled from Bordeaux to Paris ("near 500 miles") were John, "Captain Palmes, sent to Paris by Captain Tucker to receive the orders of the Commissioners, of Dr. Noel a French Surgeon of the Boston who went [as] our Interpreter, of Master Jesse Deane (son of Silas Deane), and of my little Son, and my Domestic Servant"; "[Personal Receipts and Expenditures, 1778–1779.]," Founders Online, National Archives.

50. "1779. February 11," Founders Online, National Archives.

51. The *Adams Papers* editors added here "Perhaps 'kiss'; this word is heavily scratched out." "John Adams to Abigail Adams, 25 April 1778," Founders Online, National Archives, note 2.

52. "John Adams to Abigail Adams, 25 April 1778," Founders Online, National Archives.

53. "Abigail Adams to John Adams, 30 June 1778," Founders Online, National Archives.

CHAPTER THIRTEEN: "LABOUR AND RATES DEVOUR THE PROFFETS"

1. "Abigail Adams to Daniel Roberdeau, 15 December 1777," Founders Online, National Archives.
2. "Abigail Adams to Hannah Quincy Lincoln Storer, 1 March 1778," Founders Online, National Archives.
3. "Abigail Adams to Hannah Quincy Lincoln Storer, 1 March 1778," Founders Online, National Archives.
4. "Abigail Adams to John Adams, 21 October 1778," Founders Online, National Archives.
5. "Abigail Adams to John Adams, 21 October 1778," Founders Online, National Archives.
6. "John Adams to Abigail Adams, 12 April 1778," Founders Online, National Archives.
7. "Abigail Adams to John Thaxter, 9 April 1778," Founders Online, National Archives.
8. In 1778 Abigail's cousin, John Thaxter, Jr. was clerking for the congressional secretary.
9. "Abigail Adams to John Thaxter, 9 April 1778," Founders Online, National Archives.
10. "Abigail Adams to John Thaxter, 9 April 1778," Founders Online, National Archives.
11. "Abigail Adams to John Thaxter, 9 April 1778," Founders Online, National Archives.
12. "Abigail Adams to John Adams, 15 July 1778," Founders Online, National Archives.
13. "Abigail Adams to John Adams, 10 June 1778," Founders Online, National Archives.
14. "Abigail Adams to John Adams, 15 July 1778," Founders Online, National Archives.
15. "Abigail Adams to John Adams, 15 July 1778," Founders Online, National Archives.
16. "Abigail Adams to John Adams, 15 July 1778," Founders Online, National Archives.
17. "Abigail Adams to John Adams, 15 July 1778," Founders Online, National Archives.
18. "Abigail Adams to John Adams, 13 December 1778," Founders Online, National Archives.
19. "John Adams to Abigail Adams, 6 November 1778," Founders Online, National Archives.
20. "John Adams to Abigail Adams, 6 November 1778," Founders Online, National Archives.
21. "Abigail Adams to John Adams, 13 December 1778," Founders Online, National Archives.
22. "Abigail Adams to John Adams, 21 October 1778," Founders Online, National Archives.
23. "Abigail Adams to John Adams, 21 April 1776," Founders Online, National Archives.
24. "Abigail Adams to John Adams, 29 September 1778," Founders Online, National Archives.
25. "Abigail Adams to John Adams, 2 January 1779," Founders Online, National Archives.
26. "Abigail Adams to John Adams, 27 December 1778," Founders Online, National Archives.
27. "John Adams to Abigail Adams, 2 December 1778," Founders Online, National Archives. The *Adams Papers* editors added their own accounting to John's estimate: "The editors' count is only eighteen, surviving or alluded to, including the present letter."
28. "Abigail Adams to John Adams, 12–23 November 1778," Founders Online, National Archives.
29. "John Adams to Abigail Adams, 28 February 1779," Founders Online, National Archives.
30. "John Adams to Abigail Adams, 20 February 1779," Founders Online, National Archives.
31. "Abigail Adams to John Adams, 20 March 1779," Founders Online, National Archives.
32. "Abigail Adams to John Adams, 20 March 1779," Founders Online, National Archives.
33. "John Adams to Abigail Adams, 14 May 1779," Founders Online, National Archives.
34. *Adams Papers* editors: "Recently reelected a Braintree representative to the Massachusetts House, Cranch was particularly active at this time as a member of a committee conducting the sale of confiscated loyalist estates in Suffolk County. See the Confiscation Acts of 30 April and 1 May as published in the *Boston Gazette*." "Abigail Adams to John Adams, 8 June 1779," Founders Online, National Archives.
35. "Abigail Adams to John Adams, 8 June 1779," Founders Online, National Archives.
36. "From John Adams to Benjamin Franklin, 31 March 1779," Founders Online, National Archives; AA would meet Capt. John Paul Jones much later when she was in Paris with John. Her written comments about Jones are less than flattering.
37. "Constitution of the Commonwealth of Massachusetts, 1780," National Humanities Institute http://www.nhinet.org/ccs/docs/ma-1780.htm.
38. "Constitution of the Commonwealth of Massachusetts, 1780," chapter 5, section 2; National Humanities Institute http://www.nhinet.org/ccs/docs/ma-1780.htm.

39. *John Adams, Revolutionary Writings, 1775–1783*, ed. Gordon Wood, Massachusetts Historical Society, Library of America (New York: Penguin, 2011), 711.

40. JQA balked at a second trip, but it was Abigail who pressed him to go. Her reasoning is in a letter of January 19, 1780, to JQA after he had sailed.

41. Joseph Stevens had also been an assistant to JA and passenger the year before on that first rough voyage.

42. For a full description of the adventure, see John L. Smith, Jr., "The Remarkable Spanish Pilgrimage of John Adams," *Journal of the American Revolution*, November 23, 2016, https://allthingsliberty.com/2016/11/remarkable-spanish-pilgrimage-john-adams/.

43. "[December 1779]," Founders Online, National Archives.

44. "Abigail Adams to John Quincy Adams, 19 January 1780," Founders Online, National Archives.

CHAPTER FOURTEEN: "A FEW NECESSARIES FOR THE FAMILY"

1. "John Adams to Abigail Adams, 16 March 1780," Founders Online, National Archives.

2. "Abigail Adams to John Quincy and Charles Adams, 26 February 1780," Founders Online, National Archives.

3. "John Adams to Abigail Adams, 12 February 1780," Founders Online, National Archives.

4. "Abigail Adams to John Adams, 18 January 1780," Founders Online, National Archives.

5. The Adams Papers editors added, "The winter of 1779–1780, when for the only time in recorded history the harbors of both Boston and New York froze solidly, was long known as 'the Hard Winter.' Its effects were felt from Maine to Georgia and from Detroit to New Orleans." "Abigail Adams to John Adams, 26 February 1780," Founders Online, National Archives.

6. "John Adams to Abigail Adams, 17 June 1780," Founders Online, National Archives.

7. "Abigail Adams to John Adams, 1 May 1780," Founders Online, National Archives.

8. "Abigail Adams to John Adams, 24 July 1780," Founders Online, National Archives.

9. "John Adams to Abigail Smith, 14 February 1763," Founders Online, National Archives.

10. "Abigail Adams to John Adams, 1 May 1780," Founders Online, National Archives.

11. "Jean de Neufville & Son to Abigail Adams, 25 May 1781," Founders Online, National Archives.

12. The use of the word "politician" then meant someone who was actively engaged in politics, but was not a candidate for any election.

13. "Abigail Adams to John Adams, 5 July 1780," Founders Online, National Archives.

14. A "tinkling cymbal" a biblical term from the apostle Paul's first letter to the Corinthians: "Though I speak with the tongues of men and of angels, and have not charity, I am become as sounding brass, or a tinkling cymbal" (13:1). It signified an emptiness in the words being spoken, in this case by John Hancock.

15. "Abigail Adams to John Adams, 5 July 1780," Founders Online, National Archives.

16. "John Adams to Abigail Adams, 12 May 1780," Founders Online, National Archives.

17. "From John Adams to Jonathan Jackson, 8 November 1782," Founders Online, National Archives.

18. "Benjamin Franklin to Samuel Huntington, 9 Aug. 1780," *The Writings of Benjamin Franklin*, 10 vols. (New York: Macmillan, 1905–1907), ed. Smyth, 8:128.

19. "Abigail Adams to John Adams, 23 April 1781," Founders Online, National Archives.

20. "Abigail Adams to John Adams, 17–18 July 1782," Founders Online, National Archives.

21. "Coverture" was the status of a married woman which was merged with that of her husband.

22. "Abigail Adams to John Adams, 17–18 July 1782," Founders Online, National Archives.

23. "Abigail Adams to John Adams, 9 December 1781," Founders Online, National Archives.

24. "John Adams to Abigail Adams, 12 October 1782," Founders Online, National Archives.

25. "From John Adams to James Warren, 17 June 1782," Founders Online, National Archives.

26. "Abigail Adams to John Adams, 29 September 1781," Founders Online, National Archives.

27. "Abigail Adams to John Adams, 9 December 1781," Founders Online, National Archives.

28. This mysterious illness which struck John for nearly three months has been analyzed by historians ever since. The predictive diagnoses run from malaria, typhus, Grave's Disease, and even a psychosomatic cause. JA raved about the curing effects from "Peruvian bark" (quinine) several times in letters after his recovery.

29. "From John Adams to James Warren, 9 April 1783," Founders Online, National Archives.

30. "John Adams to Abigail Adams, 11 July 1781," Founders Online, National Archives.

31. "From John Adams to Boston Patriot, 8 February 1810," Founders Online, National Archives.

32. "John Adams to Abigail Adams, 11 July 1781," Founders Online, National Archives, note 2. The Adams Papers editors note: "Major William Jackson (1759–1828), under whose particular care JA had placed CA during the voyage, was a Charlestonian who had served under Maj. Gen. Benjamin Lincoln in the latter's southern campaign and had come to Europe with John Laurens' mission to obtain further aid for the American military effort."

33. "John Adams to Abigail Adams, 11 July 1781," Founders Online, National Archives, note 2. The Adams Papers editors say: "The erratic conduct of Gillon led to an early and bitter quarrel between him and Jackson; they parted in Spain and afterward fought a duel in America, in which Jackson was wounded."

34. Both Cornwallis and Washington assigned the acceptance of surrender swords to seconds-in-command.

35. "John Adams to Abigail Adams, 12 October 1782," Founders Online, National Archives.

36. "Abigail Adams to John Adams, with a List of Articles wanted from Holland, 17 June 1782," Founders Online, National Archives.

37. "Abigail Adams to John Adams, with a List of Articles wanted from Holland, 17 June 1782," Founders Online, National Archives.

38. "Abigail Adams to John Adams, with a List of Articles wanted from Holland, 17 June 1782," Founders Online, National Archives.

39. "Abigail Adams to John Adams, with a List of Articles wanted from Holland, 17 June 1782," Founders Online, National Archives.

40. "John Adams to Abigail Adams 2d, 16 October 1782," Founders Online, National Archives.

CHAPTER FIFTEEN: "TO HAZARD THE WATERY ELEMENT"

1. "Sensibility" can be defined by having the capacity for emotional reactions to people and things.

2. "Abigail Adams to John Adams, 8 October 1782," Founders Online, National Archives.

3. "Abigail Adams to John Adams, 17–18 July 1782," Founders Online, National Archives.

4. The Harvard graduation ceremony was a popular event to attend in the Boston region, whether the attendee had a friend or relative graduating or not.

5. "Abigail Adams 2d to John Adams, 10 May 1783," Founders Online, National Archives.

6. "Abigail Adams 2d to Elizabeth Cranch, 22 December 1782," Founders Online, National Archives.

7. "Abigail Adams to John Adams, 17–18 July 1782," Founders Online, National Archives.

8. "John Adams to Abigail Adams, 22 January 1783," Founders Online, National Archives.

9. "John Adams to Abigail Adams, 22 January 1783," Founders Online, National Archives.

10. "Abigail Adams to John Adams, 23 December 1782," Founders Online, National Archives.

11. "John Adams to Abigail Adams, 22 January 1783," Founders Online, National Archives.

12. "Abigail Adams to John Adams, 23 December 1782," Founders Online, National Archives.

13. "John Adams to Abigail Adams, 22 January 1783," Founders Online, National Archives.

14. "Abigail Adams to John Adams, 19 October 1783," Founders Online, National Archives.

15. "Abigail Adams 2d to Elizabeth Cranch, June 1782," Founders Online, National Archives.

16. "Abigail Adams to John Adams, 5 August 1782," Founders Online, National Archives.

17. "Abigail Adams to John Adams, 5 August 1782," Founders Online, National Archives.

18. Dr. Benjamin Waterhouse later became co-founder and professor at Harvard Medical School.

19. "Abigail Adams to John Adams, 5 August 1782," Founders Online, National Archives.

20. "Abigail Adams to John Adams, 5 September 1782," Founders Online, National Archives.

21. "Abigail Adams to John Adams, 23 December 1782," Founders Online, National Archives.

22. "Abigail Adams to John Adams, 7 May 1783," Founders Online, National Archives.

23. "John Adams to Abigail Adams, 4 February 1783," Founders Online, National Archives.

24. *Journal of the Continental Congress*, volume 24: *January 1, 1783, to August 29, 1783* (Washington, D.C.: Government Printing Office, 1922), 321 (May 1, 1783).

25. "John Adams to Abigail Adams, 7 September 1783," Founders Online, National Archives.

26. "Abigail Adams to John Adams, 17–18 July 1782," Founders Online, National Archives.

27. "Abigail Adams to John Adams, 7 April 1783," Founders Online, National Archives; "Phillips Academy, founded in 1778 and legally incorporated in 1780, enrolled twenty-eight students in 1782, and thirty-five in 1783. They varied widely in age, but many were at the age of CA (12) and TBA (10). See *Biographical Catalogue of the Trustees, Teachers and Students of Phillips Academy Andover, Andover, Mass.*, 1903." *Adams Papers* editors.

28. "1783 Tuesday. Feb. 18," Founders Online, National Archives.

29. "From Benjamin Franklin to Vergennes, 17 December 1782," Founders Online, National Archives.

30. "John Adams to Abigail Adams, 10 June 1783," Founders Online, National Archives.

31. "From Benjamin Franklin to Robert R. Livingston, 22[–26] July 1783," Founders Online, National Archives.

32. "Abigail Adams to John Adams, 20 September 1783," Founders Online, National Archives.

33. The *Oxford English Dictionary* defines "strangery" as a urinary tract blockage.

34. Abigail's parents, Rev. William Smith, Sr. and Elizabeth Quincy Smith, are buried in the cemetery adjacent to the Smiths' house and the gravesites are still accessible to the public.

35. "Will of Reverend William Smith, 12 September 1783," Founders Online, National Archives; William Smith, Jr. died soon afterward, in 1787, of alcoholism.

36. "Will of Reverend William Smith, 12 September 1783," Founders Online, National Archives.

37. "Will of Reverend William Smith, 12 September 1783," Founders Online, National Archives.

38. "Will of Reverend William Smith, 12 September 1783," Founders Online, National Archives.

39. "Will of Reverend William Smith, 12 September 1783," Founders Online, National Archives. *Adams Papers* editors: "It is interesting to note that Rev. Smith made this manumission provision shortly after Chief Justice William Cushing of the Massachusetts Supreme Judicial Court, in a charge to the jury in the case of *Commonwealth vs. Jennison* (April 1783), argued that slavery was illegal under the Massachusetts Constitution of 1780." Note 1.

40. The original name had been Stoneyfield. The purchase was made on behalf of the Adams by Cotton Tufts in 1787 while they were in Europe.

41. "Abigail Adams to Cotton Tufts, 5 October 1789," Founders Online, National Archives.

42. However, that didn't include in highly speculative out-of-state land in Vermont.

43. "LM" was "Lawful Money"—consolidated State of Massachusetts bank notes.

44. "Abigail Adams to John Adams, 3 January 1784," Founders Online, National Archives.

45. "Abigail Adams to John Adams, 3 January 1784," Founders Online, National Archives.

46. "Abigail Adams to John Adams, 11 February 1784," Founders Online, National Archives.

47. "Abigail Adams to Cotton Tufts, 18 June 1784," Founders Online, National Archives.

48. "Abigail Adams to Cotton Tufts, 18 June 1784," Founders Online, National Archives.

49. "Abigail Adams to Cotton Tufts, 18 June 1784," Founders Online, National Archives.

50. The *Adams Papers* editors: "John Briesler and Esther Field married in London while serving the Adamses, and Esther gave birth to a daughter on 28 May 1788 on shipboard, as the Brieslers were returning with AA and JA to America. The Brieslers continued to serve the Adamses into the 1790s." "Abigail Adams to John Adams, 11 February 1784," Founders Online, National Archives; note 4. The servant AA wanted to go with her was Jane Glover Newcomb (Jinny). "The one I expected to have come with me undertook to get married and dissapointed me." "Abigail Adams to John Adams, 25 May 1784," Founders Online, National Archives, note 7.

51. "Abigail Adams to John Adams, 11 February 1784," Founders Online, National Archives.

52. "Abigail Adams to John Adams, 11 February 1784," Founders Online, National Archives.

53. "Abigail Adams to Cotton Tufts, 18 June 1784," Founders Online, National Archives.

54. "Abigail Adams to John Adams, 11 February 1784," Founders Online, National Archives.

55. "Sunday June 20 1784," Founders Online, National Archives. This trip was one of the few times AA kept a diary or journal. Her sister Mary Cranch had asked for one.

56. "Abigail Adams' Diary of her Voyage from Boston to Deal, 20 June–20 July 1784," Founders Online, National Archives.

57. AA apparently had expected Capt. Lyde to be a crude, salty sea captain, possibly from her initial evaluation of his eyes and face (her use of physiognomy). She admitted her first opinion was wrong. He was "an admirable Seaman, nothing cross or Dictatorial in his Manners, a much more agreable Man than I expected to find him." "Abigail Adams to Mary Smith Cranch, 6–30 July 1784," Founders Online, National Archives.

58. "Sunday June 20 1784," Founders Online, National Archives.

CHAPTER SIXTEEN: "IN A LAND OF ENCHANTMENT"

1. "Abigail Adams to Mary Smith Cranch, 6–30 July 1784," Founders Online, National Archives.

2. "Abigail Adams to Mary Smith Cranch, 6–30 July 1784," Founders Online, National Archives.

3. "Abigail Adams to Mary Smith Cranch, 6–30 July 1784," Founders Online, National Archives.

4. "Abigail Adams to Mary Smith Cranch, 6–30 July 1784," Founders Online, National Archives.

5. "Abigail Adams to Mary Smith Cranch, 6–30 July 1784," Founders Online, National Archives.

6. "Abigail Adams to Mary Smith Cranch, 6–30 July 1784," Founders Online, National Archives.

7. "Abigail Adams to Elizabeth Smith Shaw, 11 July 1784," Founders Online, National Archives.

8. "Abigail Adams to Mary Smith Cranch, 6–30 July 1784," Founders Online, National Archives.

9. "Abigail Adams to Mary Smith Cranch, 6–30 July 1784," Founders Online, National Archives; note 16. Explanation by the *Adams Papers* editors.

10. "Abigail Adams to Mary Smith Cranch, 6–30 July 1784," Founders Online, National Archives.

11. "Abigail Adams to Mary Smith Cranch, 6–30 July 1784," Founders Online, National Archives.

12. "Abigail Adams to Mary Smith Cranch, 6–30 July 1784," Founders Online, National Archives.

13. "Abigail Adams to Mary Smith Cranch, 6–30 July 1784," Founders Online, National Archives.

14. "Abigail Adams to Mary Smith Cranch, 6–30 July 1784," Founders Online, National Archives.

15. "Abigail Adams to Mary Smith Cranch, 6–30 July 1784," Founders Online, National Archives.

16 "Abigail Adams to Mary Smith Cranch, 6–30 July 1784," Founders Online, National Archives.

17. "Abigail Adams to Mary Smith Cranch, 6–30 July 1784," Founders Online, National Archives.

18. Mentioned throughout AA's journal and letters were "Mr. Storer" (Charles Storer, JA's secretary since 1782), "Mr. Smith" (William Smith, AA's Boston cousin), and "Mr. Spear" (an amiable fellow sailing passenger).

19. *Abigail Adams: Letters* (New York The Library of America–Literary Classics of the United States, 2016), 1062–1063.

20. "Abigail Adams to John Adams, 23 July 1784," Founders Online, National Archives.

21. "John Adams to Abigail Adams, 26 July 1784," Founders Online, National Archives.

22. "John Adams to Abigail Adams, 26 July 1784," Founders Online, National Archives.

23. "Abigail Adams to Elizabeth Smith Shaw, 28–30 July 1784," Founders Online, National Archives.

24. "Abigail Adams to Elizabeth Smith Shaw, 28–30 July 1784," Founders Online, National Archives.

25. "Abigail Adams to Mary Smith Cranch, 6–30 July 1784," Founders Online, National Archives.

26. "Abigail Adams to Mary Smith Cranch, 6–30 July 1784," Founders Online, National Archives.

27. "Abigail Adams to Mary Smith Cranch, 6–30 July 1784," Founders Online, National Archives; *Adams Papers* editors: "Although Copley retained possession of the painting to have engravings made, it did not 'belong to him'; JA had already paid for it. AA's description of the portrait is not entirely accurate: JA is not holding a map of Europe, and only one female figure is visible in the background." Note 43. The original painting is now in the Harvard University Portrait Collection.

28. "Abigail Adams to Mary Smith Cranch, 6–30 July 1784," Founders Online, National Archives. The Oxford English Dictionary's "first definition for slut is 'a woman of dirty, slovenly, or untidy habits or appearance; a foul slattern.'" https://www.thedailybeast.com/the-surprising-roots-of-the-word-slut.

29. "Abigail Adams to Mary Smith Cranch, 6–30 July 1784," Founders Online, National Archives.

30. "Abigail Adams to Mary Smith Cranch, 6–30 July 1784," Founders Online, National Archives.

31. "Abigail Adams to Mary Smith Cranch, 6–30 July 1784," Founders Online, National Archives.

32. "Abigail Adams to Mary Smith Cranch, 6–30 July 1784," Founders Online, National Archives.

33. "Abigail Adams to Mary Smith Cranch, 6–30 July 1784," Founders Online, National Archives.

34. "John Adams to Abigail Adams, 1 August 1784," Founders Online, National Archives.

35. "John Adams to Abigail Adams, 1 August 1784," Founders Online, National Archives.

36. "Abigail Adams to Mary Smith Cranch, 6–30 July 1784," Founders Online, National Archives.

37. "Abigail Adams to Mary Smith Cranch, 6–30 July 1784," Founders Online, National Archives.

38. *Journal and Correspondence of Miss Adams, Daughter of John Adams,* "edited by Her Daughter [Caroline Amelia (Smith) de Windt]," 2 vols. (New York and London, 1841–1842), i:viii.

39. "Abigail Adams to Lucy Cranch, 5 September 1784," Founders Online, National Archives.

40. "Abigail Adams to Lucy Cranch, 5 September 1784," Founders Online, National Archives.

41. The French word "Hôtel" could also mean a very large house. In this case, it was the home of Comte de Rouault.

42. "From the Diary of John Adams [August17, 1784]," Founders Online, National Archives.

43. "Abigail Adams to Mary Smith Cranch, 5 September 1784," Founders Online, National Archives.

44. "Abigail Adams to Elizabeth Cranch, 5 September 1784," Founders Online, National Archives.

45. "Abigail Adams to Mary Smith Cranch, 5 September 1784," Founders Online, National Archives.

46. "Abigail Adams 2d to Elizabeth Cranch, 4 September 1784," Founders Online, National Archives.

47. "Abigail Adams to Lucy Cranch, 5 September 1784," Founders Online, National Archives.

48. "Abigail Adams to Mary Smith Cranch, 5 September 1784," Founders Online, National Archives.

49. Among many other visitors were Thomas Jefferson, Antoine Lavoisier, Charles-Maurice de Talleyrand, Jean-Antoine Houdon, Napoléon Bonaparte, and of course Dr. Benjamin Franklin (who reportedly asked for her hand in marriage but was turned down).

50. "Abigail Adams to Cotton Tufts, 8 September 1784," Founders Online, National Archives.

51. "Abigail Adams to Mary Smith Cranch, 5 September 1784," Founders Online, National Archives.

52. "Abigail Adams to Cotton Tufts, 8 September 1784," Founders Online, National Archives.

53. "Abigail Adams to Mary Smith Cranch, 5 September 1784," Founders Online, National Archives.

54. "Abigail Adams to Cotton Tufts, 8 September 1784," Founders Online, National Archives.

55. "Abigail Adams to Mary Smith Cranch, 5 September 1784," Founders Online, National Archives.

56. "Abigail Adams to Cotton Tufts, 8 September 1784," Founders Online, National Archives.

57. "Abigail Adams to Mary Smith Cranch, 5 September 1784," Founders Online, National Archives.

58. "Abigail Adams to Cotton Tufts, 8 September 1784," Founders Online, National Archives.

CHAPTER SEVENTEEN: "THE BUSINESS OF LIFE HERE [IS] PLEASURE"

1. "Abigail Adams to Mercy Otis Warren, 5 September 1784," Founders Online, National Archives.

2. "Abigail Adams to Mary Smith Cranch, 7 January 1785," Founders Online, National Archives.

3. "Abigail Adams to Mercy Otis Warren, 5 September 1784," Founders Online, National Archives.

4. "Abigail Adams to Elizabeth Smith Shaw, 15 October 1786," Founders Online, National Archives.

5. "Abigail Adams to Mercy Otis Warren, 5 September 1784," Founders Online, National Archives.

6. "About one-third of the children abandoned in Paris during the eighteenth century came from the provinces and, thus, were at least a few days old and already sick and underfed. Many of these babies died before reaching the ancient hospital, the Hôtel-Dieu, which also served as a foundling home. In 1772, the king prohibited this transfer of infants to Paris, but the flow continued. The ban was renewed in 1779 but with no better results, and at the end of the ancien régime, between 6,000 and 7,000 newborn babies were being abandoned in the capital each year. The mortality of these children was horrifying. More than 80 percent died." "Breast Milk and Artificial Infant Feeding," Antoinette Fauve-Chamoux, *Cambridge World History of Food,* ed. Kenneth F. Kiple and Kriemhild Conee Ornelas, volume 1 (Cambridge, UK: Cambridge University Press, 2000).

7. "Abigail Adams to Elizabeth Smith Shaw, 11 January 1785," Founders Online, National Archives.

8. "Abigail Adams to Cotton Tufts, 3 January 1785," Founders Online, National Archives.

9. For example: "the consideration of Colo. Hamilton's being a member of my family." Washington called his small group of military secretaries and aides-de-camp his "family." Lafayette was certainly a valuable one. "From George Washington to William Gordon, 3 May 1780," Founders Online, National Archives.

10. "Abigail Adams to Mary Smith Cranch, 9 December 1784," Founders Online, National Archives.

11. "Abigail Adams to Mary Smith Cranch, 15 April 1785," Founders Online, National Archives.

12. "Abigail Adams 2d to Elizabeth Cranch, 30 September 1784," Founders Online, National Archives.

13. "Abigail Adams to Elizabeth Smith Shaw, 14 December 1784," Founders Online, National Archives.

14. "Abigail Adams to Mary Smith Cranch, 9 December 1784," Founders Online, National Archives.

15. "Abigail Adams to Mary Smith Cranch, 9 December 1784," Founders Online, National Archives.

16. "Abigail Adams to Mary Smith Cranch, 20 February 1785," Founders Online, National Archives.

17. "Abigail Adams to Charles Storer, 3 January 1785," Founders Online, National Archives.

18. Gen. George Washington was an excellent dancer by all accounts.

19. "Elizabeth Smith Shaw to Abigail Adams, 25 April 1785," Founders Online, National Archives.

20. "Elizabeth Smith Shaw to Abigail Adams, 15 October 1784," Founders Online, National Archives.

21. "Abigail Adams to Elizabeth Smith Shaw, 11 January 1785," Founders Online, National Archives.

22. "Catharine Louisa Salmon Smith to Abigail Adams, 26 October 1785," Founders Online, National Archives.

23. "Catharine Louisa Salmon Smith to Abigail Adams, 26 October 1785," Founders Online, National Archives.

24. "The Congress of the Confederation" was Congress's post-war name during the times of the Articles of Confederation. The name was then changed by the Constitution to the "United States Congress."

25. The French term for a noble knight.

26. "Abigail Adams to Elizabeth Cranch, 3 December 1784," Founders Online, National Archives.

27. "Thursday. May 13th," Founders Online, National Archives.

28. "Abigail Adams to Thomas Jefferson, 6 June 1785," Founders Online, National Archives.

29. "Abigail Adams to Mary Smith Cranch, 8 May 1785," Founders Online, National Archives.

30. "Abigail Adams to Elizabeth Cranch, 8 March 1785," Founders Online, National Archives.

31. *Journal and correspondence of Miss Adams, daughter of John Adams, second president of the United States. Written in France and England, in 1785* (New York: Wiley and Putnam, 1841–42), 18. This was not the historic first flight of a hot air balloon, but the sight was still amazing to the congregated assembly.

32. "Abigail Adams to Mary Smith Cranch, 8 May 1785," Founders Online, National Archives.

33. "John Adams to Cotton Tufts, 24 April 1785," Founders Online, National Archives.

34. "John Adams to Cotton Tufts, 24 April 1785," Founders Online, National Archives.

35. Mercy Otis Warren sarcastically called such pompous, insecure husbands *"The Lord of the universe"*; "Mercy Otis Warren to Abigail Adams, 15 March 1779," Founders Online, National Archives.

36. "John Adams to Cotton Tufts, 24 April 1785," Founders Online, National Archives.

37. "Abigail Adams to Cotton Tufts, 26 April 1785," Founders Online, National Archives. Dr. Woody Holton brought to prominence AA's phrase *"With this money which I call mine."* Holton reminds the readers that according to "the common-law doctrine of coverture," married women were prevented from owning anything personal. My sincere thanks to Holton and his 2009 book *Abigail Adams* (New York, Free Press, 2009).

38. Holton, *Abigail Adams*, 213. Abigail's phrase and much documentation for AA's financial intelligence were unveiled largely by Holton in his book.

39. "Abigail Adams to Cotton Tufts, 26 April 1785," Founders Online, National Archives.

40. "Abigail Adams to Elizabeth Smith Shaw, 8 May 1785," Founders Online, National Archives.

41. "Abigail Adams to Thomas Jefferson, 6 June 1785," Founders Online, National Archives.

42. "Abigail Adams to Thomas Jefferson, 6 June 1785," Founders Online, National Archives.

43. "Abigail Adams to Mary Smith Cranch, 24 June 1785," Founders Online, National Archives.
44. "Abigail Adams to Thomas Jefferson, 6 June 1785," Founders Online, National Archives.
45. Abigail and Nabby had stayed at the Strand in July 1784.
46. "Abigail Adams to Thomas Jefferson, 6 June 1785," Founders Online, National Archives.
47. "Abigail Adams to John Quincy Adams, 11 August 1785," Founders Online, National Archives.
48. "Abigail Adams to Thomas Welsh, 25 August 1785," Founders Online, National Archives.
49. "Abigail Adams to Thomas Jefferson, 6 June 1785," Founders Online, National Archives.

CHAPTER EIGHTEEN: "THE TORY VENOM HAS BEGUN TO SPIT"

1. "From John Adams to Elbridge Gerry, 2 May 1785," Founders Online, National Archives.
2. The Marquis of Carmarthen, Sir Clement Cottrell Dormer, Baron Lynden van Blitterswyck, Baron De Nolken, Under Secretary Mr. Frasier.
3. "From John Adams to John Jay, 2 June 1785," Founders Online, National Archives.
4. *London Morning Herald and Daily Advertiser*, June 8, 1785.
5. "From John Adams to John Jay, 2 June 1785," Founders Online, National Archives.
6. "Abigail Adams to Mary Smith Cranch, 24 June 1785," Founders Online, National Archives.
7. "Abigail Adams to Mary Smith Cranch, 24 June 1785," Founders Online, National Archives.
8. "Abigail Adams to Mary Smith Cranch, 24 June 1785," Founders Online, National Archives; note 4.
9. "Abigail Adams to Mary Smith Cranch, 24 June 1785," Founders Online, National Archives; note 4.
10. "Small talk" is an old term, still used, for idle chit-chat. AA even used that term in her letter to her sister.
11. "Abigail Adams to Mary Smith Cranch, 24 June 1785," Founders Online, National Archives.
12. King George III bought "Buckingham House" in 1761 as a wedding present for Queen Charlotte, but the court was still at St. James's Palace. By 1827, Buckingham Palace had been remodeled enough to officially serve as the Royal Family home and the administrative offices of the monarchy. https://www.royal.uk/royal-residences-buckingham-palace.
13. "Abigail Adams to Mary Smith Cranch, 24 June 1785," Founders Online, National Archives.
14. "Abigail Adams to Mary Smith Cranch, 24 June 1785," Founders Online, National Archives.
15. "Abigail Adams to John Quincy Adams, 26 June 1785," Founders Online, National Archives.
16 "Abigail Adams to Mary Smith Cranch, 24 June 1785," Founders Online, National Archives.
17. "Abigail Adams to John Quincy Adams, 26 June 1785," Founders Online, National Archives.
18. "Abigail Adams to Charles Williams, 1 July 1785," Founders Online, National Archives.
19. "Abigail Adams to Lucy Cranch, 2 April 1786," Founders Online, National Archives.
20. Charlotte Augusta Matilda, Augusta Sophia, Elizabeth, and George, Prince of Wales, later King George IV. The *Adams Papers* editors; "Abigail Adams to Mary Smith Cranch, 30 September 1785," Founders Online.
21. "Abigail Adams to Mary Smith Cranch, 30 September 1785," Founders Online, National Archives.
22. "Abigail Adams to Mary Smith Cranch, 11 September 1785," Founders Online, National Archives.
23. "Abigail Adams to Mary Smith Cranch, 15 August 1785," Founders Online, National Archives.
24. "Abigail Adams to Mary Smith Cranch, 15 August 1785," Founders Online, National Archives.

25. "Abigail Adams 2d to Royall Tyler, 11 August 1785," Founders Online, National Archives.

26. "Abigail Adams to Charles Storer, 22 May 1786," Founders Online, National Archives.

27. "The Ton of London" meant the most popular attraction or trend. "Abigail Adams to Lucy Quincy Tufts, 3 September 1785," Founders Online, National Archives.

28. "Abigail Adams to Lucy Quincy Tufts, 3 September 1785," Founders Online, National Archives.

29. "Abigail Adams to Lucy Quincy Tufts, 3 September 1785," Founders Online, National Archives.

30. "Abigail Adams 2d to John Quincy Adams, 4 July 1785 – 11 August 1785," Founders Online, National Archives.

31. "Abigail Adams to Elizabeth Smith Shaw, 4 March 1786," Founders Online, National Archives.

32. "Abigail Adams to William Stephens Smith, 18 September 1785," Founders Online, National Archives.

33. "Abigail Adams to Cotton Tufts, 10 January 1786," Founders Online, National Archives.

34. "Abigail Adams to Mary Smith Cranch, 26 February 1786," Founders Online, National Archives.

35. "Abigail Adams to Mary Smith Cranch, 26 February 1786," Founders Online, National Archives; note 9.

36. "Abigail Adams to Elizabeth Smith Shaw, 4 March 1786," Founders Online, National Archives.

37. "Abigail Adams to Mary Smith Cranch, 24 April 1786," Founders Online, National Archives.

CHAPTER NINETEEN: "IRONING IS VERY BAD FOR YOU"

1. "Abigail Adams 2d to John Quincy Adams, 9 February 1786," Founders Online, National Archives.

2. "Abigail Adams 2d to John Quincy Adams, 9 February 1786," Founders Online, National Archives.

3. "Abigail Adams 2d to John Quincy Adams, 9 February 1786," Founders Online, National Archives.

4. "Abigail Adams 2d to John Quincy Adams, 9 February 1786," Founders Online, National Archives.

5. "Abigail Adams 2d to John Quincy Adams, 9 February 1786," Founders Online, National Archives.

6. "Abigail Adams 2d to John Quincy Adams, 9 February 1786," Founders Online, National Archives.

7. "Abigail Adams 2d to John Quincy Adams, 9 February 1786," Founders Online, National Archives.

8. "Abigail Adams 2d to John Quincy Adams, 9 February 1786," Founders Online, National Archives.

9. "Abigail Adams 2d to John Quincy Adams, 9 February 1786," Founders Online, National Archives.

10. "Abigail Adams 2d to John Quincy Adams, 9 February 1786," Founders Online, National Archives.

11. Any popular trend or fad. "Abigail Adams to Mary Smith Cranch, 6 April 1786," Founders Online, National Archives.

12. "Abigail Adams to Mary Smith Cranch, 6 April 1786," Founders Online, National Archives.

13. "Abigail Adams to Mary Smith Cranch, 6 April 1786," Founders Online, National Archives.

14. "Abigail Adams to Elizabeth Smith Shaw, 19 July 1786," Founders Online, National Archives.

15. "Abigail Adams to Charles Storer, 23 March 1786," Founders Online, National Archives.

16. Different sources cite the wedding date as June 12 (which was a Monday in 1786). In AA's letters she labeled the wedding date of "Sunday the 12 of June." One would suppose the Sabbath

Day (Sunday) would stand out more to her than a one-day date error. Therefore, the author uses Sunday, June 12.

17. "Abigail Adams to Mary Smith Cranch, 21 May 1786," Founders Online, National Archives.

18. "Abigail Adams to Mary Smith Cranch, 13 June 1786," Founders Online, National Archives.

19. "Abigail Adams to Thomas Jefferson, 23 July 1786," Founders Online, National Archives; including note 6.

20. "Abigail Adams to Mary Smith Cranch, 4 July 1786," Founders Online, National Archives.

21. "Mary Smith Cranch to Abigail Adams, 19 July–7 August 1785," Founders Online, National Archives.

22. "Mary Smith Cranch to Abigail Adams, 10 July 1786," Founders Online, National Archives.

23. "Abigail Adams to Mary Smith Cranch, 4 July 1786," Founders Online, National Archives.

24. "Abigail Adams to Elizabeth Cranch, 18 July 1786," Founders Online, National Archives.

25. "Abigail Adams to Mary Smith Cranch, 12 September 1786," Founders Online, National Archives.

26. "Abigail Adams to Mary Smith Cranch, 12 September 1786," Founders Online, National Archives.

27. "Abigail Adams to Mary Smith Cranch, 12 September 1786," Founders Online, National Archives.

28. "Abigail Adams to Mary Smith Cranch, 12 September 1786," Founders Online, National Archives.

29. "Abigail Adams to Mary Smith Cranch, 12 September 1786," Founders Online, National Archives.

30. "Abigail Adams to Abigail Adams Smith, 15 August 1786," Founders Online, National Archives.

31. "Abigail Adams to Mary Smith Cranch, 12 September 1786," Founders Online, National Archives.

32. "Abigail Adams to Mary Smith Cranch, 12 September 1786," Founders Online, National Archives.

33. "Abigail Adams to Mary Smith Cranch, 26 February 1786," Founders Online, National Archives.

34. "Mary Smith Cranch to Abigail Adams, 9 October 1786," Founders Online, National Archives.

35. "Mary Smith Cranch to Abigail Adams, 24 September 1786," Founders Online, National Archives.

36. Royall Tyler went on to father eleven children from those long, dark Vermont winters. Even with his playboy reputation, Royall went on to accomplish much. He reenlisted with the militia and helped quell Shays' Rebellion. He eventually became Chief Justice of the Vermont Supreme Court, as well as Professor of Jurisprudence at the University of Vermont. He also had been a popular playwright, penning the comedy *The Contrast* in 1787 shortly after his breakup with Nabby Adams. *The Contrast* was the first American play to be performed by professional actors. Even President George Washington enjoyed it.

37. "Mary Smith Cranch to Abigail Adams, 9 October 1786," Founders Online, National Archives.

38. "Mary Smith Cranch to Abigail Adams, 9 October 1786," Founders Online, National Archives.

39. "Mary Smith Cranch to Abigail Adams, 9 October 1786," Founders Online, National Archives.

40. Husband Richard Cranch frequently traveled on business, as he was doing at this time.

41. "Abigail Adams to Mary Smith Cranch, 12 October 1786," Founders Online, National Archives.

42. "Abigail Adams to Mary Smith Cranch, 12 October 1786," Founders Online, National Archives; as a stand-alone sentence, this quote may have been taken slightly out of context.

43. "To Thomas Jefferson from Abigail Adams, 29 January 1787," Founders Online, National Archives.

44. "From Thomas Jefferson to Abigail Adams, 22 February 1787," Founders Online, National Archives.

45. "Abigail Adams to Cotton Tufts, 24 January 1787," Founders Online, National Archives.

46. "Abigail Adams to Cotton Tufts, 24 January 1787," Founders Online, National Archives.

47. "Richard Cranch to John Adams, 18 January 1780," Founders Online, National Archives.

48. "Abigail Adams to Cotton Tufts, 24 January 1787," Founders Online, National Archives; note 3.

49. "Abigail Adams to John Adams, 27 December 1783," Founders Online, National Archives.

50. "Abigail Adams to John Adams, 27 December 1783," Founders Online, National Archives.

51. "Abigail Adams' Diary of her Return Voyage to America, 30 March–1 May 1788," Founders Online, National Archives.

52. "Abigail Adams to Elizabeth Smith Shaw, 15 August 1785," Founders Online, National Archives.

53. "Abigail Adams to Thomas Jefferson, 12 August 1785," Founders Online, National Archives.

54. "Abigail Adams to Mary Smith Cranch, 1 October 1785," Founders Online, National Archives.

55. "From John Adams to John Jay, 25 January 1787," Founders Online, National Archives. JA addressed his resignation letter of intent to John Jay, the president of the Continental Congress.

CHAPTER TWENTY: "A BEAUTIFUL COUNTRY"

1 "Abigail Adams to Mary Smith Cranch, 20 January 1787," Founders Online, National Archives.

1. "Abigail Adams to Lucy Cranch, 26 April 1787," Founders Online, National Archives.

2. "Abigail Adams to Lucy Cranch, 26 April 1787," Founders Online, National Archives.

3. "Abigail Adams to Lucy Cranch, 26 April 1787," Founders Online, National Archives.

4. "Robert Young taught a twelve-week lecture series discussing 'the Mechanism and Motions of the Universe,' which began on 30 January. The lectures were held at No. 43, Gerard Street, in Soho (*London Daily Universal Register*, 27 Jan. 1787)."

5. "Abigail Adams to Lucy Cranch, 26 April 1787," Founders Online, National Archives, note 3.

6. "Abigail Adams to Lucy Cranch, 26 April 1787," Founders Online, National Archives.

7. "Abigail Adams to John Quincy Adams, 20 March 1787," Founders Online, National Archives.

8. "Abigail Adams to John Quincy Adams, 17 January 1787," Founders Online, National Archives.

9. "Abigail Adams to John Quincy Adams, 20 March 1787," Founders Online, National Archives.

10. "Abigail Adams to Thomas Jefferson, 27 June 1787," Founders Online, National Archives.

11. "From Thomas Jefferson to Francis Eppes, [30 August 1785]," Founders Online, National Archives.

12. "Abigail Adams to Thomas Jefferson, 26 June 1787," Founders Online, National Archives.

13. "Abigail Adams to Thomas Jefferson, 27 June 1787," Founders Online, National Archives.

14. "Abigail Adams to Thomas Jefferson, 6 July 1787," Founders Online, National Archives; her Virginia aunt, Elizabeth Wayles Eppes.

15. "Abigail Adams to Thomas Jefferson, 6 July 1787," Founders Online, National Archives.

16. "Abigail Adams to Thomas Jefferson, 6 July 1787," Founders Online, National Archives.

17. "Thomas Jefferson to Abigail Adams, 10 July 1787," Founders Online, National Archives.

18. "Abigail Adams to Mary Smith Cranch, 16 July 1787," Founders Online, National Archives.

19. "Abigail Adams to Elizabeth Smith Shaw, 2 May 1787," Founders Online, National Archives.

20. "Abigail Adams to Mercy Otis Warren, 14 May 1787," Founders Online, National Archives.

21. There were nine people in their party: John, Abigail, Nabby, Nabby's baby William and his nurse, Esther Field, the coachman, footman, and postilion (one who guides the lead horse).

22. "Abigail Adams to Mary Smith Cranch, 15 September 1787," Founders Online, National Archives; note 1.

23. "Abigail Adams to Mary Smith Cranch, 15 September 1787," Founders Online, National Archives.

24. "Abigail Adams to Mary Smith Cranch, 15 September 1787," Founders Online, National Archives.

25. John Adams's diary: "Sunday 23 [i.e., 22 July.]," Founders Online, National Archives.

26. "Abigail Adams to Mary Smith Cranch, 15 September 1787," Founders Online, National Archives.

27. "Abigail Adams to Mary Smith Cranch, 15 September 1787," Founders Online, National Archives.

28. "John Adams to Cotton Tufts, 27 August 1787," Founders Online, National Archives.

29. "From John Adams to Cotton Tufts, 1 July 1787," Founders Online, National Archives.

30. "Catharine Louisa Salmon Smith to Abigail Adams, 26 October 1785," Founders Online, National Archives.

31. "Abigail Adams to Mary Smith Cranch, 20 October 1787," Founders Online, National Archives.

32. "Abigail Adams to Mary Smith Cranch, 10 February 1788," Founders Online, National Archives.

33. "Abigail Adams Smith to John Quincy Adams, 10 February 1788," Founders Online, National Archives.

34. "Abigail Adams Smith to John Quincy Adams, 10 February 1788," Founders Online, National Archives.

35. "Abigail Adams to Thomas Jefferson, 21 February 1788," Founders Online, National Archives.

36. "Abigail Adams to Thomas Jefferson, 26 February 1788," Founders Online, National Archives.

37. Thomas Jefferson lived in debt for his entire life. TJ's experts at Monticello say that he always kept a ledger which listed his debits and credits, but never balanced it.

38. "To James Madison from Thomas Jefferson, 25 May 1788," Founders Online, National Archives.

39. "Abigail Adams to Mary Smith Cranch, 10 February 1788," Founders Online, National Archives.

40. Interestingly enough, the *Adams Papers* editors noted, "In later years, the family apparently 'revised' the Brieslers' marriage date back to Sept. 1787; see JQA's Diary entry for 14 Aug. 1838, D/JQA/33, APM Reel 36." "Abigail Adams to Mary Smith Cranch, 10 February 1788," Founders Online, National Archives; note 6.

41. "Abigail Adams to Abigail Adams Smith, 7 July 1788," Founders Online, National Archives.

42. "Abigail Adams' Diary of her Return Voyage to America, 30 March–1 May 1788," Founders Online, National Archives; note 7.

43. "Abigail Adams' Diary of her Return Voyage to America, 30 March–1 May 1788," Founders Online, National Archives; note 7.

44. "Abigail Adams to Abigail Adams Smith, 7 July 1788," Founders Online, National Archives.

45. "Abigail Adams to Abigail Adams Smith, 7 July 1788," Founders Online, National Archives.

46. "Abigail Adams to Abigail Adams Smith, 7 July 1788," Founders Online, National Archives.

47. The 12th Amendment adopted in 1804 changed the national election ticket nomination process. From then on, two people of like minds of a particular ticket were voted for rather than just the two people who received the most votes winning.

48. "Abigail Adams to John Adams, 15 December 1788," Founders Online, National Archives.

49. "Abigail Adams to John Adams, 15 December 1788," Founders Online, National Archives.

50. "Abigail Adams to John Adams, 15 December 1788," Founders Online, National Archives.

51. "Abigail Adams to John Quincy Adams, 5–6 May 1789," Founders Online, National Archives; Peter Boylston Adams ended up reconsidering the request by the Adamses.

52. "I presume there will be more than an hundred packages," "Abigail Adams to John Adams, 14 June 1789," Founders Online, National Archives.

53. "Abigail Adams to John Quincy Adams, 5–6 May 1789," Founders Online, National Archives.

54. "John Adams to Abigail Adams, 19 December 1793," Founders Online, National Archives.

55. Article 1, section 3. https://constitution.congress.gov/browse/article-1/section-3/.

56. "Abigail Adams to John Adams, 19 February 1797," Founders Online, National Archives.

CHAPTER TWENTY-ONE: "THIS WHIRLIGIG OF A WORLD"

1. "John Adams to Abigail Adams, 13 May 1789," Founders Online, National Archives.

2. "Abigail Adams to John Adams, 31 May 1789," Founders Online, National Archives.

3. "Abigail Adams to John Adams, 31 May 1789," Founders Online, National Archives.

4. "John Adams to Abigail Adams, 6 June 1789," Founders Online, National Archives.

5. "[P]ray get an oz of glober salts and half oz manna & take immediately, an oz of antimonial wine & take 30 drops three time a day." "Abigail Adams to John Adams, 14 June 1789," Founders Online, National Archives.

6. "Abigail Adams to John Adams, 14 June 1789," Founders Online, National Archives.

7. "Abigail Adams to Mary Smith Cranch, 28 June 1789," Founders Online, National Archives.

8. Nabby had also met Thomas Brand Hollis when she was in Britain with her parents. She and Colonel Smith, her husband, named their third son Thomas Hollis Smith.

9. "Abigail Adams to Thomas Brand Hollis, 6 September 1790," Founders Online, National Archives.

10. "Abigail Adams to Mary Smith Cranch, 28 June 1789," Founders Online, National Archives.

11. "Abigail Adams to Mary Smith Cranch, 28 June 1789," Founders Online, National Archives.

12. "Abigail Adams to Mary Smith Cranch, 28 June 1789," Founders Online, National Archives; note 7.

13. "Abigail Adams to Mary Smith Cranch, 12 July 1789," Founders Online, National Archives.

14. "Abigail Adams to John Adams, 6 December 1794," Founders Online, National Archives.

15. "Abigail Adams to Cotton Tufts, 6 February 179[1]," Founders Online, National Archives.

16. "Abigail Adams to John Quincy Adams, 7 November 1790," Founders Online, National Archives.

17. "To John Adams from Mercy Otis Warren, 7 May 1789," Founders Online, National Archives.

18. "Abigail Adams to James Lovell, 22 April 1789," Founders Online, National Archives.

19. The process of franking allowed for free mailing services for governmental business.

20. "Abigail Adams to Mary Smith Cranch, 5 January 1790," Founders Online, National Archives.

21. "Abigail Adams to Mary Smith Cranch, 9 August 1789," Founders Online, National Archives.

22. "Abigail Adams to Mary Smith Cranch, 5 January 1790," Founders Online, National Archives.

23. "Abigail Adams to Mary Smith Cranch, 5 January 1790," Founders Online, National Archives.

24. "Abigail Adams to Mary Smith Cranch, 5 January 1790," Founders Online, National Archives.

25. "Abigail Adams to Mary Smith Cranch, 3 November 1789," Founders Online, National Archives.

26. "Abigail Adams to Mary Smith Cranch, 9 August 1789," Founders Online, National Archives.

27. "Abigail Adams to Mary Smith Cranch, 28 April 1790," Founders Online, National Archives.

28. "Abigail Adams to Mary Smith Cranch, 3 November 1789," Founders Online, National Archives.

29. "Abigail Adams to Mary Smith Cranch, 3 November 1789," Founders Online, National Archives.

30. Congress Hall, Chestnut Street at Sixth Street, should not be confused with Independence Hall. From 1790–1800 Congress worked out of Congress Hall until the move to Washington City (DC) could be completed. George Washington (his second term) and John Adams took their oaths there.

31. It was an estimated $40 million in domestic debt, $12 million in foreign debt, and $25 million in state debt. The value of $77 million today would be $125 billion: https://www.measuringworth.com/dollarvaluetoday/?amount=77000000&from=1790.

32. "Abigail Adams to Mary Smith Cranch, 1 September 1789," Founders Online, National Archives.

33. "Abigail Adams to Cotton Tufts, 18 April 1790," Founders Online, National Archives.

34. "Abigail Adams to Cotton Tufts, 18 April 1790," Founders Online, National Archives. The *Adams Papers* editors explain, "Several lotteries were open at the time, including lotteries to finance the construction of a free school in Williamstown and to raise money for the town of Charlestown. On 2 March, the Mass. General Court also passed legislation calling for a semiannual lottery to raise £10,000 for the state. An advertisement appeared in the Boston *Independent Chronicle*: 'As the object of this Lottery is to ease the taxes of the people, and to promote public credit, the Managers flatter themselves, that principles of patriotism, as well as a spirit of adventure, will conduce to a speedy sale of the Tickets.' (*Independent Chronicle*, 11, 18 March, 9 April)." Ibid., note 6.

35. The *Federalist Papers* were written and published to support the effort to ratify the US Constitution. James Madison was one of the three authors; the other two were John Jay and Alexander Hamilton.

36. There is no record of Abigail ever riding a horse. However, John preferred to ride horseback.

37. "Abigail Adams to John Adams, 27 December 1795," Founders Online, National Archives.

38. "Abigail Adams to John Adams, 27 December 1795," Founders Online, National Archives.

39. "Cotton Tufts to Abigail Adams, 7 January 1791," Founders Online, National Archives.

40. "Abigail Adams to Mary Smith Cranch, 10 October 1790," Founders Online, National Archives.

41. "The Treaty of New York" sought to identify each Creek Indian tribe as a sovereign nation and was not to be encroached on by illegal immigration. *National Archives* editors added, "Within two years, the treaty had been rendered meaningless; the US government was unable to halt white settlement in Creek territory." "Abigail Adams to Mary Smith Cranch, 8 August 1790," Founders Online, National Archives, note 3.

42. "Abigail Adams to Mary Smith Cranch, 8 August 1790," Founders Online, National Archives.

43. "Abigail Adams to Mary Smith Cranch, 8 August 1790," Founders Online, National Archives.

44. "Abigail Adams to Mary Smith Cranch, 25 October 1790," Founders Online, National Archives; the *Adams Papers* editors offer the possible explanation of Abigail's illness, "Intermittent fever and use of quinine suggest she may have been suffering from malaria rather than influenza." Ibid., note 2.

45. "Abigail Adams to Mary Smith Cranch, 25 October 1790," Founders Online, National Archives. Aside from having crossed the Atlantic Ocean twice as well as the English Channel, Abigail still did not like crossing bodies of water such as rivers. The upcoming trip required crossing three bodies of water.

46. "Abigail Adams to John Quincy Adams, 12 September 1790," Founders Online, National Archives.

47. "Abigail Adams to Abigail Adams Smith, 21–28 November 1790," Founders Online, National Archives.

48. "Abigail Adams to Mary Smith Cranch, 9 January 1791," Founders Online, National Archives.

49. "Abigail Adams to Abigail Adams Smith, 21–28 November 1790," Founders Online, National Archives.

50. "Abigail Adams to Abigail Adams Smith, 21–28 November 1790," Founders Online, National Archives.

51. "Abigail Adams to Mary Smith Cranch, 9 January 1791," Founders Online, National Archives.

52. "Abigail Adams to Mary Smith Cranch, 28 April 1790," Founders Online, National Archives.

53. "Abigail Adams to Mary Smith Cranch, 12 March 1791," Founders Online, National Archives.

54. "Abigail Adams to Abigail Adams Smith, 26 December 1790," Founders Online, National Archives.

55. "Abigail Adams to Abigail Adams Smith, 26 December 1790," Founders Online, National Archives.

CHAPTER TWENTY-TWO: "A DEVISION OF THE SOUTHERN & NORTHERN STATES"

1. "Abigail Adams to Cotton Tufts, 6 February 179[1]," Founders Online, National Archives.
2. "Abigail Adams to Cotton Tufts, 18 December 1791," Founders Online, National Archives.
3. "Abigail Adams to Cotton Tufts, 18 December 1791," Founders Online, National Archives.
4. "Abigail Adams to Cotton Tufts, 18 December 1791," Founders Online, National Archives.
5. "From Thomas Jefferson to George Washington, 15 May 1791," Founders Online, National Archives.
6. "Abigail Adams to Mary Smith Cranch, 12 March 1791," Founders Online, National Archives.
7. "John Adams to William Stephens Smith, 19 June 1791," Founders Online, National Archives.
8. "From Thomas Jefferson to Lafayette, 2 April 1790," Founders Online, National Archives.
9. "Abigail Adams to Mary Smith Cranch, 12 March 1791," Founders Online, National Archives.
10. "Abigail Adams to Mary Smith Cranch, 20 April 1792," Founders Online, National Archives.
11. "Abigail Adams to Mary Smith Cranch, 29 April 1792," Founders Online, National Archives.
12. Abigail's description of James hinted that he was an indentured servant.
13. "Abigail Adams to Mary Smith Cranch, 12 March 1791," Founders Online, National Archives.
14. James would become a very inspiring example of Abigail's equal educational rights struggle.
15. "Abigail Adams to Mary Smith Cranch, 12 March 1791," Founders Online, National Archives.
16. "Abigail Adams to John Adams, 10 May 1794," Founders Online, National Archives.
17. "Abigail Adams to Mary Smith Cranch, 20 April 1792," Founders Online, National Archives.
18. "Abigail Adams to Mary Smith Cranch, 20 April 1792," Founders Online, National Archives.
19. "Abigail Adams to John Adams, 29 December 1792," Founders Online, National Archives.
20. "From John Adams to Tench Coxe, 20 August 1791," Founders Online, National Archives.
21. "From John Adams to Tench Coxe, 20 August 1791," Founders Online, National Archives.
22. "Abigail Adams to Mary Smith Cranch, 20–21 March 1792," Founders Online, National Archives.

23. "Abigail Adams to Abigail Adams Smith, 8 January 1791," Founders Online, National Archives.

24. "Abigail Adams to Abigail Adams Smith, 8 January 1791," Founders Online, National Archives. Abigail and Nabby "had both likely seen Elizabeth Farren when she appeared as Lady Teazle in Richard Brinsley Sheridan's 'The School for Scandal' at Drury Lane in London in 1785 and 1786." Note 2.

25. "Abigail Adams to Mary Smith Cranch, 20 April 1792," Founders Online, National Archives.

26. "Abigail Adams to Mary Smith Cranch, 20 April 1792," Founders Online, National Archives. It's possible that the forty-seven-year-old Abigail was describing menopause.

27. "Abigail Adams to Abigail Adams Smith, 8 January 1791," Founders Online, National Archives.

28. "Abigail Adams to Mary Smith Cranch, 20 April 1792," Founders Online, National Archives.

29. Essentially, one of the same causes of the market crash of 1929.

30. "Abigail Adams to Mary Smith Cranch, 29 April 1792," Founders Online, National Archives.

31. "Abigail Adams to Mary Smith Cranch, 25 June 1795," Founders Online, National Archives.

32. "John Adams to Abigail Adams, 5 December 1792," Founders Online, National Archives.

33. "Abigail Adams to John Adams, 4 December 1792," Founders Online, National Archives.

34. The remaining 55 electoral votes were scattered between George Clinton (50), Thomas Jefferson (4), and Aaron Burr (1).

35. "John Adams to Abigail Adams, 1 December 1793," Founders Online, National Archives.

36. "John Adams to Abigail Adams, 22 December 1793," Founders Online, National Archives.

37. "John Adams to Abigail Adams, 1 December 1793," Founders Online, National Archives.

38. The Jacobins were an extremist and ruthless political mob during the time of the French Revolution's "Reign of Terror."

39. "John Adams to Abigail Adams, 6 January 1794," Founders Online, National Archives.

40. "Abigail Adams to John Adams, 26 February 1794," Founders Online, National Archives.

41. "Abigail Adams to John Adams, 26 February 1794," Founders Online, National Archives.

42. "Abigail Adams to John Adams, 26 February 1794," Founders Online, National Archives.

43. "John Adams to Abigail Adams, 10 February 1794," Founders Online, National Archives.

44. "John Adams to Abigail Adams, 24 January 1793," Founders Online, National Archives.

45. Genêt was arrested and was being extradited to France when Washington halted the process. Knowing that Genêt would be executed in France, Washington pardoned Genêt. Genêt became an American citizen and even married into the New York family of Governor Clinton.

46. "Abigail Adams to Thomas Boylston Adams, 10 January 1795," Founders Online, National Archives.

47. "John Adams to John Quincy Adams, 2 December 1794," Founders Online, National Archives.

48. "John Adams to Charles Adams, 31 December 1795," Founders Online, National Archives.

49. "John Adams to Charles Adams, 31 December 1795," Founders Online, National Archives.

50. Abigail was possibly referring to one of the two new lambs that were just born, "We have got two Lambs already." "Abigail Adams to John Adams, 12 February 1794," Founders Online, National Archives.

51. "Abigail Adams to John Adams, 12 February 1794," Founders Online, National Archives.

52. "Abigail Adams to John Adams, 13 February 1795," Founders Online, National Archives.

53. "Abigail Adams to John Adams, 26 February 1794," Founders Online, National Archives.

54. "Elizabeth Smith Shaw to Abigail Adams, 24 January 1795," Founders Online, National Archives.

55. "Elizabeth Smith Shaw Peabody to Abigail Adams, 28 February 1796," Founders Online, National Archives.

56. "Abigail Adams to John Adams, 20 February 1796," Founders Online, National Archives.

57. "Abigail Adams to John Adams, 20 February 1796," Founders Online, National Archives.

CHAPTER TWENTY-THREE: "IN HIS WICKED EYES . . . THE VERY DEVIL"

1. "Autocratrix" means "A female sovereign who is independent and absolute; a title given to the empresses of Russia." The Free Dictionary by Farlex, https://www.thefreedictionary.com/Autocratrix.

2. "John Adams to Abigail Adams, 24 January 1793," Founders Online, National Archives.

3. "Abigail Adams to John Adams, 9 February 1793," Founders Online, National Archives.

4. "John Adams to Abigail Adams, 30 December 1796," Founders Online, National Archives. Martha Bland Blodget Corran was a thrice-married plantation manager and "plantation mistress" in Prince George County, Virginia.

5. "John Adams to Abigail Adams, 28 December 1795," Founders Online, National Archives.

6. Sara Georgini, *Women in George Washington's World* (Charlottesville: University of Virginia Press, 2022), 138.

7. Julian Ursyn Niemcewicz, "Man of the Enlightenment, His Portrait of America 1797–1799, 1805, *Travels through America*, 8 November 1797," *Polish Review* 46, no. 3 (2001), 261–270. Access: JSTOR.

8. Sheila Skemp, *First Lady of Letters: Judith Sargent Murray and the Struggle for Female Independence* (Philadelphia: University of Pennsylvania Press, 2011), 290.

9. "Unselfish" could be a modern substitution for "disinterested."

10. "Abigail Adams to John Adams, 28 January 1797," Founders Online, National Archives. "Physiognomy" was a pseudo-scientific theory which Abigail believed in. The essence was that one could discern a person's innermost feelings by studying the facial features of the subject.

11. "Abigail Adams to John Adams, 20 February 1796," Founders Online, National Archives.

12. "Abigail Adams to John Adams, 20 February 1796," Founders Online, National Archives.

13. "Abigail Adams to John Adams, 21 February 1796," Founders Online, National Archives.

14. "Abigail Adams to John Adams, 21 February 1796," Founders Online, National Archives.

15. "John Adams to Abigail Adams, 27 February 1796," Founders Online, National Archives.

16. "John Adams to Abigail Adams, 27 February 1796," Founders Online, National Archives.

17. "Abigail Adams to John Quincy Adams, 28 November 1796," Founders Online, National Archives.

18. "Abigail Adams to John Adams, 1 January 1797," Founders Online, National Archives.

19. "Abigail Adams to John Adams, 1 January 1797," Founders Online, National Archives. Although AA mentioned "Sooth sayers" regarding her premonition dream, she did not believe in fortune tellers. This was unlike Ronald and Nancy Reagan who checked in occasionally with Joan Quigley, a famed astrologer of the 1970s and 1980s.

20. "Abigail Adams to John Adams, 1 January 1797," Founders Online, National Archives.

21. The Warrens may have harbored a grudge after John wouldn't give some or all of their sons a federal job.

22. "Abigail Adams to John Adams, 15 January 1797," Founders Online, National Archives.

23. "John Adams to Abigail Adams, 24 February 1797," Founders Online, National Archives.

24. "Abigail Adams to John Adams, 1 March 1797," Founders Online, National Archives.

25. "John Adams to Abigail Adams, 17 March 1797," Founders Online, National Archives.

26. "Abigail Adams to John Adams, 13 February 1797," Founders Online, National Archives.

27. "Abigail Adams to John Adams, 13 February 1797," Founders Online, National Archives.

28. "Abigail Adams to John Adams, 13 February 1797," Founders Online, National Archives.

29. "Abigail Adams to John Adams, 13 February 1797," Founders Online, National Archives.

30. "Abigail Adams to John Adams, 13 February 1797," Founders Online, National Archives.

31. "Abigail Adams to John Adams, 13 February 1797," Founders Online, National Archives.

32. "John Adams to Abigail Adams, 27 March 1797," Founders Online, National Archives.

33. "John Adams to Abigail Adams, 27 March 1797," Founders Online, National Archives.

34. "John Adams to Abigail Adams, 22 March 1797," Founders Online, National Archives.

35. "John Adams to Abigail Adams, 27 March 1797," Founders Online, National Archives.

36. "From John Adams to Benjamin Rush, 30 September 1805," Founders Online, National Archives.

37. "Abigail Adams to John Adams, 6 February 1797," Founders Online, National Archives.
38. "John Adams to Abigail Adams, 11 April 1797," Founders Online, National Archives.
39. "Abigail Adams to John Adams, 23 April 1797," Founders Online, National Archives.
40. "Abigail Adams to Mary Smith Cranch, 16 May 1797," Founders Online, National Archives.
41. "Abigail Adams to John Quincy Adams, 15 June 1797," Founders Online, National Archives.
42. "Abigail Adams to Mary Smith Cranch, 16 May 1797," Founders Online, National Archives.
43. "Abigail Adams to Mary Smith Cranch, 24 May 1797," Founders Online, National Archives.
44. "Mary Smith Cranch to Abigail Adams, 13 June 1797," Founders Online, National Archives.
45. "Mary Smith Cranch to Abigail Adams, 13 June 1797," Founders Online, National Archives.
46. "Abigail Adams to Mary Smith Cranch, 23 June 1797," Founders Online, National Archives.
47. "Abigail Adams to Mary Smith Cranch, 3 June 1797," Founders Online, National Archives.
48. "Abigail Adams to John Quincy Adams, 15 June 1797," Founders Online, National Archives.
49. "John Quincy Adams to Charles Adams, 17 May 1795," Founders Online, National Archives.
50. "John Quincy Adams to Charles Adams, 17 May 1795," Founders Online, National Archives.
51. "Abigail Adams to John Adams, 28 January 1797," Founders Online, National Archives.
52. "Abigail Adams to Mary Smith Cranch, 26 December 1797," Founders Online, National Archives.
53. "Abigail Adams to Mary Smith Cranch, 3 July 1798," Founders Online, National Archives.
54. "Did you know Women and African Americans could vote in NJ before the 15th and 19th Amendments?," National Park Service [https://www.nps.gov/articles/voting-rights-in-nj-before-the-15th-and-19th.htm].
55. "Abigail Adams to Mary Smith Cranch, 15 November 1797," Founders Online, National Archives.
56. "Abigail Adams to John Quincy Adams, 23 November 1797," Founders Online, National Archives.
57. "Abigail Adams to Elizabeth Ellery Dana, 27 June 1797," Founders Online, National Archives.

CHAPTER TWENTY-FOUR: "MUCH OF THE SCUM RISING"

1. "Abigail Adams to Catherine Nuth Johnson, 2 March 1798," Founders Online, National Archives.
2. The first official presidential "chief of staff" was John Steelman in the Truman administration 1946–1953.
3. "Fisher Ames to Rufus King, 24 September 1800," University of Wisconsin–Madison, Center for the Study of the American Constitution; https://csac.history.wisc.edu/multimedia/ founders-on-the-founders/abigail-adams/.
4. "Abigail Adams to Mary Smith Cranch, 26 May 1798," Founders Online, National Archives.
5. https://www.archives.gov/exhibits/treasures_of_congress/text/page5.
6. "Abigail Adams to John Quincy Adams, 12 June 1798," Founders Online, National Archives.
7. "Abigail Adams to John Quincy Adams, 2 December 1798," Founders Online, National Archives.
8. "Abigail Adams to Mary Smith Cranch, 5 January 1798," Founders Online, National Archives.
9. "Abigail Adams to Mary Smith Cranch, 7 April 1798," Founders Online, National Archives.
10. "Abigail Adams to Mary Smith Cranch, 9 April 1798," Founders Online, National Archives.
11. "Abigail Adams to Mary Smith Cranch, 7 April 1798," Founders Online, National Archives.

12. "Abigail Adams to Mary Smith Cranch, 28 April 1787," Founders Online, National Archives.
13. "Abigail Adams to Mary Smith Cranch, 26 May 1798," Founders Online, National Archives.
14. "Abigail Adams to Mary Smith Cranch, 3 July 1798," Founders Online, National Archives.
15. "Abigail Adams to Mary Smith Cranch, 24 July 1798," Founders Online, National Archives.
16. "John Adams to George Washington, 9 October 1798," Founders Online, National Archives.
17. "Abigail Adams to John Adams, 20 January 1799," Founders Online, National Archives.
18. "Abigail Adams to Cotton Tufts, 8 June 1798," Founders Online, National Archives.
19. "Abigail Adams to John Adams, 29 November 1798," Founders Online, National Archives.
20. "Abigail Adams to John Adams, 29 November 1798," Founders Online, National Archives.
21. "John Adams to Abigail Adams, 25 December 1798," Founders Online, National Archives.
22. "John Adams to Abigail Adams, 5 January 1799," Founders Online, National Archives.
23. "Abigail Adams to John Adams, 27 February 1799," Founders Online, National Archives.
24. "Abigail Adams to Elizabeth Smith Shaw Peabody, 19 July 1799," Founders Online, National Archives.
25. "John Adams to Abigail Adams, 12 October 1799," Founders Online, National Archives.
26. "Abigail Adams to Mary Smith Cranch, 15 November 1799," Founders Online, National Archives.
27. "Abigail Adams to Mary Smith Cranch, 22 December 1799," Founders Online, National Archives.
28. "Abigail Adams to Abigail Adams Smith, 4 May 1800," Founders Online, National Archives.
29. "Abigail Adams to Mary Smith Cranch, 5 March 1800," Founders Online, National Archives.
30. "Abigail Adams to Mary Smith Cranch, 24 April 1800," Founders Online, National Archives.
31. "Abigail Adams to Hannah Phillips Cushing, 4 April 1800," Founders Online, National Archives.
32. "Abigail Adams to Elizabeth Smith Shaw Peabody, 16 April 1800," Founders Online, National Archives.
33. "Abigail Adams to Mary Smith Cranch, 24 April 1800," Founders Online, National Archives.
34. "Abigail Adams to Mary Smith Cranch, 15 March 1800," Founders Online, National Archives.
35. "Abigail Adams to Mary Smith Cranch, 14 March 1798," Founders Online, National Archives.
36. "Abigail Adams to Mary Smith Cranch, 24 April 1800," Founders Online, National Archives.
37. *The Prospect Before Us, Volume 1*, by James Thomson Callender (Richmond, VA: S. Pleasants, Jr., J. Lyon; 1800).
38. Thomas Jefferson's Monticello website acknowledges that this contemporary source quote has not been found and therefore is of dubious authenticity. "Its earliest known appearance in print is in a collection of New England folk tales, *The Jonny-Cake Papers* first published in 1879." https://www.monticello.org/site/research-and-collections/son-half-breed-indian-squaw-quotation.
39. "Abigail Adams to Mary Smith Cranch, 26 May 1800," Founders Online, National Archives.
40. "Letter from Alexander Hamilton, Concerning the Public Conduct and Character of John Adams, Esq. President of the United States [24 October 1800]," Founders Online, National Archives.
41. "Letter from Alexander Hamilton, Concerning the Public Conduct and Character of John Adams, Esq. President of the United States [24 October 1800]," Founders Online, National Archives.
42. "Abigail Adams to Thomas Boylston Adams, 15 August 1800," Founders Online, National Archives.

43. "From John Adams to Benjamin Rush, 25 January 1806," Founders Online, National Archives.

44. "From John Adams to Benjamin Rush, 11 November 1806," Founders Online, National Archives.

45. Lesley Kennedy, "6 Things You May Not Know About the White House," History, December 21, 2020, https://www.history.com/news/white-house-history-facts-presidents. "The stone exterior of the building was first painted with a lime-based whitewash in 1798 to protect it from the elements and freezing temperatures. According to the White House Historical Association, the 'White House' moniker began to appear in newspapers before the War of 1812. But it was President Theodore Roosevelt, who, in 1901, designated the official name of the residence of the U.S. president to be the White House. (Previous names included the Presidents' House, the Executive Mansion, the Presidential Palace and the Presidential Mansion.) It also commonly goes by 'The People's House.'" Ibid.

46. "John Adams to Abigail Adams, 2 November 1800," Founders Online, National Archives. "But when JA took up residence on 1 November 1800, walls were wet or unplastered, few furnishings were in place, and only one of three staircases was built. Despite offers of private lodgings, JA resolved to remain in the President's House as his work continued. When Thomas Jefferson moved in on 19 March 1801, he ordered numerous architectural changes, and the building was not completed until 1802." Note 1.

47. "John Adams to Abigail Adams, 2 November 1800," Founders Online, National Archives.

48. "Abigail Adams to Mary Smith Cranch, 21 November 1800," Founders Online, National Archives. The names of Abigail's nine persons are unknown.

49. "Abigail Adams to Mary Smith Cranch, ca. 18 October 1800," Founders Online, National Archives.

50. "Abigail Adams to Mary Smith Cranch, 10 November 1800," Founders Online, National Archives.

CHAPTER TWENTY-FIVE: "I WANT TO SEE THE LIST OF JUDGES"

1. "Abigail Adams to Mary Smith Cranch, 21 November 1800," Founders Online, National Archives.

2. "Abigail Adams to Mary Smith Cranch, 21 November 1800," Founders Online, National Archives.

3. "Abigail Adams to Mary Smith Cranch, 21 November 1800," Founders Online, National Archives.

4. "Abigail Adams to Mary Smith Cranch, 21 November 1800," Founders Online, National Archives.

5. "Abigail Adams to Mary Smith Cranch, 21 November 1800," Founders Online, National Archives.

6. "Abigail Adams to Mary Smith Cranch, 21 November 1800," Founders Online, National Archives.

7. "Abigail Adams to Mary Smith Cranch, 21 November 1800," Founders Online, National Archives.

8. "Abigail Adams to Abigail Adams Smith, 21 November 1800," Founders Online, National Archives.

9. "Abigail Adams to Cotton Tufts, 28 November 1800," Founders Online, National Archives.

10. "Abigail Adams to Mary Smith Cranch, 10 November 1800," Founders Online, National Archives; Charles probably died of a liver infection, dropsy, and a consumptive cough.

11. "Abigail Adams to Mary Smith Cranch, 10 November 1800," Founders Online, National Archives.

12. "Abigail Adams to Cotton Tufts, 15 January 1801," Founders Online, National Archives.

13. Mummery was a hypocritical, pretentious ceremony. "Abigail Adams to Mary Smith Cranch, 7 February 1801," Founders Online, National Archives.

14. "Abigail Adams to Thomas Boylston Adams, 3 January 1801," Founders Online, National Archives.

15. "Abigail Adams to Mary Smith Cranch, 21 December 1800," Founders Online, National Archives.

16. "Abigail Adams to Mary Smith Cranch, 21 December 1800," Founders Online, National Archives.

17. "Abigail Adams to Mary Smith Cranch, 21 December 1800," Founders Online, National Archives.

18. "Abigail Adams to Mary Smith Cranch, 21 December 1800," Founders Online, National Archives.

19. "Abigail Adams to Mary Smith Cranch, 21 December 1800," Founders Online, National Archives.

20. "Abigail Adams to Mary Smith Cranch, 21 December 1800," Founders Online, National Archives.

21. "Abigail Adams to Mary Smith Cranch, 21 December 1800," Founders Online, National Archives.

22. "Abigail Adams to Mary Smith Cranch, 21 December 1800," Founders Online, National Archives.

23. Abigail Adams to Thomas Boylston Adams, 13 [December] 1800," Founders Online, National Archives.

24. "Abigail Adams to Thomas Boylston Adams, 25 January 1801," Founders Online, National Archives.

25. "Abigail Adams to Mary Smith Cranch, 21 December 1800," Founders Online, National Archives.

26. Despite some physical disabilities, "Billy" became an excellent writer and lawyer. He later founded the Boston Athenaeum.

27. "William Smith Shaw to Abigail Adams, 25 February 1801," Founders Online, National Archives.

28. "Abigail Adams to William Smith Shaw, 14 February 1801," Founders Online, National Archives.

29. "Abigail Adams to William Smith Shaw, 14 February 1801," Founders Online, National Archives.

30. "Abigail Adams to John Adams, 21 February 1801," Founders Online, National Archives. Following the sentence "I want to see the list of judges" and blotted out for some reason was "pray tell all who inquire after me."

31. "Midnight appointments," some not requiring congressional approval, are still practiced by outgoing presidents to this day. The activity today also includes presidential pardons and other favors. One of John Adams's unreproachable appointments was to elevate John Marshall to Chief Justice of the Supreme Court.

32. "Abigail Adams to John Adams, 21 February 1801," Founders Online, National Archives.

33. "From John Adams to Thomas Boylston Adams, 15 September 1801," Founders Online, National Archives.

34. "From Abigail Smith Adams to Thomas Boylston Adams, 12 July 1801," Founders Online, National Archives.

35. "From Abigail Smith Adams to Thomas Boylston Adams, 27 December 1801," Founders Online, National Archives.

36. Louisa Catherine Adams, *Diary and Autobiographical Writings of Louisa Catherine Adams, Volume 2 1778–1849*, edited by Judith S. Graham et al., 2 vols. (Cambridge, MA: Belknap Press of Harvard University Press, 2013), https://www.hup.harvard.edu/catalog.php?isbn=97806740 58682&content=toc.

37. "From Abigail Smith Adams to Ann Frances Harrod, 19 February 1805," Founders Online, National Archives.

38. "From Abigail Smith Adams to Thomas Boylston Adams, 28 February 1802," Founders Online, National Archives.

39. Never said, but implied that the arrangement was necessary to guard against the prying eyes of John.

40. "From Abigail Smith Adams to Thomas Boylston Adams, 28 February 1802," Founders Online, National Archives.

41. "Claim Against the Estate of Norton Quincy, 15 February 1802," Founders Online, National Archives.

42. "From Abigail Smith Adams to Thomas Boylston Adams, 26 April 1803," Founders Online, National Archives.

43. "From Abigail Smith Adams to Thomas Boylston Adams, 26 April 1803," Founders Online, National Archives.

44. "From Abigail Smith Adams to Thomas Boylston Adams, 26 April 1803," Founders Online, National Archives.

45. "From John Quincy Adams to Abigail Smith Adams, 15 March 1804," Founders Online, National Archives.

46. Now called "John Adams Birthplace" and "John Quincy Adams Birthplace."

47. John Quincy Adams, *Memoirs of John Quincy Adams: comprising portions of his diary from 1795 to 1848, Volume 1,* edited by Charles Francis Adams, 12 vols. (Philadelphia: J. B. Lippincott & Company, 1874–1877), 1:264.

48. "From Abigail Smith Adams to John Quincy Adams, 30 December 1804," Founders Online, National Archives.

49. "From John Adams to Thomas Boylston Adams, 15 September 1801," Founders Online, National Archives.

50. "From John Adams to Samuel Dexter, 23 March 1801," Founders Online, National Archives.

51. Mary Jefferson Epps had died in childbirth.

52. "From Abigail Smith Adams to Thomas Jefferson, 20 May 1804," Founders Online, National Archives.

53. "From Thomas Jefferson to Abigail Smith Adams, 13 June 1804," Founders Online, National Archives.

54. "From Thomas Jefferson to Abigail Smith Adams, 13 June 1804," Founders Online, National Archives.

55. The first was Abigail's innocent letter of condolence; the second was Jefferson's attack on Abigail regarding John's "midnight appointments."

56. The same Meriwether Lewis would lead the Lewis and Clark expedition.

57. "From Abigail Smith Adams to Thomas Jefferson, 1 July 1804," Founders Online, National Archives.

58. "From Abigail Smith Adams to Thomas Jefferson, 25 October 1804," Founders Online, National Archives.

59. "From Abigail Smith Adams to Thomas Jefferson, 25 October 1804," Founders Online, National Archives.

CHAPTER TWENTY-SIX: "A HAPPY DOMESTIC CIRCLE"

1. "From Abigail Smith Adams to Thomas Jefferson, 15 December 1816," Founders Online, National Archives.

2. "From Abigail Smith Adams to Elizabeth Smith Shaw Peabody, 10 June 1807," Founders Online, National Archives.

3. "From Abigail Smith Adams to Louisa Catherine Johnson Adams, 30 November 1807," Founders Online, National Archives.

4. Benjamin Rush, *A Memorial Containing Travels Through Life or Sundry Incidents in the Life of Dr. Benjamin Rush* (Library of Congress, 1901).

5. It is generally discarded today as a valid source of history due to its bias.

6. "From Thomas Jefferson to Mercy Otis Warren, 8 February 1805," Founders Online, National Archives.

7. Today, Mercy's history books are generally discredited by historians for their inaccuracies and blind favoritisms. John Adams was essentially correct in his reviews.

8. "From John Adams to Mercy Otis Warren, 11 July 1807," Founders Online, National Archives.

9. "From John Adams to Mercy Otis Warren, 11 July 1807," Founders Online, National Archives.

10. "To John Adams from Mercy Otis Warren, 28 July 1807," Founders Online, National Archives.

11. "To John Adams from Mercy Otis Warren, 1 August 1807," Founders Online, National Archives.

12. "To John Adams from Mercy Otis Warren, 27 August 1807," Founders Online, National Archives.

13. "To John Adams from Mercy Otis Warren, 27 August 1807," Founders Online, National Archives.

14. "To John Adams from Mercy Otis Warren, 27 August 1807," Founders Online, National Archives.

15. "To John Adams from Mercy Otis Warren, 27 August 1807," Founders Online, National Archives.

16. "To John Adams from Mercy Otis Warren, 27 August 1807," Founders Online, National Archives.

17. "From Mercy Otis Warren to Abigail Smith Adams, 9 January 1810," Founders Online, National Archives.

18. "From Abigail Smith Adams to Mercy Otis Warren, 31 December 1809," Founders Online, National Archives.

19. "From Abigail Smith Adams to Abigail Amelia Adams Smith, 8 December 1808," Founders Online, National Archives.

20. "From Abigail Smith Adams to Elizabeth Smith Shaw Peabody, 5 June 1809," Founders Online, National Archives.

21. "From Abigail Smith Adams to John Quincy Adams, 29 November 1805," Founders Online, National Archives.

22. "From John Adams to James Lloyd, 5 April 1815," Founders Online, National Archives; in fact, 10 of William Steuben's fellow prisoners were found guilty, beheaded, and had their heads posted about town.

23. "From Abigail Smith Adams to Louisa Catherine Johnson Adams, 30 November 1807," Founders Online, National Archives.

24. Charles Francis Adams became a Harvard lawyer, a state and national politician, curator of the Adams Family Papers, and builder of the first presidential library housed in the Stone Library at Peacefield for his father John Quincy. As a diplomat he was appointed by President Abraham Lincoln to be envoy to the United Kingdom during the American Civil War. He was vital in keeping Britain's neutrality.

25. "From Abigail Smith Adams to John Quincy Adams, April 1808," Founders Online, National Archives.

26. "From John Quincy Adams to Abigail Smith Adams, 24 February 1808," Founders Online, National Archives.

27. In 1824 the Democratic-Republican Party fractured into two parties. One dropped the "Republican" part of its name and became the Democratic Party; the other half became the Whig Party.

28. "From Louisa Catherine Johnson Adams to Abigail Smith Adams, 7 January 1810," Founders Online, National Archives.

29. "From Abigail Smith Adams to Caroline Amelia Smith De Windt, 9 December 1809," Founders Online, National Archives. After marrying John Peter De Windt she was Caroline Amelia Smith De Windt.

30. "From Abigail Smith Adams to Caroline Amelia Smith De Windt, 9 December 1809," Founders Online, National Archives.

31. "From Abigail Smith Adams to Caroline Amelia Smith De Windt, 9 December 1809," Founders Online, National Archives.

32. "From Abigail Smith Adams to Caroline Amelia Smith De Windt, 9 December 1809," Founders Online, National Archives.

33. "From Abigail Smith Adams to Caroline Amelia Smith De Windt, 9 December 1809," Founders Online, National Archives.

34. "From Abigail Smith Adams to Elizabeth Smith Shaw Peabody, 29 December 1811," Founders Online, National Archives.

35. "From John Quincy Adams to Abigail Smith Adams, 30 June 1811," Founders Online, National Archives.

36. "From Louisa Catherine Johnson Adams to Abigail Smith Adams, 7 January 1810," Founders Online, National Archives.

37. "From Louisa Catherine Johnson Adams to Abigail Smith Adams, 7 January 1810," Founders Online, National Archives.

38. "To James Madison from Abigail Adams, 1 August 1810," Founders Online, National Archives.

39. "To James Madison from Abigail Adams, 1 August 1810," Founders Online, National Archives.

40. "From John Quincy Adams to Abigail Smith Adams, 30 June 1811," Founders Online, National Archives.

41. "From John Quincy Adams to Abigail Smith Adams, 30 June 1811," Founders Online, National Archives.

42. "From Abigail Smith Adams to Louisa Catherine Johnson Adams, 28 April 1811," Founders Online, National Archives.

43. "From William Stephens Smith to Abigail Smith Adams, 12 August 1811," Founders Online, National Archives.

44. "From Abigail Amelia Adams Smith to Benjamin Rush, 12 September 1811," Founders Online, National Archives.

45. "From Abigail Amelia Adams Smith to Benjamin Rush, 12 September 1811," Founders Online, National Archives.

46. "To John Adams from Benjamin Rush, 20 September 1811," Founders Online, National Archives.

47. "From John Adams to Benjamin Rush, 13 October 1811," Founders Online, National Archives.

48. "From Abigail Smith Adams to John Quincy Adams, 17 November 1811," Founders Online, National Archives.

49. "From Abigail Smith Adams to John Quincy Adams, 17 November 1811," Founders Online, National Archives.

50. "From Abigail Smith Adams to John Quincy Adams, 17 November 1811," Founders Online, National Archives.

51. "From John Adams to Benjamin Rush, 2 November 1811," Founders Online, National Archives.

CHAPTER TWENTY-SEVEN: "MY FIRE IS OUT, MY WIT DECAYED"

1. "From John Adams to Benjamin Rush, 21 December 1809," Founders Online, National Archives.

2. "To John Adams from Benjamin Rush, 17 October 1809," Founders Online, National Archives.

3. "To John Adams from Benjamin Rush, 17 October 1809," Founders Online, National Archives.

4. "To John Adams from Benjamin Rush, 17 October 1809," Founders Online, National Archives.

5. "From John Adams to Thomas Jefferson, 15 July 1813," Founders Online, National Archives.

6. "From Abigail Smith Adams to John Quincy Adams, 5 January 1812," Founders Online, National Archives.

7. "From Abigail Smith Adams to John Quincy Adams, 24 July 1811," Founders Online, National Archives.

8. "From Abigail Smith Adams to John Quincy Adams, 27 February 1814," Founders Online, National Archives.

9. "From Abigail Smith Adams to Elizabeth Smith Shaw Peabody, 12 May 1814," Founders Online, National Archives.

10. "From Elizabeth Smith Shaw Peabody to Abigail Smith Adams, 17 January 1814," Founders Online, National Archives.

11. "From Abigail Smith Adams to Abigail Amelia Adams Smith, 13 May 1809," Founders Online, National Archives.

12. "From Abigail Smith Adams to Caroline Amelia Smith De Windt, 26 February 1811," Founders Online, National Archives.

13. "From Abigail Smith Adams to Elizabeth Smith Shaw Peabody, 11 September 1812," Founders Online, National Archives.

14. "From Abigail Smith Adams to Elizabeth Smith Shaw Peabody, 11 September 1812," Founders Online, National Archives.

15. "From Abigail Smith Adams to Elizabeth Smith Shaw Peabody, 17 July 1812," Founders Online, National Archives.

16. "From Abigail Smith Adams to George Washington Adams, 9 January 1813," Founders Online, National Archives.

17. "From Abigail Smith Adams to Mercy Otis Warren, 30 December 1812," Founders Online, National Archives.

18. "From Abigail Smith Adams to Mercy Otis Warren, 30 December 1812," Founders Online, National Archives.

19. "To John Adams from Benjamin Rush, 20 September 1811," Founders Online, National Archives.

20. Laudanum was a mixture of 10 percent opium powder in a solution with alcohol.

21. "From Abigail Smith Adams to Mercy Otis Warren, 8 August 1813," Founders Online, National Archives.

22. "From Elizabeth Smith Shaw Peabody to Abigail Smith Adams, 19 August 1813," Founders Online, National Archives.

23. "From John Adams to Thomas Jefferson, 16 August 1813," Founders Online, National Archives.

24. "From Abigail Smith Adams to Julia Stockton Rush, 24 September 1813," Founders Online, National Archives.

25. "From Thomas Jefferson to Abigail Smith Adams, 22 August 1813," Founders Online, National Archives.

26. "From Abigail Smith Adams to Thomas Jefferson, 20 September 1813," Founders Online, National Archives.

27. "From Abigail Smith Adams to John Quincy Adams, 8 December 1811," Founders Online, National Archives.

28. "From John Quincy Adams to Abigail Smith Adams, 30 November 1811," Founders Online, National Archives.

29. "From John Quincy Adams to Abigail Smith Adams, 21 September 1812," Founders Online, National Archives.

30. "From Abigail Smith Adams to John Quincy Adams, 27 February 1814," Founders Online, National Archives.

31. "From François Adriaan Van der Kemp to Abigail Smith Adams, 5 November 1813," Founders Online, National Archives.

32. "From Abigail Smith Adams to François Adriaan Van der Kemp, 23 February 1814," Founders Online, National Archives.

33. "From Abigail Smith Adams to Mercy Otis Warren, 16 January 1803," Founders Online, National Archives.

34. "From Abigail Smith Adams to John Quincy Adams, 27 February 1814," Founders Online, National Archives.

35. "From Abigail Smith Adams to John Quincy Adams, 28 February 1815," Founders Online, National Archives.

36. "From Abigail Smith Adams to John Quincy Adams, 10 March 1815," Founders Online, National Archives.

37. This was a common phrase from the eighteenth century.

38. "From Abigail Smith Adams to Louisa Catherine Johnson Adams, 14 April 1815," Founders Online, National Archives.

39. "From Abigail Smith Adams to John Quincy Adams, 24 December 1815," Founders Online, National Archives.

40. "From Abigail Smith Adams to John Quincy Adams, 24 December 1815," Founders Online, National Archives.

41. "Abigail Adams to John Adams, 18 November 1798," Founders Online, National Archives.

42. "From Abigail Smith Adams to Louisa Catherine Johnson Adams, 14 April 1815," Founders Online, National Archives.

43. "From Abigail Smith Adams to John Quincy Adams, 27 February 1814," Founders Online, National Archives.

CHAPTER TWENTY-EIGHT: "HER LETTERS YET REMAIN"

1. "From Abigail Smith Adams to Louisa Catherine Johnson Adams, 20 March 1816," Founders Online, National Archives.

2. "From Abigail Smith Adams to Louisa Catherine Johnson Adams, 20 March 1816," Founders Online, National Archives.

3. "From Abigail Smith Adams to John Quincy Adams, 27 August 1816," Founders Online, National Archives.

4. "From John Adams to John Quincy Adams, 26 July 1816," Founders Online, National Archives.

5. "From Abigail Smith Adams to John Quincy Adams, 11 September 1815," Founders Online, National Archives.

6. John Quincy Adams eventually also became a Unitarian Universalist.

7. "From Abigail Smith Adams to John Quincy Adams, 5 May 1816," Founders Online, National Archives.

8. "From Abigail Smith Adams to Louisa Catherine Johnson Adams, 20 March 1816," Founders Online, National Archives.

9. "From Abigail Smith Adams to Harriet Welsh, 18 August 1817," Founders Online, National Archives.

10. "From John Adams to François Adriaan Van der Kemp, 23 June 1817," Founders Online, National Archives.

11. "From John Adams to Benjamin Rush, 21 June 1811," Founders Online, National Archives.

12. "From Abigail Smith Adams to John Quincy Adams, 5 November 1816," Founders Online, National Archives.

13. David McCullough, *John Adams* (New York: Simon & Schuster, 2001), 622.

14. "From Abigail Smith Adams to John Quincy Adams, 8 June 1815," Founders Online, National Archives.

15. "From Abigail Smith Adams to Louisa Catherine Johnson Adams, 20 March 1816," Founders Online, National Archives.

16. "From Abigail Smith Adams to Louisa Catherine Johnson Adams, 12 December 1817," Founders Online, National Archives.

17. The Battle of New Orleans was fought and won after the close of the War of 1812.

18. "From Abigail Smith Adams to John Quincy Adams, 10 March 1815," Founders Online, National Archives.

19. "From Abigail Smith Adams to Louisa Catherine Johnson Adams, 27 February 1818," Founders Online, National Archives.

20. "From Abigail Smith Adams to Louisa Catherine Johnson Adams, 27 February 1818," Founders Online, National Archives.

21. "From Abigail Smith Adams to John Quincy Adams, 30 December 1804," Founders Online, National Archives. We know from letters that Juno lived until at least summer 1811. Juno reportedly was the puppy offspring from John Adams's dog that he kept while he lived in the President's House for four months. That dog was named Satan, probably inspired by various newspaper writers and editors of the day.

22. "From Abigail Smith Adams to Louisa Catherine Johnson Adams, 21 August 1818," Founders Online, National Archives.

23. "From John Adams to Thomas Jefferson, 20 October 1818," Founders Online, National Archives.

24. Dr. Benjamin Waterhouse was a Revolutionary War veteran and a physician. He was a family friend to the Adamses, and co-founder and professor at the Harvard Medical School.

25. "From Harriet Welsh to Caroline Amelia Smith De Windt, 1 November 1818," Founders Online, National Archives.

26. "From Harriet Welsh to Louisa Catherine Johnson Adams, 22 October 1818," Founders Online, National Archives.

27. "From Harriet Welsh to Louisa Catherine Johnson Adams, 26 October 1818," Founders Online, National Archives.

28. "From Harriet Welsh to Caroline Amelia Smith De Windt, 1 November 1818," Founders Online, National Archives.

29. "From Thomas Boylston Adams to John Quincy Adams, 1 November 1818," Founders Online, National Archives.

30. "To John Adams from Thomas Jefferson, 13 November 1818," Founders Online, National Archives.

31. "From Thomas Boylston Adams to John Quincy Adams, 1 November 1818," Founders Online, National Archives.

32. In 2022 a beautiful, tree-lined mall was dedicated in downtown Quincy which passes between the Hancock Cemetery and the United First Parish Church. A new statue of Abigail was also dedicated at the church. The church rightfully calls itself "The Church of the Presidents." The Adams family tomb in the Hancock Cemetery still holds the remains of Nabby, John and Abigail's daughter, along with George Washington Adams and John Adams II, sons of John Quincy and Louisa Adams.

33. "From Louisa Catherine Johnson Adams to Harriet Welsh, 4 November 1818," Founders Online, National Archives.

34. "Will of Abigail Adams, 18 January 1816," Founders Online, National Archives.

35. "Will of Abigail Adams, 18 January 1816," Founders Online, National Archives.

36. "Will of Abigail Adams, 18 January 1816," Founders Online, National Archives.

37. "From Abigail Smith Adams to Harriet Welsh, 15 March 1815," Founders Online, National Archives.

38. "From Abigail Smith Adams to Louisa Catherine Johnson Adams, 21 January 1811," Founders Online, National Archives.

39. "Abigail Smith Adams, Obituary Notice, 28 October 1818," Founders Online, National Archives.

40. "Abigail Smith Adams, Obituary Notice, 28 October 1818," Founders Online, National Archives.

41. "From Abigail Smith Adams to Abigail Amelia Adams Smith, 3 October 1808," Founders Online, National Archives.

Further Reading

PRIMARY SOURCES

Adams, Abigail. *Abigail Adams: Letters* (Library of America, 2016).

Adams, John; Abigail Adams, "Adams Family Papers." Adams Family Papers: An Electronic Archive. Massachusetts Historical Society.

National Archives. Founders Online: https://founders.archives.gov.

SECONDARY SOURCES

Abrams, Jeanne E., *First Ladies of the Republic* (New York: New York University Press, 2018).

———, *Revolutionary Medicine: The Founding Fathers and Mothers in Sickness and in Health* (New York: New York University Press, 2013).

———, *A View from Abroad: The Story of John and Abigail Adams in Europe* (New York: New York University Press, 2021).

Akers, Charles W., *Abigail Adams, A Revolutionary American Woman* (New York: Library of American Biography, 2006).

Belton, Blair, ed. *Abigail Adams in Her Own Words* (New York: Gareth Stevens Publishing, 2014).

Bober, Natalie S., *Abigail Adams, Witness to a Revolution* (New York: Aladdin Paperbacks, 1995).

Bowen, Catherine Drinker, *John Adams and the American Revolution* (Boston: Little, Brown, 1950).

Brown, Ralph A., *The Presidency of John Adams* (Lawrence: University Press of Kansas, 1975).

Butterfield, L.H., Friedlaender, Marc, Kline, Mary-Jo, eds., *The Book of Abigail and John* (Cambridge, MA: Harvard University Press, 1975).

Cobbs, Elizabeth, *Fearless Women, Feminist Patriots from Abigail Adams to Beyoncé* (Cambridge, MA: Belknap Press of Harvard University Press, 2023).

Ellis, Joseph J., *First Family: Abigail and John* (New York: Vintage Books, 2010).

Ferling, John, *John Adams: A Life* (New York: Henry Holt and Company, 1992).

"First Lady Abigail Adams." CSPAN. https://www.c-span.org/video/?310725-1/lady-abigail-adams.

Gelles, Edith B., *Abigail Adams: Letters* (New York: Library of America, 2016).

———, *Abigail Adams: A Writing Life* (New York: Twayne Publishers, 1998).

———, *Portia: The World of Abigail Adams* (Indianapolis: Indiana University Press, 1992).

Hogan, Margaret A., Taylor, C. James, eds., *My Dearest Friend: Letters of Abigail and John Adams* (Cambridge, MA: Belknap Press of Harvard University Press, 2007).

Holton, Woody, *Abigail Adams* (New York: Free Press, 2009).

Hom, Annika, "The Untold Stories of Slaves Who Lived in Abigail Adams's Birthplace." BostonGlobe.com (February 6, 2019).

Jacobs, Diane, *Dear Abigail* (New York: Ballantine Books, 2014).

Levin, Phyllis Lee, *Abigail Adams, A Biography* (New York: St. Martin's Press, 2001).

Lewis, Charlene M. Boyler, Boudreau, George, eds., *Women in George Washington's World* (Charlottesville: University of Virginia Press, 2022).

McCullough, David, *John Adams* (New York: Simon & Schuster, 2001).

Michals, Debra, *"Abigail Adams."* National Women's History Museum, 2015.

Mitchell, Stewart, ed., *New Letters of Abigail Adams 1788—1801* (Cambridge, MA: Riverside Press, 1947).

Norton, Mary Beth, *Liberty's Daughters: The Revolutionary Experience of American Women, 1750–1800* (New York: Little, Brown, 1980).

Orihel, Michelle, "Remember the Ladies: Teaching the Correspondence of John and Abigail Adams in the Age of Social Media." *Common-Place: The Interactive Journal of Early American Life* (2018).

Shepherd, Jack, *The Adams Chronicles: Four Generations of Greatness* (Boston: Little, Brown, 1975).

Smith, Page, *John Adams, Volumes I & II* (Garden City, NY: Doubleday, 1962).

White House Historical Association. "Abigail Adams Used the East Room to Dry the Laundry." *Whitehousehistory.org.*

Withey, Lynne, *Dearest Friend: A Life of Abigail Adams* (New York: Touchstone Free Press, 1981).

Acknowledgments

Ⓣhis book would not exist without the letters written by Abigail Adams. She was aware that her spelling and penmanship were below par for the time, so she often reminded the receiver to burn her letters after reading. Luckily, few if any of her correspondents did. Abigail's letters reveal an extraordinary woman living during those dark times when American revolutionary success was starkly uncertain. Her intelligence, adaptability, and quiet strength served her well—and equally well for her husband, John Adams—as the infant American country was going through its growing pains. She should be considered one of this country's most significant Founders.

The late David McCullough said, "The advantage of being an historian is that you get to read other people's mail." Reading Abigail's many letters, probably numbering in the thousands in total, has now been made very easy to do. Since 2010, the National Archives, the National Historical Publications and Records Commission (NHPRC), and the University of Virginia Press have created an accessible website called Founders Online. As I browsed through the remarkable collection during the pandemic—an intriguing and enjoyable exercise— I first became aware of the existence of Abigail's very engaging letters. They opened the door to her many adventures and the remarkable people she had met. I was smitten with Abigail.

A book about the Founding Era takes a steady stream of encouraging words and advice for the print and words to come alive.

A thank you goes out to Dr. Page Smith at UCSC for planting the American Revolution bug deep inside me during the 1970s. I'd find him out in his rustic writing cabin behind the main house where he had written his two-volume work on John Adams. Abigail, of course, frequently entered our conversation.

My sincere gratitude extends to all my friends, acquaintances, and tutors during the creation of this project—especially Todd Andrlik and Don Hagist. I'd met Dr. Lynn Price Robbins when she was an editor of the *Papers of George Washington*. She offered me much valuable direction and encouragement. I also owe a debt of thanks to Bruce H. Franklin, owner and publisher of Westholme Publishing, for his valued support and direction on this project. Copy editor Noreen O'Connor-Abel masterfully edited this manuscript, no simple feat. Sara Georgini of the *Adams Papers* and Daniel T. Hinchen both at the Massachusetts Historical Society provided very knowledgeable and in-person guidance on Abigail during my enjoyable visit there. Cathy Torrey, president of the Abigail Adams Historical Society, couldn't have been more courteous during her generous tour of Abigail's birth home in Weymouth, Massachusetts. But most importantly, my heartfelt appreciativeness remains for Hugh T. Harrington, the editor emeritus of the *Journal of the American Revolution*. His unswerving friendship and excellent advice made all the difference to me in my struggling days of writing. I will be forever grateful to him.

Index

as Smith trust administrator, 151, 204
Creek treaty celebration, 220–221
culture and social life
  of England, 158–161, 167–168, 177–
    178, 180–182, 184–192, 198
  of France, 162–165, 167–170, 172
  of the Netherlands, 192–193
  of Philadelphia, 221–223, 231, 258–
    259
  of Washington, DC, 265–266
Cunningham, Ann Boylston, 62
currency, value of, 108, 109, 110, 114, 117
Cushing, Thomas, 40
Custis, Daniel Parke, 267

Dana, Elizabeth Ellery, 250
Dana, Francis, 131, 139
De Windt, Caroline Amelia (granddaugh-
    ter). *See* Smith, Caroline Amelia
    (granddaughter; wife of John Peter
    De Windt)
De Windt, John Peter, 304–305
Deane, Silas, 43, 102, 115, 120
Declaration of Independence, 92–93, 99,
    180, 287, 292
Democratic-Republican Party
  anger of, over JA's "midnight appoint-
    ments," 269
  and the embargo of 1807, 284
  and the French Revolution, 228
  John Quincy Adams's switch to, 285
  origins of, 202
  and the peaceful transition of power,
    243
  and the presidential election of 1796,
    240, 260, 266
  and the presidential election of 1800,
    257
Dexter, Rebecca, 308
Dickinson, John, 59, 75
Direct House Tax of 1798, 245
dogs. *See* pets
Dorchester Heights fortification, 83
dysentery epidemic of 1775, 68–72

economic and financial matters
  AA's fund for the poor, 153, 175, 227–
    228
  bequests in AA's will, 310–311

British economic system, 203
  cancellation of Cranch's debt, 216–217
  Charles's loss of John Quincy's invest-
    ments, 248
  Cranch family's financial problems, 102
  Dutch loan to America, 141, 261
  French backing of Continental currency,
    114
  government bonds, 152–153, 196–197,
    205, 218–220, 254–255
  importation and sale of European goods,
    125–126, 128–129, 134–136
  income effect of service in Congress, 38–
    39
  James Lovell's inside information on,
    117
  market crash of 1792, 231
  real estate investments, 138–139, 152,
    166, 174–175, 272–273
  resale of pins, 60, 62, 66, 74
  Stamp Act's effect on income, 20
  value of currency, 108, 109, 110, 114,
    117
  wartime shortages, 62, 66, 109
education
  of AA, 4, 7
  of Charles, 137, 150, 192
  coeducation of blacks with whites, 243–
    244
  female education, 97–98, 121, 191,
    199–200, 236
  JA on, 50, 78, 97, 121
  of John Quincy, 40–41, 49, 137, 192
  mothers' responsibility for, 32
  of Nabby, 49–50
  of Thomas, 150, 192
England
  editorials about JA in the British press,
    180–181
  JA's appointment as ambassador to,
    175–176
  vacation in the south of, 202–203
  and the War of 1812, 293, 300
  Washington's neutrality policy towards,
    233, 234
  See also London, England
entertainment. *See* culture and social life
Estaing, Jean-Baptiste-Charles-Henri-Hec-
    tor, 121, 122–123

Smith, Isaac, Jr. (cousin), 4–5, 29–30
Smith, Isaac, Sr. (uncle), 4, 23, 89, 153
Smith, John Adams (grandson), 208, 231
Smith, Louisa Catherine (niece), 311
Smith, Mary "Polly" (niece), 246
Smith, Mary (sister; wife of Richard
        Cranch)
    to AA, on state of Peacefield, 247
    to AA, on the caretaker of the Adams's
        house, 194–195
    AA to, on Betsy, 37
    AA to, on British press, 180–181
    AA to, on editing JA's presidential let-
        ters, 253
    AA to, on "fall disorder," 183
    AA to, on fashion, 259
    AA to, on finding servants in Philadel-
        phia, 222
    AA to, on folk medicine, 19
    AA to, on France, 161, 168–169
    AA to, on George Washington's death,
        257
    AA to, on getting lost on way to Wash-
        ington, DC, 264–265
    AA to, on grandmotherhood, 199
    AA to, on health issues, 231
    AA to, on her visit to the Netherlands,
        192–193
    AA to, on homesickness, 191
    AA to, on Indians, 220–221
    AA to, on JA's absence, 22
    AA to, on missing brother, 204
    AA to, on Nabby's marriage, 190
    AA to, on Nabby's missing husband,
        246
    AA to, on Patience Wright, 159
    AA to, on pet bird, 173
    AA to, on returning to Braintree from
        Philadelphia, 229
    AA to, on royal introductions, 181, 182
    AA to, on scattered family, 220
    AA to, on servants' marriage, 206
    AA to, on slavery, 268
    AA to, on the election process, 258, 260
    AA to, on the health of, 262
    AA to, on the Quincy lineage, 202–203
    AA to, on tiring of the election process,
        260
    AA to, on trip to Quincy, 254

AA to, on visiting Mount Vernon, 267
AA to, on voting rights for women, 249
AA to, on William Stephens Smith,
        186–187
AA's and JA's purchase of Mount Wol-
        laston from, 272
AA's and JA's visits with, in Salem, 21
AA's cancellation of husband's debt,
        216–217
AA's financial support of, 227–228
Adams boys' stay with, 195–196
death of, 289
education of, 4
evacuation of, from Boston, 62
financial problems of, 102
in Germantown cove, 18–19
inheritance of, 152
marriage of, 9
move of, to Boston, 39–40
move of, to Salem, 15–16
Richard Cranch's interest in, 8
on women's education and rights, 191
Smith, Page, 282
Smith, Sarah "Sally" (daughter-in-law; wife
        of Charles), 234–235, 246, 257,
        262, 289–290
Smith, William, Jr. "Billy" (brother), 8,
        151, 171, 204
Smith, William (father)
    death and bequests of, 151–152, 204
    and education of AA, 4
    JA on, 8
    marriage of, to Elizabeth Quincy, 5
    as slave owner, 6
Smith, William Stephens (son-in-law)
    AA on, 186–187
    appointment of, as surveyor and port in-
        spector, 255
    disappearance of, 246
    financial success of, 235
    JA to, on the state of public affairs,
        1791, 228
    marriage of, to Nabby, 190–191
    money-making scheme of, 215
    move of, to the wilderness, 284
    and Nabby's breast cancer, 288
    at Nabby's death, 296
    participation of, in failed effort to liber-
        ate Venezuela, 282–284